"This impressive work demonstrates that the Global War On Terror (GWOT) is both ineffective and inhumane, and that there are better, more ethical ways to deal with political violence. Especially praiseworthy is the variety of voices the book contains: prominent academics and activists, as well as victims. It should be required reading for anyone seeking a critical understanding of our present dilemma."

Charles Lindholm, *Boston University, USA*

"This is a timely work that combines insight with style. It offers a fine example of engaged scholarship. It is a book well worth reading!"

Stephen Eric Bronner, *Rutgers University, USA*

Assessing the War on Terror

This volume is a collection of articles that critically examine the efficacy, ethics, and impact of the War on Terror as it has evolved since 9/11.

During the decade and a half of the Global War on Terror (GWOT), numerous books have considered the political, psychosocial, and economic impacts of terrorism. However, there has been little systematic effort to examine the effectiveness of the GWOT in achieving its goals. Furthermore, there is virtually nothing that presents a comparative analysis of the GWOT by the people most directly affected by it—citizens and scholars from conflict zones in the Middle East. There is, therefore, great need for a book that analyzes the strategies, tactics, and outcomes of the GWOT and that also presents facts and ideas that are missing or underrepresented in the dominant public narratives. The contributions in this volume were chosen to specifically address this need. In doing so, it uniquely provides not only Western perspectives of the GWOT, but also importantly includes perspectives from the Middle East and those most directly affected by it, including contributions from scholars and policy makers. Overall, the contributions demonstrate how views differ based on geographical location, and how views have changed during the course of the still-evolving War on Terror.

The book will be of much interest to students and scholars of terrorism and counter-terrorism, foreign policy, Middle Eastern politics, security studies and IR, as well as policy makers.

Charles Webel is the Delp-Wilkinson Chair and Professor of Peace Studies at Chapman University, USA, and Professor of International Economic Relations at the University of New York in Prague, Czech Republic. He is author/editor of eights books, including *Terror, Terrorism, and the Human Condition* (2007) and *Peace and Conflict Studies, 3rd edition* (with D. Barash, 2014).

Mark Tomass is an economist and instructor at Harvard University, USA, and author of *The Religious Roots of the Syrian Conflict: The Remaking of the Fertile Crescent* (2016).

Contemporary Terrorism Studies

Conducting Terrorism Field Research
A Guide
Edited by Adam Dolnik

US–UK Counter-Terrorism after 9/11
A Qualitative Approach
Edgar B. Tembo

Transforming Violent Political Movements
Rebels Today, What Tomorrow?
Kevin Grisham

Radicalization in Western Europe
Integration, Public Discourse and Loss of Identity among Muslim Communities
Carolin Goerzig and Khaled Al-Hashimi

Putting Terrorism in Context
Lessons from the Global Terrorism Database
Gary LaFree, Laura Dugan and Erin Miller

Al Qaeda's Global Crisis
The Islamic State, Takfir, and the Genocide of Muslims
V. G. Julie Rajan

Social Networks, Terrorism and Counter-Terrorism
Radical and Connected
Edited by Martin Bouchard

Understanding Lone Actor Terrorism
Past Experience, Future Outlook, and Response Strategies
Edited by Michael Fredholm

Hamas, Popular Support and War in the Middle East
Insurgency in the Holy Land
Richard Davis

Social Movement De-Radicalisation and the Decline of Terrorism
The Morphogenesis of the Irish Republican Movement
Gordon Clubb

Understanding Deradicalization
Methods, Tools and Programs for Countering Violent Extremism
Daniel Koehler

Assessing the War on Terror
Western and Middle Eastern Perspectives
Edited by Charles Webel and Mark Tomass

Assessing the War on Terror
Western and Middle Eastern Perspectives

**Edited by
Charles Webel and
Mark Tomass**

LONDON AND NEW YORK

First published 2017
by Routledge
2 Park Square, Milton Park, Abingdon, Oxon OX14 4RN

and by Routledge
711 Third Avenue, New York, NY 10017

Routledge is an imprint of the Taylor & Francis Group, an informa business

© 2017 selection and editorial material, Charles Webel and Mark Tomass; individual chapters, the contributors

The right of the editors to be identified as the authors of the editorial material, and of the authors for their individual chapters, has been asserted in accordance with sections 77 and 78 of the Copyright, Designs and Patents Act 1988.

All rights reserved. No part of this book may be reprinted or reproduced or utilized in any form or by any electronic, mechanical, or other means, now known or hereafter invented, including photocopying and recording, or in any information storage or retrieval system, without permission in writing from the publishers.

Trademark notice: Product or corporate names may be trademarks or registered trademarks, and are used only for identification and explanation without intent to infringe.

British Library Cataloguing in Publication Data
A catalogue record for this book is available from the British Library

Library of Congress Cataloging in Publication Data
Names: Webel, Charles, editor. | Tomass, Mark, 1961– editor.
Title: Assessing the War on Terror : Western and Middle Eastern perspectives / edited by Charles Webel and Mark Tomass.
Description: Abingdon, Oxon ; New York, NY : Routledge, 2017. | Series: Contemporary terrorism studies | Includes bibliographical references and index.
Identifiers: LCCN 2016041380| ISBN 9781138204560 (hardback) | ISBN 9781315469171 (ebook)
Subjects: LCSH: War on Terrorism, 2001–2009. | Terrorism–Prevention–Evaluation.
Classification: LCC HV6431 .A84424 2017 | DDC 363.325/16–dc23
LC record available at https://lccn.loc.gov/2016041380

ISBN: 978-1-138-20456-0 (hbk)
ISBN: 978-1-315-46917-1 (ebk)

Typeset in Times New Roman
by Wearset Ltd, Boldon, Tyne and Wear

Contents

List of tables x
Notes on contributors xi

Introduction 1
CHARLES WEBEL

PART I
Framing and assessing the War on Terror 5
MARK TOMASS

1 **The evil scourge of terrorism** 7
  NOAM CHOMSKY

2 **The complex relationship between peacebuilding and terrorism approaches: towards post-terrorism and a post-liberal peace?** 18
  OLIVER P. RICHMOND AND IOANNIS TELLIDIS

3 **Trauma and the city: the psychology of America's terrorism trauma** 45
  SARTON WEINRAUB

PART II
Hearing from the victims of terror-inflicted regions 57
MARK TOMASS

4 **The Syrian tragedy: the role of the West, a government insider's account** 60
  BOUTHAINA SHAABAN

Contents

5 Iraq: a victim of terror and the War on Terror 82
ANWAR SAID AL-HAIDARI

6 The ideological origins of ISIS: fighting terror with common sense 108
MARK TOMASS

7 Winning the hearts and minds of the Pukhtuns of Afghanistan and Northwest Pakistan with altruism, public health and development, not by terrorism and counterterrorism 137
SHER MOHAMMED KHAN

PART III
Calculating the costs of the War on Terror 145
MARK TOMASS

8 The global war on terrorism: how ethical and effective? 147
CHARLES P. WEBEL AND JOHN A. ARNALDI

9 Led astray: legal and moral blowback from the global War on Terror 163
WILLIAM A. COHN

10 Terror from above and within: the hidden cultural and political costs of lethal drones 196
LAURIE CALHOUN

PART IV
Analyzing, negotiating with, and ending terror groups 215
MARK TOMASS

11 A dialogue on why Western youth are attracted to ISIS 218
SCOTT ATRAN AND MARK TOMASS

12 Negotiating with the Taliban: not war on terrorism, but dialogue for solutions 228
JOHAN GALTUNG

13	**A tale of two CTs: a ground-level counterinsurgency perspective on Belgian counter-terrorism measures** CASEY DOUGLAS CARR	234
14	**The 'war on terrorism': what does it mean to win?** AUDREY KURTH CRONIN	253
	Conclusion CHARLES WEBEL	273
	Index	285

Tables

2.1	Interactions between terrorism and peacebuilding	38
5.1	Number of victims injured during five months of 2015	100
5.2	Provinces with largest number of victims within five months of 2015	101
6.1	Comparative practice of Islam 1	121
6.2	Comparative practice of Islam 2	122

Contributors

John A. Arnaldi is a life coach who taught the Applied Ethics of War and Peace in the Honors College at the University of South Florida (USF). He is the co-editor, with Charles Webel, of *The Ethics and Efficacy of the Global War on Terrorism*.

Scott Atran is Presidential Scholar at the John Jay College of Criminal Justice, and is Research Director in Anthropology at the National Center for Scientific Research in Paris. He is also a senior research fellow at Harris Manchester College, Oxford University, co-founder of ARTIS Research and Risk Modeling, and has been a Visiting Professor of Psychology and Public Policy at University of Michigan. He is the author of *Cognitive Foundations of Natural History: Towards an Anthropology of Science; In Gods We Trust: The Evolutionary Landscape of Religion;* and *Talking to the Enemy: Faith, Brotherhood, and the (Un)Making of Terrorists*.

Laurie Calhoun, a philosopher and cultural critic, is the author of *We Kill Because We Can: From Soldiering to Assassination in the Drone Age*, *War and Delusion: A Critical Examination; Philosophy Unmasked: A Skeptic's Critique*, and dozens of essays on war.

Casey Douglas Carr is an MA candidate in International Conflict and Security at the University of Kent in Brussels. Having a background in psychology with the U.S. military, including overseas combat service from 2008–2010, he obtained his BA in the subject at the University of New York in Prague, concentrating his course load on social and psychological aspects of disaster, conflict, and crisis. His research investigates individual and collective radicalization processes, where his current work focuses on Islamic political activism and radicalization in Belgium.

Noam Chomsky is one of the world's most influential linguistics scholars and political analysts. He has published scores of books in both fields. He is currently Professor Emeritus in Linguistics and Philosophy at The Massachusetts Institute of Technology, and he has lectured and taught at many universities worldwide.

William A. Cohn is an attorney and constitutional law scholar, he has practiced and taught law since 1993, working with clients, judges, international organizations, bar associations and scholars, lecturing and publishing extensively on matters of law and policy. His scholarship focuses on law and ethics; and on innovative methods to promote critical thinking skills, media literacy, and the rule of law.

Audrey Kurth Cronin is Professor of International Security at the School of International Service, American University in Washington, D.C. and Senior Research Associate at the Changing Character of War Programme, University of Oxford, UK. She is the author of several books, including *How Terrorism Ends: Understanding the Decline and Demise of Terrorist Campaigns*.

Johan Galtung, from Norway, is widely recognized as a founder of peace studies. He also founded the world's first Peace Research Institute in Oslo and has since helped initiate many centers for peace and reconciliation throughout the world. He founded the *Journal of Peace Research*. In 1993, he created TRANSCEND, a global Peace, Development and Environment Network. Prof. Galtung is the founder and current rector of the TRANSCEND Peace University. Over the last five decades, he has mediated over 100 international conflicts, often successfully. He has published over 1,500 articles and more than 150 books, with translations into 33 languages. He has been a consultant to the United Nations and its family of organizations. His commitment to peace has been recognized with 13 honorary doctorates and professorships and an Alternative Nobel Prize, the High Livelihood Award, in 1987.

Anwar Said al-Haydari, a political scientist at the University of Baghdad, Iraq, has written scholarly papers on the Islamists in Israeli political thought, the revolution and counter revolution in Egypt, the electoral systems in Iraq, the politics of the Israeli religious parties regarding the Palestinians.

Sher Mohammad Khan, from the Swat valley, Pakistan, is a medical doctor with Master's degree in Nuclear Medicine. He served in the National Health Service of the UK. In 1974, he joined Pakistan's Atomic Energy Commission to establish peaceful uses of atomic energy in medicine. As head of the Institute of Radiotherapy and Nuclear Medicine, he dealt medically with displaced persons from Afghanistan. As Honorary Chairman of the Red Crescent/Red Cross society, he was involved in humanitarian work with persons who have been displaced due to "man-made" and natural disasters in northwest Pakistan. After retirement, Dr. Khan joined a private medical care facility where the majority of the patients come from Afghanistan.

Oliver P. Richmond is currently a Professor of International Relations and Peace and Conflict Studies in the Department of Politics and Humanitarian and the Conflict Response Institute, at the University of Manchester, UK. Prof. Richmond was previously at the University of St. Andrews (Scotland), where he directed the Centre of Peace and Conflict Studies. He is the author of numerous books, most recently *A Very Short Introduction to Peace*, and is a leading analyst of "liberal peace."

Bouthaina Shaaban, a nominee for the Noble Peace Prize in 2005, is Political and Media Advisor for the Syrian Presidency, and former Minister of Expatriates in Syria. She has served in the Syrian government as minister and in different capacities for 20 years, and is also a writer and professor at Damascus University. Before assuming her ministerial position, Shaaban was Director of the Foreign Media Department at the Ministry of Foreign Affairs in Syria and a spokesperson for Syria. Shaaban's career has been dedicated to changing the social injustices that befall women in the Arab world. In 1990–1991 she had a Fulbright Research Fellowship at Duke University. She was also a Distinguished McAndless Professor at Eastern Michigan University. In 2005, she received the award for "The Most Distinguished Woman in a Governmental Position in the Arab World" from the League of Arab States. Dr. Shaaban has published nine books and many articles in Arabic and English, trying to create a bridge between East and West. Her latest book is *Damascus Diary: An Inside Account of Hafez al Assad Peace Diplomacy*.

Ioannis Tellidis is Associate Professor of International Relations at the College of International Studies, Kyung Hee University, South Korea, and Associate Editor of the journal *Peacebuilding*. His interests include terrorism and political violence, peace and conflict studies and the role of technology in peacebuilding. His research has been published in *Cooperation and Conflict*, *Critical Studies in Terrorism*, *Global Governance*, *International Studies Review*, *Peace Review* and *Terrorism and Political Violence*, and he is the co-editor of *Researching Terrorism, Peace and Conflict: Interaction, Synthesis and Opposition* (Routledge 2015) and *Terrorism, Peace and Conflict Studies: Investigating the Crossroad* (Routledge 2014).

Mark Tomass, an economist and instructor at Harvard University, bases his research on the Middle East on his experience as a native of Syria and from living through the Lebanese civil war of 1975–1990 and the Muslim Brothers' revolt of 1976–1982. His contributions to understanding civil conflict include "Religious Identity, Informal Institutions, and the Nation States of the Near East," "Game Theory Models with Instrumentally Irrational Players: A Case Study of Civil War and Sectarian Cleansing," and his book entitled: *The Religious Origin of the Syrian Conflict: The Remaking of the Fertile Crescent*. His book employs economic and anthropological concepts that highlight the role of political entrepreneurs in the formation of the religious map of the Middle East and the civil conflicts they have generated.

Charles P. Webel is a Fulbright Specialist in Peace and Conflict Resolution and Professor at the University of New York in Prague. Dr. Webel also currently holds the Delp-Wilkinson Chair and is Professor and Department Chair of

Peace Studies at Chapman University in Orange, CA. He has previously studied and taught at the University of California at Berkeley and Harvard University. Dr. Webel also served as Director of the Centre for Peace Studies, at the University of Tromsø, Norway. Prof. Webel has eight books currently in print, including *Peace and Conflict Studies* (with David Barash), the standard text in the field; *Terror, Terrorism, and the Human Condition*, and *The Politics of Rationality*. He is working on several new books, including *The Rationalization of the World?* He is also a four-time Fulbright Scholar, most recently to Myanmar.

Sarton Weinraub is a licensed clinical psychologist in private practice in New York City specializing in the practice of Humanistic (Person-Centered) Psychotherapy. Dr. Weinraub is the Director of the New York Person-Centered Resource Center, a humanistic mental health treatment center in New York City. He received his doctorate from Saybrook University in California, and he also received training in the Person-Centered Approach from the Independent Consultation Center in New York City and in psychodynamic-psychotherapy from the New York University Psychoanalytic Institute.

Introduction

Charles Webel

September 11, 2016 marked the fifteenth anniversary of the most lethal terrorism attack in American history. But although most Americans and virtually all global media appropriately "remembered" the tragic day 15 years earlier, few paused to analyze the reasons for the attacks and the "effectiveness" of the world war that has ensued. Even fewer performed a dispassionate "cost/benefit" analysis of the "Global War on Terrorism" (GWOT), both from strategic and ethical standpoints.

The U.S.-led counterterrorist strategy initiated by the Bush administration and largely preserved by Obama's should be re-examined—and significantly modified if not abandoned—because it has been shown to be largely ineffective in reducing the global incidence and lethality of acts of political violence Western leaders brand "terrorist," notwithstanding the widely publicized assassinations of Osama bin Laden and other high-ranking leaders of terrorist groups, and the absence to date of another successful major terrorist attack on U.S. soil since 9/11. This realpolitik strategy of negative peacemaking, put into effect in September 2001—about a decade and a half decade ago—has not defeated radical Islamism or any other violent ideology, has resulted in many thousands of casualties, has led to a global clash between extreme elements of Western and Islamist civilizations, and threatens to escalate to a war of the world in which non-state terrorists and state counterterrorists may both employ weapons of mass destruction.

A principal aim of this book is to examine official mainstream constructions of "terrorists," "terrorism" and "counterterrorism" as powerful rhetorical frames used to sell the GWOT and the justifications for initiating and continuing it. These frames also underlie numerous ethical assumptions–attempts to justify the morality of killing in "war"—which we also call into question.

We suggest an alternative construction for understanding the roots of terrorism and for devising "antiterrorism" strategies to replace the largely ineffective "counterterrorism" policies being used to deal with terrifying acts of political violence. This framework is based both on an empirical analysis of how groups labeled "terrorist" end, as well as on a normative assessment of the utility and morality of "fighting terror with terror."

During the approximately 15 years of "the war on terrorism," numerous books have been published that consider the political, psychosocial, and economic impacts of terrorism. However, there has been little systematic effort to examine the "effectiveness" of the GWOT in achieving its goals in making the world in general, and the United States, the United Kingdom, and the rest of the West in particular, more secure by reducing the number and lethality of officially-designated terrorist attacks. And there is virtually nothing that presents comparative analyses of the GWOT by the people most directly affected by it—citizens and refugees from conflict zones in the Middle East and the West.

As a result, in this book we include in-depth analyses of the strategies, tactics, and outcomes of the Global War on Terror, and we present facts and ideas that are missing or underrepresented in the dominant narratives found in public discourse. Furthermore, we also document the concrete effects of terrifying political violence on its victims. Consequently, we include first-person narratives by survivors of the 9/11 and the 2016 Brussels attacks, as well as on-site accounts by witnesses and survivors of the direct and long-term violence perpetrated by terrorists and counterterrorists in Afghanistan, Iraq, Pakistan, and Syria.

Assessing the War on Terror: Western and Middle Eastern Perspectives presents readers with provocative articles that critically examine the efficacy, ethics, and impact of the War on Terror as it has evolved over the past 15 years. These contributions were included because they effectively address specific aspects of the war—from Western and Middle-Eastern perspectives on terrorism—that are missing or underrepresented in political discourse since 9/11.

The book includes a mix of article types: theory, lecture, research, and participant observation. It includes contributions written at different times since 9/11 and the present, thus reflecting the immediacy of the times when they were written and providing a necessary socio-historical context for understanding these complex events and historical processes. There would be no way to do justice to such a broad area of topics and events taking place over the past 15 years without sampling political discourses at discrete points in time and without including different, and sometimes controversial and conflicting, voices and narratives.

Among the key questions addressed in the book are:

- How is terrorism defined and what are the implications of these definitions?
- Do decision-makers' and terrorized citizens desires for retribution mean that nations must engage in wars around the world, or are there more effective alternatives?
- How can effective counterterrorism and antiterrorism strategies be developed and implemented?
- What does it mean to "win," "lose," or be "frozen" in a "Global War on Terror?"
- How should we weigh the risks, costs, and benefits of conducting a War on Terror?
- What have been the human and financial costs of the GWOT, and who bears the responsibility for civilian casualties, a.k.a., "collateral damage?"
- What is ISIS (or the Islamic State) and what might be done to deal with it?

- How do a representative of the Syrian government, a prominent Iraqi intellectual and political analyst, and a Pukhtun physician from the borderlands of Afghanistan and Pakistan view the civil wars racking their countries?
- What moral and strategic issues are involved in modern air warfare, including drones?
- Is it possible, and desirable, to negotiate with such "terrorist" groups as the Taliban, al-Qaeda, and ISIS?
- Have the strategies and tactics the West and Russia are using to confront terrorism been effective, or should they be changed?
- How do terrorist groups end?
- How and why are people, including young Westerners, "radicalized?"
- What do people on the ground in such current and past conflict zones as New York City on 9/11, Pakistan/Afghanistan, Iraq, Brussels, and Syria think and feel about acts of terror, who perpetrated them, and what should be done to cope with and possibly to end them?

From our perspective, while all acts of terrorism are unethical and must be confronted, current rationales for the War on Terror fail to meet universalistic normative standards, and the military means deployed on behalf of this effort have been both unethical and ineffective. Accordingly, in this book we propose a counter-strategy, called antiterrorism, which may be both more ethical and more efficacious than the failed Global War on Terrorism in addressing the roots of and rationales for terrifying political violence.

Part I

Framing and assessing the War on Terror

Mark Tomass

In the opening essay of this book, Noam Chomsky uses the official definition of "terrorism" in US and British law, "the calculated use of violence or threat of violence to attain goals that are political, religious, or ideological in nature ... through intimidation, coercion, or instilling fear," to show that the US has employed state-directed international terrorism since the Monroe Doctrine has been a guide for foreign policy. While Ronald Reagan's "War on Terror," which he declared in 1981, produced an unusually extreme record of terrorism inflicted upon the third world, especially in Latin America, that era was not a departure from the norm. In that war, Reagan used the phrase "the evil scourge of terrorism," a cover term for his "War on Terror," to enforce the US right to dominate the American continent and beyond. Accordingly, US policymakers used violence and economic strangulation to subdue defiant states and to provide haven to international terrorists, whose names would be common knowledge in the West if the US were serious about fighting terrorism.

Chomsky claims that successive US administrations' policies have inspired, not defeated, radical Islamist terrorism by promoting a deficient moral and intellectual culture. In 2010, the US celebrated the twentieth anniversary of "the fall of the tyranny of the enemy" after the collapse of the communist regimes in Eastern and Central Europe, while it kept mum "about the culmination of the hideous atrocities" in US domains that are "so glaring that it takes real dedication to miss it."

To end the evil of terrorism, Chomsky makes three policy recommendations: First, end the West's role as a perpetrator of terrorism. Second, attempt to address legitimate grievances. Third, deal with an act of terror, like any criminal act, by identifying and apprehending the suspects and carrying out an honest judicial process, as opposed to using the current techniques that enhance rather than mitigate the threat of terrorism.

In the second essay, Oliver P. Richmond and Ioannis Tellidis argue that what they call "orthodox" approaches to terrorism normally rest on the "exclusion" of terrorist actors until they renounce the use of violence. Such exclusion produces a "catch 22" situation in which terrorists must give up their leverage before arriving at the negotiating table, which makes an "orthodox" approach to terrorism more like "state-building" than "peacebuilding." In contrast, Richmond and Tellidis present a "post-terrorism" and "post-liberal" approach that focuses on the need to develop a broad and inclusive peace process to induce all actors away from supporting political or structural violence and toward negotiating a sustainable compromise. They advocate the development of institutions that bridge local and international differences, thus producing a hybrid and more inclusive model that may gain wide acceptance, including by extremists. In their "post-terrorism" approach, they encourage engaging with the root causes of violence and its prevention. Building on the commonly accepted fact that responses to terrorism may prevent peace processes from proceeding, Richmond and Tellidis argue that orthodox approaches to both analyzing and combating terrorism have tended to replicate the conditions of conflict. Top-down policies often obscure efforts that seek to produce a durable and sustainable peace because they exacerbate the motives that terrorism draw on, enable new terrorism supporters motivated by cultural, identity, or welfare exclusions, and reinforce the same institutions that produce such exclusions, thereby marginalizing local interests that facilitate the re-emergence of the conditions for violence.

After 9/11, the US and its "coalition of the willing" went to war, and the war rages on with new challenges and an unforeseeable end. The clinical psychologist, Sarton Weinraub, asks: What have we learned? Can this trauma ever be worked through? Weinraub's experiences as a survivor, New York City resident, and psychologist suggest we have a long way to go. He offers his practical insight into the psychology of those who experienced the 9/11 terrorist attacks, based on his personal experience as a survivor and as a psychological caregiver to those who faced the attacks on the ground. Weinraub's "Trauma and the City," in addition to offering samples of trauma studies relating to 9/11, claims that the phenomenon of post-traumatic stress disorder has not been given the attention it deserves, as it has impacted millions of people who experienced the events of 9/11, regardless of how far they were physically from Ground Zero.

1 The evil scourge of terrorism
Reality, construction, remedy[1]

Noam Chomsky

Erich Fromm lecture – April 3, 2010

The President could not have been more justified when he condemned "the evil scourge of terrorism." I am quoting Ronald Reagan, who came into office in 1981 declaring that a focus of his foreign policy would be state-directed international terrorism, "the plague of the modern age" and "a return to barbarism in our time," to sample some of the rhetoric of his administration. When George W. Bush declared a "War on Terror" 20 years later, he was re-declaring the war, an important fact that is worth exhuming from Orwell's memory hole if we hope to understand the nature of the evil scourge of terrorism, or more importantly, if we hope to understand ourselves. We do not need the famous Delphi inscription to recognize that there can be no more important task. Just as a personal aside, that critical necessity was forcefully brought home to me almost 70 years ago in my first encounter with Erich Fromm's work, in his classic essay on the escape to freedom in the modern world, and the grim paths that the modern free individual was tempted to choose in the effort to escape the loneliness and anguish that accompanied the newly-discovered freedom—matters all too pertinent today, unfortunately.

The reasons why Reagan's War on Terror has been dispatched to the repository of unwelcome facts are understandable and informative—about ourselves. Instantly, Reagan's War on Terror became a savage terrorist war, leaving hundreds of thousands of tortured and mutilated corpses in the wreckage of Central America, tens of thousands more in the Middle East, and an estimated 1.5 million killed by South African terror that was strongly supported by the Reagan administration in violation of congressional sanctions. All of these murderous exercises of course had pretexts. The resort to violence always does. In the Middle East, Reagan's decisive support for Israel's 1982 invasion of Lebanon, which killed some 15,000–20,000 people and destroyed much of southern Lebanon and Beirut, was based on the pretense that it was in self-defense against PLO rocketing of the Galilee, a brazen fabrication: Israel recognized at once that the threat was PLO diplomacy, which might have undermined Israel's illegal takeover of the occupied territories. In Africa, support for the marauding of the apartheid state was officially justified within the framework of the War on

Terror: it was necessary to protect white South Africa from one of the world's "more notorious terrorist groups," Nelson Mandela's African National Congress, so Washington determined in 1988. The pretexts in the other cases were no more impressive.

For the most part, the victims of Reaganite terror were defenseless civilians, but in one case the victim was a state, Nicaragua, which could respond through legal channels. Nicaragua brought its charges to the World Court, which condemned the US for "unlawful use of force"—in lay terms, international terrorism—in its attack on Nicaragua from its Honduran bases, and ordered the US to terminate the assault and pay substantial reparations. The aftermath is instructive. Congress responded to the Court judgment by increasing aid to the US-run mercenary army attacking Nicaragua, while the press condemned the Court as a "hostile forum" and therefore irrelevant. The same Court had been highly relevant a few years earlier when it ruled in favor of the US against Iran. Washington dismissed the Court judgment with contempt. In doing so, it joined the distinguished company of Libya's Qaddafi and Albania's Enver Hoxha. Libya and Albania have since joined the world of law-abiding states in this respect, so now the US stands in splendid isolation. Nicaragua then brought the matter to the UN Security Council, which passed two resolutions calling on all states to observe international law. The resolutions were vetoed by the US, with the assistance of Britain and France, which abstained. All of this passed virtually without notice, and has been expunged from history.

Also forgotten—or rather, never noticed—is the fact that the "hostile forum" had bent over backwards to accommodate Washington. The Court rejected almost all of Nicaragua's case, presented by a distinguished Harvard University international lawyer, on the grounds that when the US had accepted World Court jurisdiction in 1946, it added a reservation exempting itself from charges under international treaties, specifically the Charters of the United Nations and the Organization of American States. Accordingly, the US is self-entitled to carry out aggression and other crimes that are far more serious than international terrorism. The Court correctly recognized this exemption, one aspect of much broader issues of sovereignty and global dominance that I will put aside.

Such thoughts as these should be uppermost in our minds when we consider the evil scourge of terrorism. We should also recall that although the Reagan years do constitute a chapter of unusual extremism in the annals of terrorism, they are not some strange departure from the norm. We find much the same at the opposite end of the political spectrum as well: the Kennedy administration. One illustration is Cuba. According to long-standing myth, thoroughly dismantled by recent scholarship, the US intervened in Cuba in 1898 to secure its liberation from Spain. In reality, the intervention was designed to prevent Cuba's imminent liberation from Spain, turning it into a virtual colony of the United States. In 1959, Cuba finally did liberate itself, causing consternation in Washington. Within months, the Eisenhower administration planned in secret to overthrow the government, and initiated bombing and economic sanctions. The basic thinking was expressed by a high State Department official: Castro would be removed "through disenchantment and disaffection based on economic dissatisfaction and hardship [so] every possible means should be undertaken promptly to weaken the economic life of Cuba [in order to] bring about hunger, desperation and [the] overthrow of the government."

The incoming Kennedy administration took over and escalated these programs. The reasons are frankly explained in the internal record, since declassified. Violence and economic strangulation were undertaken in response to Cuba's "successful defiance" of US policies going back 150 years; no Russians, but rather the Monroe Doctrine, which established Washington's right to dominate the hemisphere.

The concerns of the Kennedy administration went beyond the need to punish successful defiance. The administration feared that the Cuban example might infect others with the thought of "taking matters into their own hands," an idea with great appeal throughout the continent because "the distribution of land and other forms of national wealth greatly favors the propertied classes and the poor and underprivileged, stimulated by the example of the Cuban revolution, are now demanding opportunities for a decent living." That was the warning conveyed to incoming President Kennedy by his Latin America advisor, liberal historian Arthur Schlesinger. The analysis was soon confirmed by the CIA, which observed that "Castro's shadow looms large because social and economic conditions throughout Latin America invite opposition to ruling authority and encourage agitation for radical change," for which Castro's Cuba might provide a model.

Ongoing plans for invasion were soon implemented. When the invasion failed at the Bay of Pigs, Washington turned to a major terrorist war. The president assigned responsibility for the war to his brother, Robert Kennedy, whose highest priority was to bring "the terrors of the earth" to Cuba, in the words of his biographer, Arthur Schlesinger. The terrorist war was no slight affair; it was also a major factor in bringing the world to the verge of nuclear war in 1962, and was resumed as soon as the missile crisis ended. The terrorist war continued through the century from US territory, though in later years Washington no longer undertook terrorist attacks against Cuba, but only provided the base for them, and continues to provide haven to some of the most notorious international terrorists, with a long record of these and other crimes: Orlando Bosch, Luis Posada Carriles, and numerous others whose names would be well-known in the West if the concerns about terrorism were principled. Commentators are polite enough not to recall the Bush doctrine declared when he attacked Afghanistan: those who harbor terrorists are as guilty as the terrorists themselves, and must be treated accordingly, by bombing and invasion.

Perhaps this is enough to illustrate that state-directed international terrorism is considered an appropriate tool of diplomacy across the political spectrum. Nevertheless, Reagan was the first modern president to employ the audacious device of concealing his resort to "the evil scourge of terrorism" under the cloak of a "War on Terror."

The audacity of Reaganite terrorism was as impressive as its scale. To select only one example, for which events in Germany provided a pretext, in April

1986, the US Air Force bombed Libya, killing dozens of civilians. To add a personal note, on the day of the bombing, at about 6:30 pm, I received a phone call from Tripoli from the Mideast correspondent of ABC TV, Charles Glass, an old friend. He advised me to watch the 7 pm TV news. In 1986, all the TV channels ran their major news programs at 7 pm. I did so, and exactly at 7 pm, agitated news anchors switched to their facilities in Libya so that they could present, live, the US bombing of Tripoli and Benghazi, the first bombing in history enacted for prime time TV—no slight logistical feat: the bombers were denied the right to cross France and had to take a long detour over the Atlantic to arrive just in time for the evening news. After showing the exciting scenes of the cities in flames, the TV channels switched to Washington, for sober discussion of how the US was defending itself from Libyan terror, under the newly devised doctrine of "self-defense against future attack." Officials informed the country that they had certain knowledge that Libya had carried out a bombing of a disco in Berlin a few days earlier in which a US soldier had been killed. The certainty reduced to zero shortly after, as quietly conceded well after its purpose had been served. And it would have been hard to find even a raised eyebrow about the idea that the disco bombing would have justified the murderous assault on Libyan civilians.

The media were also polite enough not to notice the curious timing. Commentators were entranced by the solidity of the non-existent evidence and Washington's dedication to law. In a typical reaction, the NYT editors explained that "even the most scrupulous citizen can only approve and applaud the American attacks on Libya ... the United States has prosecuted [Qaddafi] carefully, proportionately—and justly," the evidence for Libyan responsibility for the disco bombing has been "now laid out clearly to the public," and "then came the jury, the European governments to which the United States went out of its way to send emissaries to share evidence and urge concerted action against the Libyan leader." Entirely irrelevant is that no credible evidence was laid out and that the "jury" was quite skeptical, particularly in Germany itself, where intensive investigation had found no evidence at all; or that the jury was calling on the executioner to refrain from any action.

The bombing of Libya was neatly timed for a congressional vote on aid to the US-run terrorist force attacking Nicaragua. To ensure that the timing would not be missed, Reagan made the connection explicit. In an address the day after the bombing Reagan said:

> I would remind the House [of Representatives] voting this week that this arch-terrorist [Qaddafi] has sent $400 million and an arsenal of weapons and advisers into Nicaragua to bring his war home to the United States. He has bragged that he is helping the Nicaraguans because they fight America on its own ground.

—namely America's own ground in Nicaragua. The idea that the "mad dog" was bringing his war home to us by providing arms to a country we were attacking with a CIA-run terrorist army based in our Honduran dependency was a nice touch, which did not go unnoticed. As the national press explained, the bombing of Libya should "strengthen President Reagan's hand in dealing with Congress on issues like the military budget and aid to Nicaraguan 'contras'."

This is only a small sample of Reagan's contributions to international terrorism. The most lasting among them was his enthusiastic organization of the jihadi movement in Afghanistan. The reasons were explained by the CIA station chief in Islamabad, who directed the project. In his words, the goal was to "kill Soviet Soldiers," a "noble goal" that he "loved," as did his boss in Washington. He also emphasized that "the mission was not to liberate Afghanistan"—and in fact it may have delayed Soviet withdrawal, some specialists believe. With his unerring instinct for favoring the most violent criminals, Reagan selected for lavish aid Gulbuddin Hekmatyar, famous for throwing acid in the faces of young women in Kabul and now a leader of the insurgents in Afghanistan, though perhaps he may soon join the other warlords of the western-backed government, current reports suggest. Reagan also lent strong support to the worst of Pakistan's dictators, Zia ul-Haq, helping him to develop his nuclear weapons program and to carry out his Saudi-funded project of radical Islamization of Pakistan. There is no need to dwell on the legacy for these tortured countries and the world.

Apart from Cuba, the plague of state terror in the Western hemisphere was initiated with the Brazilian coup in 1964, installing the first of a series of neo-Nazi National Security States and initiating a plague of repression without precedent in the hemisphere, always strongly backed by Washington, hence a particularly violent form of state-directed international terrorism. The campaign was in substantial measure a war against the Church. It was more than symbolic that it culminated in the assassination of six leading Latin American intellectuals, Jesuit priests, in November 1989, a few days after the fall of the Berlin wall. They were murdered by an elite Salvadoran battalion, fresh from renewed training at the John F. Kennedy Special Forces School in North Carolina. As was learned last November, but apparently aroused no interest, the order for the assassination was signed by the chief of staff and his associates, all of them so closely connected to the Pentagon and the US Embassy that it becomes even harder to imagine that Washington was unaware of the plans of its model battalion. This elite force had already left a trail of blood of the usual victims through the hideous decade of the 1980s in El Salvador, which opened with the assassination of Archbishop Romero, "the voice of the voiceless," by much the same hands.

The murder of the Jesuit priests was a crushing blow to liberation theology, the remarkable revival of Christianity initiated by Pope John XXIII at Vatican II, which he opened in 1962, an event that "ushered in a new era in the history of the Catholic Church," in the words of the distinguished theologian and historian of Christianity Hans Küng. Inspired by Vatican II, Latin American Bishops adopted "the preferential option for the poor," renewing the radical pacifism of the Gospels that had been put to rest when the Emperor Constantine established

Christianity as the religion of the Roman Empire—"a revolution" that converted "the persecuted church" to a "persecuting church," in Küng's words. In the post-Vatican II attempt to revive the Christianity of the pre-Constantine period, priests, nuns, and laypersons took the message of the Gospels to the poor and the persecuted, brought them together in "base communities," and encouraged them to take their fate into their own hands and to work together to overcome the misery of survival in brutal realms of US power.

The reaction to this grave heresy was not long in coming. The first salvo was Kennedy's military coup in Brazil in 1964, overthrowing a mildly social democratic government and instituting a reign of torture and violence. The campaign ended with the murder of the Jesuit intellectuals 20 years ago. There has been much debate about who deserves credit for the fall of the Berlin wall, but there is none about the responsibility for the brutal demolition of the attempt to revive the church of the Gospels. Washington's School of the Americas, famous for its training of Latin American killers, proudly announced as one of its "talking points" that liberation theology was "defeated with the assistance of the US army"—given a helping hand, to be sure by the Vatican, using the gentler means of expulsion and suppression.

As you recall, last November was dedicated to celebration of the twentieth anniversary of the liberation of Eastern Europe from Russian tyranny, a victory of the forces of "love, tolerance, nonviolence, the human spirit and forgiveness," as Vaclav Havel declared. Less attention—in fact, virtually zero—was devoted to the brutal assassination of his Salvadoran counterparts a few days after the Berlin wall fell. And I doubt that one could even find an allusion to what that brutal assassination signified: the end of a decade of vicious terror in Central America, and the final triumph of the "return to barbarism in our time" that opened with the 1964 Brazilian coup, leaving many religious martyrs in its wake and ending the heresy initiated in Vatican II—not exactly an era of "love, tolerance, nonviolence, the human spirit and forgiveness."

We can wait until tomorrow to see how much attention will be given to the thirtieth anniversary of the assassination of the Voice of the Voiceless while he was reading mass, a few days after he wrote a letter to President Carter pleading with him—in vain—not send aid to the military junta, who "know only how to repress the people and defend the interests of the Salvadoran oligarchy" and will use the aid "to destroy the people's organizations fighting to defend their fundamental human rights." As happened. And we can learn a good bit from what we are unlikely to see tomorrow.

The contrast between the celebration last November of the fall of the tyranny of the enemy, and the silence about the culmination of the hideous atrocities in our own domains, is so glaring that it takes real dedication to miss it. It sheds a somber light on our moral and intellectual culture. The same is true of the retrospective assessments of the Reagan era. We can put aside the mythology about his achievements, which would have impressed Kim il-Sung. What he actually did has virtually disappeared. President Obama hails him as a "transformative figure." At Stanford University's prestigious Hoover Institution Reagan is revered as a colossus whose "spirit seems to stride the country, watching us like a warm and friendly ghost." We arrive by plane in Washington at Reagan international airport—or if we prefer, at John Foster Dulles international airport, honoring another prominent terrorist commander, whose exploits include overthrowing Iranian and Guatemalan democracy, installing the terror and torture state of the Shah and the most vicious of the terrorist states of Central America. The terrorist exploits of Washington's Guatemalan clients reached true genocide in the highlands in the 1980s while Reagan praised the worst of the killers, Rioss Montt, as "a man of great personal integrity" who was "totally dedicated to democracy" and was receiving a "bum rap" from human rights organizations.

I have been writing about international terrorism ever since Reagan declared a War on Terror in 1981. In doing so, I have kept to the official definitions of "terrorism" in US and British law and in army manuals, all approximately the same. To take one succinct official definition, terrorism is "the calculated use of violence or threat of violence to attain goals that are political, religious, or ideological in nature ... through intimidation, coercion, or instilling fear." Everything I have just described, and a great deal more like it, falls within the category of terrorism, in fact state-directed international terrorism, in the technical sense of US–British law.

For exactly that reason, the official definitions are unusable. They fail to make a crucial distinction: the concept of "terrorism" must somehow be crafted to include their terrorism against us, while excluding our terrorism against them, often far more extreme. To devise such a definition is a challenging task. Accordingly, from the 1980s there have been many scholarly conferences, academic publications, and international symposia devoted to the task of defining "terrorism." In public discourse the problem does not arise. Well-educated circles have internalized the special sense of "terrorism" required for justification of state action and control of domestic populations, and departure from the canon is generally ignored, or if noticed, elicits impressive tantrums.

Let us keep, then, to convention, and restrict attention to the terror they commit against us. It is no laughing matter, and sometimes reaches extreme levels. Probably the most egregious single crime of international terrorism in the modern era was the destruction of the World Trade Center on 9/11, killing almost 3,000 people, a "crime against humanity" carried out with "wickedness and awesome cruelty," as Robert Fisk reported. It is widely agreed that 9/11 changed the world.

Awful as the crime was, one can imagine worse. Suppose that al-Qaeda had been supported by an awesome superpower intent on overthrowing the government of the United States. Suppose that the attack had succeeded: al-Qaeda had bombed the White House, killed the president, and installed a vicious military dictatorship, which killed some 50,000–100,000 people, brutally tortured 700,000, set up a major center of terror and subversion that carried out assassinations throughout the world and helped establish "National Security States" elsewhere that tortured and murdered with abandon. Suppose further that the dictator brought in economic advisers who within a few years drove the economy to one of the worst disasters in its history while their proud mentors collected Nobel Prizes and received other accolades. That would have been vastly more horrendous even than 9/11.

And as we all should know, it is not necessary to imagine, because it in fact did happen: in Chile, on the date that Latin Americans sometimes call "the first 9/11," September 11, 1973. The only change I have made is to per capita equivalents, an appropriate measure. But the first 9/11 did not change history, for good reasons: the events were too normal. In fact, the installation of the Pinochet regime was just one event in the plague that began with the military coup in Brazil in 1964, spreading with similar or even worse horrors in other countries and reaching Central America in the 1980s under Reagan—whose South American favorite was the regime of the Argentine generals, the most savage of them all, consistent with his general stance on state violence.

Putting all of this inconvenient reality aside, let us continue to follow convention and imagine that the War on Terror re-declared by George W. Bush on 9/11 2001 was directed to ending the plague of international terrorism, properly restricted in scope to satisfy doctrinal needs. There were sensible steps that could have been undertaken to achieve that goal. The murderous acts of 9/11 were bitterly condemned even within the jihadi movements. One constructive step would have been to isolate al-Qaeda, and unify opposition to it even among those attracted to its project. Nothing of the sort ever seems to have been considered. Instead, the Bush administration and its allies chose to unify the jihadi movement in support of Bin Laden and to mobilize many others to his cause by confirming his charge that the West is at war with Islam: invading Afghanistan and then Iraq, resorting to torture and rendition, and in general, choosing violence for the purposes of state power. With good reason, the hawkish Michael Scheuer, who was in charge of tracking bin Laden for the CIA for many years, concludes that "the United States of America remains bin Laden's only indispensable ally."

The same conclusion was drawn by US Major Matthew Alexander, perhaps the most respected of US interrogators, who elicited the information that to the capture of Abu Musab al-Zarqawi, the head of al-Qaeda in Iraq. Alexander has only contempt for the harsh interrogation methods demanded by the Bush administration. Like FBI interrogators, he believes that the Rumsfeld–Cheney preference for torture elicits no useful information, in contrast with more humane forms of interrogation that have even succeeded in converting the targets and enlisting them as reliable informants and collaborators. He singles out Indonesia for its successes in civilized forms of interrogation, and urges the US to follow its methods. Not only does Rumsfeld–Cheney torture elicit no useful information: it also creates terrorists. From hundreds of interrogations, Alexander discovered that many foreign fighters came to Iraq in reaction to the abuses at Guantánamo and Abu Ghraib, and that they and their domestic allies turned to suicide bombing and other terrorist acts for the same reason. He believes that the use of torture may have led to the death of more US soldiers than the toll of the 9/11 terrorist attack. The most significant revelation in the released Torture

Memos is that interrogators were under "relentless pressure" from Cheney and Rumsfeld to resort to harsher methods to find evidence for their fantastic claim that Saddam Hussein was cooperating with al-Qaida.

The attack on Afghanistan in October 2001 is called "the good war," no questions asked, a justifiable act of self-defense with the noble aim of protecting human rights from the evil Taliban. There are a few problems with that near-universal contention. For one thing, the goal was not to remove the Taliban. Rather, Bush informed the people of Afghanistan that they would be bombed unless the Taliban turned bin Laden over to the US, as they might have done, had the US agreed to their request to provide some evidence of his responsibility for 9/11. The request was dismissed with contempt, for good reasons. As the head of the FBI conceded eight months later, after the most intensive international investigation in history they still had no evidence, and certainly had none the preceding October. The most he could say is that the FBI "believed" that the plot had been hatched in Afghanistan and had been implemented in the Gulf Emirates and Germany.

Three weeks after the bombing began, war aims shifted to overthrow of the regime. British Admiral Sir Michael Boyce announced that the bombing would continue until "the people of the country ... get the leadership changed"—a textbook case of international terrorism.

It is also not true that there were no objections to the attack. With virtual unanimity, international aid organizations vociferously objected because it terminated their aid efforts, which were desperately needed. At the time, it was estimated that some 5 million people were relying on aid for survival, and that an additional 2.5 million would be put at risk of starvation by the US–UK attack. The bombing was therefore an example of extreme criminality, whether or not the anticipated consequences took place.

Furthermore, the bombing was bitterly condemned by leading anti-Taliban Afghans, including the US favorite, Abdul Haq, who was given special praise as a martyr after the war by President Hamid Karzai. Just before he entered Afghanistan, and was captured and killed, he condemned the bombing that was then underway and criticized the US for refusing to support efforts of his and others "to create a revolt within the Taliban." The bombing was "a big setback for these efforts," he said, outlining them and calling on the US to assist them with funding and other support instead of undermining them with bombs. The US, he said, "is trying to show its muscle, score a victory and scare everyone in the world. They don't care about the suffering of the Afghans or how many people we will lose."

Shortly after, 1,000 Afghan leaders gathered in Peshawar, some of them exiles, some coming from within Afghanistan, all committed to overthrowing the Taliban regime. It was "a rare display of unity among tribal elders, Islamic scholars, fractious politicians, and former guerrilla commanders," the press reported. They had many disagreements, but unanimously "urged the US to stop the air raids" and appealed to the international media to call for an end to the "bombing of innocent people." They urged that other means be adopted to overthrow the hated Taliban regime, a goal they believed could be achieved without further death and destruction. The bombing was also harshly condemned by the prominent women's organization RAWA—which received some belated recognition when it became ideologically serviceable to express concern (briefly) about the fate of women in Afghanistan.

In short, the unquestionably "good war" does not look so good when we pay some attention to unacceptable facts.

It should not be necessary to tarry on the invasion of Iraq. Keeping solely to the effect on jihadi terror, the invasion was undertaken with the expectation that it would lead to an increase in terrorism, as it did, far beyond what was anticipated. It caused a seven-fold increase in terror, according to analyses by US terrorism experts.

One may ask why these attacks were undertaken, but it is reasonably clear that confronting the evil scourge of terrorism was not a high priority, if it was even a consideration.

If that had been the goal, there were options to pursue. Some I have already mentioned. More generally, the US and Britain could have followed the proper procedures for dealing with a major crime: determine who is responsible, apprehend the suspects (with international cooperation if necessary, easy to obtain), and bring them to a fair trial. Furthermore, attention would be paid to the roots of terror. That can be extremely effective, as the US and UK had just learned in Northern Ireland. IRA terror was a very serious matter. As long as London reacted by violence, terror, and torture, it was the "indispensable ally" of the more violent elements of the IRA, and the cycle of terror escalated. By the late 1990s, London began to attend to the grievances that lay at the roots of the terror, and to deal with those that were legitimate—as should be done irrespective of terror. Within a few years, terror virtually disappeared. I happened to be in Belfast in 1993. It was a war zone. I was there again last fall. There are tensions, but at a level that is barely detectable to a visitor. There are important lessons here. Even without this experience we should know that violence engenders violence, while sympathy and concern cool passions and can evoke cooperation and empathy.

If we seriously want to end the plague of terrorism, we know how to do it. First, end our own role as perpetrators. That alone will have a substantial effect. Second, attend to the grievances that are typically in the background, and if they are legitimate, do something about them. Third, if an act of terror occurs, deal with it as a criminal act: identify and apprehend the suspects and carry out an honest judicial process. That actually works. In contrast, the techniques that are employed enhance the threat of terror. The evidence is fairly strong, and falls together which much else.

This is not the only case where the approaches that might well reduce a serious threat are systematically avoided, and those that are unlikely to do so are adopted instead. One such case is the so-called "war on drugs." Over almost 40 years, the war has failed to curtail drug use or even street price of drugs. It has been established by many studies, including those of the US government, that by far the most cost-effective approach to drug abuse is prevention and treatment. But that approach is consistently avoided in state policy, which prefers far more expensive violent measures that have barely any impact on drug use, though they have other consistent consequences.

In cases like these, the only rational conclusion is that the declared goals are not the real ones, and that if we want to learn about the real goals, we should adopt an approach that is familiar in the law: relying on predictable outcome as evidence for intent. I think the approach leads to quite plausible conclusions, for the "war on drugs," the "War on Terror," and much else. That, however, is work for another day.

Note

1 Copyright © 2010 by Professor Dr. Noam A. Chomsky.

2 The complex relationship between peacebuilding and terrorism approaches

Towards post-terrorism and a post-liberal peace?*

Oliver P. Richmond and Ioannis Tellidis

> Approaches to terrorism and peacebuilding have a complex relationship with each other, which may be explained according to four categories outlined in this chapter. These range from blocking each others' aims, nullifying terrorism, supporting a very limited, or a broader peace process. Each of these categories has implications for the inclusion and reconciliation of a wide range of actors and the hybrid nature of the emerging peace. This relates to the critical approach of using theory to create emancipatory forms of peace, which is used as a basis for the examination of the production of hybridity via the interaction of approaches to terrorism and peacebuilding in five cases in this chapter. These include Sri Lanka, Kashmir, the Middle East, Nepal, and Northern Ireland. We argue that "post-liberal" possibilities for a hybrid form of peace (which are inherent in such conflicts) offer a "post-terrorist" potential for peace processes.

Introduction

Orthodox terrorism approaches, as with liberal peacebuilding, have become relatively empty signifiers that have lost some of the explanatory and practical traction they once had. This is due to their expropriation by policy and academic circles to support universalizing understandings of political liberalism, neoliberal ideology, national and institutional interests, and because they have been successful in co-opting academic debates, to some degree at least.[1] This has interfered with the critical job of using theory to create emancipatory forms of peace. It is well known that both terrorism and orthodox terrorism responses may prevent peace processes from proceeding, as in Northern Ireland until the mid-1990s or in Sri Lanka and Kashmir. What is less well known is the evidence that approaches to both analyzing and combating terrorism even in a critical vein may undermine and contradict peacebuilding processes, unless they themselves are in some way post-colonial and "post-liberal" (meaning a hybrid of contextual and international dynamics, institutions, norms, law, and actors). There have been often surprising hints of this evolution in various phases of the peace processes in Kashmir, Sri Lanka, the Middle East, Nepal, and Northern Ireland, offering possibilities for a hybrid form of peace. However, such an evolution has rarely been sustained. Instead the interaction of liberal peacebuilding and orthodox terrorism approaches has tended to reinforce securitized states, or virtually liberal and thinly cosmopolitan states, which themselves replicate the conditions of conflict.

Liberal peacebuilding approaches that are (more often than not) designed and executed as top-down policies, in tandem with the controversies generated by dominant approaches to terrorism, often confound efforts that seek to produce a durable and sustainable peace. They rest on exclusive normative systems and exacerbate the motives that terrorism and extremism often draw on, or enable a pool of supporters motivated by the cultural, identity, or welfare exclusions the liberal peace allows. Furthermore, they also reinforce the very state institutions that often produce such exclusions. They reflect a liberal project, wherein local interests are insufficiently represented (even marginalized in cases). This has led scholars to question the effectiveness, the appropriateness, and the legitimacy of liberal peacebuilding.[2] This is particularly problematic where "terrorism" has been used as a strategy to overturn an old order, or to attack the establishment of a new one through a peace process.[3] The intention to reconstruct stability as framed by the liberal peace and influenced by so-called orthodox understandings of terrorism and their security implications, and the concurrent neglect of the underlying sources of conflict, suggest that the nature of the "peace" that is being built is not entirely inclusive or context sensitive.[4] It normally rests on the exclusion of terrorist actors as well as perceived "non-liberal" actors, at least until they renounce the use of violence, producing a "catch 22" situation where they must give up their leverage before arriving at the negotiating table, the outcome of which is predetermined by the liberal peace's conditionalities. These include democratic majorities, political and business elites, pluralist states, a rule of law and state controlled security, neoliberal development and a civil society where individualism fragments the capacity for social control, either by states or by revolutionary or terrorist organizations. Furthermore, the peace that is being built is influenced by an externalized political, economic, and cultural geography which needs to be protected from radical difference, from non-state self-determination, and from alternative claims to legitimacy. To put it in different terms, the aforementioned are more akin to "statebuilding" rather than "peacebuilding."[5]

This chapter assesses whether the emergence of hybrid peace processes in which critical positions engage with agendas beyond liberal, orthodox, or critical frameworks may counter these dynamics in practice. It examines the impact of peace processes and the development of institutions that bridge local and international differences, thus producing a hybrid model of "local-liberal" peace, which may be more inclusive and may also gain traction and legitimacy even with the most "incorrigible" of spoilers.[6] It assesses whether this offers an opportunity to develop a post-liberal peace and a "post-terrorism" approach, which though strategically and normatively challenging, might engage more fully with root causes of violence and its prevention, with the normative aspirations of the liberal peace, and the troubling phenomena of terrorism committed in the name of peace (meaning national aspirations or claims for power and representation) or against a peace process. The term "peace process" in our article denotes a process that aims at a negotiated settlement between the main parties to the conflict, including the government, the international community, the non- or substate actors that utilize violence against the government and other liberal forces (national and international), and of course the everyday society who is more often than not the main recipient of the violence and the suffering. It is a process that is sustained over a period of time (which differs from conflict to conflict, and from one region to another), and one which deals with the main constitutional, institutional, and normative issues in the conflict.

The next section outlines our theoretical framework. This is then juxtaposed with our case studies, which offer insights from conflicts where peacebuilding efforts have been more efficient, primarily because of their elasticity when it comes to the inclusion of actors and potential hybridity. These are compared with situations where such elasticity has not been present. In Northern Ireland and Nepal, for instance, terrorists have become accepted politicians, which in turn led to a significant recession of violence and to more meaningful and focused attempts to build peace. It is for this reason that our use of the term "terrorism" goes beyond the semantics accorded to it by orthodox terrorism theories and their use by states, and indeed by all our case studies. Taking into consideration the endless debates on the definition of the phenomenon, we define "terrorism" as the incitement of, or threat to incite, terror in an attempt to maximize gains in a conflicting political relationship. Moreover, and in line with the inclusionary character of a post-liberal peacebuilding framework, our discussion of "terrorism" incorporates not only the most hard-line of actors that are ideologically opposed to liberal peace (within a terrorist organization or perhaps as "incomprehensible" as Aum Shinrikyo) but also those actors who use political violence in order to expose and rectify actual grievances concerning representation, subsistence, and identity. This is not to justify any use of violence, but to paraphrase Clausewitz, terrorism is politics by other means.[7] Peacebuilding seeks to provide politics with a non-violent normative, institutional, legal, and financial framework. Clearly one of the lessons of the last 20 years, from Cambodia to Afghanistan, is that peace processes need to be as inclusive as possible if they are to retain legitimacy and forward momentum.

Towards post-liberal peacebuilding and a post-terrorism framework

It has been established that orthodox and even critical approaches that respond to terrorism may reproduce mutual resistance, which is reflected in liberal institutions, even if they aspire to a critical role of emancipation.[8] It is also well known that there are channels of communication that transgress legality and formality even where terrorism is concerned in an effort to establish an often liberally oriented peace process. This hints at political and indeed cultural openness even in the midst of the most extreme violence. Yet, at the same time it is also clear that these dynamics often juxtapose liberal and non-liberal value systems. These

Peacebuilding and terrorism approaches 21

tensions can be harnessed not to produce the now typical deadlock over security, sovereignty, institutions, rights, or needs provision, but to produce forms of hybrid peace. This requires a hybrid peace process to bridge the polarities of mutual resistance between states, combatants, and terrorist actors, to internalize the norms of peace over violence, and to lead to a compromise which preserves everyday integrity especially relating to rights and needs.[9] This also raises the question of how to negotiate a new hybrid peace between terrorists, militants, and other actors who use violence for political reasons and liberal states to produce a hybrid, post-liberal form of peace. This would interrogate the claims made by those using political violence as well as the liberal peace in the areas of rights, needs, governance, and security. It also raises the issue of whether a hybrid peace will mainly represent the state, liberal actors, those who control the means of violence (i.e., it mainly represents power), or whether it will resolve the structural conditions of conflict (i.e., it represents everyday forms of peace)?[10]

Contemporary approaches to liberal peacebuilding aim to produce states which have significant institutions, control of security and territory, but intervene little in local or global markets and provide only limited safety nets or public services. Thus, it fails to benefit those who most need a sustainable and durable peace. It may exacerbate the types of polarization that occur that feed terrorism in society. This might be because of a range of exclusions and proscriptions decided either internally or externally, or because it fails to focus on resolving root causes (especially relating to material and structural matters),[11] or because the social, economic, and political inappropriateness of the project exacerbates and reproduces frictions and conflicts rather than eliminating them. Moderate and inclusive grassroots actors that are far more reliable and trustworthy, or have a localized perspective on where causal factors emanate from and which actors are involved, and also may have access to localized strategies to disempower those who want to use violence, are repeatedly overlooked by the international community. Instead, the latter seems to favor negotiations with local power-brokers who are often exclusionary and extremist (perhaps covertly) from the perspective of many local commentators who are outside government, the state, or whose connections with international actors are minimal.

The nature of extremist and exclusionist local power-brokers holds the key to the manifestation of terrorism in conflicts where peacebuilding efforts are taking place. To exclude such actors because of their methods and because they may hold taboo positions or aspire to controversial ideologies and norms, denies the peace process access and the capacity to negotiate over these. The point of any such negotiation would be to minimize any demanded compromise on basic human rights and needs and to provide both to the general population as quickly as possible. Failure to do so may result in illiberal and negative forms of peace and the construction of a security state apparatus (as in Kashmir, the Middle East, or in Northern Ireland until the Good Friday Agreement), with its attendant long term failures to cement an inclusive peace. Or it produces a victor's peace, if elite or international actors have sufficient coercive capacity, based on terrorists' complete exclusion, as recently occurred in Sri Lanka. Both strategies are well known to be contradictory to a liberal peace, and its norms and rights. In many cases for long periods of time the internationals' mantra was not to negotiate with terrorists, thereby disabling significant local actors and aspects of a plausible peace process aimed at creating the liberal state. Moreover, the readiness with which both states and the internationals have equated entire communities with "terrorists" in certain cases, made the realization of a liberal peace even more remote.[12] The outcome has been heavily militarized and illiberal states where poverty has dominated and been the marker, together with identity, of division.

This also connects with a key dynamic in the inter-relationship between orthodox terrorism and liberal peacebuilding approaches. Spoiling attacks on liberal peacebuilding tend to be taken as acts of insurgency or terrorism, and have as a result empowered a conservative rather than emancipatory version of the liberal peace.[13] This conservative version rests on high levels of securitisation[14] and a focus on institutions over everyday life, which has an impact on budgets, policies, political and state objectives, and the amounts of resources individuals have access to in order to provide material substance to liberal rights, law, and potential. It is not emancipatory, so offers little hope of a self-sustaining peace: it cannot provide a social contract because it works by excluding segments of the population. In turn, as is evident in virtually all our case studies, this exclusion often leads to the empowerment of terrorist discourses. Thus root causes remain unaddressed, and securitization of both state and its opposition intensifies, in a guerrilla war of attrition whose centralized power is ill suited to respond legitimately.

Critical approaches to understanding terrorism[15] appear to be more suited to liberal peacebuilding approaches, and offer more capacity for a peace at the everyday level, maintaining rights, law, and needs. However, though these are focused on cosmopolitan solutions to conflict, they also demand that potential interlocutors in any liberal peace process adopt the praxis of the liberal peace and liberal institutionalism (in other words, "become liberal"), without necessarily taking into consideration the potential inherent in grassroots and/or civil society movements.[16] This denies, to a lesser extent than more orthodox approaches, alterity and difference, which are also significant at the everyday level, the rejection of which may well be a causal factor of terrorist and political violence. In cases where all parties can be seen to be connected to, relate to, or are part of a liberal polity, progress in liberal peacebuilding can be very plausible. In cases where peace processes involve actors aspiring to different or multiple identities, liberal peacebuilding is relatively ineffective.

A post-terrorism/post-liberal hybrid peace process would capitalize on the dynamics of hybridity, both emerging and needed. It would require more open forms of negotiation, more engagement with all actors who have a stake in local, state, and regional politics, an engagement with "local-local" dynamics, needs as well as rights. This represents a struggle for legitimacy in an international and regional terrain, a state terrain, and a local terrain. At the international level, the orthodox terrorism and liberal peacebuilding approach are in tension over international legitimacy: this represents security versus peace, or the realist architecture of the securitized state versus the liberal architecture of the institutionalized, law-governed, civil society and market oriented state. At the local level, especially beneath civil society (at the local-local level where alterity is present)[17] there is a mixture of marginal legitimacy for terrorism aims (though not necessarily their tactics), support for a liberal state, and strong legitimacy for hybridity resulting from local agency and identity.

This represents a possibility for a local-liberal hybrid form of peace,[18] and offers some opportunities, if recognized for a negotiation of the frameworks of peace, the negation of terrorist violence, the acceptance of difference, and to some degree the maintenance of liberal and cosmopolitan norms. It rests on hybrid forms of politics, rescues peace processes from terrorism, the liberal peace from a lack of local consent, and develops local-liberal hybridity which offers the chance of a more sophisticated peace than that which has emerged in orthodox environments, such as in Kashmir or Sri Lanka. Contrary to realist and orthodox frameworks that seek to guarantee the actors' security before any peace is established, post-terrorism seeks to incorporate and reconcile even those actors whose agenda is opposed to liberal institutionalist approaches as the peace itself is negotiated and formed. To some degree there may be glimmers of this post-terrorism approach in Nepal and in Northern Ireland. Making clear that this is a post-liberal peace process would offer "incorrigible" actors the incentive of constructing a hybrid order drawing on their own identities, customs, and interests, as well as those of the liberal peace and its benefits. It gives all a stake in the outcome of a peace process which probably surpasses their stake in an outcome configured by relations of power, victory, or defeat.

Of course, this does not mean the acceptance of violence—far from it—but it does mean that more nuanced and localized understandings of legitimacy at the local level need to be seen as complementary to international and state legitimacy, and indeed constitutive of a broader legitimacy for approaches to terrorism and peacebuilding where they interact. It would be far more commensurate with security, democracy, law, and rights embodied in stable institutions, as well as representative of contextual alterity which might modify them.

This analysis gives rise to a number of categories, as indicated by our case studies, with a range of implications, relating to the interplay of terrorism approaches and peacebuilding.

1. The first category indicates that orthodox terrorism approaches justify a conservative liberal peace and is used to prevent the latter progressing towards a more stable version, resting on nationalism. Key actors are excluded and hybridity is denied by all sides in the dispute, often through force.
2. The second indicates that an orthodox terrorism approach might lead to an orthodox form of liberal peace but this depends on the conflict actors

forming their own state, resting on ethnonationalist understandings of legitimacy. Hybridity is blocked or managed by separation but contacts between disputants may be more flexible.

3   The third indicates that critical terrorism approaches can support liberal peacebuilding, but may block a move to a more contextual form of peacebuilding in a context where liberal values are not widely held, and especially where secessionism is feared. All actors are included in the peace process, but hybridity favors the state and formal actors.
4   The final category indicates how post-terrorism approaches might support an inclusive and hybrid form of post-liberal peace that has international and local legitimacy and promotes a wider reconciliation.

In the next section, we turn to illustrations from our case studies which illustrate these dynamics.

Orthodox categories of terrorism and liberal peacebuilding

Sri Lanka: orthodox terrorism with elements of a conservative liberal peace approach

The change of government and western attitudes towards the Liberation Tigers of Tamil Eelam (LTTE) in Sri Lanka is indicative of the effect of 9/11 on anti-terrorist and/or statebuilding discourses. The initial priority of Prime Minister Wickremesinghe's government during 2001–2002, with international donor assistance, was the development of the Tamil region and a concurrent peace process, quietly facilitated by Norwegian diplomats, assuming that this would be enough to turn a substantial number of LTTE supporters against the use of political violence and for the peace process. Yet, neither state nor non-state terrorism subsided completely because the political solutions brought forward did not address the root issue of autonomy and independence. At the start of the peace process, the government referred to the extremists as the LTTE, recognizing them as a political entity, opponents and/or group with a specific and particular socio-political agenda. After 9/11 the term used to describe LTTE by governmental forces and agencies was simply "terrorists." The same change in attitude became evident in the general population who, after 2005, referred to LTTE as "terrorists" as the full force of the state was turned against them.[19] This had a commensurate effect on the peace process which rapidly came to be seen as implausible.

The collapse of the peace process cannot be solely attributed to the incongruence and discord between the two main actors. Nor can it be blamed on the intermediaries, or the lack of a peace dividend for the state and its citizens. The liberal expectations and agendas of the international community, seeking an immediate improvement on democracy and human rights, did not reflect the preparedness of either the government or the LTTE, nor was their much local or international sincerity in their application. The hurried international attempts after 2002 to bring about a successful completion of the peace process, without the necessary understanding by the local actors of the need to incorporate and implement democratic and human rights reforms, are equally to blame, in the absence of a significant capacity to redistribute a material peace dividend, though development was certainly experienced in parts of the LTTE controlled areas.

For, while the Sri Lankan government accepted that the LTTE would need time to accept such proposals, the international community continued to put pressure on the government despite the fact that there were no international actors that could exert leverage over LTTE. Instead of incremental measures, negotiations, and compromises, the international community in essence adopted the same stance as Prabakharan's[20] personal agenda: no compromise.[21] Initially, while the peace process was still owned by local actors, it looked promising. As soon as they could, the international community stepped in and not only took over as the primary promoter of peace, but sidelined the local actors and even undermined the Norwegian efforts that until then had brought the possibility of a sustainable peace closer than ever before.[22]

As the process began to collapse, perhaps more importantly as well as cynically, branding the LTTE as a terrorist organization excluded them from a series of rounds of negotiations that took place in Western capitals,[23] thus hindering from within all efforts to promote and establish a durable and sustainable peace. The LTTE should not be absolved from the crimes and abuses of human rights it committed, but this also does not justify Prabakharan's personal strategy.[24] His politics alienated a substantial part of the Tamil population but, more significantly, they allowed the government to justify its human rights abuses in the name of national security—as the recent UN Human Rights Report attests.[25] A better understanding of the context is necessary in both cases because rather than merely resting on identifying terrorist actors and agendas or maintaining a liberal peace agenda, it can provide the international community with an understanding of those actors capable and willing to participate in the production of a hybrid peace: one that may incorporate liberal institutional norms tailored to and fomented by local particularities, but not securitized either by terrorism or orthodox terrorism praxis. Unfortunately, Prabakharan's agenda was to produce an exclusive form of peace which continues to favor the Sinhala majority.

Yet the main lesson to be learned from more recent events in Sri Lanka is that the international community's and state actors' discourse of liberal peace is more often than not camouflaged as a pure counter-terrorist strategy, with little concern for the liberal norm of human rights protection and democratic rule.[26] Thus liberal peacebuilding parallels orthodox terrorism and the securitization of the state. It favors a state with a firm grip on security and a rule of law over human rights and welfare. Yet at the same time liberal peacebuilding is clearly blocked by orthodox terrorism approaches applied by the state and international community. The Norwegian mediation efforts that came closer than ever to a compromise that would have seen a share in power, some degree of self-rule, and the elimination of violence, were spoiled by the Sinhalese government because they were deemed to be working in favor of Tamil rights and independence, even if they seemed to offer a critical bridge between ending terrorism and making peace.[27] Similarly, with local NGOs that attempted to foment some kind of peace: for the government, any such non-governmental actor has been equated with the LTTE, and under counter-terrorist laws all NGOs had to inform local police stations before they engaged in any initiative.[28] A combination of international complicity,[29] Chinese strategic support, the legitimacy of a counter-terrorism strategy, and the success of the Rajapaksa government made this confluence seem plausible. Orthodox terrorism approaches undermined liberal peacebuilding and evacuated local alterity in conformity with the nationalist Sinhala strategy of the post-independence era.

In May 2009, governmental forces defeated the LTTE and put an end to 25 years of violence. This chapter does not wish to engage in an evaluation of military anti- or counter-terrorist strategies. Instead, we wish to highlight the alternative routes that could have been possible and perhaps more effective (as will be shown in the following sections) had the international community upheld its very own norms of the protection of human rights and the promotion of democratic administration, while also accommodating local contextuality (often termed "local ownership" and participation). In the case of Sri Lanka, the importance of state security was superior to the guarantee of human rights,[30] both towards the end of the conflict where civilians were intentionally targeted,[31] as well as after the LTTE had been defeated: the detention of 14,000 suspects, a further 130,000 refugees placed in camps, and videos of extra-judicial killings bear testament to this.[32] It raises a further question of whether there are steps that might now be taken to prevent a reversion to violence despite the fact that the LTTE agenda remains extant, that a nationalist Sinhala government has a firm grip on power, strong international support as well as condemnation exists, and there is a government-held aversion to third party assistance or accountability?

In this case dynamics of hybridity have long been in existence at the social level, but these have been less visible from the state and international perspective than the institutional and counter-terrorist discourses. The latter have controlled formal modes of legitimacy, and local actors have generally fallen into line with ethnonationalist discourses, apart from a few key NGOs. Thus, the orthodox terrorism and liberal peacebuilding approach support the notion of a state but contradict each other over the issue of a nationalist or pluralist form of state. The dominant Sinhala majority have embraced the liberal architecture of the institutionalized, law-governed, civil society and market oriented state. At the local level, the local-liberal hybrid is more apparent, and was so particularly during the Norwegian backed peace process, where there were opportunities for a negotiation of the frameworks of peace, the negation of terrorist violence, the acceptance of difference, and to some degree the maintenance of liberal and cosmopolitan norms. This emergence of a post-terrorism and post-liberal approach, however, was blocked by the return to a more nationalist and orthodox terrorism approach under President Rajapaksa which has ironically undermined the liberal state, though it also blocked the possible negotiated secession of the LTTE.

Kashmir: balancing orthodox terrorism and conservative liberal peace

In Kashmir, unlike in Sri Lanka, an orthodox approach to terrorism has blocked peacemaking since the start of the conflict, due to the fact that it constitutes an issue of discord between two nuclear superpowers with aspirations to maintain nationhood status and territorial control, and that are against secessionism or self-determination. Since 2004 the two sides have taken incremental rapprochement steps with the aim of reducing tensions, violence, and fatalities. These have included the opening of back-channel/track II diplomatic contacts, the reopening of a trade route that had been shut for over 60 years, and the formation by the Indian PM of advisory groups whose aim is the negotiation and improvement of issues of everyday life, independence/self-determination, violence, and reduction of army presence. The Indian redeployment of 5,000 of its troops from Jammu and Kashmir is indicative of that effort and the overall discourse of peace that could be seen to be emerging, though of course this was mainly subservient to national rather than everyday interests, and such developments have more recently been halted.

Nevertheless, the peace process has always been too weak, top down, and elitist, focused on sovereignty, national prestige, territory and borders, to be seriously effective—let alone sustained and self-sustainable. It is a peace process in which the subjects are the states of Pakistan and India, rather than the people who live in the region. Political, military, social, and economic elites at either side of the border have a vested interest in the continuation of the conflict.[33] Furthermore, the armies of both countries impose their own will and understanding on the situation: Pakistan's military has fueled violence by aiding extremist groups and by fomenting radicalization among the population, even as recently as January 2010;[34] while the Indian military has a very strong presence in the area (800,000 troops) and even when announcements of troops withdrawal are made, these retired officers are then turned into paramilitaries in order to fight insurgents and extremist groups.[35] Thus, India seems to succumb to international pressures to de-escalate the crisis, without necessarily loosening its tight grip. This means that an orthodox approach to terrorism makes more sense to either side than a liberal peacebuilding approach does, because it would aid irredentist or secessionist impulses through the move towards rights and majoritarian notions of democracy.[36] The problem with this is that it reifies the territorial, sovereign, and nationalist side of the conflict, places its resolution in the hands of the elites invested in these dynamics, and disempowers local populations. This opens the way for some to exploit the situation through violence, the marginalization of civil society, and the loss of a social contract. Those who refrain from violence risk becoming both the victims of terrorism and of nationalism just as those who do not refrain. This means there needs to be an approach which rewards democratic politics over violence and nationalism.

However, the general view in national capitals on both sides of the Line of Control (LoC) is "why talk to local Kashmiri politicians if we are already engaged in talks with Pakistan [or India]?"[37] This is exacerbated by the fact that there are few political interlocutors in Kashmir that could be considered credible by Delhi politicians—and vice versa.[38] They are regarded as a front for terrorism or secessionism, or oppression. These perceptions revolve around a toxic mix of state sovereignty and identity where inflexible versions of both deny both. Orthodox terrorism perspectives enable this dead end, and liberal peace exacerbates competing demands for statehood because it is interpreted in a conservative manner—as statebuilding. The relatively recent and brief turn to politics and abandonment of violence by local representatives did not carry enough weight to convince the central authorities to seek serious dialogue with the region's politicians, in parallel with the peace talks and Confidence Building Measures (CBMs) that took place between India and Pakistan. It was argued that India is very good at negotiating with militants, but not really adept at running multi-track peace processes.[39] Its viewpoint is ingrained with the assumptions of orthodox terrorism and it is resistant to the liberal peace for Kashmir, because of its broader implications for its relations with Pakistan, and implicitly the state itself.

This implies that Kashmir has been left purposefully undeveloped and under the constant watch of the Indian army. In terms of employment as a way of ameliorating aspects of everyday life and providing some sense of security and stability to the local population, violence has made it impossible to generate private investment given state investment is limited by its high security bill for the region. Yet most facilities in Kashmir are state-owned and state-regulated, which makes for few opportunities and very little infrastructure.[40] Even though international development organizations (the World Bank, the Asian Development Bank, and the United Nations Development Program) suggested that the valley should be declared a free economic zone that enables trade across the LoC, both the Indian and Pakistani governments are very reluctant to support Kashmiri development, despite its potential.[41] As such, even the much-celebrated opening of the road to Muzaffarabad (capital of Pakistani Kashmir) did not yield much because clearance across the LoC is too cumbersome.

Any territorial and constitutional change in Kashmir generates fears in Delhi of a snowball effect that will make other Indian states seek independence.[42] The Indian government is also weary of benevolent outside help in terms of peacebuilding. Responding to an offer of assistance made by the U.S. Ambassador in New Delhi in 2009, the Indian government highlighted the significance of it being seen to engage willfully and unaided in the amelioration of the situation. For that purpose, it pointed to a series of CBMs that are currently in place, and others that are pending implementation. These included the release of prisoners who have been incarcerated longer than their court sentence; the release of prisoners who are not hard core militants and do not pose any threat; the transparent and public prosecution of force personnel involved in human rights violations; and generous development spending.[43] These measures, among others, are the ones that confirm the orthodox character of the state counter-terrorist discourse and its complicity in reinforcing the power relationship at the expense of a more sophisticated peace: why are non-threatening individuals held? Why have individuals been kept longer than their sentences dictated? Why have force personnel involved in human rights violations not been publicly prosecuted until now? Despite the CBMs, however, and with the exception of the city of Jammu (explained partly by higher levels of development compared to other areas in Kashmir), resentment for the Indian government remains widespread and deeply rooted. The division between autonomists and separatists in the ranks of local Kashmiri politicians mirrors the overall population's will. In a survey conducted in August 2007,[44] 87 percent of those asked in Srinagar favored an independent Kashmir, as they could not identify with either Pakistan or India. Ninety-five percent, however, of those asked in Jammu stated that Kashmir should not secede from India.

Orthodox notions of territoriality have been reproduced at the expense of rights, needs, and ambitions, even when they are expressed in non- or anti-violent terms. Eighty thousand deaths in the region have made the vast majority of the population reluctant to support any type of militants. Yet the orthodox policies and attitudes of both governments also alienate the citizenry.[45] As is typical with the liberal frameworks of peacebuilding, the individual and communal perceptions of peace are excluded, sidelined, and overlooked when compared to those of officialdom and elites.[46] It reflects a disciplinary framework that rests on coercion, a lack of consent, conditionality, and the prioritization of elite interests.[47]

These latter consequently connect to orthodox terrorism approaches which cement the dynamics the conflict feeds on by militarizing the territory and confirming both ethnic and state nationalism. Security and multiple forms of identity coexist in permanent tension with secession confirming the ontology of orthodox terrorism which drives a conservative version of liberal peacebuilding as relying on state security first, along with institutions, the rule of law, human rights, and civil society. Unanswered questions over which state, what type of state, and whose security is at stake means the liberal agenda is never achieved. Yet its focus on the state and institutions seems to confirm the orthodox agenda, meaning a no-war, no-peace situation[48] has become the status-quo. This highlights both the internal contradictions of liberal peace and terrorism approaches, as well as their mutual complementarity—albeit with its unintended consequences of reinforcing conflict and debilitating peace.

In this case a pluralist set of political institutions are clearly required to organize politics at the local level to reflect the very obvious need to include a broader range of actors in the peace process and to produce hybrid institutions and territorial arrangements. Liberal peacebuilding might offer these but for the determination of both states to maintain power. Orthodox terrorism theory supports these antagonistic positions. More critical and emancipatory versions of both might help unravel these positions, and would imply post-liberal and post-terrorist understandings of the conflict. The question of legitimacy is multi-faceted in Kashmir, but clearly both states and both civil societies have differing opinions, and never have been able to impose themselves full on the other.

A focus on local-local notions of legitimacy, and their relationships with both states might transcend arteriosclerotic positions such as the aforementioned. This would again represent a local-liberal hybrid.

Israel/Palestine: a hybrid state, but neither post-terrorism nor post-liberal

The aforementioned approach of exploiting peace processes in order to preserve territorial integrity and advance state-security, so hardening the liberal peace into a conservative, securitization, and institutional model is also evident in the Middle East, where military and political elites are very skeptical when it comes to accepting—let alone promoting—an emancipatory peace that is established through liberal governance and its institutions. Unlike other conflicts, where the implementation of liberal conditionalities imposed by the international community is more visible,[49] the international organizations that have intervened in the Middle East have often been sidelined and/or ignored. The reasons for this are twofold. On the one hand, the initiatives of such institutions are either not trusted by local elites because they are not sufficiently invested in their identities, or they are seen as representative of a set of conditions that seek to undermine the political and cultural gains of one group over the other.[50] On the other hand, Israel has always been perceived of by liberal elites as part of the society of liberal states. Thus, international strategy has been mainly that pressure should be placed upon the Palestinians to develop the liberal reflexes that will allow them to build and develop those institutions necessary for the establishment and promotion of a liberal state.

It is this framework that led to the proposition of a two-state solution in the region, first expressed in the 1947 UN General Assembly Resolution 181.[51] Ever since then, and particularly after the end of the Cold War, when the liberal peace was promoted as the most viable solution for inter- and intra-state conflicts, every attempt to reach a compromise in the region was centered on the creation of a Palestinian state. Nevertheless, failure to do so cannot solely be attributed to the lack of will of the conflicting parties—for instance terror attacks and targeted killings that continued on both sides, the issue of settlements that to this day threaten the derailment of the most recent round of negotiations,[52] and the eruption of the second intifada. The Oslo Peace Accords, or Declaration of Principles (DoP) were undoubtedly derailed and condemned to failure because of the parties' lack of will to reach peace in partnership, partly because of very orthodox understandings of terrorism and the inflexibility of a conservative understanding of the liberal peace. The DoP failed to bear fruit because it ignored what had by then become the core root of the conflict: the socio-economic conditions that affected most Palestinians—implying a broader inequality in material and identity terms—and which were brought to the fore with the first Intifada. While the DoP for the first time ever accorded an equal status to Palestinians and Israelis, it too fell victim to the traps of statebuilding camouflaged as peacebuilding. First, the symmetry it accorded to the actors was virtual for it was an agreement between an "occupying power and an occupying people."[53] Second, the DoP favored the creation of a Palestinian state without taking into consideration internal political divisions and factions vying for power. Nor did it comprehend the difficulty of the day-to-day operation of a Palestinian state without the constant involvement of Israel.

In that sense, therefore, the DoP (along with most other peace efforts in the region) did not attempt to address the needs of the grassroots actors for whom it was supposedly promoting a liberal state. In fact, as it was argued by independent peacebuilding NGOs, not only has the grassroots level not been addressed but it has even been undermined by Track I approaches.[54] Peace efforts have adopted an overtly political top-down approach, thus regurgitating and recycling state-centric notions of peace and security.[55] This places power in the hands of elites who focus on nationalist goals, on related identity matters, and then construct a security narrative on that basis. In this sense, liberal statebuilding has developed in an intimate relationship with orthodox understandings of terrorism as a security threat which requires a liberal state (strong for Israel and weak for Palestinians) which guarantees security. But the state is internationally and locally contested, and its legitimacy is in doubt.

The credibility of the liberal peace framework in the region has continued to be undermined even after the failure of the Oslo Accords. From the international point of view, the most poignant example is the international community's refusal to accept the electoral result that saw Hamas winning 76 of the 132 parliamentary seats in January 2006. This reaction is indicative of the liberal peace model's inability—even in critical or cosmopolitan form—to engage in dialogue with actors who are seen as "unacceptable"—even though they were politically empowered, legitimated, and electorally mandated by the very people the liberal model claims to want to serve. What makes this attitude even more significant is the inability of the internationals to recognize the reasons behind Hamas' electoral results: namely, the weariness of Palestinians with the corrupt, ineffective, and in cases indifferent regime of Fatah (as well as strategic regional support).[56] Progress even towards a liberal peace is blocked by the heavily securitized discourse associated with orthodox terrorism. Israel's assassination and arrest of so many elected Hamas officials, for instance, undermines the Palestinians' faith in electoral mechanisms, thus undercutting the liberal end of hybridity.[57] Instead, the focus is on state security and liberal institutions over human needs associated with liberal peace theory. Thus local legitimacy has been lost because territory, sovereignty, rights, and justice have been compromised by both Israel and external actors. Neoliberal economic strategies have been applied to deal with poverty and its causal dynamics.[58] Thus, the peace and state that has emerged since the early 1990s is one where its territory and security is controlled by Israel, its economy is also to be integrated into the global economy often via Israel, its budget is supported by external donors (mainly the EU), and its institutions are based on those of liberal democracy, modified informally by local networks of patronage. It is a neoliberal and hybrid state without sovereignty, and without the capacity to sustain itself or to meet basic liberal norms of human rights applied equally to all citizens and communities in the region.

This highlights the inconsistency between the theory and the practice of liberal peace frameworks, as well as the commitment of Western states to human rights, something that has even been criticized by the Special Rapporteur on the situation of human rights in the Palestinian territories.[59] In other words, employing orthodox terrorism discourses in order to debilitate a violent group might in fact reinvigorate its social and political acceptance by those segments of the population which the peacebuilders attempt to incorporate into the peace efforts. Furthermore, it may lead to a type of state that has little chance of viability, and be almost completely dependent on external support. This discourse denies alterity, even where it is deeply ingrained in culture, identity, religion, and political processes, and reifies a form of sovereignty which is instrumental in blocking meaningful negotiations or engagements with everyday life.

In the context of the Israeli–Palestinian conflict, the liberal peace model is connected to an orthodox state discourse that promotes exclusionary notions of security even where territorial pluralism has marked recent history, and recognizes, negotiates with, and politically enriches already and/or traditionally established elites. For these elites, a difficult path between aiming at maintaining international credibility by accepting the liberal peace framework as well as the orthodox terrorism framework must be charted. In addition, localized constituencies must be maintained. These elaborate constraints produce a range of responses which contradict in public and private transcripts, sometimes separately, at local, state (embryonic or recognized), and international levels. It is a hybrid, agonistic, and post-liberal process, in which compromises and concessions appear to be driven by contradictory norms of peace, rather than the more liberal and orthodox forms of strategic and securitized interests, borders, and territory. The peace process has fluctuated between being inclusive and exclusive and the much needed hybridity that has emerged represents power rather than the diversity of an everyday peace as a consequence.

Rather than offering a basis for emancipation, the Middle East remains trapped in a sovereign discourse about security, and the neat but impractical connection of national identity with territorial claims, as opposed to pragmatic everyday requirements for peace. What is necessary is an attitude and a framework that promotes human security in more inclusive terms, transcends the political use of terrorism as a practice of violence and a discourse of exclusion, and the use of the liberal peace as an alien set of institutions and normative standards where they are not consented to in situ. Post-terrorist, post-sovereign, post-colonial, and post-liberal sensibilities are required by local, state, and international actors to transcend such blockages and to reconstruct local, regional, and international legitimacy for the Middle East which reflects the consent of each constituency. In other words, then, what is needed is a post-liberal introspection of the liberal peace frameworks that may well lead to a new era of post-terrorist politics. This recognition and mutual renegotiation of legitimacy would represent the local-liberal hybrid, rescuing the peace processes from terrorism and the liberal peace and its state model from a lack of local consent. This would be again far more commensurate with democracy and rights embodied in stable institutions, as well as representative of contextual alterity which might modify them.

Towards a post-terrorism, post-liberal peace category

Nepal: post-terrorism but not post-liberal

Following the events of 9/11, Maoist extremists decided to switch their strategy and, in exchange for political recognition and participation in the government, they declared that they would renounce their violent tactics.[60] Both sides agreed to this, transcending the exclusive claims of legitimacy and sovereignty of one side, and the argument for representation and the use of violence on the other. This change coincided with the severe counter-terrorist measures of the government that led to both the abuse of human rights and the weakening of the Maoists. The Comprehensive Peace Agreement (CPA) signed between the Nepalese government and the (Maoist) Unified Communist Party of Nepal in November 2006 has produced a peace of sorts between the two groups, with the help of the UN, which has maintained the process of liberal statebuilding and the maintenance of sovereignty. Terrorism has ended though acute political tensions remain over powersharing, security, and the reconfiguration of power. Nevertheless, the conflict is now adopting a more ethnic dimension, with groups in the South like the Terai people (who claim to constitute 40 percent of Nepal's population) making their own claims for autonomy and representation. Furthermore, UN's mandate[61] is significantly limited to facilitating processes between a bipolar nexus (government and Maoists), without substantial involvement at the grassroots level.

Under the CPA, the government forces are limited inside their barracks whereas the Maoist combatants are confined inside cantonments monitored by the UN Mission in Nepal (UNMIN). As a result, state security is undermined and armed groups in the South operate relatively freely. The majority of these groups were allied to the Maoists before the peace process began. However, support for the Maoists has dwindled when they failed to meet promises of ethnic proportional representation and local empowerment. Lacking the organization of the Maoists, these groups are now more a conglomeration of warlords than a political threat to the government—although the security of the state is actively undermined because, unlike the Maoists, these groups increasingly target civilians. The violence exhibited by these groups represents a continuation of the Maoist tactics, not because they will generate direct results but because they are noticed by the government and by internationals.[62] Preoccupied exclusively with the Maoists at the political level, the government does not seem to want to engage with any of the southern groups calling for federation and/or autonomy, thus marginalizing all other moderate, non-violent voices that raise the same issue(s).

While even senior figures in Kathmandu admit that lack of development is a serious issue that exacerbates violence in the southern regions,[63] government and Maoists suppress grassroots attempts to establish a peace that provides for human security. The lack of an institutional framework that secures the work of human rights activists means that NGOs are very limited in their interactions with grassroots movements in the affected regions. The peace process is an "empty process"[64] because the Maoists and the government have marginalized the human rights and civil society networks that sparked the 1996 peace movement.[65] Even where local NGOs are active, widespread corruption means that they are probably a front for political involvement rather than addressing everyday grassroots issues. The result is that those who manage the liberal peace also manage political constituencies and the flow of aid/development capital.[66] International NGOs, on the other hand, have come under attack because, instead of reflecting their very own messages of social inclusion and participation/representation, they in fact reproduce and reinforce class and caste divisions.[67]

The attitude of the international community towards the Nepalese grassroots is highly ambivalent. Most international actors seemed to be more concerned with the international attributes of the liberal peace (elections, institutions-building, etc.) than with the everyday, local characteristics and needs as they emerge after a significant cessation of violence. These are seen from the government and international level to be retrogressive. More importantly, donors ignore the highly unequal socioeconomic and socio-political foundations on which the old regime was resting, thus fomenting incentives for exiting the peace process for large sections of the population.[68] The UN's limited mandate means that Terai and Madhesi groups cannot enter talks with the government, unless the government accepts such calls for talks. The government does not wish to grant them any recognition. Both the government and the Maoists have co-opted the international community in order to continue their political game.

The peace that came forward with the CPA has never fully addressed the reasons why grassroots movements sided with the Maoist rhetoric. Nor did it address the means by which such support was received by the Maoist leadership. Consequently, this "bipolar" peace is one that fails to satisfy not only the need for human security brought forward by sectors of its population, but also the need for its own, national security. The "peace paradox" in Nepal is that, despite the lack of orthodox terrorism approaches, the liberal peace project has not flourished precisely because it was not allowed to be owned and developed at the everyday level—which would have generated a hybrid form—but instead has been influenced by an externalized set of standards and perspectives. It has been left with the same castes and elites to administer and manage it according to their political interests. This has meant that the contextual dynamics of civil society peacebuilding have not been able to infuse the state or the elite level peace process sufficiently. As a result, the peace process has rested mainly on the elites' and international legitimacy level. While a post-terrorism approach allowed a negotiation process with the Maoists, the elitist and Eurocentric nature

Peacebuilding and terrorism approaches 35

of the liberal peace's focus has meant much of the population remains excluded by its priorities.

As a first step away from an orthodox terrorism approach there are many lessons to be learned here. Unfortunately, the focus on an orthodox liberal peace approach has meant that the peace process has been elite focused, driven by external values and institutional frameworks, and has become trapped by the contradictory views of opposing groups rather than dealing with the everyday issues of the population. In this sense, a negotiation process has come into being, despite concerns about violence and its political intent, but the negotiations are limited by the contradictions inherent in classical concerns about sovereignty, boundaries, the control of power, as well as the locally depoliticizing and decontextualized, external agendas promoting the liberal peace.

Clearly, in this case, to some degree the peace process coexists with violence but this is mitigated by the critical approach to terrorism and that the liberal peace process has adopted the praxis of the liberal peace. However, it has done less well in taking into consideration the potential inherent in grassroots and/or civil society movements, for which the Maoists and other groups have had to use strong arm tactics to gain traction. To some degree this has denied alterity and difference but some space has been left to begin the difficult process of embracing it. This may result in something more than a virtually liberal state, if the twin issues of securitization and poverty can also be addressed. The emergence of localized hybridity would suggest that both needs and rights issues in their contextual settings would be focused on in order to develop a more embedded form of legitimacy. This would fulfil the potential for a hybrid and post-liberal peace which moves beyond the representation of power and into the everyday.

Northern Ireland: post-terrorism and post-liberal peacebuilding?

In Northern Ireland, a further step away from orthodox terrorism and orthodox liberal peace approaches was taken, with very significant results, but only after a long phase of more orthodox engagements was tried and had clearly failed to break the deadlock. The next step towards a post-liberal process was taken in the sense that the polity that was negotiated included both former combatants (using tactics associated with terrorism or state oppression) and a softening of some of the components of the liberal peace.[69] This included modifications to sovereignty, shared between local actors, the UK, and the Republic of Ireland (to limited degrees); powersharing alterations to democracy; a move towards a notion of shared and porous sovereignty and borders where localized territorializing remained in more limited form; massive state and EU investment to deal with poverty and inequality, including in civil society; deviations from the standard rule of law and human rights regimes; and the "Europeanization" of the peace process. This led to alternative and competing local forms of legitimacy which also connected to the liberal peace model, while offering some innovations. The shift from the formal liberal framework in Northern Ireland, however, is very limited because, broadly speaking, most parties have accepted the liberal framework (especially its neoliberal variant), much as they may have been influenced in the past by religion, socialism, or other varied alternatives.

Northern Ireland is the only one of our cases that exhibits a more durable and sustainable peace, mainly for two reasons. First, the peace process began as diametrically opposed to orthodox understandings of counter-terrorism, and involved at the official level a struggle against various security services that had become embedded in these approaches. It was based on a process of communicational exchange that looked beyond the orthodox fears and securitized anxieties of the past. While back-channels were open and working since the 1970s,[70] it was not until the Labour government of Tony Blair that a more critical approach to Northern Irish terrorism began taking shape. Taking advantage of the back-channels that existed between them and the IRA, the British government (in close collaboration with the Irish government) reformulated its understandings of sovereignty and security in exchange for peace. It was also aided in this effort by the war-weariness of the local population and the anti-violence grassroots movements that began developing and that put pressure on the terrorist factions to find alternative ways to achieve their goals. Paradoxically, some of our sources have indicated that the only reason why peace emerged was because the British government did not want any more violence in mainland Britain, and particularly London.[71] Belfast, then, was subordinated to the interests of London.[72]

Second, the international community seemed as committed as the UK and Ireland in helping creating a space that would be conducive to peace. EU funding is still considered to be the most important contribution to the peace process. But more than that, the EU offered new understandings of regionalism, sovereignty, and coexistence that were welcomed at least by the state level actors. The supranational character of the Union as well as its focus on its regions (rather than solely its member-states)[73] meant that decentralization and devolution of power to regions from the state were not seen as succumbing to interests, or debilitating to central powers and authorities or their sovereignty.[74] Furthermore it enabled an introspective re-imagining and redefinition of the territorial identities espoused by the two communities.[75] Once this move had been made, the territorialized, securitized, orthodox approaches to terrorism and for peacebuilding appeared as problems rather than solutions. More than anything, the EU is the very reason why the British and Irish governments co-operated so closely.[76]

Of course, funding was equally crucial and unlike other conflicts examined in our article, the anti-violent and reconciliatory grassroots movements of Northern Ireland were significantly aided. Furthermore, it was appropriately used for redressing social, economic, and rights inequalities, and for developing an economy that was previously virtually inexistent because of the risks imposed by violence. Finally, the U.S. government had an equally important role to play, albeit during (rather than before or after) the peace process.[77]

What makes Northern Ireland's case poignant is the move away from orthodox frameworks of security, and towards an emancipatory dimension of the liberal peace that provides vital space for grassroots movements and the civil society to own and direct the peace process themselves, rather than having it imposed by (and tailored to) the interests of the state and/or the international society. Citizens were also given material capacity through a range of private investment, state, EU, and donor resources to enact their rights more equally. Many of the initiatives of external and local actors, from the EU, UK, to localized politics, enabled a move away from orthodox terrorism approaches on all sides, as well as a decisive shift towards a liberal peace.[78] But on close examination, many of the tenets of the liberal peace, especially those related to a clear and Westphalian notion of sovereignty have been compromised on to provide ambiguous political institutions, territorial boundaries, powersharing, prosperity (from massive intergovernmental support), and an active role of civil society closely allied to sectarian identities as well as liberal norms. Here there is a clear hybridization of the local with the liberal international. International assistance to peacebuilding should be precisely that—assistance. What differentiates the Northern Ireland case from the others already explored in this chapter is the engagement of policy makers, peacebuilders, NGOs, and donors with local civil society's potential to initiate and sustain a peaceful polity in a range of different but overlapping contextual frames. Civil society also found ways of expressing itself separately to institutions and formal channels, and much of this agency was facilitated by massive public investment in infrastructure, living conditions, for jobs, and opportunities. Everyday life in the end proved more important than sectarian pre-negotiation objectives, which have remained but as partially symbolic and historical aspirations associated with the historical process of changing identities.

The shift towards liberal peacebuilding in Northern Ireland indicated an engagement with root causes and a move away from orthodox terrorism approaches. This led from a situation where peace processes and violence coexisted to one where a peace process became the focus of political action and violence was marginalized. All the interlocutors adopted the praxis of the liberal peace and liberal institutionalism, and more importantly took into consideration the potential inherent in grass-roots and/or civil society movements. All parties related to a liberal polity but even so this indicates perhaps the development of a post-terrorism/post-liberal hybrid process in that legitimacy began to be mutually constructed in line with international, regional, state, and local preferences. This rescued the peace process from terrorism, the liberal peace from a lack of local consent, and developed local-liberal hybridity to respond to the structural aspects of the conflict.

Conclusion

Hybrid and more flexible peace processes are obviously required, but the four categories that emerge from the interaction of approaches to terrorism, as indicated by our case studies, have varying implications for the creations of an inclusive peace process and a hybrid form of peace (meaning post-terrorism and post-liberalism) (see Table 2.1). The first category of relationship between

Table 2.1 Interactions between terrorism and peacebuilding

	Conservative liberal peace	Orthodox liberal peace	Post-liberal peace
Orthodox terrorism	Prevents a stable peace from forming; key actors are excluded; hybridity is denied	Rests on exclusive, often ethnonationalist legitimacy; depends on actors possessing their own Weberian state	Room for only partial hybridity (mimicry) because security, legitimacy, sovereignty and territorial integrity of the state are paramount
Critical terrorism	No room for Conservative Liberal Peace because a state's discriminatory policies have led to the manifestation of terrorism/excludes key actors	All actors are included in peace process, but state and formal/cosmopolitan actors are favoured	Theoretically more possible, but critical terrorism focuses on the normative role of the state as opposed to the potential of the local/everyday
Post-terrorism	Not applicable because key actors may not conform to liberal ideology	Very limited applicability because non-liberal or hybrid actors will still be marginal	Leads to a more inclusive, post-liberal peace, with international, national and local legitimacy combined inclusively Peace processes focus on inclusivity and pluralism, institutionalised in both international and everyday socio-historical contexts.

terrorism and peacebuilding tends to be self-defeating in terms of producing peace as can be seen in Kashmir and the Middle East, and may be the case in Sri Lanka, where hybrid peace processes and forms of peace have been blocked or used to maintain the power of the dominant state actor. The second category where an orthodox terrorism approach might lead to a liberal peace may arise in the Middle East and even Kashmir, depending on whether the conflict actors receive their own state and can express more localized, if ethnonationalist understandings of legitimacy. But even this seems tenuous in these cases as hybridity represents power and states are under pressure to separate (as in all the above cases to some degree). Again, a more flexible and open approach that can embrace hybrid identities, institutions, and sovereign arrangements is clearly required. The third category provides strong support, as in the case of Nepal, that critical terrorism approaches can support liberal peacebuilding, but again though flexibility in the peace process over its inclusiveness has not translated into the hybridity of that process and its resultant institutions. Hybridity has again represented the state as a dominant actor. Indeed, it appears to have blocked a move to

Peacebuilding and terrorism approaches 39

a more contextual form of peacebuilding even though liberal values in Nepal are not widely held, and remain contained within an elite strata of the political class and civil society. The final category, for which the sole exemplar is Northern Ireland, indicates how critical terrorism approaches enable a peace process to emerge, especially where significant material incentives exist for the populations. However, unlike Nepal, it is difficult to use this case to support a post-liberal form of peace because of the fact that liberal values are already widely held. However, in a perverse way—as all of the other categories also suggest—there may be significant traction in hybridity being a legitimate goal in peacebuilding where diverse and pluralist ontologies exist.

Clearly, all of these cases hint at the need for a post-terrorist approach which enables at least the possibility of a hybrid and post-liberal peace, by allowing issues such as territory, sovereignty, rights, needs, and identity to become part of a negotiation process to shape the nature of state, institutions, norms, economy, and civil society. This post-terrorism, post-liberal approach would lead to an outcome commensurate with both local alterity and the ways in which they might be bridged with dominant conceptions of international norms and security. Strong hints of this approach are present in the cases of Nepal and Northern Ireland, which are the most successful of the cases examined. By comparison, Sri Lanka, Kashmir, and the Middle East have at times also benefited from, or may in the future benefit from, such an approach.

A post-terrorism approach is integral to a post-liberal approach to peacebuilding in which a range of actors are brought into the processes for an end—state or form of peace—which is determined by that negotiation process, rather than by external interests, by orthodox assumptions of security for liberal states, and the latter's use as a blue print for conflict management around the world. It is precisely this consent and the engagement of peace process with the everyday life of the local populations that need to be engaged with to bring forward a hybrid model of peace: one that not only rests on (and foments) the liberal principles of a positive peace, but also one that incorporates local sensitivities, attitudes, and particularities. As our analysis of the Northern Ireland peace process has shown, it is easier for any peace process to be accorded legitimacy by grassroots movements when it takes into account the everyday needs of the local populations; when it does not marginalize grassroots in favor of elites; and when power-relations are not replicated at the expense of representation and legitimacy.

A post-liberal, post-terrorism agenda entails a praxis that would enable political, social, and economic organizations and institutions to represent and respect the communities they are effectively in a contractual relationship with. As a consequence, international forms of peacebuilding would be more likely to be participatory, empathetic, locally owned, and self-sustaining, socially, politically, economically, and environmentally speaking.[79] They provide a via media between different identities and interests, and they can guard against direct or structural violence, thus providing justice and equity.[80] What is more important, however, is that a post-liberal agenda also opens up the possibilities of post-terrorist frameworks and conducts of behavior. The conflicts in Kashmir and

Nepal highlight this possibility. In the first case, orthodox understandings of security, legitimacy, and representation (or lack thereof) have pushed the local populations towards the arms of "imported" terrorist groups, who rely on local feelings of oppression, opposition, and resentment towards the central authorities to implement and carry out their violent strategies. In the second case, more critical understandings on the part of internationals allowed for a more inclusive process—though with limitations. Since it is in the disputants' interest to maintain or foment conflict, the onus falls upon the international community to provide a via media, a dialogue between disputants and internationals of all levels that would make evident an ethical and acceptable discourse and praxis by which a post-liberal and post-terrorist peace might be achieved. In other words, the attitude and behavior of the internationals is important when it comes to local populations rejecting or legitimizing terrorists violence[81] and opening inclusive peace processes. Reconciliation requires internationals not limiting their objectives to those contained solely within a liberal epistemology, especially where local actors are struggling to represent alterity rather than similarity. Post-terrorism and post-liberal approaches indicate the need for the rapid development of a broad and inclusive peace process that has the necessary material, cultural, ideational, and normative breadth to induce all actors away from supporting political or structural violence and negotiating a sustainable compromise.

Notes

* This chapter was first published as Oliver P. Richmond, and Ioannis Tellidis (2012) The Complex Relationship Between Peacebuilding and Terrorism Approaches: Towards Post-Terrorism and a Post-Liberal Peace? *Terrorism and Political Violence* 24:1, 120–143. Reproduced with permission of Taylor and Francis.

1 See among others, Richard Jackson, *Writing the War on Terrorism. Language, Politics and Counter-Terrorism* (Manchester: Manchester University Press, 2005); K. McEvoy and B. Gormally, "'Seeing' is believing: Positivist terrology, peacemaking criminology, and the Northern Ireland peace process," *Critical Criminology* 8, no. 1 (2007): 9–30; Jason Franks, *Rethinking the Roots of Terrorism* (London: Palgrave, 2006); Bruce Hoffman, *Inside Terrorism* (London: Weidenfeld & Nicholson, 1998); John Horgan and Michael Boyle, "A case against 'critical terrorism studies,'" *Critical Studies on Terrorism* 1, no. 1 (2008): 51–64.

2 First among these is John Paul Lederach's *Building Peace* (Washington DC: United States Institute of Peace, 1997). For more recent analyses, see among others Roland Bleiker, *Popular Dissent, Human Agency and Global Politics* (Manchester: Cambridge University Press, 2000); Mark Duffield, *Global Governance and the New Wars: The Merging of Development and Security* (London: Zed Books, 2001); Ian Clark, *The Post-Cold War Order: Spoils of Peace* (Oxford: Oxford University Press, 2001); Roland Paris, *At War's End* (Cambridge: Cambridge University Press, 2004); Oliver P. Richmond, *The Transformation of Peace* (Basingstoke: Palgrave, 2007); Vivienne Jabri, *War and the Transformation of Global Politics* (London: Palgrave, 2007); Michael Pugh, Neil Cooper, and Mandy Turner, *Whose Peace? Critical Perspectives on the Political Economy of Peacebuilding* (London: Palgrave, 2008); Oliver P. Richmond and Jason Franks, *Liberal Peace Transitions: Between Statebuilding and Peacebuilding* (Edinburgh: Edinburgh University Press, 2009).

3 See in particular an earlier article from this research project, Oliver P. Richmond and Jason Franks, "The impact of orthodox terrorism discourses on the construction of the liberal peace: Internalisation, resistance or hybridisation?," *Critical Studies on Terrorism* 2, no. 2 (2009): 201–218.
4 Edward Newman, Roland Paris, and Oliver P. Richmond, "Introduction," in Edward Newman, Roland Paris, and Oliver P. Richmond (eds.), *New Perspectives on Liberal Peacebuilding* (Tokyo: United Nations University Press, 2009), 3–25, quote at p. 4.
5 Richmond and Franks, *Liberal Peace Transitions* (see note 2 above).
6 See Paul Wilkinson, *Terrorism Versus Democracy* (London: Frank Cass, 2001); Edward Newman and Oliver P. Richmond (eds.), *Challenges to Peacebuilding: Managing Spoilers During Conflict Resolution* (Tokyo: UNU Press, 2006).
7 Ioannis Tellidis, *Preventing Terrorism? Conflict Resolution and Nationalist Violence in the Basque Country* (Unpublished PhD Thesis, University of St. Andrews, 2008), 148. http://research-repository.st-andrews.ac.uk/bitstream/10023/426/6/Ioannis%20 Tellidis%20PhD %20thesis.pdf (accessed July 7, 2011).
8 Oliver P. Richmond and Jason Franks, "The impact of orthodox terrorism discourses on the construction of the liberal peace: Internalisation, resistance or hybridisation?," *Critical Studies on Terrorism* 2, no. 2 (2009): 201–218.
9 Oliver P. Richmond, *A Post-Liberal Peace* (London: Routledge, 2011), conclusion. For a cosmopolitan view see Andrew Linklater, "Dialogic politics and the civilising process," *Review of International Studies* 31 (2005): 141–154. For a post-structural view see W. E. Connolly, *Identity/Difference* (Minneapolis, MN: University of Minnesota Press, 1991).
10 See Homi Bhabha, *The Location of Culture* (London: Routledge, 1994).
11 Paris, *At War's End* (see note 2 above); Edward D. Mansfield and Jack Snyder, "Prone to Violence: The Paradox of the Democratic Peace," *National Interest* 82 (Winter 2005/6): 39–45.
12 Perhaps the war-like rhetoric employed by (both state and non-state) political and military figures is a discursive obstacle to peace processes, since it is very difficult to revert to a pro-peace discourse without losing face. Roger Mac Ginty, Personal Communication.
13 Newman and Richmond (see note 6 above). For the gradations of the liberal peace, see Richmond, *The Transformation of Peace* (see note 2 above), conclusion.
14 Barry Buzan, Ole Wæver, and Jaap de Wilde, *Security: A New Framework for Analysis* (London: Lynne Rienner, 1998).
15 Franks, *Rethinking the Roots of Terrorism* (see note 1 above); Richard Jackson, "The core commitments of critical terrorism studies," *European Journal of Political Science* 6, no. 3 (2007): 244–251; Richard Jackson, Marie Breen-Smyth, and Jeroen Gunning (eds.), *Critical Terrorism Studies: A New Research Agenda* (Abingdon: Routledge, 2009).
16 Ioannis Tellidis, "Orthodox, Criticals and the missing context: Basque civil society reaction(s) to terrorism," *Critical Studies on Terrorism* 4, no. 2 (2011): 181–197.
17 For more on locality in peacebuilding, see Richmond, *A Post-Liberal Peace* (see note 9 above) introduction.
18 Ibid., chapter 5.
19 Confidential Source, Personal Interview, Colombo, April 4, 2007.
20 Founder of LTTE and leader of the organization until his death in the government's offensive in 2009.
21 Paikiasothy Saravanamuttu, Centre for Policy Alternatives, Personal Interview, Colombo, April 5, 2007.
22 Confidential Source, Personal Interview, Colombo, April 4, 2007.
23 Confidential Source, International Centre for Ethnic Studies, Personal Interview, Colombo, April 4, 2007; Confidential Source, Consortium of Humanitarian Agencies, Personal Interview, Colombo, April 4, 2007.

24 Jannie Lilja, "Trapping constituents or winning hearts and minds? Rebel strategies to attain constituent support in Sri Lanka," *Terrorism and Political Violence* 21, no. 2 (2009): 306–326.
25 United Nations, "Report of the Secretary General's Panel on Accountability in Sri Lanka," March 31, 2011. www.un.org/News/dh/infocus/Sri_Lanka/POE_Report_Full.pdf (accessed April 27, 2011); Confidential Source, Centre for Peace Building and Reconciliation, Personal Interview, Colombo, April 5, 2007.
26 Deirdre McConnell, "The Tamil people's right to self-determination," *Cambridge Review of International Affairs* 21, no. 1 (2008): 59–76.
27 Confidential Source, UN, Personal Interview, Colombo, April 6, 2007; Amita Shastri, "Ending ethnic civil war: the peace process in Sri Lanka," *Commonwealth and Comparative Politics* 47, no. 1 (2009): 76–99; Kristine Höglund and Isak Svensson, "Damned if you do, and damned if you don't: Nordic involvement and images of third-party neutrality in Sri Lanka," *International Negotiation* 13 (2008): 341–364.
28 Confidential Sources, Centre for Peace Building and Reconciliation, Personal Interviews, Colombo, April 9, 2007.
29 Roger Mac Ginty, "Social network analysis and counter-insurgency: a counterproductive strategy?," *Critical Studies on Terrorism* 3, no. 2 (2010): 209–226, quote at p. 217.
30 McConnell, "The Tamil people's right to self-determination" (see note 26 above).
31 United Nations, "Report of the Secretary General's Panel on Accountability in Sri Lanka" (see note 25 above).
32 Saroj Pathirana, "Sri Lanka's Tamil Tiger suspects 'won't be freed soon'." http://news.bbc.co.uk/1/hi/world/south_asia/8450914.stm (accessed April 19, 2011).
33 Professor Radha Kumar, Nelson Mandela Centre for Conflict Resolution, Personal Interview, Delhi, September 10, 2007; Professor Noor Ahmed Baba, University of Kashmir, Personal Interview, Srinagar, September 13, 2007.
34 Syed Shoaib Hasan, "Why Pakistan is 'boosting Kashmir militants,'" *BBC News*, March 3, 2010. http://news.bbc.co.uk/1/hi/world/south_asia/4416771.stm (accessed June 15, 2010).
35 Confidential Source, Wilson Centre, Personal Interview, Delhi, September 11, 2007.
36 U.S. Embassy (New Delhi) Cable 140972: Confidential, February 12, 2008. www.hindu.com/2011/04/04/stories/2011040452111100.htm (accessed April 19, 2011).
37 Confidential Source, International Committee of Red Cross, Sunder Nagar, September 4, 2007.
38 Confidential Source, Personal Interview, Srinagar, September 13, 2007.
39 Confidential Source, International Centre for Ethnic Studies, Personal Interview, Colombo, April 4, 2007.
40 Mubeen Shah, President of Chamber of Commerce, Personal Interview, Srinagar, September 14, 2007.
41 Ibid.
42 Shri Chari, "Protecting human rights in times of conflict: an Indian perspective," *Terrorism and Political Violence* 17, nos. 1 and 2 (2005): 217–228; Confidential Source, Action Aid, Personal Interview, Srinagar, September 13, 2007.
43 U.S. Embassy (New Delhi) Cable 230893: Confidential, October 22, 2009. www.hindu.com/2011/03/30/stories/2011033056191500.htm (accessed April 19, 2011).
44 "Majority in Kashmir valley want independence: poll," *Reuters*, August 13, 2007. www.reuters.com/article/idUSDEL29179620070813 (accessed August 22, 2010).
45 Rajen Harshe, "India–Pakistan conflict over Kashmir: Peace through development co-operation," *South Asian Survey* 12, no. 1 (2005): 47–60.
46 Richmond, *The Transformation of Peace* (see note 2 above).
47 Oliver P. Richmond, "Eirenism and a post-liberal peace," *Review of International Studies* 35, no. 3 (2009): 557–580, quote at p. 560.
48 Roger MacGinty, *No War, No Peace: The rejuvenation of Stalled Peace Processes and Peace Accords* (Basingstoke: Palgrave, 2006).

49 Confidential source, Van Leer Institute for Peace, Personal Interview, Jerusalem, June 28, 2007.
50 Confidential Military source, Personal Interview, Jerusalem, July 1, 2007.
51 UN General Assembly, Resolution 181 (II). Future Government of Palestine, A/RES/181 (II), November 29, 1947. http://domino.un.org/unispal.nsf/0/7f0af2bd897689b785256c330061d253 (accessed September 11, 2010).
52 Crispian Balmer, "Middle East peace push faces settlement deadline," *The Independent*, September 26, 2010. www.independent.co.uk/news/world/middle-east/middle-east-peace-push-faces-settlement-deadline-2090147.html (accessed November 4, 2011).
53 Nils Butenschon, "The Oslo Agreement: from the White House to Jabal Abu Ghneim," in G. Giacaman and D. Jorund Lonning (eds.), *After Oslo: New Realities, Old Problems* (London: Pluto Press, 1999), 19.
54 Shimshom Zelniker, Director, Van Leer Institute for Peace, Personal Interview, Jerusalem, June 27, 2007.
55 Ron Pundak, Director, Peres Centre for Peace, Personal Interview, Tel Aviv, June 27, 2007.
56 Richmond and Franks, *Liberal Peace Transitions* (see note 2 above), 166.
57 Roger Mac Ginty, Personal Communication.
58 Raja Khalidi and Sobhi Samour, "Neoliberalism as Liberation: The Statehood Programme and the Remaking of the Palestinian National Movement," *Journal of Palestine Studies* 40, no. 2 (2001): 6–25.
59 UN Human Rights Council, "Report of the Special Rapporteur on the situation of human rights in the Palestinian Territories occupied since 1967," UNDoc A/HRC/4/17, January 29, 2007.
60 Brig. Gen. Ramindra Chhetri, Nepalese Army, Personal Interview, Kathmandu, September 26, 2007.
61 UN Security Council Resolution 1740, January 23, 2007.
62 Nathalie Hicks, Country Director, International Alert, Personal Interview, Kathmandu, August 21, 2007; Confidential Source, Focus Group, Purbanchal University, Personal Interview, Biratnagar, September 23, 2007.
63 Avanindra Kumar Shrestha, Minister of Home Affairs, Personal Interview, Kathmandu, August 21, 2007.
64 People refer to it as "*murda shanty*" (dead peace).
65 Confidential Source, Human Rights NGO, Personal Interview, Biratnagar, September 23, 2007.
66 OECD, *Do No Harm: International Support for State Building* (Paris: OECD Publishing, 2010), 46.
67 Ibid., 86.
68 Ibid., 39.
69 Daniel Byman, "The decision to begin talks with terrorists: Lessons for policymakers," *Studies in Conflict and Terrorism* 29, no. 5 (2007): 403–414.
70 Jonathan Powell, *Great Hatred, Little Room* (London: Bodley Head, 2008).
71 This was the case in our meetings with policy-makers, ex-prisoners, NGOs, and a group of scholars at INCORE, University of Ulster, Londonderry, December 4, 2007.
72 Sir Ken Bloomfield, Former Head of NI Civil Service and member of Victims Association, Personal Interview, Belfast, December 3, 2007.
73 John McGarry, "Globalisation, European Integration and the Northern Ireland Conflict," in Michael Keating and John McGarry (eds.), *Minority Nationalism and the Changing International Order* (Oxford: Oxford University Press, 2001), 295–324, quote at p. 313.
74 Etain Tannam, "The European Commission and conflict in Northern Ireland," *Cambridge Review of International Affairs* 11, no. 1 (1997): 8–27.

75 Cathal McCall, "Post-modern Europe and the resources of communal identities in Northern Ireland," *European Journal of Political Research* 33, no. 3 (1998): 389–411.
76 Elizabeth Meehan, "Europe and the Europeanisation of the Irish Question," in Michael Cox, Adrian Guelke, and Fiona Stephen (eds.), *A Farewell to Arms? Beyond the Good Friday Agreement* (Manchester: Manchester University Press, 2006), 338–356.
77 Paul Dixon, "Rethinking the International and Northern Ireland: a critique," in Cox, Guelke and Stephen (eds.), *A Farewell to Arms?*, 409–426.
78 Roger Mac Ginty, "The liberal peace at home and abroad: Northern Ireland and liberal internationalism," *British Journal of Politics and International Relations* 11, no. 4 (2009): 690–708.
79 For this definition of peace, see Oliver P. Richmond, *Peace in IR* (London: Routledge, 2008), conclusion.
80 Richmond, *A Post-Liberal Peace* (see note 9 above), quote at pp. 572–573.
81 Ioannis Tellidis, "Terrorist conflict vs. civil peace in the Basque Country," in Oliver Richmond (ed.), *Palgrave Advances in Peacebuilding: Critical Developments and Approaches* (Basingstoke: Palgrave, 2010), 415–438.

3 Trauma and the city
The psychology of America's terrorism trauma

Sarton Weinraub

Introduction

Have New Yorkers been traumatized by September 11? Countless personal accounts of September 11 and numerous studies on September 11-related PTSD point to levels of trauma experienced by people who were directly and indirectly affected by the events of that day. I have witnessed trauma in all shapes and forms: I was in the immediate vicinity of Ground Zero on September 11, and I have worked as a psychotherapist in New York since 2001. As I reflect on trauma following September 11, and as I reflect on the nature of trauma itself, I find the origins and course of trauma are difficult to generalize because its experience is diverse.

New York before and after September 11

New York City prior to the 9/11 attacks was a very different place. I was living in Los Angeles at that time (in the late 1990s) when many of us thought of Manhattan and the outer boroughs as episodes of "Sex and the City." I am told by those who were then living in New York at the time, that the city was more raw, more diverse, more affordable, more relaxed, more dangerous, and much more fun.

Experiencing trauma here in New York City feels different than in other parts of the country and possibly even the world. It feels both simple yet quite complex. On the one hand, living here is so tough that it feels as if the people of this city are familiar with trauma on a daily basis. On the other hand, seeing the variety of faces that appear each day on the subway, it seems that for many NYC is filled with boundless joy and opportunity. The behavior of New Yorkers is often considered harsh or downright mean by visitors. Yet I find the directness of the average New Yorker satisfying and I am not afraid of unforeseen retaliation.

Often, I see a familiar pattern of acclimation to the city. Those who have just moved here (usually those in their twenties) are nervous, yet excited. Usually, for the first time in their lives they are able to freely live life. They find ways to live cheaply. They work, they love, they party, they hurt, and they learn, some faster than others. Then, the desire for family comes. Some stay and some go. Usually the Europeans, unless they are very rich or have American partners, go home. Those who stay may take on a new form of cynicism. I state this without judgment but as an observable phenomenon. And for some, this is a place where once you evolve past any trauma, you learn to live life with a greater depth of awareness.

In many ways, it feels like 9/11 was a blip on the screen for New York City. It came, brought a major yet brief traumatic event to the city, and went away. Yes, there were a few who got scared and moved out, but those stories are limited. Yet the speed and fervor with which gentrification followed 9/11 in New York City is incredible. In many ways, it is hard to understand what actual and lasting effect 9/11 has had on New York City. Was there widespread trauma brought on by the events of 9/11? Certainly, a small number of citizens witnessed unspeakable horrors, lost loved ones, and risked their own lives to save others. But what about the rest of us who took part but were not overtly affected? Were we traumatized as well?

Personal experiences on September 11

I did not work or live near what would later be called "Ground Zero," so it was strange that I was near the World Trade Center on the morning of September 11, 2001. I was there to accompany my partner at the time while she was looking at a potential artist's studio to rent on Beaver Street, about four blocks from the World Trade Center (WTC). Beaver Street was one of the last remaining small streets in the Wall Street area where artists could still find space. The night before I had been to my first Yankees game and I was a bit hung over. I had just moved to New York to begin my career as a psychologist. That morning we rode our bikes from the East Village down Broadway, noticing the World Trade Towers on our way. We even discussed going to the top of the World Trade Center for the city view.

Inside the studio on Beaver Street, we did not hear or notice the first plane hitting the towers, but the second plane rattled the building we were in. We looked outside to see what was going on, and we could see a plume of smoke high in the sky coming from the direction of the towers. Looking out, to us people seemed a bit frenzied, but we could not yet see panic on their faces.

Sensing something had happened, we left the Beaver Street studio to look further. As we walked toward the direction of the towers, a woman passed us crying terribly. Having no idea what she had just seen I asked her if she needed help? She looked at me, and in a state of shock said "no, thank you." I did not know what to think, but as we turned the corner we could see both towers on fire; then I knew that woman must have come from the buildings. I felt horrible. What could I have done for her?

I looked at the World Trade towers from the southeast. From our vantage point it appeared as if bombs had gone off simultaneously in planned explosions. From where we were, there was no sign that planes had hit the towers. Thank God we did not see anyone jumping off the buildings. Staring at the towers burning, I thought it strange, as the view was so enormous. Yet, from our vantage point it seemed so small compared to the size of the buildings. We stood there gawking, as a state of shock over took us. I knew I was witnessing a historic event. I also had a sense of the enormity of the event and that more was yet to come.

Wanting more information about what had happened—this was years before the Smartphone—I ducked into a nearby shoeshine shop, where the TV was on. I asked the owner what happened; he said planes had hit the twin towers and also the Pentagon in DC. Looking at the TV, I could not believe what I was watching. I thought that this must be some media-generated scare. I could not allow myself to believe it because it would have been too scary to be true. What would come next?

After going back outside, fear began to emerge within me. Looking around, I thought everyone was in a state of shock, staring, wanting to do something but not knowing what to do. Some were awestruck, staring, doing nothing. Yet others seemed to be exhibiting signs of fear. I noticed people getting scared and expressing it in various ways. I saw a mother frantically moving her child in a stroller up the street. There were tourists scrambling for where to go next. Overall, basically everyone looked helpless. That was when we had the sense to get out of the shoeshine shop.

We had our bikes with us and, feeling numb, we casually walked them south toward the Staten Island Ferry terminal. Looking back, I see that I was now actively trying not to panic. Then, on Broadway, looking down toward the "Charging Bull" statue at Bowling Green Park, things changed. The earth shook as the first tower collapsed. We could not see it, but as I looked in the direction of the World Trade Center, hundreds of people were running toward us.

The scene in the film *The Bicycle Thief*,[1] when the crowd chases down the father with his bicycle in hand, flashed into my mind as we were seated on our bikes. Yet high above the crowd was a thick and fast moving cloud of dust that began high in the sky but was quickly coming down. As people ran past us, the cloud quickly engulfed us. There was nowhere to ride our bikes, so, stupidly, I locked them to the nearest post and then we moved south toward the river. The smoke became thicker and heavier. Running was no longer an option. Which direction should we go? Everyone around us began to cough and was struggling to breathe. I took my shirt off to use as a facemask. Still coughing, we now could not see where the smoke began and ended. A black man walked past me completely covered white with dust.

My friend wanted to hide in a nearby shelter, but I wanted to keep moving. We got to the edge of the East River near the Staten Island Ferry terminal. Looking north toward the South Street Sea Port, we saw that the smoke was still very thick but dissipating as it mixed with the air from the East River. Hundreds of people were climbing over huge road medians to get closer to the water to breathe freely. I could see the Brooklyn Bridge from where I was in Manhattan, and it looked like thousands of people were moving across it, going to Brooklyn.

By now, we were in a crowd of thousands, moving together west under the Westside Highway along the water heading toward Canal Street. I was in shock, but I began to feel that people around us were supportive and caring for one another in this mass exodus under the FDR Highway. I noticed people around us sharing cloths to protect themselves from the smoke. A random person walking next to me gave me the rest of his water, which we shared. This gift from a stranger would have been unheard of 20 minutes earlier.

It was a moment of amazing support and community; one I have not experienced either before or after. But then, just as we began to feel some bit of camaraderie, we heard fighter jets rip through the air above; everyone looked up in fear. Because of the smoke, we could not see the jets, so panic swept through the crowd as if there might be an air battle above us. We did not know what was going on. What we did know is that we all had to keep moving to get out of the smoke. We did not know where or when the smoke would end. But moving north was our only option.

Luckily, as we entered and crossed Canal Street on the Lower East Side, the smoke cleared, and before us we could see New York City once again. Looking southwest, we could see the origin of the smoke coming from where one of the World Trade towers had been. The other one was still standing strong. With the smoke clearing, people cheered and a feeling of temporary relief could be seen on the face of every person who crossed Canal Street. Honestly, I had the feeling of moving to a place of safety. Everyone seemed scared, and it was clear that the people on the other side of Canal Street who had not been in the smoke looked scared too, not knowing what to do.

There were deli owners in front of their store selling water bottles as though we were at a baseball game, which, in hindsight, was very tacky. But what could we do but move on toward what we hoped would be safety? Still, in what is considered Chinatown, we were moving north toward the Lower Eastside, when we saw neighbors. It was clear there was a difference between those who were emerging from the dust and those who had not experienced it.

I felt they looked upon us as pitiful souls; they seemed to want to engage us but, considering the large numbers of people coming out of the smoke, they were not able to help us. So we walked on, heading for the East Village, trying to ignore where we had been and hoping for something better ahead.

We were exhausted now. My head hung low; I was scared, in shock, but feeling as if I had found safety. Then, as if the gods were calling us back, the ground rumbled, and turning around quickly we all had a bird's eye view of the second tower crumbling. I remember from where I was standing that it looked as if a giant was emptying out a bag of quarters.

What we saw was horrifying. I remember praying that people in the area had been able to evacuate. After what we had just come from, this sight was too much. Now that we were out of the smoke, we could see fear on the faces of the people around us. In hindsight, this marked the moment that a state of shock consumed me.

Knowing that our apartment was close, we pushed on. Walking through the East Village, the quiet was noticeable. Because of the buildings now separating us, from seeing the ruins of the WTC, we could no longer hear nor see further carnage. Yet we knew carnage was there. It was a workday, and yet the neighborhood seemed empty. The few who were there noticed our clothes covered with dust and asked what we had witnessed. We told them what we could. The horror on the faces of people who had not been there seemed even more terrifying.

As we reached the apartment, we all needed to use the toilet. When it was my turn, I found the toilet seat cover ripped from its base. My friend had been so scared that she must have done this unconsciously; I knew at that moment we all were trying to hide the deep fear within. Phone service was scarce and we did not have any working Internet. My neighbor had cable TV, which was functional, so we went to her apartment to watch the news. We ate, bathed, and thought about what we could do to help. Many of us tried to go to local hospitals to give blood, but we were turned away as they did not need blood donations. Most of the victims were in, or near the WTC, were already dead.

A parent's story of 9/11

A friend told me the scary story of his experience living near the World Trade Center Towers during 9/11. Having two children at two different schools in the area, he was immediately concerned about their well-being, motivating him to secure the safety of his children with speed and intensity.

I am not sure he had time to act on anything but his fight-or-flight responses. After just dropping off his second child at school, my friend saw the first plane hit the twin towers. Rushing back to get his youngest son, the school went into lockdown mode. Stuck there, helping the school go into emergency mode, he supported the children as they waited for their parents to come. Suddenly the second tower was hit.

At this time, he knew he could not stay at his first son's school. He needed to collect his second child and get both his children to safety, all the while hoping his wife was safe, since all the phones were down. Now with his youngest son by his side, he rushed to his oldest son's school on the other side of town but still in the vicinity of the twin towers' danger zone.

Rushing through the streets, he told me of the panic and horror he witnessed. They had to walk past the section of the twin towers where jumpers off the WTC were visible. He did all he could to prevent his young son from looking or even comprehending what was happening. "Keeping looking forward and stay close to me, son," he would say. Arriving at his oldest son's school, he found that a state of emergency lockdown was in effect. All the students were in the main hallway with their teachers, waiting to be picked up. He found his older son and agreed to take his neighbors' children to his building to await their parents' arrival.

Once inside his apartment, he believed they were safe. Then the first tower came down, and he did not realize they were in living in the danger zone. The apartment was covered with smoke from the top down. They all had to gather what they could and run as far as they could until they were away from the smoke. Walking uptown with his two children and four other local children, my friend then headed to his nearby friend's house and again waited.

Luckily, someone had a landline phone that did not need electricity to operate, so my friend was able to leave a message telling his wife and other neighbors where they were. For the next two weeks, they lived uptown with friends, until they moved to a new apartment. Their home was covered with ash and debris. They never were able to move back.

As he was telling me this story, I asked my friend if he felt he had been affected to the point that he had become traumatized by the events of 9/11. He told me he felt he was lucky. Being a parent, his instincts to take care of his children and find safety were primal and did not leave him time to be overwhelmed. He had reacted quickly, without feeling. As he told me this, I did not sense any hesitation or unease in him. His family had been attacked and he saved them. As he told me, "it is a parent's job."

After-effects of September 11

For the next few weeks, the city entered a state of strange utopian civility. Just about everyone stayed home the first week, taking life a bit more slowly. During the day, we wandered around the city, looking for opportunities to help one another, at home, or at community centers. Often, we went to the Westside Highway with crowds of other survivors to watch the firefighters and other workers return to "Ground Zero." With tears in our eyes, we cheered them as they arrived. It was one way to share feelings and raise our hopes bit-by-bit. Ground Zero was sectioned off and policed by officials who worked day and night to stabilize the site. One major concern was air quality. There was a mad rush to secure air filters. Yet, everyone, and I mean everyone, was friendly to one another.

To us it seemed that lower Manhattan had become the center of the world. First responders from all over the country came to New York, offering help and kindness. It lasted for a little over two weeks, but I swear, people around the city at that time were generous and caring. It eventually faded, but it did happen.

Others I knew who lived in New York City were not anywhere near the twin towers. Yet, they, too, experienced fear and worry about what had happened and what might happen again. One friend told me of waking up late and hearing of the 9/11 attacks. He hid in his apartment for a week, afraid to leave. Another friend watched the towers burn from her roof in far-off Brooklyn. However, when asked about her experience of the attacks, she stated she was so scared and she thought that she would die; these feelings haunt her to this day.

Others, who were not near ground zero that day, reported feeling as if they had also been attacked. A variety of responses included: wanting to join the military, wanting to leave the country, and for the first time feeling fear and anger toward the Muslim community. Interestingly, of all the responses to the 9/11 attacks I heard of, the reactions by those who were *not* there seemed the most extreme. Being in the city at that time, yet not experiencing the attacks directly, seems to have left a void and prevented the grieving processing from emerging.

Trauma and Post Traumatic Stress Disorder

What is trauma? Post Traumatic Stress Disorder is the mental health diagnostic label associated with clinically significant trauma, but they are not the same. The American Psychological Association (2016) defines trauma as:

> An emotional response to a terrible event like an accident, rape or natural disaster. Immediately after the event, shock and denial are typical. Longer term reactions include unpredictable emotions, flashbacks, strained relationships and even physical symptoms like headaches or nausea. While these feelings are normal, some people have difficulty moving on with their lives.[2]

The American Psychological Association (2016) then defines Post Traumatic Stress Disorder, or PTSD, as "an anxiety problem that develops in some people after extremely traumatic events, such as combat, crime, an accident or natural disaster."[3] Therefore trauma is the cause and PTSD can be understood as the effect. But does trauma occur differently for each person according to the event they are experiencing? Are the traumas of being in war the same as the traumas of growing up in an abusive family? There are so many questions and popular myths with regard to trauma.

The non-clinical definition I like to use when explaining trauma to a non-specialist comes from a New York City musician known as Cat Power. In her song "Fool," released after 9/11, Power sings that a direct hit to one's senses disconnects them. If you are a solider witnessing the horrors of war, or if you are living with an alcoholic, or if you have been through a car accident, in all cases the defining moment occurs where our senses are affected to the point that we become emotionally disconnected from our feelings. Thus, trauma is born when our senses are overwhelmed to such a point that the unknown becomes highly exacerbated. The amount of force necessary to affect each of us to the point of trauma varies depending upon a mix of internal and external factors, yet almost all humans have a common breaking point.

Studies on trauma related to 9/11

There have been very ambitious and informative studies on trauma and PTSD in people who experienced the events of September 11, both directly and indirectly.

A 2011 report published in *American Psychologist* states:

> Within the first week after 9/11, Schuster et al. (2001) conducted a national random digit-dial telephone survey of 560 adults and found that 44 percent

of participants reported substantial stress reactions. One to two months after the attacks, Schlenger et al. (2002) conducted a Web-based study with a nationally representative sample of 2,273 adults and reported a 4.3 percent prevalence of PTSD that was significantly associated with both the number of hours of television coverage of 9/11 watched and the number of 9/11-related graphic events watched on television.

These two studies were followed by a national longitudinal Web-based survey of 2,729 adults, conducted by Silver, Holman, McIntosh, Poulin, and Gil-Rivas (2002), who examined demographics, health history, lifetime exposure to stressful events, 9/11 exposures, and coping strategies. In three studies conducted (1) 9–23 days after 9/11; (2) two months after the attacks; and (3) six months after the attacks, the researchers found that within the first month, 12 percent of individuals reported acute stress symptoms and 8.9 percent reported symptoms involving functional impairment.

The researchers also found that the course of posttraumatic stress symptoms went from 17 percent at two months to 5.8 percent at six months' post attack. Taken together, these studies presented initial evidence that the 9/11 attacks, whether propagated by media images or by concerns about safety in times of war and terrorism, were significantly associated with PTSD symptoms in the general U.S. population.[4]

Another study published in 2011 in *Disaster Medicine and Public Health Preparedness* found:

> The direct exposure zone was largely concentrated within a radius of 0.1 miles and completely contained within 0.75 miles of the towers. PTSD symptom criteria at any time after the disaster were met by 35 percent of people directly exposed to danger, 20 percent of those exposed only through witnessed experiences, and 35 percent of those exposed only through a close associate's direct exposure. Outside these exposure groups, few possible sources of exposure were evident among the few who were symptomatic, most of whom had preexisting psychiatric illness.[5]

According to a 2010 study, published in the *Journal of Traumatic Stress*:

> In the general population, the mental health effects of the 9/11 attacks appear to have declined with the passage of time (Galea et al., 2003; Silver et al., 2002). In one nationally representative Web-based panel study, the proportion of adults endorsing posttraumatic stress symptoms declined from 17 percent after two months to 6 percent after three months following the attacks (Silver et al., 2002). In a representative sample of adults residing in Manhattan, the overall prevalence of posttraumatic stress disorder (PTSD) fell from 7.5 percent one month after the attacks to 1.7 percent at four months and to less than one percent six months after 9/11.
>
> (Galea et al., 2003)[6]

A study in the 2010 *Journal of Traumatic Stress* concludes:

> Following the 9/11 attacks, there was a significant decline in the prevalence of 9/11-related probable PTSD, from 9.6 percent approximately one year after 9/11 to 4.1 percent approximately four years after the attacks in this predominantly low-income, minority, primary care patient cohort. Although this pattern is consistent with most previous prospective 9/11 reports (e.g., Galea et al., 2003, Silver et al. 2002), our finding that most patients (89 percent) with baseline PTSD remitted and most patients (75 percent) with PTSD at long-term follow-up had late-PTSD was not anticipated. Previous studies in populations exposed to terrorism found lower rates of late-onset PTSD, ranging from 9 percent (North, McCutcheon, Spitznagel, and Smith, 2002) to 21 percent (North et al., 2004) 3 years and 17 months after exposure, respectively. Yet our findings are in accord with a two-year follow-up study among the general population in New York City after the 9/11 attacks, which found that 70 percent of the PTSD-positive cases at follow-up had late-onset PTSD.
>
> (Adams and Boscarino, 2006)[7]

An analysis of this small sample of studies clearly indicates that a wide range of trauma and PTSD symptoms occurred following 9/11 and affected a diverse range of people, both those who were directly and those who were indirectly exposed to the horrors of that day. These findings suggest the range of traumatic experiences is diverse and warrants further study to better understand the experience of trauma among diverse populations.

My view on trauma after September 11

As a psychologist in New York City, I've had a number of clients who were employees of businesses in the twin towers. I've also had clients who were "official" first responders—i.e., police, firemen, EMTs (Emergency Medical Technicians), and mental health workers who immediately came to the site following the buildings' collapse. My observations of, and consultations with people who worked at Ground Zero, differ from what has been widely reported.

The first responders I have worked with share harrowing stories from their experiences at Ground Zero. However, these individuals also present with low levels of diagnosable traumatic symptoms. Instead of exhibiting clear symptoms of trauma, these first responders present memories of that day that flow openly and clearly, including tears for lost friends. The experiences reported by these first responders are harrowing and downright frightening. Yet, they do not present as traumatized. Instead they show a pragmatic willingness to explore their painful memories. This suggests the actual danger they experienced had the effect of eradicating imagined fear, replacing it with the concrete experience of pain and loss.

I also consulted with individuals not at Ground Zero during the actual events but who heard about what was going on and immediately went to help. In these instances, I am not referring to first responders or those who were caught in the nightmare from the beginning. I am referring to individuals who were a safe distance away but came because they were drawn to the intense nature of the event; they were drawn to Ground Zero like a drug. It is my understanding that these individuals were not from a similar grouping in age, race, or class. Most got caught in search-and-rescue operations and did whatever other first responders asked of them.

I've heard that most of these people felt the tragedy so significantly that they were traumatized, not by the direct events but by the emotions they experienced during the clean-up. One case in particular sticks out, where the individual had no training in search-and-rescue but left his job and ended up staying at the clean-up site for two weeks; his friends and family did not know where he was. In speaking with this person, I noticed that he saw himself as a first responder, working equally alongside the police and firemen. And yet, after two weeks, he went back to his normal life, a life that had nothing in common with search-and-rescue. When I spoke with him, he told me he believed he had become a first responder and that he felt kinship with the firefighters around him. I heard he was applying for medical support to counter the toxins he inhaled at Ground Zero, as many firefighters who were also there had done.

This story raises the issue of the firefighter as a cultural phenomenon. Warren Spielberg has written of the idealization of first responders at the 9/11 site. "In becoming a cultural hero, however, the New York firefighter also becomes a fetishistic object—an object used by others to make them feel better about ourselves, often at the object's expense."[8]

As indicated by the previously-cited studies, PTSD symptoms rose in the United States as a whole following 9/11. The question is, what can be done to help treat trauma and PTSD symptoms resulting from horrific events like 9/11? Charles Whitfield, author of *Healing the Child Within* (1987), has also written about trauma. According to him, Post Traumatic Stress Disorder is a widely underutilized diagnosis. In his book, *Not crazy: You may not be mentally ill*, Whitfield states:

> Instead of their being "mentally ill" with any of the above mental illness or disorder labels, I found that most of my patients had post-traumatic stress disorder (PTSD). Some of them had a more advanced form of PTSD ... on the surface most had symptoms of various mental illnesses. But underneath was usually PTSD.[9]

For Whitfield and other trauma researchers, the origins, course, and wide range of trauma and PTSD symptoms need greater attention, including ongoing research and support for clinical practices.

Looking back, looking forward

Looking back, I was temporarily traumatized. It initially occurred the moment I experienced the first "direct hit" to my system. It happened while I was stuck in the smoke of the first tower's collapse. I heard jets fly overhead. I could not see them and I did not know if they were friend or foe. At that movement, for a brief second I did not know if I would live or die, and so the fight-or-flight response took over. Based on his study of survivors of terrorist attacks in 14 countries, Charles Webel concludes that "Terror is profoundly sensory (often auditory), and is pre- or post-verbal. The ineffability of terror is complement to, and often a result of, the unspeakable horror(s) of war(s) and other forms of collective political violence."[10] While that moment of terror was brief, in that split second all kinds of previously far-off fears rushed into my mind. Because of the smoke, we could not see the sky. We did not know whether the fighter jets above us were ours or theirs.

Even now, as I look out the window and see the city skyline from my home in Brooklyn, it is hard to not think of my experiences on 9/11. I have done my best to move on and live my life without reacting to what I experienced on 9/11. It is difficult to admit that it has not been easy. Sometimes, I will be sitting on a subway car that is not moving, and I wonder if a terror attack is imminent. Other times I will be walking down a street and see a large crowd, and, without a second thought, I consider getting away as fast as I can for my own safety.

I must admit that, since 9/11, I carry a basic fear of New York City as a whole. This fear is not debilitating, but it lies within me. The idea that we are all safe and secure is what we want to believe. However, my innocence is gone. I now know that I can die at any moment for unexpected reasons.

Maybe this is something all New Yorkers must learn to face, both pre- and post-9/11. I am aware that humans can both give and take life in equal measure. This realization makes me feel both frightened and awestruck. Over the last 15 years, I have learned how to live with this knowledge. For me, 9/11 was a birth by fire; I had just moved to this city, and overnight I became a New Yorker.

Notes

1 *The Bicycle Thief* [*Ladri di biciclette*], directed by Vittoria de Sica (1948).
2 "Trauma," American Psychological Association, accessed May 28, 2016, www.apa.org/topics/trauma.
3 "Post-traumatic Stress Disorder," American Psychological Association, accessed May 28, 2016, www.apa.org/topics/trauma/. www.apa.org/topics/ptsd/index.aspx.
4 Yuval Neria, Laura DiGrande, and Ben G. Adams, "Posttraumatic stress disorder following the September 11, 2001, terrorist attacks: A review of the literature among highly exposed populations," *American Psychologist* 66, no. 6 (September 2011): 430, doi: 10.1037/a0024791.
5 Carol S. North, David E. Pollio, Rebecca P. Smith, Richard V. King, Anand Pandya, Alina M. Surís, Barry A. Hong, Denis J. Dean, Nancy E. Wallace, Daniel B. Herman, Sarah Conover, Ezra Susser, and Betty Pfefferbaum, "Trauma Exposure and Posttraumatic Stress Disorder Among Employees of New York City Companies Affected by

the September 11, 2001 Attacks on the World Trade Center," *Disaster Medicine and Public Health Preparedness* 5, no. s2 (2011), doi: 10.1001/dmp.2011.50.
6 Yuval Neria Mark Olfson, Marc J. Gameroff, Laura DiGrande, Priya Wickramaratne, Raz Gross, Daniel J. Pilowsky, Richard Neugebaur, Julían Manetti-Cusa, Roberto Lewis-Fernandez, Rafael Lantigua, Steven Shea, and Myrna M. Weissman, "Long-Term Course of Probable PTSD After the 9/11 Attacks: A Study in Urban Primary Care," *Journal of Traumatic Stress* 23 (2010): 475, doi: 10.1002/jts.20544.
7 Neria, "Long-Term Course," 478–479.
8 Warren Spielberg, "Trauma in 9/11's Wake: The Objectification of New York City Firefighters," *Tikkun*, September 8, 2011, accessed April 28, 2016, www.tikkun.org/nextgen/trauma-in-911s-wake-the-objectification-of-new-york-city-firefighters.
9 Charles L. Whitfield, *Not Crazy: You May Not Be Mentally Ill* ([United States]: Muse House Press, 2011), 2.
10 Charles P. Webel, *Terror, Terrorism, and the Human Condition* (New York: Palgrave McMillan, 2004), 11.

Part II

Hearing from the victims of terror-inflicted regions

Mark Tomass

We are often told that terrorists' aims are political, not military. In this part, the often neglected victims of terror and the War on Terror offer us different perspectives. They tell us that new forms of terrorism have appeared in the Middle East that use military conquests to establish a new social order. We hear accounts from Syria, Iraq, and the Swat Valley of Pakistan on the past, the present, and their future prospects for peace and security.

From Syria, we hear from Buthaina Shaaban, a long-time affiliate of the Syrian government through ministerial and advisory positions. Shabaan's assessment of the consequences of US foreign policy towards the Middle East, and towards Syria in particular, is representative of the political opinions of a large segment of contemporary secular Syrians, regardless of their sectarian affiliations. Like Shaaban, that segment of Syrian society favors progressive Western social values, is thoroughly secular and feminist, and yearns to integrate Syria with the rest of the world, especially with Western and Eastern Europe and with the Americas.

In this chapter, Shaaban tells us about her personal experience in the string of events that mutated the Arab Spring uprising into one of the world's most destructive wars since World War II and led to the empowerment of the most notorious terrorist groups known in contemporary times. She argues, in contrast to the common narrative heard in US political and media circles, that the "Syrian Revolution" was not spontaneous. Rather, it was fomented with various foreign financial, political, logistical, and military means, including direct bribes offered to members of the Syrian government and street protesters. That Western and reactionary regional support not only led to massive physical destruction and safe havens for terrorist groups, but also allowed those terrorist groups to inflict catastrophic damage to Syria's cultural identity, civilizational heritage, and social cohesion.

The second chapter is from Iraq, where the number of deaths from terrorism is the highest in the world, accounting for one third of all deaths in that country, and where the highest number of suicide bombings in the world has been recorded annually since 2003, amounting to 237 in 2015 alone.[1] Anwar al-Haidari writes to us from his terror-inflicted city of Baghdad. After a detailed narration of the circumstances that led to the current state of extreme violence, al-Haidari ponders why American and Iraqi efforts against terrorism are still not unified. He concludes that, while the September 11, 2001, attacks in the US were acts of terrorism, so were many other acts perpetrated in Iraq since 2003, a fact which presents a question concerning the ethical basis upon which the United States constructed its vision for its War on Terror. Moreover, although the professed aim of fighting terrorist groups in Iraq and Syria is clear and specific, the dispute between the United States and Russia in the War on Terror reveals their different interests; it reveals also that the War on Terror is a cover for achieving those separate interests. Al-Haidari ends on a pessimistic note, wondering what the future of Iraq will look like.

In the third chapter, Mark Tomass, a native of Aleppo, Syria, outlines the ideological origins of today's Salafi-Jihadi groups and argues that their presence on the intellectual, social, and political scenes in the Middle East has surged in the past 40 years, due to the outward expansion of the Saudi–Wahhābī political alliance and the general anti-Western and anti-globalization movement reflected in the "Islamic Awakening" of the last two decades. Placing the September 11 terrorist attacks and the US invasion of Iraq in the context of the ideological expansion of the Salafi-Jihadi movement and the rise to power of a Muslim Brothers variant in Turkey, Tomass argues that the destruction of the Iraqi state and army and the significant weakening of those institutions in Syria less than a decade later couldn't have come at a better time for al-Qaeda. Both the West and al-Qaeda played similar roles in creating a power vacuum that facilitated al-Qaeda's transition to the Islamic State, in a manner which the latter had specified in detail in its 2004 manifesto "The Management of Savagery." In accordance with its complex inception, Tomass concludes that stemming the rise of al-Qaeda cannot be confined to military means. Wahhābī doctrine has gained significant ground among the Muslim masses, to the extent that in today's Syria, the vast majority of the rebel groups adhere to it, whether they organizationally belong to al-Qaeda, or to its daughter ISIL, or not. Genuine political reform in the Middle East will have to begin with challenging the hegemony of religious institutions over all aspects of life. Without such a challenge and a victory of reason over dogmatic religious ideology, the world must continue to live with a Middle East ruled either by secular authoritarian governments or by religious totalitarian ones.

Finally, while the Swat Valley from the region between Pakistan and Afghanistan is distant from today's centers of al-Qaeda and ISIS in Syria and Iraq, a native medical doctor, Sher Khan reminds us that it was the region where al-Qaeda terrorists trained prior to the 9/11 attacks and were given safe haven after they carried out those attacks. He investigates the root causes of the tradition of giving safe haven to criminals and concludes that it is partly grounded in poverty, social injustice, unemployment, and poor governance. Dr. Khan believes that prevention and early detection of these types of maladies are not only more effective, but are cheaper, than waging an unending "war on terrorism." Decision-makers need to apply an altruistic approach rather than a strategy of retaliation and revenge, such as "an eye for an eye," which leaves everyone blind. A systematic application to the problem of Rudyard Kipling's "W's" (What, Why, When, How, Where, Who) can also help address the root causes of the manmade disasters.

Note

1 *Statista: The Statistics Portal*, "Countries with the highest number of deaths by terrorism in 2014, by percentage of total deaths," www.statista.com/statistics/377061/countries-with-the-highest-number-of-deaths-by-terrorism/ and "Number of suicide attacks in 2015, by country," www.statista.com/statistics/518639/suicide-attacks-by-country/.

4 The Syrian tragedy
The role of the West, a government insider's account

Bouthaina Shaaban

Having been in Syria through the ongoing war, as I have lived here before, I shall try to present to Western readers a balanced account of what has truly happened and why, so that it may serve not only to shed light on Syria's plight, but also to act as a wake-up call to other people. The tragedy in Syria, and its ramifications, as well as the ongoing security and humanitarian catastrophe, can only be solved by simply taking a serious and brave political stand, based not on false narratives but on glaring facts.

Western policies towards Syria—since 2011—inflamed the conflict and the subsequent growth of terrorism. These policies ranged from the attempt to break up Syria's civilian and military institutions to the de-legitimization of the Syrian government, through the recognition of certain figures, without a clear legal and popular mandate, as the sole representatives of the Syrian people. Incessant attempts to procure a UN mandate for a military intervention in Syria were made at the United Nations Security Council, the failure of which led Western nations to impose suffocating unilateral and compulsory measures on Syria. The most vicious policy pursued by the West, particularly the United States, was to support a plethora of armed groups, including ones related to al-Qaeda, in order to fight the Syrian government. The last point will be scrutinized in order to highlight how the United States and its allies cynically employed extremist groups in Syria, including ISIS, to achieve geopolitical gains, leading to an outgrowth of terrorism with no regard to regional or world peace. Throughout the following points, I will give special attention to the role played by the Western mass media and the false narratives it propagated about Syria.

I subsequently examine the crucial differences between the US-led campaign against ISIS and the Russian efforts against terrorism. Using statistics and testimony, I discuss the destructive effects of both terrorist attacks and Western unilateral sanctions on Syria's institutions, infrastructure, and people. Details on the extent of material losses in important sectors of the Syrian economy will be presented below for the first time. Finally, I examine the effects of the terrorist groups' actions and ideologies on Syria's cultural identity, civilizational heritage, and social cohesion.

Beginnings

On February 15, 2011, Syria's President Bashar al-Asad headed to the Grand Umayyad Mosque in the heart of Old Damascus to join the Damascene clergy and people in prayers celebrating the birth of Prophet Mohammed. He departed the mosque, surrounded by hundreds; and by the time he got behind the wheel thousands had crammed the narrow pathway between the mosque and the millennia-old Hamidiyah Souk. The president drove his car through the crowd, both windows rolled down, greeting people along the way; his security detail was having a difficult time.[1] But there was little to worry about: 10 years at the helm of the country, carrying on an expansive reform and modernization program while keeping a country in the most turbulent region in the world safe and stable, President Asad was confident of his popularity and his personal security among his people.

Simultaneously, a meeting was taking place between members of the French intelligence services (DGSE) and members of the Libyan opposition in the coastal Libyan city of Benghazi.[2] Barely 10 days into the "protest movement" against Libya's leader, Muammar Gaddafi, an armed insurgency had sprung up in the eastern parts of the country, and a "transitional council" was formed. With no apparent legitimate political or popular mandate, this council gave a consortium of French and Italian corporations "favorable considerations" in business matters, especially concerning oil, in exchange for Western military help against the "tyrant."[3] This astonishing information was found in former US Secretary of State Hillary Clinton's emails four years later. But back in 2011, the dominant narrative was that the West needed to carry out a "humanitarian intervention" to save the Libyan people from an impending massacre; and so they did. Backed by a *fatwa* from the Al-Jazeera-based Muslim Brotherhood cleric Youssef al-Qaradawi and an invitation from the Arab League, NATO began bombing Libya. "Smart" bombs pummeled Libyan infrastructure that took decades to build. Surprisingly, for the first time in their history, Arab states such as Qatar and the UAE participated in the bombing campaign against a fellow Arab country, as opposed to just funding the venture.

The "liberation" of Libya from its military forces, state institutions, and infrastructure culminated in the unlawful murder of Colonel Gaddafi in October 2011. British Prime Minister David Cameron and French President Nicolas Sarkozy paraded in "freedom square" in Benghazi; the "tyrant" was dead, democracy—and business—could finally bloom in Libya, except it didn't. Almost five years later, Libya remains a fractured and lawless country sinking ever more into chaos and being devoured, town after town, by the so-called "Islamic State" terrorist group, while Libyan oil flows safely to French and Italian shores, generating huge profits for Western companies. Watching a fellow Arab country suffering such fierce aggression, every Syrian knew something dangerous was in the making. They were still sharing their country with 2 million Iraqis who had fled their homes in the aftermath of America's most recent attempt to spread democracy in the Arab world. Syria was the only country in the Arab League that objected to the decision to invite NATO to bomb Libya, and the only one to warn of its consequences. Instead of heeding the warnings, other Arab countries and especially the Gulf-funded media vehemently attacked Syria's position.

It was not long before the nightmarish hurricane hit Syria. Stories about Syrian security forces torturing a group of children for writing political slogans on a wall began to circulate, prompting dozens to protest in the southern city of Deraa. Yet until this very day, no search engine or media outlet could produce one photograph of those tortured children. Al-Jazeera's go-to "intellectual," Azmi Bishara, who spent countless hours on air fanning the Syrian flames, later admitted in his 2013 book, *Syria: A Way of Suffering for Freedom*, after his researchers turned every stone to find the alleged victims, that the stories of children being brutally tortured were "rumors that couldn't be substantiated."[4] He added:

> They [the rumors] were used for political mobilization, meaning that the incident was used politically against the Syrian regime to give the movement a certain importance and symbolism in a way similar to the Bouazizi incident in Tunisia and the Khalid Said incident in Egypt. This shows the effect of the Arab Spring in exaggerating events and directing them to mobilize people to protest.[5]

The true story, according to Bishara, was that the children were apprehended for hurling rocks at a traffic policeman, they were not accused of writing any political slogans, and were released shortly after.

Nonetheless, the spark was lit, and true intentions were soon unmasked. On April 10, 2011, a bus carrying off-duty soldiers was attacked, killing a dozen officers. Days later, calls for Jihad rang in the city of Homs, government buildings were hit with machine-gun fire and grenades, and several police officers were murdered, some even beheaded.[6] This would have outraged the world just three years later, if only orange jumpsuits and high-definition cameras were present in that alleyway. In Hama, a police station was attacked, and the officers were murdered. The gunmen then took the bodies of the slain policemen and hurled them into the Orontes River; this incident, however, was filmed, but the world was not outraged. In rural Homs, tens of protesters led by a Salafi cleric chanted, "The people want an Islamic Caliphate."[7] The world did not take notice, yet the video can still be found on YouTube.

The Syrian government's immediate response was reconciliatory, as some of the demonstrators had genuine demands. On March 24, 2011, the Syrian leadership convened a long and important meeting in an effort to contain what seemed to be a looming crisis. I was asked to hold a press conference at 6pm in order to acknowledge, in the name of the leadership, the people's legitimate demands and to announce decisions and measures that addressed most of these demands. On that day, I personally announced to the Syrian people the lifting of emergency laws, in place since 1963, and a comprehensive reform package that would lead to further political freedoms, a multi-party law, and the drafting of a new constitution for Syria. Next day, people told me that they went out to celebrate Syria's averting a looming crisis. A feeling of relief prevailed all over the country due to the leadership's quick response to the demands.

The President also ordered the immediate release of all those detained during the unfortunate events that took place in Deraa the week before. Thousands of Syrians from all walks of life, dozens of delegations from all Syrian cities and villages flocked to the Presidential Palace for direct dialogue with the president. I also met many delegations, including local oppositions. I was most happy to engage the youth, connect with their ideas, and listen to their aspirations; the mood was far from confrontational. Many more dialogue initiatives were taken at every level of government and civil society. This conciliatory approach, however, was met with much worse intransigence by those who claimed to represent the Syrian people and who were by then occupying much of the airtime on Al-Jazeera and al-Arabiya. These two channels played an inflammatory role, encouraging people to protest and rebel against the Syrian government, and they constituted the primary source for news about Syria to all Western media outlets.

The first major calamity, and a stark indication of what was to come, took place on June 6, 2011. Hundreds of gunmen besieged and attacked government buildings in the city of Jisr al-Shughur, bordering Turkey. At the end of the day, 120 policemen were killed; some were executed in cold blood after they ran out of ammunition. Immediately following the massacre, a fear-mongering campaign began in Gulf and Western mass media; it was "reported" that the Syrian government was going to take revenge against the people of Jisr al-Shughur to encourage people to flee Syria to Turkey. For its part, Turkey put up hundreds of tents for "Syrian refugees" before any Syrian crossed the border. Tales of a "brutal government crackdown" began to circulate in Western mass media, as told by the "refugees" in Turkey and so-called "eye witnesses" on Al-Jazeera.[8] American actress and activist Angelina Jolie visited the week-old refugee camps in Turkey to highlight the "plight" of the Syrian people there.[9] Strangely enough, Turkish government "sources" went as far as talking of setting up a military-enforced "buffer zone" in northern Syria to solve the "refugees' crisis."[10] It is only now, five years hence, that we see Turkey's major role in using Syria and the Syrian refugees as bargaining chips with the West to serve its own interests.

Most Western readers would find it hard to comprehend that such language was already in use as early as June 2011. The demonization campaign against the Syrian government was well underway. The fact, however, remains that only minor security operations were conducted in Jisr al-Shughur back then; and while the world media were speaking of atrocities, Syrian TV channels were broadcasting live images of normal life on the streets of the city. A few days later, foreign delegates based in Damascus, including the US, UK, and French ambassadors, were given a bus tour of Jisr al-Shughur, which included a visit to the mass grave in which the gunmen buried the murdered policemen. The foreign delegates did not seem to care. Needless to say, Western media did not even show this visit to Jisr al-Shughur; instead, they based their reports on the work of Al-Jazeera and Al-Arabiya's correspondents.

The Syrian leadership remained unfazed. Following a speech by President Asad, millions of Syrians took to the streets of Damascus, Aleppo, Homs, Hama, Lattakia, and every other major Syrian city. The pictures, however clear, did not reach the world media. The narrative of a brutal crackdown against a movement for democracy remained dominant.

On July 29, 2011, an obscure group of seven men, dressed in military uniforms, announced the formation of the "Free Syrian Army" on YouTube. The world was supposed to believe that out of 300,000 officers and soldiers constituting the Syrian Armed Forces, seven men were to represent a legitimate fighting force to replace that institution. Apparently, they did, at least to the West and their Turkish and Arab backers. The venture grew into 15,000 armed men based at camps in southern Turkey. Their spokesperson promised imminent action to "liberate" Syria.[11] Turkey, a member of NATO, was now hosting an army of insurgents on its territory, the composition of which was largely unknown, and who were threatening to invade a sovereign nation with the aim of overthrowing its government under the veneer of "freedom fighters." Only five years later, Western think tanks woke to the fact that "neither desertions nor defections have significantly weakened the [Syrian] military or its chain of command."[12] A study by the Carnegie Endowment's Middle East Center found that most "defections," few as they may be, happened for economic motives and were mainly towards "well-funded jihadist militias," as opposed to the so-called Free Syrian Army.[13]

The attempt to break up Syria's institutions was not limited to the armed forces. Many officials, from all levels of government, including myself, were invited, and in many ways pressured and harassed, to "defect." They were offered financial incentives and—ironically—a place in the government of "new Syria." When a government official refused the "lucrative offers," threats against their personal safety and family soon followed. Eventually, many Syrian government officials and I were sanctioned by the European Union and the United States, simply for refusing to quit our jobs and relinquish our duties. The objectives of breaking up both the military and the civilian institutions of Syria by any means necessary were clear from the onset.

On August 18, 2011, US President Barack Obama called for the ouster of President Asad.[14] The United States was yet again committing itself to changing the political regime of a sovereign country. Obama's statement constituted a green light for another serious attempt to usurp legitimacy from the Syrian government. By the end of August, a group of "opposition" figures gathered in Istanbul, under the auspices of the Turkish government, and announced the formation of the "Syrian National Council." This grouping enjoyed no popular or political legitimacy, yet Western nations and Turkey, as well as Qatar and Saudi Arabia, began to deal with them as the sole representatives of the Syrian people, aiding and abetting their intransigence and their refusal to any national dialogue initiatives that would end the crisis and the bloodshed. We cannot ascertain what sorts of deals were made under the table—similar to those between the French intelligence services and the Libyan National Transitional Council. The efforts were given a serious impetus when, in November 2011, Qatar and Saudi Arabia, backed by the nascent Muslim Brotherhood-led regimes in Egypt, Tunisia, and Libya, succeeded in freezing Syria's membership in the Arab League. The decision was followed by Arab sanctions against Syria, setting the stage for American- and European-enforced, single-measure sanctions that would prevent Syrians from acquiring many essentials, including heating fuel and cancer treatments.[15]

The anti-Syria efforts culminated in the ironically named "Friends of Syria Group" meeting in Tunisia in February 2012, which included among others the United States, France, UK, and Germany, in addition to Turkey, Qatar, Saudi Arabia, and other Arab countries. This group tried to confer legitimacy and offer support to the so-called National Council and Free Syrian Army; calling for action à la Libya that would see them replace the legitimate Syrian government.[16] The "activists" on the ground linked to the Turkey-based opposition began to circulate banners calling for a no-fly zone, a buffer zone, and international "humanitarian" intervention in Syria.[17] These demonstrators were filmed, and Western and Gulf Arab mainstream media showed the clips repeatedly; while footage showing hundreds of thousands flooding the streets of Damascus and other cities supporting their government against any foreign intervention did not make the cut.

The double veto

The "Friends of Syria" sought tirelessly to gain a UN mandate for the process of de-legitimizing the Syrian government and imposing the Turkey-based "National Council" as a representative of the Syrian people, as well as soliciting a mandate to carry on a military intervention similar to the one in Libya. These efforts to breach Syria's sovereignty were repeatedly met by Russian and Chinese vetoes at the United Nations Security Council (four in total by May 2014). The first attempt was on October 4, 2011, followed by a second one in February 2012. On the night before the second attempt was made under Chapter Seven of the UN Charter, violent clashes erupted in the central city of Homs. Media outlets reported throughout the night that Syrian security forces were committing atrocities and killing hundreds of people, just hours before the Security Council session. This behavior became a pattern. On July 19, 2012, the Security Council met to discuss another Syria-related resolution presented by the Western powers, and it was again blocked by Russian and Chinese vetoes. Just three days before this session, four of Syria's top generals were assassinated, and thousands of gunmen tried to break into Damascus—information leaked two years after the event indicated that this was a complicated American–Turkish plan to seize the Syrian capital.

Russia's foreign minister, Sergey Lavrov, explained the reasoning behind the veto(es):

The veto [right] is not a privilege but a great responsibility. Thanks to the veto imposed by Russia and China several times we can say that a chance for transition to the political settlement process has emerged in the Syrian crisis. And it is absolutely true that the Russia–China veto has prevented Syria's transformation into Libya.[18]

Outside the Security Council, an international working group, which in addition to the Arab League, France, Britain, and the United States, included Russia and China, met in Geneva in June 2012. The group issued the "Geneva Communiqué," which advocated a Syrian-led political solution for the crisis, based on dialogue between Syrians. Western powers, however, largely ignored the outcomes of the meeting, and they began to recognize the Syrian National Coalition (or the SNC, the offspring of the National Council) as the sole legitimate representative of the Syrian people. The Arab League, under Qatari leadership, went as far as giving the SNC Syria's seat at the 2013 Arab Summit in Doha. This unelected "coalition," like its predecessor, enjoyed no legitimate popular mandate, little presence on the ground in Syria, and many of its members had ties to terrorist organizations. Conferring legitimacy on this group of Istanbul-based figures enabled them to call on Western and Arab countries to fund and arm the so-called Free Syrian Army. This "army," however, proved to be no more than a franchise name; arms and funding actually went to the real forces on the ground, i.e., the Jihadi terrorist groups. Thus, Western nations, especially the United States, time and again fed the intransigence of the so-called opposition and stymied any attempt at a political settlement, leading Syria to spiral more and more into violence.

The chemical factor

On March 19, 2013, a rocket carrying a chemical agent hit the Syrian town of Khan al-Assal, west of Aleppo, killing and injuring dozens of soldiers and civilians. The following day, the Syrian government asked the United Nations to send a team of its experts to investigate the attack. Even though Russia, in addition to a senior member of the UN commission of inquiry on Syria, Carla Del Ponte, accused the "rebels" of carrying out a chemical attack.[19]

Western and Arab media persisted in accusing the Syrian government of carrying out several chemical attacks—with no evidence to back the claim. The US also refused to look at evidence the Russians provided on the terrorists' use of chemical weapons.[20] "Outrage" with the Syrian government over the alleged attacks prompted US President Barack Obama to pledge on June 14, 2013, to provide "direct American military aid" to the "Syrian opposition."[21] Obama did not, however, specify which groups would receive this military aid, as the dominant forces on the ground were the Jihadi groups. Furthermore, the CIA had already been arming many militant groups, including the extremist ones, since 2012—long before the "chemical excuse."[22]

The UN investigators finally arrived in Damascus on August 18, 2013. Three days later, while the UN mission was preparing to begin its work, another chemical attack occurred on the outskirts of Damascus. The United States, before any investigation was conducted, pointed fingers at the Syrian government. US Secretary of State John Kerry was quick to threaten unilateral American military action against Syria to punish it for crossing Obama's "red line." The weeks that followed witnessed hectic diplomatic movements, especially on the part of Russia, which culminated in an agreement that averted military conflict. Russian President Vladimir Putin, who met Obama at the G20 summit shortly after the US had issued the ultimatum, offered to put Syria's chemical stockpiles under international monitoring, before they were eventually destroyed under the UN's auspices.[23] On September 14, 2013, the United States and Russia agreed to a framework that would facilitate the dismantling of Syria's chemical arsenal by mid-2014.

By June 2014, Syria had, with UN verification, complied with its end of the bargain. The dismantling of the chemical arsenal, however, did not spare Syria from repeated unsubstantiated US allegations of using chemical weapons during the conflict, with the main culprit now being chlorine gas, so as to keep the specter of military intervention looming over the Syrian government's head in order to extort political concessions whenever necessary. On the other hand, ISIS and the other terrorist organizations continue to launch chemical attacks against the Syrian Army[24]—with little "outrage" on part of the United States.

The dismantling of Syria's chemical stockpiles was supposed to be the first joint action between Russia and the United States that might lead to a political solution of the Syrian crisis. It was in this spirit that both the US and Russia called for convening the Geneva II Conference, in January and February 2014. Although Sergey Lavrov and John Kerry agreed to conciliatory opening speeches, Kerry's speech may be described as a war speech against the Syrian government. Two important things preceded the speech. First, the US's total rejection of Iran's presence at the Geneva Conference, despite the fact that the UN Secretary-General had already sent an invitation to Iran and was forced to rescind it. Second, the United States and Turkey rejected the presence of any Syrian opposition except the Turkey-based "Syrian National Coalition." In the two rounds of talks in January and February 2014, the representative of the Syrian government stressed that the top priority in Syria was the fight against terrorism, and that all countries should participate in this effort because terrorism in Syria constituted a real threat to the region and the world at large. No one was prepared to heed the warnings of the Syrian government or to take the dangers to world peace seriously.

Hand in hand with al-Qaeda

It only took 14 years after the tragic events of 9/11 for a representative of a jihadi group closely linked to al-Qaeda to be able to write an op-ed for a major American publication: the *Washington Post*. Labib Nahhas, the head of foreign relations for the Ahrar al-Sham group, wrote an article calling on the United States to join efforts with his organization to "end the reign" of Bashar al-Asad.[25]

Ahrar al-Sham is, of course, a terrorist organization that adopts Salafi-Jihadism as its ideology and is part of the Jaysh al-Fatah (Army of Conquest) coalition, which also includes Jabhat al-Nusra, the official al-Qaeda branch in Syria. Al-Qaeda had taken advantage of the chaos in Syria, as it did in Iraq and Libya, to appear on the scene first as al-Nusra, and then later it was joined by the so-called Islamic State of Iraq and Syria (formerly al-Qaeda in Iraq). Yet when the Syrian government first warned of al-Qaeda's presence in Syria, the declaration was met with doubts, and at times ridicule, from the Western mass media, even though Syria had suffered terrorist attacks in the decade before. When al-Nusra claimed responsibility for a dual car bombing in Damascus on December 23, 2011, the Istanbul-based Syrian opposition accused the Syrian government of fabricating the whole episode.

Al-Qaeda in Syria, in both its al-Nusra and ISIS manifestations, is however very real, as the world was soon to find out. In fact, so real was al-the Qaeda threat in Syria that the US would come to create a wobbly coalition, whose simple purpose is exterminating ISIS.[26]

After 9/11, the Syrians sympathized with the US, saying: "We know how you feel, we have been there before in the 1980s, when terrorism struck in the heart of our towns and cities." We actually shared intelligence with them and were thanked by the Bush Administration for helping save American lives during a 2006 terrorist attack on the American Embassy in Damascus.[27] We expected the same from Americans—both the people and the government—but instead, we got nothing but a vicious media campaign and US backing for an ugly sectarian war.

When violence escalated in Syria, the "Free Syrian Army" franchise quickly disappeared from the battlefield, but not from the media. The real forces on the ground were al-Nusra, Jaysh al-Islam (Army of Islam), Ahrar al-Sham, Jaysh al-Mujahedeen (Army of Mujahedeen), and other jihadi groups—including ISIS. These groups, with foreign support, soon turned major cities such as Aleppo and Homs into battlefields, barricading themselves in residential areas and causing a mass exodus of civilians. The Syrian Army was soon fighting on an endless number of fronts. It had to protect neighborhoods and towns, power lines and water sources, factories and public institutions. Everything and everyone was under attack. Jihadis from dozens of countries, including veteran Chechen ones, soon joined the terrorists in Syria.[28] NATO weapons were smuggled from war-torn Libya to jihadis in Syria.[29] Terror tactics never seen before were used against the Syrian people. Terrorists would dig tunnels underneath residential areas, fill them with explosives, and then detonate them, knocking down entire buildings. They would relentlessly shell city centers with mortars, rockets and "hell canons"—a nightmarish weapon that lobs canisters loaded with hundreds of pounds of explosives and shrapnel.

It wasn't long before the Islamic State of Iraq and Syria began to dominate the scene. Yet when the organization scored its first big "victory" in the summer of 2013, overrunning the Menagh airbase north of Aleppo with its erstwhile ally al-Nusra, after dozens of suicide attacks, the Istanbul-based opposition issued a statement congratulating the Syrian people for this "achievement."[30] Al-Jazeera interviewed, from within the Menagh airbase, ISIS's war chief Omar al-Shishani (a Chechen), a man who would mastermind the organization's biggest atrocities, from beheadings to the Mount Sinjar tragedy.

The reader might notice a discrepancy here; I am mostly citing Western media sources, yet at the same time criticizing them. The reason is quite simple. Even though the world media reported the jihadi surge, the dominant narrative was that all of it was in response to Syrian government atrocities, claiming that the "regime" had purposely transformed the country into a magnet for terrorists. This narrative remained in place even when ISIS became the West's "number one enemy" in the region, in addition to its onetime sidekick al-Nusra. However, no one was asking the real and necessary question: How were all these jihadis able to group in the tens of thousands, arm and fund themselves, and cross into Syria?

Regardless of what was being presented to the world, decision makers in the West, and especially the United States, not only knew very well the factors behind the escalation of the conflict in Syria, but also helped them grow. The weapon shipments from Libya, mentioned above, were actually funneled through a CIA and MI6-run back-channel highway dubbed the "rat line."[31] These weapons crossed from southern Turkey into Syria and into the hands of the jihadis, al-Nusra, and ISIS.[32] Furthermore, Western powers knew exactly the eventual outcome of these actions.

A recently declassified secret US intelligence report, written in August 2012, predicted—and even welcomed—the prospect of a "Salafist principality" in eastern Syria and an al-Qaeda-controlled Islamic State in Syria and Iraq.[33] The American Defense Intelligence Agency document identifies al-Qaeda in Iraq (which morphed into ISIS) and fellow jihadi groups as the "'major forces driving the insurgency in Syria,' and states that 'western countries, the Gulf states and Turkey' were supporting the opposition's efforts to take control of Eastern Syria."[34]

> Raising the "possibility of establishing a declared or undeclared Salafist principality," the Pentagon report goes on, "this is exactly what the supporting powers to the opposition want, in order to isolate the Syrian regime, which is considered the strategic depth of the Shia expansion (Iraq and Iran)."[35]

In a rare bout of frankness, US Vice President Joe Biden complained to students at the Kennedy School of Harvard University that America's biggest problem was its allies.

> The Turks, the Saudis, the Emirates, etc., what were they doing? They were so determined to take down [President Bashar] al-Asad and essentially have a proxy Sunni-Shia war, what did they do? They poured hundreds of millions of dollars and tens, thousands of tons of weapons into anyone who would fight against Asad.[36]

He also said that Turkey admitted it had let too many foreign fighters cross its border into Syria. These policies ended up helping militants linked to al-Qaeda (i.e., al-Nusra Front) and ultimately ISIS, Biden explained.[37] Biden eventually apologized for making these remarks, which came weeks after the United Nations Security Council adopted a set of resolutions barring countries and individuals from funding and arming both ISIS and al-Nusra. Nevertheless, these resolutions were never truly implemented, as no action has been taken against countries or individuals known to be financing, arming, or facilitating movements of terrorists.

The United States blacklisted al-Nusra Front in 2012 and bombed its headquarters in 2014. Nonetheless, by early 2015, America and its allies were preparing another strike against the Syrian government, the spearhead of which was none other than al-Qaeda's Nusra Front. In the spring of 2015, Saudi Arabia, Turkey, and Qatar put together a nightmarish amalgamation of jihadist groups to strike in northern Syria. "The Army of Conquest" coalition included, in addition to Ahrar al-Sham and al-Nusra Front, groups of Central Asian, Chechen, and Chinese-Uyghur jihadis.[38] Advancing from their bases in southern Turkey, the terrorist horde stormed the Syrian province of Idleb. Outrageously, the US-run Military Operations Center (also known as "the MOC"), based in the Turkish city of Antioch, planned the offensive.[39] Furthermore, the United States supplied some groups it deemed "moderate" with US-made TOW anti-tank missiles to help with the Idleb offensive.[40] These missiles were launched at the Syrian Army's tanks and vehicles, clearing the way for the jihadi army to overrun the cities of Idleb, Ariha, and Jisr al-Shughur, killing and displacing thousands of innocent civilians—many of whom eventually found their way to Europe across the Mediterranean.

During the nearly 15 years since the tragedy of September 11 and the long War on Terror that followed, which has cost the lives of thousands of Americans and millions of Afghans and Iraqis, Western, and especially, American policies and actions have rendered large parts of Syria a safe haven for a double-headed al-Qaeda monster. The Al-Nusra Front, loyal to Osama Bin Laden's successor Ayman al-Zawahiri, and the Islamic State, loyal to the self-proclaimed Caliph Abu Bakr al-Baghdadi, aided by a flood of money, weapons, and foreign fighters coming through the porous Turkish border, were able to capture entire Syrian provinces and turn them into safe havens for thousands of jihadis from all around the world, many of whom are plotting attacks against the West itself—similar to the November 13, 2015 Paris attacks. All the while, Western governments, media, and policies, especially the sanctions regime, have worked to weaken, de-legitimize, and even demonize the only party truly fighting terrorism in Syria: the Syrian government and its institutions.

The phony war

In August 2014, the United States and a coalition of 60 countries (including Saudi Arabia and Qatar), decided it was time to "degrade" and eventually destroy ISIS. Dr. Frankenstein was coming after the monster he created; except, in reality, he was not.

The supposed US-led military campaign against ISIS is, for all intents and purposes, a phony war. In a year of airstrikes, the US-led coalition conducted an average of some 15 airstrikes per day against an organization controlling a territory the size of Great Britain.[41] To put this number into perspective, during Operation Desert Storm in 1991, the United States launched 1,000 airstrikes a day against Iraq. During the 2003 invasion of Iraq, the American Air Force carried out some 700 airstrikes a day. The air campaign against ISIS, which Obama promised would help eventually destroy it, was little more than a slap on the wrist. Consequently, in a year of American airstrikes, the terrorist group was able to increase the area it controls, conquering the Iraqi city of Ramadi (capital of Anbar province) and the ancient Syrian city of Palmyra. ISIS was so at ease in its areas of control that it began to mint coins, establish schools, and carry out a systematic destruction of ancient ruins in both Iraq and Syria. World Heritage sites in Palmyra, Nimrod, and Nineveh were razed; American satellites captured images of the destruction, but apparently failed to notice those who placed the bombs.

Looking for foot soldiers in Syria to join its campaign, the US opted to arm "moderate" Syrian opposition groups for the purpose of fighting ISIS. For the Idleb offensive against the Syrian government, the United States and its allies were able to group and equip 50,000 fighters (mostly jihadis), but when it came to fighting terrorism, the US training program drew in a whopping 50 "moderates." The 50 men enjoyed a lavish training program paid for with half a billion dollars of American taxpayers' money. But when they entered Syria, al-Qaeda's Nusra front took away their American-supplied weapons and threw them in prison.[42] The US eventually cancelled the program, but the farce did not end there.[43] The Obama administration decided to airdrop 50 tons of weapons directly into the hands of the "moderates," now calling themselves the Syrian Democratic Forces (SDF).[44] How many shipments would follow and in whose hands would they end up? No one knows.

If the United States and its allies are not out to destroy ISIS, then what is their real objective? I would not like to delve into much speculation, but one cannot ignore facts on the ground. Since the US-led coalition began its campaign ISIS has expanded. The terrorist group is attracting more foreign recruits, as the Turkish border with Syria remains wide open. In Mount Sinjar in Iraq, the United States did not allow Kurdish Peshmerga forces in control of commanding heights to target the road linking the ISIS-controlled cities of Mosul and Raqqah. On November 12, 2015, the United States reversed its decision, and in one day the Kurdish Peshmerga replaced ISIS in the Sinjar province.

But where did the men of ISIS go? My conjecture is that they shaved their beards and changed their uniforms, and joined the SDF. Many former ISIS, al-Nusra, and Ahrar al-Sham members have switched allegiances and joined the SDF, alongside the Kurdish YPG, under the banner of "tribal fighters." The ultimate aim of this American-backed group is not to fight ISIS, but to establish a separatist Kurdish entity in northern Syria as a prelude to partitioning the country—the same goes for Iraq.

Other terrorist groups such as al-Nusra and Jaysh al-Fatah also continue to expand, with support from the US and its allies. Is this failure the result of flawed policies? Does the United States and its allies badly misunderstand the region? Or is there a deliberate course of action to achieve certain geopolitical gains and, perhaps, redraw the maps of both Iraq and Syria? In any case, the Syrian people and their government are the ones facing the mortal threat of the so-called Islamic State and the host of other terror organizations. While American and other Western decision-makers could afford the luxury of trial and error from the comfort of their offices halfway around the earth, Syrians have paid a high price in both their blood and their livelihood, standing up courageously against global terrorism. Decisive action should have been taken, if anybody wanted a way out for Syria, but the West did not take it.

In his speech before the seventieth session of the UN General Assembly in September 2015, Russia's President Vladimir Putin criticized the export of the so-called "democratic" revolutions, which unleashed poverty and violence instead of the triumph of democracy, especially in the Middle East. He cited the examples of Iraq and Libya, where the United States changed political regimes by force in defiance of international laws and norms, creating power vacuums that in turn led to the emergence of lawless areas, which immediately started to be filled with extremists and terrorists. Putin said:

> We think it is an enormous mistake to refuse to cooperate with the Syrian government and its armed forces who are valiantly fighting terrorism face to face ... we should finally acknowledge that no one but President Asad's armed forces and Kurdish militia are truly fighting Islamic State and other terrorist organizations in Syria.

The Russian president then proposed the joining of efforts and the creation of a broad international coalition against terrorism. He also proposed discussions at the UN Security Council about a resolution aimed at coordinating forces to confront ISIS and other terrorist organizations, based on the principles of the UN Charter.

Putin's speech reflected Russia's ample understanding of the situation in Syria since 2011, which stems largely from the continuous strategic dialogue between Damascus and Moscow. This dialogue goes back decades, and it has intensified dramatically during the Syrian crisis. Since 2014, Russia has been providing technical military assistance to Iraq, Syria, and other states in the region, with the goal of combating extremism and ISIS. Politically, Russia has worked tirelessly to establish a broad regional and international coalition against terrorism, months before Putin's speech at the UN. Upon meeting President Putin in Moscow in June 2015, Syria's foreign minister, Mr. Walid Moualem, and I welcomed Russia's efforts in trying to establish such a coalition. However, Syria seriously doubted that support from the United States and its allies, especially Turkey and Saudi Arabia, would be forthcoming. Our estimate was accurate; the United States and its allies responded negatively to all initiatives, leaving Russia no alternative but to act decisively against the terrorist threat endangering Syria, the Middle East, and Russia itself, if not the entire world.

So, on September 30, 2015, upon a request from the Syrian government, the Russian air force began conducting airstrikes against the different terrorist groups operating on Syrian soil. At the moment of this writing, the strikes are ongoing, coupled with a massive ground offensive by the Syrian Army on many fronts to weed out the terrorists and liberate Syrian cities and villages.

The performance of the Russians in Syria has embarrassed the United States. The Russians presented the Americans with satellite pictures showing ISIS terrorists moving for miles on the roads to Palmyra, while US satellites observed, with no action whatsoever taken against them by the American-led coalition. The Russians also presented the United States with other satellite pictures showing ISIS terrorists moving oil from the north of Syria to Sinjar in Iraq, where the oil is sold through Iraqi Kurdistan in exchange for weapons and ammunition that go back to Syria. All this happens along a road in the midst of a desert, which makes those involved an easy target for American airstrikes had there been a will to do that. On the other hand, after only two months of the Russian airstrikes in Syria, the Syrian Army was enabled to liberate large areas from ISIS and al-Nusra Front—including the ancient city of Palmyra. As a result, the Russians are gaining credibility in Syria and the Arab world at large, while the Americans and the West no longer enjoy the trust of the Arab people.

The price we paid

Before 2011, Syria's economy was rapidly growing, standing at the apex of a decade-long shift from a planned economy to a social market one, which opened up the country and its people to countless new opportunities. The shift did cause certain pressures on the more vulnerable segments of society. The Syrian government, however, worked tirelessly to ease those pressures. Syria continued to be a welfare state, providing huge subsidies, universal free healthcare, and free education at all levels.

Unfortunately, the systematic attack on Syria's public institutions, infrastructures, and population by both the terrorists and their regional and international backers drove the country into an unmitigated disaster, the likes of which the world has rarely seen. Terrorist attacks were not, however, the only culprit. American and European sanctions and pressures against the Syrian government's institutions, the private sector, and individuals were just as damaging. There was hardly a sector left intact. As a whole, Syria's gross domestic product (GDP) fell from $60 billion in 2010 to $30 billion in 2013, and continues to retract by an average of 15 percent every year.[45] On the other hand, inflation went through the roof, robbing Syrians of their monthly wages and life savings. The destruction of the country's industrial base and the suffocating American and European sanctions led Syria's foreign trade to drop by more than 90 percent since 2011.[46]

In 2010, only 10 percent of Syria's population fell under the lowest poverty line, and the Syrian government set the target of decreasing this rate to 7 percent in 2015. Today, more than 80 percent of the population has sunk below the line. The Syrian pound also took a severe blow as its exchange rate fell from 46 pounds to $1 US dollar in 2010, to 650 pounds to the dollar as of this writing.

Despite the destructive war, the Syrian government still provides free universal healthcare to all Syrians, which is needed now more than ever. The fact that the healthcare system in Syria still functions today is incredible, considering the extent of the damage it has suffered. Hospitals were first on the terrorists' target list, to be looted in order to procure medications and equipment for their field hospitals. Some hospitals were attacked ruthlessly, such as al-Kendy hospital in Aleppo, which was the largest facility specializing in cancer treatment in Syria and the fourth largest in the region before it was knocked down by two huge suicide-bomb trucks in 2014. All in all, 76 public hospitals and 692 clinics were damaged, with 33 hospitals and 373 clinics completely destroyed, in addition to 325 ambulances.[47] Syria's pharmaceutical industry, one of the most advanced in the Middle East, also suffered heavy damages. Many public and private factories were attacked, robbed, and razed to the ground—such as the Tameco factory complex in Damascus, the largest and most advanced drug manufacturing facility in Syria. Other factories went out of commission because American and European sanctions prevented them from procuring necessary materials for the production of medications or denied them much-needed machinery and spare parts. These criminal, unilateral, compulsory measures have also denied Syrian hospitals quantities of advanced equipment and prevented Syrian patients from getting necessary medications—especially cancer treatments.

Education in Syria is still free and accessible to all at every level. Yet the education sector has also suffered substantial damage. This is perhaps one of the most dangerous aspects of the war, since it directly affects the future of millions of children and young people, those who should go on to shape the future of Syria as skilled and educated professionals. Children are not only losing education, they are also suffering from severe psychological trauma due to the circumstances in which most Syrians live today.

Back in 2010, 96 percent of Syria's children completed primary education, a percentage 16 points higher than the Arab average; by 2013, this number was halved.[48] Four years of destruction have cost the education sector 240 billion Syrian pounds (around $720 million at the current exchange rate).[49] In addition to educational facilities, 210 cultural centers were destroyed across Syria.[50] Over 1,000 educators and 566 children lost their lives as a result of terrorist attacks against schools and universities.[51] The most horrendous attack of all took place in January 2014, when a suicide bomber walked into the Ikrima al-Makhzoumy elementary school in Homs, killing 31 innocent children and injuring dozens.

Another dangerous aspect relating to education is the pseudo-institutions established by the terrorist groups in their areas of control. ISIS, al-Nusra, and other terrorist groups have set up their own "schools," in which they feed young children their poisonous ideologies. Furthermore, these terrorist organizations have organized "Jihad Camps," which, in addition to indoctrinating young children, teach them how to use weapons and explosives. Even if those areas are liberated from the terrorists' grip today, the long-term effects of this phenomenon will undoubtedly linger for years to come.

In addition, when children who are still in school want to study at night, they often can't, because the lights are out. Syria's infrastructure, which took decades to build and modernize, is under repeated attacks from both the terrorists and the West. Terrorist groups often target power lines, water mains, and oil and gas pipelines. Nearly a third of the power lines in Syria are out of service, as well as many power plants and transfer stations, with damages reaching upwards of $1 billion (at the current exchange rate).[52] This is not to mention the lost lives of hundreds of engineers and maintenance workers who were attacked while trying to repair as much infrastructure damage as possible. The power plants that are still intact often run out of spare parts and/or generator fuel due to the suffocating American and European sanctions, which lead to more power outages. The sanctions targeting Syria's energy exports and imports, in addition to the terrorist groups' destroying and taking control of oil and gas infrastructure, have cost the country $48.3 billion over the past four years.[53] Illegal trade in stolen oil, most of which is smuggled across the border to be sold in black markets in Turkey, is still flourishing in areas under the terrorists' control. Furthermore, the bulk of Syria's civil aviation fleet remains grounded due to American and European sanctions, leaving more Syrians out of jobs and the country cut off from the rest of the world.

This extensive damage to the country's infrastructure has rendered most economic activities impossible, robbing millions of Syrians of their livelihoods. As a result of the damages to the infrastructure and energy shortages, industrial productivity in Syria has decreased sharply. Thousands of factories have also been attacked and looted. The example of the Aleppo industrial park, one of the largest in the region, stands out. Since 2012, when the industrial park came under the terrorists' control, hundreds of production lines have been dismantled and hauled across the border to Turkey. The Turkish authorities were not only complacent, but acted as accomplices to one of the biggest robberies in history. Turkish engineers helped to dismantle the production lines; only to reassemble them in newly opened factories in Turkey.[54] The sum of direct and indirect material losses to the industrial sector in Syria as of October 2015 is close to $4 billion.[55]

The agricultural sector, another main pillar of the Syrian economy, suffered a similar fate. Huge tracts of land lie uncultivated due to the conflict, while the loss of equipment and other investments is estimated at almost $1 billion.[56] These lands cannot be easily recultivated once the conflict is over; that will take years of work and rehabilitation, not to mention extensive investments and water resources. Losses to Syria's agricultural sector exceed the quantities of production in the realm of research and development. For decades, the Syrian government has given special attention to scientific research in the field of agricultural engineering, as Syria aimed to remain self-sufficient in terms of food production, especially wheat. The headquarters for the International Center for Agricultural Research in the Dry Areas, or ICARDA, was located in Syria, just south of Aleppo. Established in 1977, ICARDA's activities included the development of new crop varieties, water harvesting, conservation agriculture, the diversification of production systems, and integrated crop/rangeland/livestock production systems, for the benefit of all mankind. Sadly, ICARDA was attacked and destroyed by the terrorists, forcing the center to relocate to Beirut, but only after losing invaluable material from its inventories in Aleppo. These losses prompted the first ever withdrawal from the "doomsday seed vault" in Norway, necessary in order to carry out ICARDA's vital research.[57]

The effects of the war on Syria exceed material losses; indeed, this war has come after Syria's very soul. Over 1,000 mosques and churches were damaged by terrorist attacks, many of them of great historical significance.[58] The terrorists brought down the minaret of the Umayyad Mosque in Aleppo, one of the earliest mosques in Islam, as it was completed in 715 AD, which is 35 years after the establishment of the Umayyad dynasty and 83 years after the death of the Prophet. Shrines of great Muslim scholars and companions of the prophet, such as the Uwais al-Qarani's shrine in Raqqah, were blown up by ISIS and al-Nusra in accordance with Wahhabi dictates.

The terrorists attacked Maaloula, the only village in the world where Western Aramaic, the language of Christ, is still spoken and taught. Many historical churches, artifacts, and manuscripts from Maaloula were either destroyed or looted and sold in black markets. A countless number of other historical sites were attacked, looted, or used as bases for the terrorists; black markets for stolen items from Syria's archeological sites are flourishing in Lebanon, Turkey, and Europe (especially in London). In May 2015, the so-called Islamic State occupied Palmyra, the jewel of the Syrian Desert and one of the world's greatest archeological sites. Their first heinous act there was to murder professor Khalid al-Asaad, the curator of Palmyra's ancient sites and one of the greatest archeologists in the world today. Dr. Asaad was a personal friend; he refused to leave his beloved Palmyra, even when ISIS threatened his life. The terrorists then started a systematic destruction of Palmyra's treasures, from Bel's Temple to the arch of triumph; a campaign is still ongoing at this writing, while the world sits quietly and watches. A French historian once said: "Every civilized man has two homelands, his own and Syria." Yet the world today stands idly by, merely speaking hollow words of sorrow from a safe distance, as the birthplace of civilization itself is picked clean by fanatics and robbers.

One of the things that has distinguished Syria from all other countries over the years, is the unique social cohesion and the extraordinary family ties, which have lasted over centuries. It is probably one of the few countries in the world that has enjoyed such an excellent level of social solidarity. A mixture of spiritual education and long-entrenched healthy habits produced this Syrian way of life. At both happy and sad occasions, Syrians took pride in expressing solidarity and practicing generosity. No sect or religion stood as a hindrance to this social behavior. Even the refugees who fled to Syria from the Ottoman massacres in 1915, or from Palestine in 1948 and 1967, or from Iraq in 2003, or Lebanon in 2006 were never called refugees. Those arriving from Turkey constituted the Armenian and Assyrian communities in Syria, of which the Syrian people are very proud. Not one single tent was set up for almost three million Iraqis who immediately earned the right to go to schools and universities and also to set up their businesses. It is this beautiful social cohesion that was a major target for the terrorists and their sectarian language and ideology.

Conclusion: Palmyra, Aleppo, and the future of peace for Syria

Between the mid-1970s and the mid-1980s a wave of violence led by the Muslim Brotherhood terrorist organization hit Syria, costing the lives of thousands of innocent people. In wake of the tragic events, President Hafez al-Asad called on the international community to agree on defining the concept of "terrorism." Syria repeated this call for decades, especially after the events of September 11, and the devastating wars that followed in Afghanistan and Iraq, but the call was ignored by the Western powers.

Syria defined, and still defines, "terrorists" as those who attack innocent civilians and government institution with the aim of mindless murder, overthrowing order and establishing an extremist rule. Unfortunately, even though many groups operating in Syria—apart from ISIS and al-Qaeda—fit this description, the United States, Europe, and especially Turkey not only refuse to acknowledge their terrorist nature but have aided their campaign against the Syrian government. Groups such as Army of Islam and Ahrar al-Sham can never be acknowledged as "moderates," let alone as credible negotiating partners; they attack civilians, harbor extremist ideologies, and rely on foreign fighters. Furthermore, the so-called "Syrian opposition" remains highly fractured. There are several "oppositions," created by many countries, with diverse, and at times contradictory, loyalties and agendas. What they all have in common, however, is the lack of any control over militant groups on the ground, especially jihadist groups. This is similar, again, to the Libyan case; for those who arrived from Paris and London with the aim to rule Libya were soon ousted by men with guns—and jihadist ideologies.

Nonetheless, the Syrian government respected the will of the international community, and approached the third round of the Geneva talks with a positive attitude, aiming to achieve a political solution. The Syrian government has also adhered to the cessations of hostilities agreed to by Russia and the United States. This has allowed humanitarian relief to reach many areas, and rendered many fronts silent. It has also allowed the Syrian Army—with the help of the Russian air force—to liberate the historical city of Palmyra and drive back the ISIS militants to their home base in Raqqah.

There are, however, regional players unhappy with both the prospect of a political solution in Syria and the Syrian government making great advances against the terrorist groups—hence becoming a credible international partner in the war on ISIS. Saudi Arabia, Qatar, and Turkey—the latter in particular, worked to sabotage the Geneva talks and destroy the fragile truce. At Ankara's insistence, the "Riyadh-based opposition" withdrew from the talks, and militant groups allied to Turkey began a fierce shelling campaign on the government-held parts of the city of Aleppo. Turkey also injected 8,000 jihadist fighters onto the battleground around Aleppo, who attacked the Syrian Army across the entire frontline.

This latest episode is a mere continuation of the pattern Turkey, Saudi Arabia, and Qatar have followed since 2011—with Western support. Tens of thousands of foreign fighters, tons of armaments, and billions of dollars poured into Syria. Cities and towns were turned into battlefields causing an unspeakable death toll among both civilians and the military units trying to protect the major urban centers. The West, and the United States in particular, have contributed to the mayhem; above all, they still refuse to provide a clear classification on who is a terrorist and who is not—despite Syrian and Russian insistence.

Today, there seems to be no genuine American will to actually defeat ISIS and the other terrorist organizations. The US approach to the war on ISIS has taken a more sinister turn, aiming to reshape the future of Syria and Iraq in accordance with American geopolitical interests. It is at this juncture that the Kurdish issue becomes crucial.

Unilaterally announcing federalism in northern Syria, the so-called "Syrian Democratic Forces" are now vowing to protect the illegal federal entity. And even though the United States did not directly support the creation of this federal entity, it had no problem in breaching Syria's sovereignty—yet again—by sending 250 "advisors" from its Special Forces to help the SDF in consolidating power in northern Syria. At the same time, the US still refuses to acknowledge the role of the main force fighting ISIS on the ground: The Syrian Arab Army.

This chapter has shed a light on Western policies in Syria, offering a different narrative to the one the Western mass media propagate. What I want Western readers to understand is that their governments' policies have had negative effects on the raging conflict in Syria. All we ask is for Western policy makers to take into consideration the views of those Syrians who stood with their government in the face of the Wahhabi and the Muslim Brotherhood's violent onslaught on Syria's army, secular institutions, and cultural identity.

Notes

1 YouTube, February 15, 2011. www.youtube.com/watch?v=tNBZcMo9I5E.
2 Julian Pecquet, "Emails to Hillary contradict French tale on Libya war," *Al-Monitor*, June 23, 2015. www.al-monitor.com/pulse/originals/2015/06/libya-gadhafi-french-spies-rebels-support.html.
3 Ibid.
4 Azmi Bishara (2013) *Syria: A Way of Suffering for Freedom* (Doha: Arab Center for Research and Policy Studies), p. 84.
5 Ibid.

The Syrian tragedy 79

6 Fares Sa'ad, "How the revolution happened before my eyes: A neutral tale of Baba Amro," *Le Monde Diplomatique*, January 4, 2013.
7 YouTube, July 3, 2011. www.youtube.com/watch?v=ogOi4pQ_z5w.
8 Hasnain Kazim, "Seeking Safety in Turkey: Syrian Refugees Describe Horrors of Assad Crackdown," *Der Spiegel*, June 17, 2011. www.spiegel.de/international/world/seeking-safety-in-turkey-syrian-refugees-describe-horrors-of-assad-crackdown-a-769029.html.
9 "Angelina Jolie visits Syrian refugees in Turkey," *CNN*, June 18, 2011. http://edition.cnn.com/2011/WORLD/europe/06/18/turkey.jolie.visit/.
10 Andrew Osborn, "Turkey to create military 'buffer zone' within Syria for refugees," *Telegraph*, June 16, 2011. www.telegraph.co.uk/news/worldnews/middleeast/syria/8580603/Turkey-to-create-military-buffer-zone-within-Syria-for-refugees.html.
11 Ruth Sherlock, "'15,000 strong' army gathers to take on Syria," *Telegraph*, November 3, 2011. www.telegraph.co.uk/news/worldnews/middleeast/syria/8868027/15000-strong-army-gathers-to-take-on-Syria.html.
12 Dorothy Ohl, Holger Albrecht, and Kevin Koehler, "For Money or Liberty? The Political Economy of Military Desertion and Rebel Recruitment in the Syrian Civil War," Carnegie Middle East Center, November 24, 2015. http://carnegieendowment.org/2015/10/24/for-money-or-liberty-political-economy-of-military-desertion-and-rebel-recruitment-in-syrian-civil-war/ilqf.
13 Ibid.
14 Scott Wilson, "Assad must go, Obama says," *Washington Post*, August 18, 2011. www.washingtonpost.com/politics/assad-must-go-obama-says/2011/08/18/gIQAelheOJ_story.html.
15 Neil MacFarquhar and Nada Bakri, "Isolating Syria, Arab League Imposes Broad Sanctions," *New York Times*, November 27, 2011. www.nytimes.com/2011/11/28/world/middleeast/arab-league-prepares-to-vote-on-syrian-sanctions.html?_r=0.
16 Arshad Mohammed and Christian Lowe, "Friends of Syria condemn Assad but see more killing," *Reuters*, February 24, 2012. www.reuters.com/article/us-syria-meeting-tunis-idUSTRE81N16820120224.
17 "Annan renews call for UN unity on Syria," *Al-Jazeera*, March 16, 2012. www.aljazeera.com/news/middleeast/2012/03/2012327153111767387.html.
18 "Chance to begin political settlement process in Syria exists – Lavrov," *Russia Beyond the Headlines*, April 20, 2015. http://rbth.com/news/2015/04/20/chance_to_begin_political_settlement_process_in_syria_exists_-_lavrov_45362.html.
19 "UN's Del Ponte says evidence Syria rebels used sarin," *BBC*, May 6, 2013. www.bbc.com/news/world-middle-east-22424188. See also Joe Lauria, "Russia Says Syrian Rebels Used Sarin Gas," *The Wall Street* Journal, July 9, 2013. www.wsj.com/articles/SB10001424127887324507404578596153561287028.
20 Ibid.
21 "US says it will give military aid to Syria rebels," *BBC News*, June 14, 2013. www.bbc.com/news/world-us-canada-22899289.
22 Seymour M. Hersh, "The Red Line and the Rat Line," *The London Review of Books*, 36 (8): 21–24, April 17, 2014. www.lrb.co.uk/v36/n08/seymour-m-hersh/the-red-line-and-the-rat-line.
23 "Syria crisis: Russia's Putin issues plea to US over Syria," *BBC News*, September 12, 2013. www.bbc.com/news/world-middle-east-24058529.
24 Jack Moore, "ISIS Carries Out Chemical Weapon Attack On Syrian Army: State TV," *Newsweek*, April 5, 2016. http://europe.newsweek.com/isis-carries-out-chemical-weapon-attack-syrian-army-state-news-agency-444213?rm=eu.
25 Labib al-Nahhas, "The deadly consequences of mislabeling Syria's revolutionaries," *Washington Post*, July 10, 2015. www.washingtonpost.com/opinions/the-deadly-consequences-of-mislabeling-syrias-revolutionaries/2015/07/10/6dec139e-266e-11e5-aae2-6c4f59b050aa_story.html.

26 Eric Shmitt, "Al Qaeda Turns to Syria, With a Plan to Challenge ISIS," *New York Times*, May 15, 2016. www.nytimes.com/2016/05/16/world/middleeast/al-qaeda-turns-to-syria-with-a-plan-to-challenge-isis.html?emc=eta1&_r=0.
27 "U.S. lauds Syrian forces in embassy attack," *CNN*, September 12, 2006. http://edition.cnn.com/2006/WORLD/meast/09/12/syria.embassy/.
28 Thomas Grove and Mariam Karouny, "Syria War: Rebels Joined By Chechnya Islamic Militants In 'Jihad' Against Assad," *The Huffington Post*, June 3, 2013. www.huffingtonpost.com/2013/03/06/syria-war-rebels-chechnya-islamic-militants_n_2821197.html.
29 C. J. Chivers, Eric Schmitt, and Mark Mazzetti, "In Turnabout, Syria Rebels Get Libyan Weapons," *New York Times*, June 21, 2013. www.nytimes.com/2013/06/22/world/africa/in-a-turnabout-syria-rebels-get-libyan-weapons.html.
30 Nour Malas and Rima Abushakra, "Islamists Seize Airbase Near Aleppo," *The Wall Street Journal*, August 6, 2013. www.wsj.com/articles/SB10001424127887323420604578652250872942058.
31 Seymour M. Hersh, "The Red Line and the Rat Line," *The London Review of Books*, 36 (8): 21–24, April 17, 2014. www.lrb.co.uk/v36/n08/seymour-m-hersh/the-red-line-and-the-rat-line.
32 Ibid.
33 Seumas Milne, "Now the truth emerges: how the US fueled the rise of Isis in Syria and Iraq," *Guardian*, June 3, 2015. www.theguardian.com/commentisfree/2015/jun/03/us-isis-syria-iraq.
34 Ibid.
35 Ibid.
36 Barbara Plett Usher, "Joe Biden apologized over IS remarks, but was he right?" *BBC News*, October 7, 2014. www.bbc.com/news/world-us-canada-29528482.
37 Ibid.
38 Caleb Weiss, "Turkistan Islamic Party in Syria involved in new Idlib offensive," *The Long War Journal*, April 23, 2015. www.longwarjournal.org/archives/2015/04/turkistan-islamic-party-in-syria-involved-in-new-idlib-offensive.php.
39 Charles Lister, "Why Assad is Losing," *Foreign Policy Magazine*, May 5, 2015. http://foreignpolicy.com/2015/05/05/why-assad-is-losing-syria-islamists-saudi/.
40 Ibid.
41 "Special Report: Operation Inherent Resolve," The United States Department of Defense, October 6, 2015. www.defense.gov/News/Special-Reports/0814_Inherent-Resolve.
42 "U.S.-trained Syrian rebels gave equipment to Nusra: U.S. military," *Reuters*, September 26, 2015. www.reuters.com/article/us-mideast-crisis-usa-equipment-idUSKCN0RP2HO20150926.
43 Jim Milkaszewski, Erik Ortiz, and Laura Saravia, "Pentagon Ends Program to Train Syrian Rebels, Starts Revamped Initiative," *MSNBC*, October 9, 2015. www.nbcnews.com/storyline/isis-terror/pentagon-ending-program-train-equip-syria-rebels-n441601.
44 Barbara Starr, "U.S. delivers 50 tons of ammunition to Syria rebel groups," *CNN*, October 12, 2015. http://edition.cnn.com/2015/10/12/politics/syria-rebel-groups-ammunition-50-tons/.
45 "Conflict in the Syrian Arab Republic: Macroeconomic implications and obstacles to achieving the millennium development goals," The United Nations Economic and Social Commission for Western Asia (ESCWA), June 2014, p. 2.
46 Ibid., p. 3.
47 "Damages estimate," Syrian Arab Government: Ministry of Health, September 2015.
48 "Conflict in the Syrian Arab Republic," ESCWA, p. 28.
49 "Damages estimate," Syrian Arab Government: Ministry of Education and Ministry of Higher Education, September 2015.
50 "Damages estimate," Syrian Arab Government: Ministry of Culture, September 2015.

51 "Damages estimate," Syrian Arab Government: Ministry of Education, September 2015.
52 "Damages estimate," Syrian Arab Government: Ministry of Electricity, September 2015.
53 "Damages estimate," Syrian Arab Government: Ministry of Oil and Mineral Reserves, September 2015.
54 "Syrian militants profit on ruins of former industrial capital," *Russia Today*, November 22, 2014.
55 "Damages estimate," Syrian Arab Government: Ministry of Industry, September 2015.
56 "Damages estimate," Syrian Arab Government: Ministry of Agriculture and Agrarian Reform, September 2015.
57 "Arctic 'Doomsday Vault' opens to retrieve vital seeds for Syria," *CNN*, October 19, 2015. http://edition.cnn.com/2015/10/19/europe/svalbard-global-seed-vault-syria/.
58 "Damages estimate," Syrian Arab Government: Ministry of Religious Affairs, September 2015.

5 Iraq

A victim of terror and the War on Terror

Anwar Said al-Haidari
Translated from Arabic by Mark Tomass

Introduction

The organized state terrorism that was practiced by Saddam Hussein's regime in Iraq, the totalitarian ideology adopted by that regime's members, the absence of state power after its collapse as a result of the 2003 war, the regional powers' exploitation of the social diversity in Iraq for the purpose of partitioning it along sectarian and ethnic lines, and the presence of the multinational occupying forces have all been factors contributing to the activation of terrorist operations under the pretext of resisting foreign occupation. While disguised by a sectarian cloak, that terrorism was and still is carried out against civilians and their infrastructure

The first administration of former Iraqi Prime Minister Nouri al-Maliki[1] cooperated with the United States, succeeded in limiting terrorist operations, and reduced the level of violence, as the United States was able to disengage al-Qaeda from its supporting communities in the Sunni-dominated regions of Iraq. However, the subsequent breakout of the Syrian crisis, coinciding with the 2011 withdrawal of the US military from Iraq, worsened the security situation in Iraq.

The Western world, led by the United States and its allies in the region, sided against the government of Syria, while Iraq took a neutral position, knowing that the escalation of violence would not solve the crisis. Accordingly, US military support for the Iraqi army diminished, and accusations of sectarianism were leveled against al-Maliki's government based on the Prime Minister's Shia identity, which the Sunna viewed as hostile to them and to their interests. As a result, the Iraqi army withdrew from the western, Sunni dominated provinces of Iraq, which in turn weakened the army's relationship with the local inhabitants. The weakening of that relationship accompanied the country's abandonment of the political process, as a "tribal revolt" paved the way for the expansion of the Islamic State of Iraq and [Greater] Syria (ISIS). This enabled ISIS to occupy the city of Mosul in June of 2014, with the support of "tribal revolutionaries." The subsequent US formation of an international coalition to intervene after ISIS moved to take over the city of Arbil (Erbil) has not led to positive results, as American and Iraqi efforts have not been unified, and the future of Iraq is still unclear.

The chapter concludes that while the September 11, 2001, attacks in the US were acts of terrorism, so were many acts perpetrated in Iraq since 2003. This fact presents a question concerning the ethical basis upon which the United States constructed its vision of its War on Terror. Moreover, although the aim of fighting terrorist groups in Iraq and Syria is clear and specific, the dispute between the United States and Russia in the War on Terror reveals their different interests, and that the War on Terror is a cover for achieving those interests.

The War on Terror

It is no secret that the US war against Iraq in 2003 was directly related to the Global War on Terror, launched after the September 2001 events in the United States. Since then, Iraq has become a scene for the activities of terrorist groups that have operated under various names.

Al-Qaeda's terrorist operations in Iraq began after the US occupation in April 2003. With the absence of the Iraqi state and the dismantling of the Iraqi Army by Iraq's de facto governor, Paul Bremer, in May 2003, al-Qaeda inaugurated its terrorist operations with the bombing of the Jordanian Embassy. In August 2003, it destroyed the United Nations headquarters in Baghdad and killed its representative, Sergio de Mello. In the same month, it followed up by assassinating the Iraqi religious scholar Ayatollah Mohammad Baqer al-Hakim, along with 80 other people, during Friday prayers at the Imam Ali shrine in Najaf. It also assassinated the president of the Governing Council, Ezzedine Salim, at the entrance in the international Green Zone. Since then, al-Qaeda's terrorist operations have spread to other parts of Iraq, on a large scale and carried out by the Islamic State of Iraq and Syria, and by Baathist militias. Terrorist operations have penetrated into the heart of Baghdad, near the Green Zone and its entrances, as well as other places, severing the road between Baghdad and the central and southern provinces of Iraq, while people dubbed the area the "triangle of death."

Iraq came close to drifting into civil war between the Sunna and Shia after the February 2006 bombing of the mausoleums of the revered tenth and eleventh Shia Imams in Samarra, which the Twelver Shia[2] consider a sacred shrine; this act of terrorism received widespread international condemnation. These events took place while the Shia militias known as the Mahdi Army were active and successful in fighting al-Qaeda. However, Nuri al-Maliki's assumption of the prime ministerial post in the same year changed the equation.

In May 2006, al-Maliki became Prime Minister after an arduous process, although he was neither prepared for the post nor was he a candidate for it. However, he had personal traits that enabled him to hold that post, which also, under the Iraqi constitution, made him the Commander in Chief of the Armed Forces. In these times, the security situation in Iraq was in its worst stages, with terrorist activities hitting almost all parts of the country. The outskirts of Baghdad were almost empty of its inhabitants, who had been displaced, uprooted, or physically liquidated. This was a time in the period known to Baghdadis as "sectarianism."[3] This was also the period where forces opposed to the political process were backed by regional Arab states that intended to thwart the American project in Iraq and expected the collapse of the Maliki government and the crumbling of the political process as a whole because of the terrorist strikes that swept the country.

On a parallel level, the Iraqi leadership was skeptical about the seriousness of the United States in its War on Terror in Iraq, but that suspicion was limited to the US Embassy in Baghdad and did not include the US administration in Washington. More specifically, the Afghan origin of the then US ambassador in Iraq, Zalmay Khalilzad, made him suspect, and this suspicion found support in several incidents. Among them were the prevention of US troops and Iraqi forces' pursuit of terrorists after their attacks, the intervention by the US Embassy to release terrorists from custody after the Iraqi authorities had caught them redhanded, and cases where terrorists were in possession of US documents. The most common incidents consisted of terrorist groups carrying out operations under the watchful eye of US forces, who did nothing to prevent them. In one case, a terrorist den for the manufacturing of car bombs was discovered in the house of one of the heads of a political bloc in the Iraqi parliament; the US Embassy intervened to prevent the Iraqi government from taking legal action against him.

This parliamentarian continued to make booby-traps for cars in his home, where his bodyguards, led by his own son, directed terrorist activities in the area with the protection of the US Embassy. At the same time, his brother-in-law, who was an appointed minister in the Iraqi government, had been accused of terrorism and murder for killing the two sons of an Iraqi lawmaker, but managed to escape from the judiciary by leaving Iraq. As a precaution against the threat posed by this member of parliament's terrorist activities, a curfew was imposed every Friday. However, at a later stage, and after the replacement of Ambassador Khalilzad, when the parliamentarian continued to make car bombs in his home, the security apparatus blew up a booby-trapped car parked at his home, arrested his mother-in-law and his son, and placed him under house arrest until he departed from Baghdad and settled in Amman. From that time on, terrorist activities were eradicated in that area and normal life returned to it.

The frequency of such incidents increased Iraqi suspicions that the US Embassy had something to do with terrorism. Discussions between a number of American officials, politicians, and US Ambassador Khalilzad increased those doubts. For example, Dr. Nadim al-Jabri, who was a member of parliament and leader of a political party and a candidate for prime minister, told me that he discussed this matter with the US ambassador multiple times, whereon Khalilzad told him that he was "undertaking the role of a stabilizer" between the Shia and Sunna. He followed up by saying, "You are like someone learning how to ride a bicycle. We are teaching you how to balance; if you tilt to the right, we return your balance to you from the left, or vice versa." Dr. Jabri replied jokingly: "What if you push us strongly from the back and we lose our balance and fall?" Khalilzad replied, smiling, "We do not do that; Iran does it."

Among the duties of the US forces was to handle the two parts of Baghdad, al-Karkh for the Sunna and al-Rusafa for the Shia. They did not allow Iraqi forces to enter al-Karkh, which during those days was mostly under the control of al-Qaeda.

It seems that the "idea of the bicycle" was, according to Vice President Dick Cheney, also present in the thinking of General John Abizaid and General George William Casey, while President Bush attributed it to Donald Rumsfeld.[4]

In addition, the American side was in constant disagreement with Baqir al-Zubaidi, a former commander of the Badr Brigades (the Iran-officered military wing of the Iran-based Shia Islamic party, Supreme Council for Islamic Revolution in Iraq) and the interior minister in the government of Ibrahim al-Jaafari, an Iraqi politician who was Prime Minister of Iraq in the Iraqi Transitional Government from 2005 to 2006, and who has been Minister of Foreign Affairs since 2014. Al-Zubaidi has often hindered his ministry's activity in fighting terrorism. He waged a media campaign against al-Jaafari, accusing him of sectarianism and violating human rights. He also opposed his appointment in Maliki's first government.

Al-Maliki and his crew realized that in order to make progress in the fight against terrorism, it would be necessary to bypass the US Embassy in Baghdad and contact the US administration directly, at the highest levels. They saw that it would not also be necessary to prepare an alternative plan for the fight against terrorism away from the Embassy. Indeed, a plan was prepared to accomplish this task with a meeting between al-Maliki and President Bush, scheduled to be held in the Jordanian capital, Amman.

On the eve of the al-Maliki/Bush meeting in 2006, the Iraqi parties opposing the political process moved to Amman in anticipation of the results of the meeting, expecting a sharp change in the political process that would stunt the much-desired democratic transformation, thus reaping the fruits of the pressure imposed on the process by terrorist operations. Individuals in government circles within the Iraqi delegation reported that a meeting took place between al-Maliki and Jordan's King Abdullah II, in which the two sides discussed the relations between their countries. The Iraqi side highlighted the tensions in those relations, including the existence of elements operating within Jordanian territories, which had carried out terrorist activities in Iraq and discriminated against Iraqis who travel to Jordan based on their sectarian identities. At that meeting, King Abdullah asked the Iraqi side to inform him of the message they would like him to convey to President Bush. The crucial Iraqi response was that they would not accept the mediation of any third party in their dealings with the US side and that Jordan's role in the process would be confined to hospitality and would not include mediation.

Al-Maliki later met with US National Security Adviser Steve Hadley, and they discussed the political and security situation in Iraq. Amid demands from various parties for the withdrawal of United States troops, sources attending the meeting noted that Hadley advised al-Maliki to develop a rapport with President Bush. Hadley believed Bush was deeply concerned about how the outcome of the United States military campaign in Iraq would bear on his legacy, and therefore his state of mind was such that he would welcome sincere suggestions on what needed to be done to stabilize Iraq. The Iraqi delegation took that advice and set a date to meet with President Bush.

When al-Maliki met with Bush, he expressed the Iraqi government's fears that terrorist activities may end the political process in Iraq and lead to the failure of the American project and the era of President Bush in Iraq. Al-Maliki also openly expressed his doubts about the US role in the fight against terrorism in Iraq. When President Bush asked al-Maliki to suggest an alternative plan to fight terrorism, he responded with a well-thought-out plan and briefed him about it. After a debate, President Bush approved the plan. When President Bush asked for feedback on what was required at this stage, al-Maliki emphasized the need to keep the trio of Abizaid, General George Casey, and Khalilzad away from the Iraqi file at this stage. President Bush thought a bit about it and then told the Iraqi delegation that he had agreed to this request, and he would find those three alternative posts that would not detract from their status. It was also agreed that Bush would reduce the circle of intermediaries between the two leaders, Bush and al-Maliki, to the absolute minimum and conduct teleconferenced meetings between them when necessary, which is what happened later.

The Kurds also played a supporting role in the Iraqi government, as they recognized that any setback for the political process in Iraq would hurt the gains they had achieved thus far. This coincided with the US administration's recognition of the need to change the strategy led and carried out by the tripartite Abizaid, Casey, and Khalilzad, by taking the Iraqi file away from them and replacing them with the duo General David Petraeus-Ambassador Ryan Crocker and replacing Defense Minister Rumsfeld with William Gates (which Bush later did). The new strategy was to initiate a surge in United States troops, commanded by General Petraeus, while Ambassador Crocker took over the political and diplomatic file. From then onward, Bush and al-Maliki agreed to be jointly in charge of making important decisions themselves.[5]

That meeting was an important station in the War on Terror in Iraq, for it allowed al-Maliki to launch his so-called "law enforcement" plan without American restrictions; this enabled him to eliminate terrorist centers in Iraqi cities. As a result, terrorist operations were reduced in frequency and remained focused on fewer important targets.[6] This improvement in security was helped by the fact that al-Qaeda undertook a terrorist act in the Jordanian capital of Amman, prompting Jordan to cooperate in sharing intelligence with the Iraqi side. The main success was a joint US-Iraqi operation on June 7, 2006, which eliminated the Jordanian Abu Musab al-Zarqawi, whom al-Qaeda's then leader, Osama bin Laden, had appointed as the head of al-Qaeda in Mesopotamia. Al-Zarqawi's death was a big setback for al-Qaeda and strengthened the Iraqi forces, while the War on Terror took a positive turn, in favor of the prestige and security of the Iraqi state and its institutions. The United States also worked on disengaging al-Qaeda from its support base and reached an agreement with Sheikh Ahmed Abu Risha (a Sunni leader in al-Anbar province and formerly head of the movement of Sunni tribesmen known as the Anbar Salvation Council), whom President Bush met during his visit to Anbar in May 2007.[7] Then US Secretary of State Condoleezza Rice also visited al-Anbar and met with tribal Sunni leaders there.[8] The result of these meetings was the formation of what became known as the

Sunni-led "Awakening Movement," which undertook the burden of the War on Terror in the predominantly Sunni areas.

In an operation called "The Charge of the Knights," al-Maliki turned in 2008 to fight the Mahdi Army (an armed group linked to Iraq's Shia community and a revival of the army initially created by the Iraqi Shia cleric Muqtada al-Sadr in 2003 and disbanded in 2008). The latter took advantage of its role in protecting the Shia-majority areas from the terrorist attacks and the weakness of official security institutions in those areas. As a result, the government's security institutions began to impose control, and there were signs of the emerging prestige of the Iraqi state, while terrorist activities and violence subsided somewhat significantly.

However, the relationship between the American and Iraqi sides took a downward turn during President Obama's first term, and the subsequent withdrawal of US troops from Iraq and signing of the strategic framework agreement between the two countries. The relationship between the two sides deteriorated during al-Maliki's second term (2010–2014), when the War on Terror took a different direction, especially after the outbreak of violence in Syria in 2011. This also led to a competition between the United States and Iran over their roles in Iraq.

In 2011, the Arab Spring uprisings set an example for a parallel movement of protests in the predominantly Sunni Iraqi city of al-Anbar, where there was widespread popular rejection of the political process as a whole, as well as rejection of the presence of the Iraqi army in the Sunni-majority provinces. This movement threatened to storm the capital city, under the slogan "We are coming, Baghdad," and accompanied by sectarian speeches that appeared especially tailored by elements in al-Qaeda, which was involved in the sit-ins. The Anbar movement was supported the Gulf countries and Turkey, with the participation of a number of parties involved in the political process.

While the Anbar movement proceeded, the government's efforts in the fight against terrorism were not up to the necessary level. Ethnic and sectarian divisions were the most prominent features of the ruling political class's behavior from all sides, and corruption was rampant in the Iraqi state institutions, including the military. Accordingly, Article 4 of the Iraqi Anti-Terrorism Act became controversial and lent justification to the demands for the withdrawal of security forces from Sunni areas. The Iraqi government, on the other hand, sensed that the withdrawal of its forces from these areas meant opening the door to ISIS. Indeed, in June 2014, the northern city of Mosul, near the Syrian-Iraqi border, fell because of the combination of these factors, followed by the withdrawal of Iraqi and Kurdish forces from the city, as well as the fall to ISIS of the Iraqi provinces of Kirkuk and Saladin, and the activation of sleeper cells within Mosul.

With the rapid collapse of the Iraqi defenses, the religious authorities, led by Imam al-Sistani, announced "Voluntary Holy War" (*al-Jihad al-Kifā'i*). This was in accordance with Islamic belief, which holds that the clerics have the power to declare jihad and mobilize the faithful to defend their homeland in the face of any attack. While jihad is the duty of every believer—it is one of the Five

Pillars of Islam (together with prayer, fasting, alms-giving, and a pilgrimage to Mecca)—"*Voluntary* Jihad" is not a duty of every Muslim believer.

The call for a voluntary holy war on the fifteenth of the month of Shaaban (the eighth month of the Islamic calendar) coincided with an important religious event for Shia Muslims: the anniversary of the birth of the Twelfth Imam of the Twelver Shia, Imam Muhammad ibn al-Hasan, known as al-Mahdi. The Shia believe that al-Mahdi is the promised Savior, currently in a state of occultation (i.e., of being "hidden" from the world by God), who upon reappearance will fill the earth with equity, justice, and peace. It is the duty of the Shia to wait for him in his absence and prepare for his appearance to help with accomplishing his mission.

The coinciding of religious ceremonies performed by millions of Shia in the holy city of Karbala to mark the birth anniversary al-Mahdi with ISIS's occupation of Mosul and its sectarian call to eliminate the other sect, created a morally significant momentum. Millions of volunteers were inspired to join the ranks of the official military institution in support of the Iraqi army in the fighting in order to overcome the psychological defeat, which had been followed by a military defeat. The Popular Mobilization (*al-Hashd al-Sha'bi*), as they were officially called, brought back a psychological balance to the army and to the Iraqi people. In fact, those who cannot decipher the Iraqi reality from inside Iraq cannot understand the ideological dimension that provides the volunteers with moral support. Critics saw the Iraqi volunteers as "agents of Iran," including, for example, the US Vice President Joe Biden.[9]

The volunteer groups formed their own organizations, which bore several different names. They were associated as a new body called the Popular Mobilization Authority, which in turn was associated with the Prime Minister, who also held the post of General Commander of the Armed Forces. Among the most prominent of the organizations that joined the popular crowd were those Shia groups resisting the United States' occupation prior to its withdrawal, most notably, the League of the Righteous; Hezbollah Brigades; the peace brigades, inheritor of the Mahdi Army after it was disbanded by the order of al-Sayyed Muqtada al-Sadr, and the Badr Organization.[10]

Iraq in the midst of terrorism

Iraqis, like many of the peoples of the world, have suffered from totalitarian rule and from the tyranny of absolute rule. Similar political models have been in place in many other Arab countries, including those nations that have commercial and security interests with the United States. In the latter cases, the United States has not made its own domestic social and political values—such as democracy, liberalism, individualism, and human rights—benchmarks of its foreign policy. The US preferred stability to freedom. Stability meant ensuring the US's interests. However, the result in the Middle East was a loss of both freedom and stability.

Saddam Hussein, who seized power in Iraq in 1979, had enjoyed United States' support throughout the 1980s, under the Reagan Administration. His violations of human rights in Iraq reached its peak in his use of weapons of mass destruction against the Iraqi people, beginning with the Kurds. The United States provided political, economic, intelligence, and military support that eventually inflated the Iraqi regime's capabilities and resulted in its possession of weapons of mass destruction. This boosted Saddam Hussein's aggressiveness and encouraged him to invade Kuwait in 1990. The United States' support for that action followed the backing of his invasion of Iran, in an effort to contain the alleged "Persian danger against our Sunni friends," as Condoleezza Rice termed it.[11]

This image of the United States is ingrained in the Iraqi memory and was brought to reality during the events of the second Gulf War, when President George H. W. Bush called on Iraqis to the overthrow the Iraqi regime. When Iraqis rose up, the United States helped the regime to suppress the uprising with the utmost cruelty. Mass graves swallowed tens of thousands of Iraqi civilians, with their families. That US position was also supported by the Arab regional order.

With the outbreak of the popular uprising in Iraq after Saddam's defeat in the war to liberate Kuwait in March 1991, southern, central, and northern Iraqi cities were liberated from the regime's control, and the regime itself was about to fall. However, United States' policymakers feared that the fall of Saddam's regime under those circumstances would increase Shia power, and Washington believed the Shia were under Tehran's influence. In this regard, the then American Secretary of State James Baker said that, as much as Saddam's neighbors want his disappearance, they fear that a weak Iraq benefits the Iranian theocracy, which would spread Islamic fundamentalism with the help of Iraq's Shia and would quickly strengthen Iran's regional hegemony. This was a real obsession with the first Bush administration and its allies.[12]

Saddam's fall also enhanced the aspirations of the Kurds, who were demanding an independent state, a source of concern for Washington's ally Ankara. These reasons prompted the United States to decline assistance to those who carried out the uprising; James Baker described them as "rebels," and also described the uprising as an "insurgency." Contributing to the abortion of the uprising, United States' troops allowed Saddam's regime to use helicopters and military aircraft in situations that did not pose a risk to American soldiers. The Pentagon decided not to shoot down the aircrafts even after it began to attack the masses.

The Pentagon also opposed the establishment of a demilitarized zone in southern Iraq, making it easier for Saddam to move heavy weapons and infantry that were not involved in any fighting in Desert Storm and to crush the uprising, killing tens of thousands of civilians and displacing hundreds of thousands of others in full view of United States troops. In that situation, Baker said, "Our critics accused us of inciting the Kurds and Shia to rebel against Saddam in the days immediately following the end of the war and then leaving them to face their fate, refusing to provide them with assistance."[13] Ambassador Martin Indyk recalled in this connection:

We allowed Saddam, without explanation, to use helicopters to quell the Shia rebellion in southern Iraq after Bush had called on the Iraqi people to rise up in the face of the dictator. Saddam's loyalists massacred around 60,000 Iraqi Shia, while US troops stood idly by, and then he moved in the Iraqi Republican Guard teams that were stationed in the north against the Iraqi Kurds, killing 20,000 of them and forcing 2 million to flee across the border to Turkey.[14]

If what took place were clear violations of human rights, as Indyk suggested, then United States policymakers preferred to deter a spread of Iranian influence even at the expense of human rights, maintaining "the tradition of preferring stability to freedom."[15] As a result, Iraq's Shia lost confidence in the United States. As former Vice President Dick Cheney said, in trying to explain the United States policy failure in Iraq, "they were afraid, and they are right, that we would let them down again."[16]

Terrorist organizations, such as al-Qaeda and its successors, had no presence in Iraq prior to the US occupation, but the regime maintained Salafi cells operating under the control of the security service. The Baath regime in Iraq was secular and propagated Arab nationalist slogans up until the regime's occupation of Kuwait in August 1990. As Kuwait is an Arab country, and because the international coalition to liberate Kuwait included a number of Arab countries from the Gulf region, in addition to Egypt and Syria, the Saddam Hussein regime transformed its slogans into a religious discourse. Accordingly, Saddam added new titles to his previous series of titles.

Saddam began his series of titles with "Comrade Struggler," a title Baathists normally give themselves. He later adopted the title of the "National Liberation Hero." However, since national liberation seemed entirely inconsistent with the occupation of an Arab country, Saddam changed his discourse toward the religious, with "Abdullah the Believer" and "the Holy Warrior Leader Aided by God." Saddam continued this approach in the media and referred to it as the "Faith Campaign," and then took the title of "Commander of the Faith Campaign."

Under these conditions, Salafi features in Iraqi society began to appear; like most of the Salafi groups in the world, they were backed by Saudi ideology and money. The Iraqi regime's goal was to use the Salafi groups as a social force to counter the rise of Shia religious sentiments. These reached their peak under the leadership of Grand Ayatollah al-Sayyed Muhammad Sadiq al-Sadr, whom the regime assassinated in February 1999, after a series of assassinations of Shia religious authorities and clerics.[17]

The Salafi movement is one of the Sunni sects that oppose pluralism in Islam. Its main center at the present time is Saudi Arabia, which adopts its own Wahhabi version and funds parallel Salafi groups throughout the world. The Salafi Wahhabi movement uses modern technology in its broadcasting activities while simultaneously propagating a reactionary medieval ideology that rejects all other views of Islam. They see other groups through medieval lenses. Thus, they view contemporary Christians as Crusaders, Shia as infidels, and members of other Sunni sects as apostates, all of whom deserve to be killed, beginning with the Shia.

The Salafi Wahhabi movement was first used outside Saudi Arabia by the United States during the Afghan war, to fight the Soviet Union in Afghanistan with the intellectual and financial support of Saudi Arabia and the Gulf countries. Their unifying force was the Taliban, the main host of al-Qaeda, who eventually declared the Caliphate after the Soviet withdrawal and who also gained the recognition of three United States' allies: Saudi Arabia, the United Arab Emirates, and Pakistan. However, the terrorist attacks of September 11, 2001, transformed the relationship between al-Qaeda and the United States into an open war. While the United States earned the world's sympathy, Iraq remained in a state of international and regional isolation from the time of its invasion of Kuwait in 1990. The US then invaded Iraq in 2003 under the false pretexts that it aided and abetted al-Qaeda and possessed weapons of mass destruction.

The United States' invasion of Iraq was neither welcomed internationally nor regionally, and not even by Iraqis. The regional Arab regimes were similar to Saddam's in many respects. They had totalitarian aspects, power was concentrated in the hands of a few individuals, and their sectarian affiliation was Sunni. As for Iran, it was not ready to welcome the United States into its western neighborhood in addition to having US forces in its eastern neighborhood in Afghanistan. As for the Iraqi opposition, it preferred weakening Saddam's regime and then gradually undermining it in a manner that avoided both chaos and a reputation for collaborating with a foreign occupation. Remarkably, the Shia majority in southern Iraq resisted the occupation, while Sunni-majority provinces surrendered,[18] and the Kurds in northern Iraq officially celebrated the arrival of United States forces led by General Jay Garner.

The fall of Saddam's regime caused alarm in a region that lacked peaceful mechanisms to transfer authority; it also lacked equal citizenship rights and acceptance of diversity and pluralism. Most Arab regimes have a Sunni identity that does not allow equal citizenship or democracy. Internally, they rely on the devices of a police state, and externally on United States support. Placing Iraq on the path of democratic transformation, the adoption of a multiparty system, and the peaceful transfer of power meant the withdrawal of Iraq from the value system of the other Arab regimes.

Although the Shia constitute about 60 percent of Iraq's population, they were always excluded from political power. Even the modern Iraqi state founded by Britain in 1921 handed leadership to the Sunna and withheld political power from the Shia and their leaders because of their resistance to the British occupation in 1914, which culminated in the revolt of 1920. The Shia continued to oppose successive regimes from that time until the fall Saddam's regime in 2003.[19] Therefore, the Shia participation in government for the first time in the history of Iraq also meant Iraq's exit from the Arab regional system of Sunni dominance and the recognition of religious diversity. For those reasons, the Arab powers felt it necessary to thwart the new Iraqi political experience in its infancy, before it became a model for the Arab peoples and threatened to disrupt their regimes. This situation is not peculiar to Iraq; conservative powers always fight change, and perhaps the clearest example of this is the alliance of the absolute monarchies in Europe in the face of the French Revolution.

Accordingly, the regional Arab Sunni alliance, along with remnants of the Baath regime, coordinated with al-Qaeda elements to sabotage the American project and return Iraq to its former state. They led the movement against the political process from Arab capitals, such as Amman, Damascus, Abu Dhabi, Doha, and others. Domestically in Iraq, the UN Security Council's definition of the presence of United States troops in Iraq as an "occupying force" also justified defining anti-United States' operations as "resistance" to occupation, while people debated whether that resistance should be violent or non-violent.

Under the pretext of resisting occupation, al-Qaeda infiltrated Iraq, cooperated with elements of the former Baath regime, obtained support from the Arab regimes led by Saudi Arabia, and adopted a sectarian narrative. To justify terrorist activities against Shia civilians, al-Qaeda referred to them with medieval terms, such as the "Shia Persian Safavids" who have allied themselves with the "American Crusaders"; this language made killing these "crusaders" and Shias not only justifiable, but a duty. Terrorist groups' goal and the mechanism they deployed was to drag Iraq into a Shia–Sunni civil war, as well as a confrontation between the United States and Iran. They aimed the latter at ending the Shia political presence in Iraq and draining the American military effort. However, that scenario did not succeed, because of the role of the supreme religious authority held by Imam al-Sistani, who urged Iraqis to exercise restraint and not to be entangled in retaliatory actions that would generate more community violence and serve the objectives of the terrorists.

In addition to the financial and intellectual support offered by Gulf countries, Gulf media also contributed to the promotion of the activities of the terrorist groups, describing them as "resistance." They also portrayed all the victims as participants in the occupation, ignoring the terrorist operations' civilian casualties, whom they described as "agents" of the occupation. Adding fuel to the fire was the occupation authority's blatant violation of human rights, such as the transgressions that took place in the Abu Ghraib prison and other places.

The Gulf countries' propaganda machines had a positive response in the Arab world, which had suffered a psychological defeat during the occupation and sought to overcome this with, at least, a media triumph. United States' policies in the region did not help to counter that propaganda, especially its support of totalitarian and authoritarian regimes, its interference in the internal affairs of Arab countries, and its failure in finding a just solution to the Palestinian/Israeli conflict. All of these contributed to the media's success in projecting Saddam as a "national hero" who challenged "American hegemony."

The "strategic framework agreement" between Iraq and the United States provided that the United States would support Iraq's security and its political process and would subsequently withdraw from the country, but that agreement also eliminated any pretext of "resisting the occupation" that could justify terrorist activities. For the sake of continuing their terrorist activities, terrorist groups used terms such as "agents of the occupation" and "the marginalization of the Sunna" in media discourses to portray the Iraqi government as sectarian. The Gulf Arab media promoted this image, while terrorist activities in Iraq continued and took a sharp turn toward the worst with the outbreak of the Syrian crisis.

Terrorism and the Syrian crisis

In the midst of the War on Terror in Iraq, protests broke out in the Arab world during what is known in the media as The Arab Spring. After popular protests toppled regimes in Tunisia and Egypt, the West's support of an armed rebellion overthrew the regime in Libya, and the perception was that the regime in Syria could be toppled in a similar manner. The armed groups that were formed, with foreign help, to overthrow the Syrian regime served as incubators for the increasing activities of terrorist groups led by al-Qaeda and its offshoots, such as al-Nusra and ISIS.

Iraqi Prime Minister al-Maliki's position was to stay neutral because he believed that the spark of war in Syria would extend to ignite a new war in Iraq, too. However, the United States' alliance with the Gulf countries and Turkey led them to interpret Iraq's neutrality and refusal to join them against Syria as a pro-Iranian position, Iran being an ally of the Syrian regime.

Al-Maliki wanted to have a balanced position towards Iran and the United States He was willing to improve Iraq's relations with the US, but he was not able to free Iraq from Iranian influence. With the intensification of the conflict in Syria, this centrist position was not acceptable to both parties. The regional Arab alliance cast a sectarian label on the conflict, describing the secular Baath regime as Alawi-Shia and in opposition as Sunna. When the Shia populace in Iraq realized that the Syrian opposition came from the same terrorist groups that hit them in Iraq and was targeting the Islamic holy sites in Syria, Iraqi Shia public opinion became sympathetic with the Syrian people against the terrorist groups.

To many Iraqis, the position of the United States in siding with Syrian rebel groups cast more doubt on its role in sponsoring terrorism. All of these factors combined to make al-Maliki closer to the sentiments of the Shia street, to which he belonged, regarding the Syrian crisis. As a result, he was accused of sectarianism, and he lost United States' support for his own government's war against terrorism, particularly regarding armaments, forcing him to search for alternative sources, primarily through the Russian alternative.[20]

A number of Sunni leaders favored the Western and regional project to topple the "Alawi" Assad regime in Syria and replace it with a "Sunni" one, along with toppling al-Maliki and ending the political process in Iraq. To accomplish this task, sit-ins in the Anbar province, funded by Saudi Arabia and Qatar, coincided with the Gulf media campaign against Assad and al-Maliki. These factors, in addition to the rampant corruption in Iraqi state institutions, including military and security institutions, paved the way for the fall of Mosul on June 10, 2014.

Terrorism and the fall of Mosul

The fall of Mosul to ISIS was a historically important event, in the course of the War on Terror and in relation to the history of the Iraqi state as a whole. It showed the power of terrorist organizations on one side and the weakness of the official security services on the other. This combination not only led to the fall of Mosul, but also Kirkuk and Saladin. Kirkuk, which includes Turkmen, Kurds, Arabs, and Christians, is claimed by the Kurds; Saladin is predominantly Sunni.

The depth of the divisions in Iraq also showed clearly. The Sunni Iraqi rhetoric, backed by Sunni Arab discourse, described terrorist organizations as "rebellious tribes," a metaphor for a local liberation movement against the Iraqi government, which is also described in the media as "sectarian" and "dictatorial."

While the Iraqi government announced that the fall of Mosul to ISIS was part of a plot and that it should be seen in the context of the failure of the War on Terror, Massoud Barzani, the president of the Kurdistan region, announced that the Kurds would not enter into a war against the Sunna on behalf of the War on Terror. He also announced that after June 10, 2014, Iraq no longer existed, affirming his intention to divide Iraq. Kurdish forces proceeded to control the city of Kirkuk and other areas adjacent to the Kurdistan region, the Iraqi army withdrew, and ISIS did not enter that region.

The United States, which had expected Iraqis to stand by the Iraqi government, in accord with the strategic framework agreement, kept quiet and did not intervene militarily. However, when ISIS arrived at the outskirts of the capital of Kurdistan, Arbil, and it was about to fall, the Kurdistan government called for Iranian help. Only then did the United States conduct air raids, stop ISIS's advance, and save Arbil from falling, revealing the Kurdish forces' weakness in the face of ISIS's tactics.

The crucial factor that influenced the events following the fall of Mosul was the supreme religious authority Imam al-Sistani's spiritual message encouraging hundreds of thousands of volunteers to join the ranks of the military. Al-Sistani believed that the terrorists were not only targeting the inhabitants of Nineveh, but also all Iraqis throughout Iraq, including Baghdad, Karbala, and Najaf, and he asserted that the War on Terror is everyone's responsibility. He described the terrorists as representing "dark forces who are distant from the spirit of Islam, refuse peaceful coexistence, use violence and bloodshed to stir sectarian wars to dominate other regions in Iraq and other countries."[21] The overwhelming response of the volunteer forces enabled them to regain cities from terrorists, including the provinces of Samarra, Diyala, and Saladin.

The Iraqi view of the role of the United States

The clearing of terrorists from Diyala led to a media attack, with Saudi Arabia at the forefront, which leveled against the Iraqi government the usual charge of being "a sectarian Shia militia and an agent for Iran." The liberation of Saladin was easier, as ISIS withdrew from it, and the Iraqi army, led by al-Abbadi as Commander-in-Chief of the armed forces, entered it swiftly with the help of the volunteer forces.[22] The volunteer force did not escape a media campaign waged against it that was similar to the one faced by the government in Diyala. However, despite the volunteer forces being Shia, while the inhabitants of Saladin are mainly Sunna, no sectarian violence occurred, for the government coordinated with security agencies, civil administration was restored, many locals joined the force, and local groups were given security tasks.

In my private conversations with a number of political and security officials on the successful operation in Saladin, they intimated that the American side was not happy with the growing strength of the volunteer forces because of the support they receive from Iran. For that reason, they sought to thwart any rapprochement between Sunni and Shia Iraqis in the areas of the War on Terror, particularly since the volunteer forces had succeeded in recruiting Sunni and Christian elements. Instead, the United States used the following means to hinder the progress of the Iraqi army and the volunteer forces in the Anbar province, which fell to ISIS in June 2015:

1   The US prevented the progress of Iraqi and volunteer forces in the Anbar province and in Fallujah. The latter has been a stronghold for terrorist groups since 2003. It is about 50 km to the west of Baghdad. The American hindrance of the Iraqi forces' advance into Fallujah had great significance to Iraqis. Its fall would mean a symbolic defeat for the terrorist groups; alternatively, Fallujah's liberation with forces loyal to the United States would make it a dagger in the side of the capital.
2   The US pressured the Iraqi Government not to support or arm the volunteer forces by multiple methods, most notably by exploiting the weakness of the Iraqi government in general by not delivering weapons the US had agreed to deliver or by placing conditions on their use. Those pressures were put in place with full knowledge that the volunteer forces possessed only light and medium weapons and had to face ISIS's superior weaponry, taken in battles in Syria and Iraq.
3   The US did not supply the Iraqi army with the necessary weapons, for fear that they would end up in the hands of the volunteer forces.
4   The US provided limited ammunition to armored vehicles, depleting the Iraqi army's combat capabilities, and causing the army to run out of ammunition.
5   The US did not coordinate with Iraqi forces regarding airstrikes carried out by the international coalition against terrorist group sites.
6   The US provided logistical support and weapons through direct airdrops of military equipment to groups, who in the eyes of most Iraqis, are terrorist organizations.
7   The US refused to stop ISIS's smuggling of oil, its major source of funding.
8   The US bombed Iraqi forces engaged in the fight against terrorists and then claimed that the American bombers made a mistake.

In addition, the United States' Administration continued to press the Iraqi government to establish a tribal Sunni army that would serve as its proxy. The US called this force the National Guard and named it as one of the conditions for its effectively contributing in the War on Terror in Iraq. This convinced Iraqis that the United States had no objection to keeping Anbar province under the control of ISIS, as long as the volunteer forces did not enter it. To continue its military advances, the Iraqi army ignored American pressure and decided to liberate the city of al-Ramadi, the center of Anbar province. While the Iraqi army carried out the operation on its own, the volunteer forces, to avoid being attacked by an American airstrike, had to enter al-Ramadi, which was liberated during the last week of 2015. The Americans had just bombed an Iraqi army camp, killing 20 Iraqi soldiers, injuring scores of others, and causing significant losses of military equipment.

The United States' attitude toward the Iraqi government's advances against ISIS-held territories contributed to Iraqi suspicions that the US does not intend to help Iraq build a modern, liberal nation-state, but prefers to reinforce ethno-sectarian divisions and build a state around them.

In addition, the United States' declaration that the elimination of ISIS would require three to five years raised more questions: most notably, why a superpower such as the United States is unable to take decisive steps to dismantle the known infrastructure of a terrorist group. The declaration confirmed popular suspicions that the United States is content with having terrorist groups advance America's strategic interests in Iraq and the Middle East at the expense of civilian casualties. For that reason, Iraq turned to Russia to obtain the most basic equipment it needed, such as armor-piercing missiles, with which to thwart ISIS suicide bombings, which were carried out with truckloads of explosives. Iraq's motivation to seek Russian help was reinforced by further evidence that ISIS attacks occurred before the eyes and ears of American military personnel, who also seemed at times to provide ISIS with logistical help, as in the case confirmed by Hamid Mutlaq, a member of Iraq's Council of representatives from Anbar province.[23]

Iraq and the United States' vision of the War on Terror

The United States, like many countries in the world, benefits from the absence of a legal definition of terrorism, which allows it to classify terrorist organizations in accordance with its own interests. Academic and nonofficial literature outline characteristics of a terrorist act in a manner that distinguishes it from other violent acts, such as crime, war, resistance, rebellion, or other activities with common characteristics.[24] With the absence of a legal definition of terrorism, one can at least narrow it down to the deliberate killing of civilians, but one has also to recognize that terrorist groups have their financial, material, logistical, and ideological sponsors. Using these broad criteria, one could say that the September 11, 2001, attacks in the US were acts of terrorism. However, so were many acts perpetrated in Iraq since 2003, the fact of which presents a question concerning the

Iraq: a victim of terror 97

basis upon which the United States constructed its vision of its War on Terror. The September 11 attacks were carried out on American grounds by external subjects, all of whom were killed, but they were planned and sponsored, ideologically and financially, by external parties. Who were those external parties?

The US State Department has defined four elements of its counterterrorism policy:

1 Not to make any concessions to terrorists and not to conclude any deal with them.
2 Bringing terrorists to justice for their crimes.
3 Isolate countries that sponsor terrorism and put pressure on them to get them to change her behavior.
4 Support counterterrorist capabilities of countries that are working with the United States and need help.[25]

While the United States' case against Afghanistan was that the Taliban harbored al-Qaeda's leader Bin Laden and therefore needed to be toppled by an invasion, the case against Iraq was not as solid. It was based on a suspicion that Iraq had weapons of mass destruction, which potentially could end up in the hands of terrorist groups. After it became apparent that Iraq did not possess such weapons, further American sacrifices were deemed unwarranted, even though the invasion had destroyed the institutions of the state, and the resulting power vacuum made Iraq a breeding ground for terrorists to set up shop. Still, further sacrifices to rebuild Iraq were not seen as relevant to American national security interests. While terrorist activities in Iraq were acknowledged, they were nevertheless looked upon as part of a "Sunni insurgency" and simply as Iraqi internal affairs that did not pose a threat to American interests; the conclusion was that the Iraqis should handle them on their own. Thus, terrorism was characterized as "rebellion" and terrorists were "rebels," although they were related to Al-Qaeda.[26] US Secretary of State Condoleezza Rice avoided any reference to civilian casualties caused by terrorist bombings. and she considered even the bombing of the United Nations Headquarters in Iraq in August 2003, which killed Sergio Vieira de Mello, the United Nations special representative in Iraq, along with 21 other UN employees, in the context of "rebellion," not the context of terrorism.[27]

President George W. Bush, on the other hand, had a different interpretation of the violence in Iraq. While acknowledging the existence of a "rebellion," Bush explicitly described the frequent suicide bombings that killed 120 civilians per day in the summer of 2006 as acts of terrorism, including the bombing of the revered shrines of imams in Samarra. He also admitted that terrorist acts in Iraq were perpetrated by al-Qaeda, which, in Iraq, was led by al-Zarqawi, who aimed to ignite a Sunni-Shia civil war, and that al-Zarqawi opposed the promotion of democratic institutions in Iraq.[28] Yet, even with this perspective on al-Qaeda and the need to eradicate it, Bush did not delve into the question of who was providing support for it in its war against the new Iraqi state.

Like Bush, Dick Cheney viewed the violence as a product of al-Qaeda's terrorism and was a strong critic of Rice's assessment, which was similar to those of Abizaid, Casey, and Khalilzad. The latter three saw the violence as sectarian in nature and a byproduct of a loss of Sunni power. Accordingly, they recommended that the United States should not intervene in Iraqi internal affairs unless it saw a massacre in progress similar to the one that occurred in Srebrenica in 1995, when the Bosnian Serbs slaughtered thousands of civilians.[29] Yet, even as suicide bombings targeted markets, mosques, and schools with the intent to kill as many people as possible, in addition to abductions, hostage-taking, and beheadings, let alone the destruction of Iraqi infrastructure and the killing of Iraqi and American armed forces, the view of Abizaid, Casey, and Khalilzad, which categorized the violence as sectarian as opposed to terrorist, did not change.[30]

The difference between the two perspectives stemmed from the Bush-Cheney perception of al-Qaeda as a force equally as anti-American as Iran, which, if it ousted the United Sates from Iraq and gained power there, could pose a threat to the United States' interests in the region. For that reason, Bush-Cheney supported al-Maliki politically and militarily and disengaged the Sunna from al-Qaeda in the hope of integrating them into a political process to build a new Iraq that would be politically distinct from its surrounding states.

Based on the Bush–Cheney perspective, the United Sates insisted on fighting the growing strength of al-Qaeda. They believed rebuilding Iraq according to the principles of freedom and democracy could be in the best interest of the United States, while Rice and the Abizaid–Casey–Khalilzad trio believed that the United States' mission would be accomplished by toppling Saddam in the same way the Americans' World War II mission in Europe had been completed by toppling Hitler and the Nazi regime. The US intervened in both places to eliminate the perceived threat to it and its allies; it did not intervene to spread freedom and democracy. Moreover, Rice and the trio realized from the outset that the United States' political value system could not be replicated in Iraq; its neighboring states, especially in the Gulf region, were ruled by totalitarian regimes that would not welcome a pluralistic political system. In addition, recreating the US political system in Iraq would also allow Shia Muslims access to power, and this would break the Sunni dominance in the Arab Middle East. Rice was aware that the Gulf Arab states looked upon the Shia as a virus, but it was not clear to her whether it was the Shia element or the prospect of democracy that made the Arab Gulf states nervous.[31]

While the Arabs fought democratic change in Iraq with sectarianism, the Arab Spring uprisings swept Tunisia's and Egypt's presidents from power. The Arab Gulf states rode the tide and militarized the protests in Syria while casting them in a sectarian light by associating both the Syrian and Iraqi governments with Iran. Claiming to defend the Sunna, the Arab Gulf states supported terrorist groups, and the outcome was eventually the appearance of ISIS.[32]

The United States, in turn, found its interests lined up with the Arab Gulf states against the Assad regime in Syria and against Iran, regardless of the sectarian affiliations of the conflicting parties. Although the majority of active militant groups in Iraq and Syria are totalitarian in their ideology, terrorist in their activities, and have branched out from al-Qaeda, the United States nevertheless dealt with them from the vantage point of its interests, and the extent to which they threaten American national security and the security of its allies. The US viewed them as internal movements that are not covered by the standards of the Global War on Terror; it viewed them from the same perspective that it viewed the Taliban at a later stage in the war in Afghanistan. Rice's successor, Hillary Clinton, also viewed the violence in Iraq as a form of rebellion,[33] in the same way that she viewed the Taliban insurgency inside Afghanistan and entered into negotiations with them to end the conflict in Afghanistan and withdraw American troops, having realized that it no longer posed a threat to American national security.[34]

The contradiction between values and interests was obvious in American foreign policy toward the Middle East, as was evident in Hillary Clinton's statement:

> Despite the best intentions of successive American administrations, the day-to-day reality of US foreign policy prioritized urgent strategic and security imperatives such as counterterrorism, support for Israel, and blocking Iran's nuclear ambitions over the long-term goal of encouraging internal reforms in our Arab partners.[35]

Clinton has not denied sacrificing American principles in the service of material interests, even if it required supporting dictatorships. She states:

> Championing democracy and human rights had been at the heart of our global leadership for more than half a century. Yes, we had from time to time compromised those values in the service of strategic and security interests, including by supporting unsavory anti-Communist dictators during the Cold War, with mixed results.[36]

This contradiction has been present also with the US's relations with the Arab Gulf states, specifically between American values of freedom and the totalitarian Gulf regimes' violations of human rights and export of radical ideology. Clinton states:

> Perhaps our most delicate balancing act in the Middle East was with our partners in the Persian Gulf.... The United States had developed deep economic and strategic ties to these wealthy, conservative monarchies, even as we made no secret of our concerns about human rights abuses, especially the treatment of women and minorities, and the export of extremist ideology.

Those contradictions accompanied American foreign policy toward the Gulf States and became more difficult to face after the events of September 11, 2001, when:

100 A. S. al-Haidari

> Every US administration wrestled with the contradictions of our policy toward the Gulf. The choices were never harder than after 9/11. Americans were shocked that 15 of the 19 hijackers and Osama bin Laden himself hailed from Saudi Arabia, a nation that we had defended in the 1991 Gulf War. And it was appalling that money from the Gulf continued funding extremist madrassas and propaganda all over the world.[37]

These discrepancies between values and interests in American foreign policy have cast their shadow over the Middle East, particularly regarding America's relationship with the rich Arab Gulf states allied to it. For example, the US's views in the cases of Syria and Bahrain are similar, in that it sees them as sectarian minorities ruling over majorities,[38] despite the fact that the Syrian regime is secular. However, it engaged with the two cases quite differently, based on its material interests in the Arab Gulf states, not on its professed secular values.

Saudi Arabia and the United Arab Emirates forcefully repressed the peaceful opposition in Bahrain,[39] while Saudi Arabia and Qatar armed the opposition in Syria and Clinton referred to its militant groups as rebels.[40] That vision had implications for the War on Terror in Iraq. The regional sectarian conflict that is raging between the United States' allies Saudi Arabia and Qatar and Turkey, and its foe, Iran, made Iraq and Syria fields of conflict. The result was the fall of more victims to terrorism in Iraq.

Iraq's victims of terrorism

The number of Iraqi civilians who fell at the hands of terrorist groups gives a clear indication of the scale of the terrorism suffered by the Iraqi people after the American invasion in 2003. The Iraqi Human Rights Ministry said that the number of victims of terrorism in Iraq during the period 2003–2015 was approximately 300,000 killed or injured. Within one year of ISIS's occupation of Nineveh, from June 9, 2014 to July 1, 2015, the number killed was 4,722 and the number injured 28,575, excluding Saladin and al-Anbar governorates and Kurdistan.[41]

The UN report, which was released on January 19, 2016, stated that the number of civilian casualties in Iraq during the period of January–October 2014,

Table 5.1 The numbers of victims who were injured during the listed five months of the year 2015[47]

Month	Slain		Wounded		Total
	Civilians	Non-civilians	Civilians	Non-civilians	
June	665	801	1,032	665	3,153
August	585	740	1,103	708	3,136
September	537	180	925	291	1,933
October	559	155	1,067	202	1,983
December	506	867	464	377	2,214

Table 5.2 Provinces that have seen the largest number of victims within the listed five months of the year 2015[48]

June			August			September			October			December		
Baghdad	974	30.9%	Baghdad	1,069	34%	Baghdad	840	43.5%	Baghdad	1,150	58%	Baghdad	1,048	49.3%
Diyala province	244	7.7%	Diyala province	270	8.6%	Diyala province	153	7.9%	Diyala province	233	11.7%	Nineveh	85	4%
Saladin	156	4.9%	Nineveh	72	2.3%	Saladin	151	7.8%	Nineveh	86	4.3%	Saladin	42	2%
Nineveh	27	0.9%	Saladin	36	1.1%	Nineveh	83	4.3%	Saladin	68	3.4%	Kirkuk	30	1.4%
Kirkuk	15	0.5%	Kirkuk	32	1%	Kirkuk	22	1.1%	Kirkuk	46	2.3%	Diyala province	16	0.8%

was at least 55,047, among whom 18,802 were dead and 36,245 injured.[42] As for the displaced, the report stated, "civilians continue to flee their homes and communities in massive numbers. From January 2014 through September 29, 2015, a total of 3,206,736 persons became internally displaced in Iraq, including over one million school-age girls and boys."[43] The report confirmed that ISIS is deliberately murdering civilians, kidnapping women and children based on their religious and ethnic identities and using them as sex slaves.[44] According to the report:

> ISIS continues to commit systematic and widespread violence and abuses international rights law and humanitarian law. These acts may, in some, instances, amount to war crimes, crimes against humanity, and possibly genocide.... ISIS continues to target members of different ethnic and religious communities.... The impact of the ongoing conflict and acts of terrorism on civilians remains severe and extensive.[45]

According to a report released by UNAMI (The United Nations Assistance Mission for Iraq) on January 1, 2016, the number of civilian casualties in Iraq in 2015 alone reached 22,370, including 7,515 dead and 14,855 injured.[46]

Conclusion

Fifteen years into the War on Terror and the United States' invasions of Afghanistan and Iraq, the world has entered a new phase of instability which, according to Henry Kissinger's speculations, threatens a third world war. As it is undeniable that the United States is a superpower, it is also undeniable that it has committed serious errors in its foreign policy toward the Arab and Islamic worlds and in the Middle East in particular, specifically in Iraq, a fact that is acknowledged by many American officials.

The pragmatic philosophy underpinning contemporary American political thought, along with the combination of religious and rightwing-thought that influenced President George W. Bush's policy, overshadowed the principles of democracy, liberalism, and human rights, which the United Sates has traditionally preached. This contradiction was reflected in the distorted and vague image of the United States held by the peoples of the Arab world in general and by the Iraqis in particular. After its failure to prove that Iraq possessed weapons of mass destruction, the United States also failed to establish a democratic regime in Iraq, and later it failed in its War on Terror, leaving Iraq to become a victim of ongoing terrorism since 2003.

Thus, gradually, the United States lost its credibility with the Iraqi people. Iraqis believe today that the United States is not serious in its War on Terror and may be involved in the creation of terrorist groups. This belief was strengthened after the terrorist organizations flocked to Syria; it was reinforced with the unchecked rise of ISIS and its occupation of major Iraqi cities, where it abused the inhabitants along ethnic and sectarian lines, as was seen with Christians and

Yazidis, for example. The prevailing opinion among the Iraqi intellectual elite is that, because of the United States' human and material losses in the Iraq war, it relied on nonstate actors, including al-Qaeda and its affiliates, to carry out its policies. The US therefore did not seek to destroy terrorist networks, but used them to serve its interests in the region.

The United States' policy mistake was in ignoring the peoples of the region and cooperating with dictatorships and totalitarian regimes to ensure its interests. The Iraqi people's rejoicing over the possibility of overthrowing dictatorships and transitioning towards greater democracy with the help of the largest liberal democracy in the world soon disappeared, as the United States continued its alliance with the Gulf sheikhdoms, which spearheaded the counterrevolution against the "Arab Spring," deflecting the surge towards democratization into violence and chaos and expanding the geographical reach of terrorist organizations in Iraq, Syria, Libya, Yemen, Egypt, and beyond.

Moreover, the United States did not accurately gauge the prevailing reality of the people in the Arab world. In Iraq, United States' foreign policy contributed to strengthening the divisions within Iraqi society. The US did not look at Iraqis as a people aspiring to democratic rule in accordance with the principle of equal citizenship, but as groups governed by ethno-sectarian oligarchies seeking to strengthen their power positions. It looked upon the Shia as an extension of Iran and exploited the Iraqi Sunni leaders' fear of a presumed Shia dominance, fueled by Iraq's Sunni Arab neighbors, who themselves fear the expansion of Iranian influence in the region. It exploited the Kurdish dream of an independent Kurdish state and Masoud Barzani's ambition to be the founder of that country, to ensure even more loyalty from the Kurdish leadership.

Most Iraqis have realized the serious dangers of terrorist groups, especially in the regions controlled by al-Qaeda and then ISIS. The United States, however, instead of siding with Iraqis in their War on Terror by building strong national military institutions based on equal citizenship and professional competence, has promoted divisive and even terrorist tendencies in order to establish a Sunni army based on tribal affiliations and to support Kurdish militias as a force independent from the national military establishment. It seems that this policy is a prelude for dividing Iraq according to Vice President Joe Biden's project; his name among Iraqis is now associated with a plan to divide Iraq.

Yet there is no logical relationship between dividing Iraq and the War on Terror. The United States can eliminate terrorist groups by funding and arming the Iraqi army, given that army's experience in the War on Terror, and by seeking to integrate the army's efforts in the Global War on Terror. The division of Iraq into armed ethnic and religious entities does not defuse instability in the region; those entities will be used by regional or international forces to become their proxies in future wars. In addition, dividing Iraq delivers unpredictable results in an unstable region like the Middle East, with the absence or weakness of totalitarian police states attempting to deliver stability by brute physical force.

Dividing the Arab world in the last century in accordance with the interests of the great powers did not contribute to the stability of the region and neither will dividing the divided further increase stability. Experience has shown that a trend towards global and regional union creates incentives for cooperation rather than for conflict; it is more effective in achieving international peace and security, of which the European Union stands as an example.

The policy that the United States adopted in its War on Terror is beginning to bring the world back to the bipolar model in international relations. After Russia's realization that its acceptance of working within an international consensus jeopardized its own strategic interests, it intervened in the Middle East, under the guise of the War on Terror, in order to protect its interests. Although the aim of fighting terrorist groups in Iraq and Syria is clear and specific, the dispute between the United States and Russia in the War on Terror reveals their different interests, and that the War on Terror is a cover for achieving those interests.

The Middle East has generally been within the West's sphere of influence throughout the last century. In the midst of the Israeli–Arab wars, the Soviet Union did not intervene militarily, while today Russia intervened in the Middle East directly, taking advantage of the United States' foreign policy failures in Iraq and of the "Arab Spring," which created a vacuum of power which many forces competed to fill.

Among the incentives that pushed Russia toward direct military intervention in the Syrian conflict and indirect intervention in Iraq is the fact that it has not profited from the war against Iraq and against Libya. Russia also concluded, particularly after NATO's attempt to incorporate Ukraine into its sphere, that the triumph of the West in its war against Syria would result in a siege on its eastern frontier. In addition, Russia was aware of the danger posed by terrorist groups inside the Russian Federation, as in Chechnya and in its surrounding republics of Central Asia.

The United States is aware of the same terrorist groups in that region, but because of its divergent interests from those of Russia, the US did not agree with the way Russians dealt with those groups. Accordingly, Russia feared that the United States might recycle terrorist groups currently operating in Syria and Iraq after their role has ended in those two countries, and use them against Russia in the future, either internally or externally.

Questions arise from this scenario: If terrorist organizations in Iraq and Syria are independent organizations not related to any state, then why do we see this divergence between the United States and Russia in dealing with them? Are different interests prompting these powers to take opposite positions toward the terrorist organizations?

The emergence of Russia's role in this important region of the world is an indication that a prolonged conflict will have unpredictable results and may weaken its standing in the region. Perhaps an American victory would be too costly, despite President Obama's strategic patience. From this perspective, the United States must realize the magnitude and extent of Russian interests and deal with them within a framework of a common understanding to insure its interests and dispel Russia's fears. This would stop the momentum towards a polarized position in the region.

Iraq: a victim of terror 105

The United States must also show greater objectivity in its policies towards the Middle East, where people are now more aware of international politics and live in an atmosphere of relatively greater freedom. This will enable them to contribute to policymaking, as opposed to their limited role in the era of the totalitarian regimes friendly to the United States. It is not clear to what extent and for how long the Arab regimes in the Gulf region will continue to rely on promoting terrorist groups and chaos in the Middle East, especially in Iraq, as a first line of defense, and continue to be protected by their alliance with United States.

In 2001, terrorism's stronghold was one country, Afghanistan, backed by two allies of the United States, Saudi Arabia and Pakistan. Fifteen years after the events of September 11, 2001, and the United States' declaration of the Global War on Terror, terrorism has become a global phenomenon threatening an outbreak of a Third World War. In the midst of all this, Iraq has become a victim of terrorism and of the War on Terror.

Notes

1 According to Iraq's new constitution, Prime Minister Nuri al-Maliki 2006–2014, who is also the General Secretary of the (Shia) Islamic Da'wa Party, had executive authority making his position the most powerful than the nominal presidency. The prime ministerial position was allocated to Iraq's Shia because they represent the about 60 percent of Iraq's population.
2 The Twelver Shia is the major branch of Shia Islam. The term Twelver is derived from a list of 12 Imams from the bloodline of the Prophet Muhammad through his daughter Fatima. The Imams start with Ali, the Prophet Muhammad's cousin and son in law and end with al-Mahdi, whom the Shia believe is in a state of occultation and will emerge during the Armageddon along with Jesus to bring justice to the world. (Translator's note).
3 Iraqis are used to attaching informal labels to historical events. For example, Iraqis called the first Gulf War "the Iran war," and the second Gulf War, "Bush's war," and the third Gulf War, "the fall."
4 See George W. Bush, *Qararat Masyriyya* [*Fateful Decisions*], (Beirut: Sharikat al-Matbou'at lil Tawi' wa al-Nashr, 2012), 475, 493. Also see Dick Cheney and Liz Cheney, *Fi Zamani* [*In My Time*], trans. Fadel Jtaker (Beirut: Dar al-Kuttab al-'Arab, 2012), 494.
5 For more details on President Bush's impressions from that meeting, see George W. Bush, *Qararat Masyriyya* [*Fateful Decisions*], 496–497.
6 The reduction of the number of terrorist acts has been attested in many sources including by George Bush, where he states in his memoirs that the number of deaths due to terrorist acts were 120 per day in 2006 (ibid., 448) and that they declined by 95 percent due to the weakening of al-Qaeda and "the decline of the pernicious Iranian role." (Ibid., 516).
7 For more details about that visit, see George W. Bush, *Qararat Masyriyya* [*Fateful Decisions*], 508–509. Sheikh Abu Risha was later assassinated in a terrorist bomb attack.
8 Condoleezza Rice, *Asma Marateb al-Sharaf: Zikrayat min Sinin Hayati fi Washington* [*No Higher Honor: A Memoir of My Years in Washington*], trans. Walid Shehadeh (Beirut: Bayt al-Kitab al-Arabi, 2012), 673.
9 See the remarks of Vice President Joe Biden on Iraq: "Remarks by Vice President Joe Biden on Iraq," *IIP Digital*, April 9, 2015, http://iipdigital.usembassy.gov/st/english/texttrans/2015/04/20150409314606.html#axzz3sKy1kUKN.

106 *A. S. al-Haidari*

10 With the exception of the Badr Organization, the armed wing of the Supreme Council for the Islamic Revolution in Iraq before 2003, which later became an active political organization in the government and parliament, these factions were fighting the United States' occupation, but suspended their military activities after the United States' withdrawal from Iraq, and then they returned to take up arms against ISIS.
11 See Condoleezza Rice, *Asma Marateb al-Sharaf* [*No Higher Honor*], 197.
12 James Baker, *Siyasat al-Diplomasiyya* [*Policy of Diplomacy*] (Cairo: Madbuli Library, 1999), 419–420.
13 Ibid., 417.
14 Martin Indyk, *Abria' fi al-Kaharej* [*Innocent Abroad*], trans. Omar Said al-Ayyoubi (Beirut: Dar al-Kitab al-Arabi, 2010), 51.
15 Ibid., 54.
16 Dick Cheney and Liz Cheney, *Fi Zamani* [*In My Time*], 486.
17 For more detail about the Salafists in Iraq, see Khalil al-Rubaie, *Al-Salafiyya fi al-Iraq: Dirasa fi al-Tarikh wa al-fikr* [*The Salafist in Iraq: A Study in History and Thought*] (Baghdad: Dar al-'Uloum lil Tibaa wa al-Nashr wa al-Tawzi', 2015).
18 The surrender protocol was signed in al-Anbar by Khalaf al-Olayan, who later became a Sunni political figure, then disappeared from the political scene.
19 Condoleezza Rice affirms the United States' awareness that "during the reign of Saddam Hussein, the Sunna made up about 30 percent of the population, but had nearly one hundred percent of the political power." Condoleezza Rice, *Asma Marateb al-Sharaf* [*No Higher Honor*], 424.
20 In a private meeting I had with al-Maliki in September 2015, he stated that the Americans had let him down in the War on Terror and that he had conveyed his disappointment to more than one US official.
21 A sermon to the representative of the supreme religious authority in Karbala, Sheikh Abd al-Mahdi Karbalai, *The Official Website of His Eminence Ali al-Sayyid al-Husseini al-Sistani*, June 13, 2014, www.sistani.org/arabic/archive/24918/.
22 Leaked reports stated that the Iraqi army and the volunteer forces entered Saladin as an outcome of a deal between the Iraqi Government and regional Arab states brokered by King Abdullah II and al-Sayyed Ammar al-Hakim of the Islamic Supreme Council of Iraq.
23 Mutlaq is also the representative of the Sunni Union of National Forces and a member of the Committee on defense and security in Parliament. He made his claims during his lecture on "Iraq and the Policy of Axes," delivered on November 3, 2015, at the monthly political forum featuring elite politicians, academics, and intellectuals, directed by former Minister and current Member of Parliament Dr. Ibrahim Bahr Al-Ulum.
24 Consider, for example: Charles Townshend, *al-Irhab* [*Terrorism*], trans. Mohammed Saad Hindawi Tantawi, (Cairo: Education and Culture, 2014).
25 Ibid., 130.
26 Condoleezza Rice, *Asma Marateb al-Sharaf* [*No Higher Honor*], 316. According to American sources, al-Zarqawi was, just prior to 2003, a member of the Ansar al-Islam Group, a Kurdish terrorist organization operating in northern Iraq outside the control of the Iraqi regime, and was seeking to produce weapons of mass destruction. See ibid., 212.
27 Ibid., 279, 282.
28 George W. Bush, *Qararat Masyriyya* [*Fateful Decisions*], 479, 481, 488.
29 Dick Cheney and Liz Cheney, *Fi Zamani* [*In My Time*], 504.
30 Ibid., 490.
31 Condoleezza Rice, *Asma Marateb al-Sharaf* [*No Higher Honor*], 579.
32 For more detail on the Saudi role in the face of "Arab spring revolutions," see for instance the chapter entitled "The Wahhabi counter revolution" in John R. Bradley, *Ma Ba'da al-Rabi' al-'Arabi: Kayfa Ikhtatafa al-Islamiyyoun Thawrat al-Sharq*

al-Awsat [*After the Arab Spring: How Islamists Hijacked the Middle East Revolts*], trans. Shaimaa Abd al-Hakim Taha (Cairo: Mu'asasset Hindawi Lil Ta'lim wa al-Thaqafa, 2013), 75–102.
33 See Hillary Clinton, *Khayarat Sa'ba* [*Hard Choices*], (Beirut: Sharikat al-Matbou'at Lil Tawzi' wa al-Nashr, 2015), 143.
34 Ibid., 157–174.
35 Ibid., 324–325.
36 Ibid., 133.
37 Ibid., 341–342.
38 Ibid., 342.
39 Ibid., 345–349.
40 Ibid., 433–455.
41 The Office of the United Nations High Commissioner for Human Rights (OHCHR) issued its annual report on victims in Iraq, and the United Nations confirms these data. Wakalet Huna al-Janoob al-Ikhbariyya, "*Huquq al-Insan Tusder Taqriraha al-Sanawi An Dahaya al-Iraq wa al-Umam al-Mutahida Tuakidu Irtifa al-Adad* [Human Rights Issues Its Annual Report on Iraq's Victims and the United Nations Confirms the Rise in Numbers]," January 1, 2015, www.aljanoob.org/2015/07/news/52201.
42 The United Nations states in its reports that the number of victims should be considered as the absolute minimum. See the United Nations' report on civilian casualties in Iraq, the United Nations Mission in Iraq (UNAMI), www.uniraq.org/index.php.
43 OHCHR and UNAMI, "Report on the Protection of Civilians in the Armed Conflict in Iraq: May 1–October 31, 2015," www.ohchr.org/Documents/Countries/IQ/UNAMIReport1May31October2015.pdf, i.
44 Ibid., 14.
45 Ibid., i, 8, 31.
46 "UN Casualty Figures for the Month of December 2015," United Nations Mission in Iraq (UNAMI), January 1, 2016, www.uniraq.org/index.php.
47 Ibid.
48 Ibid.

6 The ideological origins of ISIS
Fighting terror with common sense

Mark Tomass

Introduction

While Syrians tasted the bitterness of watching their men and boys being slaughtered, some Western pundits and politicians seemed to sneer at them from a distance, denying their pain and advising them to engage in dialogue with Islamist rebels. They designed for them new identities from which to negotiate and demand full authority. One day they called them moderate rebels;[1] another day they called them Islamists, but they told us they are not the terrorists from al-Qaeda, and that is why we arm them[2] and serve as their media front men.[3] Those who have not sympathized with the Islamist rebels are baffled by the Western support for them and often ask how the West is defining terrorism. Why are members of ISIS and al-Qaeda terrorists while the other rebel groups are not? In this piece, I define terror, what inspires today's terrorist acts, and which groups qualify as terrorists, so that we may begin to discuss against whom the West is waging the War on Terror and what the most effective means to mitigate it are.

Terrorism, defined as violent actions carried out by groups or states to intimidate unarmed populations or governments into submitting to their demands, has existed since time immemorial.[4] However, the current phrase "War on Terror" has specifically been used in Western circles to describe the U.S.-led reaction to the 9/11 terrorist attacks on its citizens by affiliates of al-Qaeda. That war has been a failure by any standards. Fifteen years after those attacks, al-Qaeda and its affiliates have now branched out and, in part, have transformed themselves into the Islamic State of Iraq and Syria (ISIL/ISIS); have seized vast territories; have declared an Islamic Caliphate, and have vowed to conquer lands beyond the Fertile Crescent. While the international outrage over ISIS's campaign of terror was triggered by successive videotaped beheadings of less than a handful of Westerners and subsequent shooting sprees of a few hundred civilians in the U.S. and Europe, the vast majority of ISIS's victims have been and still are Syrian and Iraqi civilians, who are by no means nor in any manner responsible for the Western "War on Terror" nor for any of the previous Gulf wars or the Arab–Israeli wars.

The mass murders of non-conformists to Sunni Muslim Law, such as Christian, Shia, and Yezidi civilians, and of Sunni Muslim civilians who did not submit to ISIS's authority, are considered by the accounts of the victims' communities to be genocidal.[5] Yet ISIS is not the only party advancing its program with violence. Today, al-Qaeda and other less infamous Salafi-Jihadi groups commit equally violent acts against civilians, but their focus is on the Middle East, not the West. For they no longer aim to advance limited political programs, as the 9/11 terrorist attacks intended to oust U.S. military presence in the Middle East. Instead, they seek to re-Islamize the Muslim World according to Wahhābī doctrine by regulating the lives of Muslims and their relationships to non-Muslims in a manner that conforms to their reading of sacred Muslim scriptures.[6] By recruiting youth with an alternative quest for recognition, purpose, and power, those Salafi-Jihadi groups are leading a cultural revolution in the Middle East, a region with richly concentrated human resources; it is a revolution that aims to revive the notion of a powerful Muslim dominion, free from non-Muslim political, social, and cultural influence.

I argue that the rise of al-Qaeda, ISIS, and similar Salafi-Jihadi groups cannot be stopped by military means alone. At the time of this writing, al-Qaeda and ISIS are receiving blows from the Syrian army from the west, the Iraqi army from the east, and Kurdish and other militias from the north. Yet those military victories, even if they proceed to eliminate those groups in Syria and Iraq, will by no means stop them from carrying out suicide bombings or vanquish the ideology that gave rise to them. Because of the increasing popularity of Salafi-Jihadi groups among Muslim youth in the Middle East and worldwide, understanding these organizations' ideological origins is necessary if secular political forces are to succeed in staunch and roll back their rising tide.

Al-Qaeda's Wahhābī doctrine has gained significant ground among Sunni Muslims, to the extent that in today's Syria the vast majority of the foreign[7] and domestic[8] rebel groups adhere to it, whether they organizationally belong to al-Qaeda, its daughter ISIS, or rival organizations that Western propaganda outlets continue to dub as "moderate rebels," such as the Army of Islam, the Free Islamic Levant, or the Soldiers of the Levant. To be effective in the fight against religiously inspired terrorist organizations, long-term solutions must first acknowledge the religious roots of the ongoing violence and then rely on sponsoring re-education programs, including logic, psychology, social psychology, philosophy, and comparative religion, within Muslim communities globally, to challenge the hegemony of dogmatic Wahhābī religious thinking over all aspects of life. Without those intellectual tools, opportunistic political entrepreneurs posing as religious authorities will continue to manipulate the unsuspecting, unsophisticated masses and advance their quests for fame, power, employment, and wealth. If the Muslim masses remain unpersuaded that the terror-producing Wahhābī doctrine, or any equally dogmatic religious doctrine, provides bad solutions for their material, social, and psychological needs, other regions of the world will continue to coexist with a Middle East ruled either by secular authoritarian police states or by their tyrannical religious alternatives, and they will thereby suffer the spillover effects of those regimes beyond the territories where they rule.

Returning to the dawn of Islam

In the eighteenth century, a religious movement in what is now Saudi Arabia spearheaded by the Medina-educated jurist Muhammad ibn Abd al-Wahhāb (1703–1792) aimed to revive a "pure and authentic" practice of Islam by returning to the way Islam was allegedly practiced by the Prophet Muhammad and his companions. During his travels outside Arabia, Ibn Abd al-Wahhāb encountered theological innovations by Sufi and Shīa Muslims that prompted him upon his return to Arabia to preach against the beliefs and practices of those groups. In addition, he also preached against those Sunni Muslims he encountered in Arabia, whom he believed were lax in their adherence to Muslim Law (*al-Sharia*).

The most influential among Ibn Abd al-Wahhāb's works is the *Book of Monotheism; Being Right of God over [His] Slaves*,[9] where he outlines each "proper" belief and practice based on a list of quotes from the *Quran*, the sayings and deeds of the Prophet Muhammad and his companions, and occasional references to Ahmad ibn Taymiyya (d. 1328). The last was also notorious for declaring the infidelity and apostasy of non-conformists to the letter of the *Quran*. Ibn Taymiyya, in turn, based his religious judgments on Ahmad ibn Hanbal (780–855), the founder of the Hanbali School of jurisprudence, who in his time resisted the rationalist intellectual movement of the *Mu'tazila* School of the eigth and ninth centuries. The *Mu'tazila*, who claimed the *Quran* was a human creation and not revealed as an ultimate word of God and argued that the power of reason is equal to revelation in its ability to arrive at religious truth, ultimately lost the battle to the traditionalists of the Hanbali and other religion-based schools.

Centered on Hanbali jurisprudence and on Ibn Taymiyya's religious judgments, Wahhābī doctrine views Islam as obedience to a set of rules that enforce the belief in one God, the performance of certain duties, and the prohibition against committing forbidden acts.[10] Wahhābī doctrine denounces beliefs or practices that potentially violate monotheism as heresies. It considers those who practice those heresies to be infidels (*Kuffar*) and apostates (*Murtaddoun*), who deserve capital punishment. It also sanctions holy war (*jihad*) against those who know of Islam but do not accept it.[11]

Wahhābī doctrine privileges adherence to the text and to transmitted tradition (*naql*) over reason ('*aql*). It forbids innovation (*Bida*'), even if it does not contradict the *Quran* or the *Hadith* (narratives or accounts of the biography and teachings of the Prophet Muhammad).[12] The doctrine permits original, independent interpretation (*ijtihad*) of an issue not specifically discussed in the *Quran* or the *Hadith* only as long as it does not contradict with those sources and if scholars overwhelmingly agree to it (*ijmā*').[13] It commands that worship and prayer in any form and for any reason be directed only to God, not to prophets or saints. It considers any form of prayer directed towards someone other than God to be a polytheistic practice. The only exception is made concerning those who approached the Prophet Muhammad during his lifetime, asking him to pray to God on their behalf.[14] To avoid falling into polytheistic practices, the doctrine forbids the veneration of graves, erecting tombs on top of them, traveling to visit them, or praying near them.[15] Moreover, a Muslim is not under obligation to follow or imitate (*taqlid*) anyone other than the Prophet Muhammad.[16]

Around 1745, Ibn Abd al-Wahhāb joined forces with Muhammad ibn Saud (d. 1765), who saw in Ibn Abd al-Wahhāb's teachings a religious mission that he could employ to satisfy his ambition for conquest.[17] Ibn Abd al-Wahhāb taught that those who do not accept his preaching and join his movement are enemies of Islam, who ought to be fought against and suffer enslavement and the confiscation of their properties. In the following religious judgments, Ibn Abd al-Wahhāb distinguished four kinds of infidels who must be fought against:

> First, that whoever is aware of the Prophet's [Muhammad] religion, but does not follow it and is also aware that he is practicing a polytheistic religion, but does not forsake it.... Second, that whoever is aware of the above and insults the religion of the Prophet of God, or favors other clerics rather than a promoter of unification [i.e., myself].... Third, that whoever knows, loves, and practices unification [monotheism], and who knows polytheism and then forsakes it, but who also hates one who comes to unification and loves one who remains a polytheist.... Fourth, that whoever is clear of all of the above, but whose countrymen declare their animosity to unification, follow polytheists, and side with them in war with us.[18]

This doctrine became the ideology that enabled Ibn Saud to establish his political dominion over rival clans; it was preached as being identical to the one practiced at the dawn of Islam, when the Prophet Muhammad is believed to have combined religious, judicial, political, and military functions in his person. Therefore, the principle of monotheism (*tawhīd*, also translated as "unification"), upon which the Wahhābīyya was based was not merely a reinstatement of the obvious belief in one and only one God. Rather, it was also enforced as a principle of political unification, whereby people pledge allegiance to the House of Saud and acknowledge its exclusive right to rule as enforcers of Wahhābī doctrine. Thus, the religious terror implied by the notion that God condemns nonbelievers and apostates to incineration in eternal hell on the Day of Judgment was appropriated by Wahhābī doctrine to maximize popular allegiance to the rule of the House of Saud. Opposition to its rule implied apostasy, which God punished by eternal fire. However, until that Day of Judgment arrived, God's Law (*sharī'atu allah*) must be enforced on earth by the threat to kill nonconformist males above the age of puberty, loot their property, enslave their women and children, and confiscate their dwellings.[19] In this way, Islam is understood as a sword (*sayf al-Islam*) to terrorize non-Muslims into submission (*islam*) and to terrorize Muslims lest they fall into apostasy (*ridda*).

This alleged revival of the era of the dawn of Islam was based on a division of powers between the Houses of Ibn Abd al-Wahhāb and Ibn Saud. An understanding was reached between the two men to cooperate and establish a state, bequeathing their power to their descendants in a manner that gave religious authority to the House of Ibn Abd al-Wahhāb (later known as the House of al-Shaykh, in reference to the title of *Shaykh* earned by Ibn Abd al-Wahhāb for his religious credentials) and temporal authority to the House of Ibn Saud. Both men pledged their Houses to enforce Wahhābī doctrine by the sword in order to establish their rule over much of the Arabian Peninsula.

Beginning in 1746, Ibn Abd al-Wahhāb and Ibn Saud formed bands that raided adjoining territories. By 1773, Riyadh fell to Muhammad ibn Saud's son, Abd al-Azīz (d. 1793). From there, the Saudi-Wahhābī alliance expanded its control over central Arabia and then between 1801 and 1805, an army led by Abd al-Azīz ibn Saud took Mecca and Medina and expanded Saudi rule farther to the north, over southern Iraq and Syria.[20] The conquests added to the Houses of Saud and of Abd al-Wahhāb considerable wealth from looting, alms-giving taxes (*zakāt*), and fines for disobedience of religious rules.[21] The Wahhābī doctrine was imposed in all of the conquered territories, which entailed the destruction of shrines venerated by non-Wahhābī Muslims.

From 1811 to 1818, Egypt's Ottoman-appointed, ethnic Albanian ruler, Muhammad Ali, sent several expeditions that ended Saudi control of the Arabian Peninsula. Later, in 1824, the Saudi-Wahhābī alliance surged again and fought with the rival clan of al-Rashid, the traditional allies of the Ottomans, over the control of territories until 1891, when it lost to al-Rashid and went into exile in the region of what is now called Kuwait. In 1902, Abd al-Azīz ibn Saud initiated a military campaign to recapture territories lost by his ancestors. By 1921, he defeated the al-Rashid clan in central Arabia, and he ousted the Hashemite clan from Mecca and Medina in 1925, establishing what is known today as the Kingdom of Saudi Arabia, where Wahhābī doctrine is enforced.

A parallel and independent movement to return to the age of the ancestors, known in Arabic as *al-Salafiyya*, also took place following the close Muslim encounters in the nineteenth century with the more advanced European military powers. It produced an intellectual movement that aimed at reversing the decline of Muslim civilization through a return to the era of the devout ancestors (*al-salaf al-sālih*), which was presumed to have prevailed in the formative years of Islam. The movement was based on the idea that the decline of Muslim power was precipitated by forsaking the practice of Islam in its purest form. Its first proponent, Jamāl al-Din al-Afghānī (1838–1897), was a Persian Shīa intellectual who attempted to reconcile Islam and science.[22] While in Egypt, he mentored the future grand mufti Muḥammad Abduh (1848–1905), who in turn collaborated with two Syrian scholars, Tāhir al-Jazāirī (1852–1920) and Jamāl al-Dīn al-Qāsimī (1866–1914). The three formed circles of friends in Egypt and Syria, criticizing the tradition of imitation (*taqlīd*) and the rigid adherence to Muslim Law. They demanded that reasoning (*ijtihād*) and consensus (*ijmā'*) be given preference over the literal text of revelation.[23]

The majority of the next generation of Salafi clerics abandoned the teachings of al-Afghānī and Abduh in favor of the literal Hanbali school of Islamic Law, the teachings of Ibn Taymiyya, and the Wahhābīyya. The remaining evolved into a form of Muslim-Arab nationalism, but eventually also endorsed the

Wahhābīyya. The nationalist trend also saw a positive role for the Umayyad dynasty in the rise of Muslim power. The fact that the Umayyad was the most Arab of the subsequent Muslim dynasties paved the way for the movement to Arabize Islam. Its chief propagator was the Syrian intellectual Muhibb al-Dīn al-Khatīb (1886–1969), a disciple of Tāhir al-Jazāirī. Al-Khatīb and others stressed the particular role of the Arabs in Islamic history and envisioned an Arab nation as a means for restoring Muslim political power.[24] However, Al-Khatīb also eventually declared his support for the House of Saud and became the most visible defender of Saudi-Wahhābī politics and religious practices.[25]

In the 1930s, the ideas of the Salafi movement were converted into political action programs by the Muslim Brothers (*al-Ikhwān al-Muslimūn*), an organization that emerged in Egypt and Syria from the fusion of Salafi Islamic societies.[26] It was founded in 1928 in Egypt, as the Association of the Muslim Brothers, by a 22-year-old public school teacher, Hasan al-Bannā (1906–1949), who is said to have memorized the Quran in his early childhood.[27] In 1933, al-Bannā gave himself the title of its Supreme Guide, which he modeled after Hitler's title as *Führer*. He appointed missionaries, who preached in mosques and in public gatherings elsewhere, recruiting new members. In this period, the activities of the Brothers centered on grassroots efforts that established religious schools and charity networks and provided limited medical services.

Al-Bannā brought the Muslim Brothers into the realm of politics after the 1936 clashes between Jewish settlers and Arabs in Palestine. His support of the Palestinian Arab cause gained him prominence in Egypt as well as in Syria, and this enabled his organization to recruit Egyptian army officers and spread its network of followers to Syria, where an association was founded in 1937 under the leadership of Mustafā al-Sibāī (1915–1965).[28]

Al-Bannā's advocacy of violent resistance to the British presence in Egypt landed him in prison in 1941. By this time, his organization had formed underground militias who wished to violently overthrow the monarchy and the parliamentary system established in 1936 by British rule. Those militias' informal participation in the 1948 Arab–Israeli war drew attention to the Brothers as an underground force posing a threat to the Egyptian government. As a result, shortly after the war, the government of Prime Minister Mahmoud al-Nuqrāshī ordered the organization to be dissolved, imprisoned many of its members, and confiscated its properties. In response, a member of the Muslim Brothers assassinated the Prime Minister on December 28, 1948. Soon after, al-Bannā himself was assassinated, on February 12, 1949, by unknown assailants. In 1965, a plot to overthrow Abd al-Nāsir's regime led to the arrests and executions of Muslim Brothers leaders, including its most prominent ideologue, Sayyid Qutb (1906–1966). Qutb, who had been sent in 1948 by the ministry of education to the United States, expressed in his writing a profound dislike of Western lifestyles and became an active member of the Muslim Brothers.[29] He attributed infidelity (*takfīr*) to the Muslim societies of his time[30] and advocated assassinations as legitimate means to ascend to power.[31] He was imprisoned and released twice before his third arrest, trial, and execution.

The doctrine of the Muslim Brothers as developed by al-Bannā, Qutb, and al-Sibāī does not differ in substance from the doctrine of the Wahhābī Salafiyya as practiced in Saudi Arabia. Both consider Islam to be a divinely revealed order that organizes all aspects of human life. For them, it is a system of belief, value, and law; a rite for worship; an identity; and an enforcement mechanism for all of these. They believe it is an order applicable to all humans at all times. Both groups oppose attempts to reconcile religion with philosophical analysis because they believe past attempts at such reconciliation led to sectarian divisions that weakened the position of Muslims in facing the Western physical, cultural, and ideological invasions.

However, the Muslim Brothers differ in appearances from the Wahhābī Salafiyya. The Brothers have abandoned their robes for Western suits and replaced their long beards with nominal ones. In their politics, they accepted the modern state instead of the caliphate and accepted elections as the means to gain power. They presented themselves as a democratic alternative to the ruling royal families. Moreover, faced with competing socialist ideas in the 1940s, Qutb and al-Sibāī formulated the notion of Islamic socialism, where the state guarantees private property but also represents the interests of the community by controlling the use of individual fortunes and deducting from them the poor tax (*zakāt*).[32] Yet, like the Wahhābī Salafiyya, the Brothers were willing to enforce Muslim law with the power of a police state and to attribute infidelity, apostasy, or heresy to anyone who challenged their self-declared monopoly over the literal interpretation of Muslim scriptures and enforcement of Muslim law.[33] In both doctrines, the state is seen as an instrument for eliminating sin as defined in Muslim scriptures rather than for maintaining peace.

The challenge for the Muslim Brothers was to deploy the power of the state to re-Islamize the many aspects of people's lifestyles in Egypt and Syria that had been "corrupted" by modern Western culture. In addition to the legal, educational, tax, and banking systems, Western influence could also be seen in women's clothing; forms of greeting; the use of foreign words in speech and the language of music, art, and ideas; and the use of the Christian calendar. The Brothers wanted to create an authentically Muslim state, but with an elected leader who would eventually embrace all the Muslim peoples. The aim of this Islamic State would be to enforce Muslim law within its borders and to send out missionaries to evangelize Islam throughout the world. Yet today, after the overthrow of the Muslim Brothers' government in Egypt and the shattering of its dream, al-Qaeda and its currently more powerful progeny, ISIS, have penetrated the ranks of the Muslim Brothers everywhere in the Arabic-speaking world. In the eyes of the believers, Wahhābī ideology has gone beyond theory and has had success on the ground that surpasses the short-lived Egyptian electoral triumph of the Muslim Brothers. This trend is clearly seen in the Palestinian circles of the Muslim Brothers, where Hamas has been penetrated by Wahhābī elements who had graduated from the religious schools in Saudi Arabia and Sudan.[34]

Inward-looking Wahhābīyya turns outward

Because of their unstable rule in the eighteenth and nineteenth centuries and their relatively meager resources, the ideological influence of the Saudi-Wahhābī alliance was largely confined to Arabia. However, the dramatic surge in oil revenue in the last quarter of the twentieth century enabled them to use this surplus to fund missionary activities, first in the Muslim world and then beyond. It initially expanded into Afghanistan with the help of a Western-supported anticommunist jihadi insurgency, and then moved into Pakistan through missionary networks and the funding of charities. In recent decades, the formation of worldwide charity networks spread Wahhābī doctrine to almost all Muslim communities around the world, a fact that helps explain the recent influx of jihadi fighters from more than 80 countries to Syria and Iraq.

In addition, Arab migrant workers in the Saudi state, who were obliged to send their children to Saudi schools, reared a new generation of non-Saudis who had absorbed the Wahhābī doctrine. Upon their return to their respective countries, they spread the Wahhābīyya through informal networks and played a crucial role in the rise of al-Qaeda in Syria, Iraq, and elsewhere by taking advantage of the power vacuum created briefly by the weakening of states where the Arab Spring uprisings erupted. Through formal and informal channels, the Saudi-Wahhābī alliance supports Salafi-Jihadi groups using various appellations. For instance, a sampling of those groups in Syria is the Army of Islam, the Islamic Free Levant, and al-Qaeda Organization in the Levant: al-Nusra Front. Among them, al-Qaeda dominates the northwestern part of Syria bordering Turkey, the Qalamoun Mountains between Syria and Lebanon, and various parts of the Golan Heights, while al-Qaeda's renegade spawn, the Islamic State of Iraq and the Levant (ISIS), rules eastern Syria and western Iraq, and also dominates large swaths of Yemen and Libya.

While the Wahhābī Salafiyya flourished in Saudi Arabia in the twentieth century, the Muslim Brothers faced leftist-nationalist military regimes in Egypt and Syria who stood against their rise to power. Having been outlawed in Egypt since January 12, 1953, many of the Brothers went into exile in Jordan, Saudi Arabia, and Qatar. But even in those countries, they still posed a threat to the royal families of the Arab kingdoms and emirates that hosted them. Accordingly, their influence was confined to the intellectual realm, while their missionary networks operated underground to spread d their doctrine.

In Syria, the Muslim Brothers demonstrated unrelenting hostility to the Baathist takeover in 1963, which led to the 1964 uprising in the city of Hama and to their being outlawed. They subsequently went underground and pursued a program of assassination against Baathist and Alawi officers from the early 1970s on, which intensified after the 1979 Aleppo Artillery School massacre, where Alawi cadets were singled out and shot, and culminated in the 1982 Muslim Brothers' takeover of the city of Hama. That armed rebellion was quelled with brutal force, and a purge of suspected sympathizers followed in what became known as the "Hama Massacre." It was not until the Arab Spring uprisings of 2011 that the Muslim Brothers of Syria and Egypt came back to the political scene, with support from two sources. One was the prince of Qatar, Hamad Āl-Thāni, who used the Brothers' patronage to transform his tiny emirate into a regional power. The other was the Justice and Development Party that rules in Turkey and aspires to restore the Ottoman Empire.[35] The Justice and Development Party that by and large adopted the ideology of the Muslim Brothers but under the rubric of "Justice and Development," played a major role in facilitating the militarization of the Syrian version of the Arab Spring uprising with the help of the United States and Qatar, under the banner of the "Free Syrian Army" (or FSA). The FSA is far from being a cohesive regular army, and is actually composed of many small armed brigades, which have mostly adopted names of historical Sunni Muslim figures or religious labels.[36]

Despite the different organizational origins of the Wahhābīyya and the Muslim Brothers, the Syrian conflict has proved that the rank-and-file of the two groups do not see fundamental differences between them, as they easily shift from one group to another, while their leaders readily brand their rivals as apostates to morally justify their execution or assassination.

Because Sunni Islam does not acknowledge religious hierarchy, it became the prerogative of any literate "pious" Muslim who acquires a following, through self-promotion, to claim the title of preacher (*dāʿiah*) and to attribute unbelief (*takfīr*) to potential infidels or apostasy (*irtidād* or *ridda*) to fellow Muslims, charges that warrant capital punishment.[37] The recent spread of satellite and internet-based media significantly contributes to the proliferation of Wahhābī-inspired religious entrepreneurship that feed off the easy business of selling hate to the susceptible Muslim masses and raises a new generation of evangelical, outward-looking jihadi fighters eager to sacrifice themselves and many others in the cause of imposing "God's Law" (*sharʿu allah*) upon "His worshippers" (*ʿibadu allah*).

From al-Qaeda to the Islamic State

The U.S. and British invasion of Iraq in 2003 provided a perfect opportunity for the new generation of Wahhābī-inspired youth to put their education into practice. The power vacuum created by the ill-fated decision by the U.S. governor in charge of Iraq, Paul Bremer, to dismantle the Iraqi state and its army created by Saddam Hussein attracted the Wahhābī cottage industry into that no man's land, where the holy warriors (*mujahedeen*) were able to hunt infidels and thereby allegedly to attain the eternal bliss promised for them by the scriptures. Among those was a Jordanian Bedouin, Ahmad al-Khalayleh, from the tribe of Bani Hassan, who dropped out of high school as soon as his father died and pursued petty criminal activities.[38] After his first imprisonment for possession of drugs and for sexual assault, his mother placed him in a religious school belonging to the Husayn bin Ali Mosque in Amman hoping to save him from a life of crime.[39] The religious education he received attracted him to join the holy warriors' in the border region between Afghanistan and Pakistan in 1989, near the end of the

U.S.- and Saudi-sponsored anti-Soviet insurgency, where he became acquainted with Osama bin Laden's network. Upon his return to Jordan around 1993, he took the name Abū Musʻab al-Zarqāwi, where Abū means "the father of"; Musʻab is the name of his son, whom he named after a distinguished self-sacrificing warrior in the army of the Prophet Muhammad; and Zarqāwi refers his birth town Zarqa in Jordan.

Al-Zarqāwi helped in recruiting Sunni Muslims to join a group named the Soldiers of the Levant (*Jund al-Sham*) and had them sent to Afghanistan for training in Bin Laden's camps, presumably to prepare for the next stage of al-Qaeda's mission to "liberate" the nation-states of the Levant (Greater Syria) from its "apostate" regimes and enforce Muslim Law. However, the arrival of the U.S. Army in Iraq presented a better opportunity for Holy War against the "Crusaders,"[40] especially after Colin Powell's UN speech prior to the U.S. invasion, which propped up al-Zarqāwi as the most dangerous terrorist after Bin Laden. That speech elevated al-Zarqāwi to stardom in the eyes of the jihadi community and facilitated his quick move into Iraq and recruitment of fighters, with whom he formed the Monotheism and Holy War Group (*Jamaʻat al-Tawhīd wa al-Jihād*). From Iraq, he pledged allegiance to Osama bin Laden and began carrying out ferocious attacks against U.S. troops and suicide bombings throughout Iraq, especially among Shia worshipers, their leading clerics, and their most sacred shrines.[41] His group then became known as the Organization of the Jihadi Base in Mesopotamia (*Tanzīm Qaidat al-Jihād fi Bilad al-Rafidayn*), commonly referred to as al-Qaeda in Iraq (AQI), while al-Zarqāwi earned the title of its Prince (*Amir*).

In 2006, al-Zarqāwi unified other armed Iraqi resistance groups under the label "the Holy Warriors' Consultative Council" (*Majlis Shoura al-Mujahedeen*). Among those who joined him were former Baathist intelligence officers whom Saddam Hussein had placed as informants during the "Islamic Awakening"[42] of the 1990s in various religious schools close to mosques, to manipulate the worshipers and steer them when needed in his desired direction. However, those officers became genuine converts, as they found religious education to be closer to their conscience than the Baath party's secular ideology, or to whatever by that time had remained of its secularism. Moreover, the U.S. discharge of more than 100,000 employed by the Iraqi security apparatus and the army, without pay, made them easy converts to al-Qaeda's organization since they had fought U.S. troops in the same trenches as had their more fanatical brethren. Indeed it was one of those officers, Abū Abd Allah al-Baghdadi, who eulogized al-Zarqāwi on June 16, 2006, 10 days following his assassination by a U.S. airstrike.

Bin Laden appointed Abū Hamza al-Muhajer (the immigrant), also known as Abū Ayyub-al-Masri (the Egyptian), to succeed al-Zarqāwi. In October 2006, al-Masri expanded "the Holy Warriors' Consultative Council" to include more jihadi factions and formed the Islamic State of Iraq (*Dawlah al-ʻIraq al-Islāmiyah*), headed jointly by Abū Omar al-Baghdadi and al-Masri; the former was its prince and the latter was its Minister of War within a 10-member cabinet.[43] In April 2010, the cleric Abū Bakr al-Baghdadi assumed leadership after al-Masri and Abū Omar al-Baghdadi were killed in a U.S.-Iraqi operation. The second al-Baghdadi, a former imam of the Ahmad ibn Hanbal Mosque in Samarra, was well versed in the literalist Hanbali tradition, the earliest precursor of the Wahhābī School and is said to have earned a doctorate in Muslim Law and lectured on the subject at the Islamic (now Iraqi) University in Baghdad.[44]

In August 2011, following the outbreak of the Syrian conflict, al-Baghdadi delegated Abū Mohammad al-Golāni (*Jolāni*) to lead a military mission into Syria under the name "the Front to Aid the Levantines (*Jabhat al-Nuṣra li-Ahl al-Shām*)," or "al-Nusra Front." The latter quickly gained presence and recruits from the ranks of Syrian rebels commonly referred to as the "Free Syrian Army" in such Sunni-dominated cities as Daraa, al-Raqqa, Idlib, Dayr al-Zor, and Aleppo.

On April 8, 2013, in a key decision to outstrip the influence of al-Qaeda, al-Baghdadi declared the reunification of al-Nusra Front with the Islamic State of Iraq to form the "Islamic State of Iraq and the Levant" (ISIS), without consultation with al-Qaeda's leader, Ayman al-Zawāhiri. In response, al-Golāni considered the reunification a hostile takeover, while many of his subjects defected from his ranks and joined ISIS. In June 2013, al-Zawāhiri ordered them to maintain the separation of the two organizations,[45] but al-Baghdadi rejected al-Zawāhiri's ruling, praised his three predecessors starting with al-Zarqāwi, rebuked al-Qaeda's leader, and declared al-Qaeda irrelevant to the new state of ISIS.[46] While al-Golāni, on the other hand, maintained his allegiance to al-Zawāhiri and renamed his faction "the Organization of al-Qaeda-al-Nusra Front."[47] Since then, both groups continue to engage in intermittent battles over the control of territories, the most recent of which is for total control of the Yarmouk Palestinian refugee camp in the southern part of Damascus.

While ISIS fought all those who refused allegiance to al-Baghdadi, al-Qaeda was more flexible. It coordinated with Wahhābī-inspired and Saudi-funded groups, such as the Army of Islam[48] and the Free Islamic Levant. Al-Qaeda also coordinated with ethnic Turkmen and groups sympathetic to the neo-Ottoman project, who were named after medieval Turkish or Mameluke conquerors, such as the Movement of Nour al-Din al-Zenki and al-Zaher Baybars. In addition, al-Qaeda worked with others affiliated with the Muslim Brothers, such as al-Tawhid Brigade and those who constituted the "Free Syrian Army,"[49] classified by the U.S. as "moderate" rebels and recipients of U.S. military aid.[50] Yet, despite that coordination, al-Qaeda maintained an upper hand over those groups and disciplined their rank and file with imprisonment and executions when they disobeyed its commands.[51]

On December 12, 2015, al-Golāni met with four journalists representing the armed Syrian rebel groups. They addressed him with the title of a religious authority, "Shaykh," and pleaded with him for over an hour to disassociate his organization, al-Nusra Front, from al-Qaeda for the sake of not bringing down the West's wrath upon the "Syrian revolution" and those whom they referred to as the "Free Syrian Army."[52] However, al-Golāni was admittedly at ease with his al-Qaeda affiliation and offered no apology or justification. Below, I paraphrase

The ideological origins of ISIS 119

his responses within (' ') marks and, where necessary, I quote him verbatim within the standard quotation marks (" ").[53]

> Al-Golāni: "We know that in reality there is no such thing as the Free Syrian Army. It is not an army or one organization, but it is a slogan and a name that people have used. It is composed of many groups and leaders. People happened to have cast on them the label of the Free Syrian Army." 'We started the jihadi movement four years ago. There is at the moment a prevailing perception among a few people that our association with al-Qaeda is a major factor that is preventing the fall of the Syrian regime. However, those people are making false assumptions.' "If tomorrow morning we were to disassociate ourselves from al-Qaeda, will that lead to the demise of Bashar al-Asad? No, it will not." 'The manner in which Americans or other international entities classify groups or countries is not based on whether they are al-Qaeda.' "Saddam Hussein, for example, was not al-Qaeda. However, he freed himself from international hegemony. The same is the case with North Korea and Cuba; they were all fought against and suffered the consequences. Whether or not one belongs to al-Qaeda has no bearing on this matter." 'The West has a problem with the ideologies of those groups or countries. We cannot meet with the West in any possible manner. "Regardless of whether we are with al-Qaeda, we will not forsake our principles. We will keep saying we want to abide by Muslim Law and will continue to seek that end and will continue with Holy War. We will not compromise or stop a battle with the enemy. This matter is an unquestionable principle of the religion of Islam. Integrating ourselves with the West would mean straying from Islam."

However, Al-Golāni continued by reassuring his audience that his organization does not seek a fight with the West:

> "At this moment, we are only seeking to fight Bashar al-Asad and Hezbollah who antagonize the Levantines. Al-Qaeda has many objectives, but we as al-Nusra Front in the Levant do not seek to fight the West." 'However, regarding our political vision for the future, we have a strategy that is constrained by Muslim Law; it is not a political policy the way the West or Americans envision a policy' because "Muslim Law is not subject to change or replacement. For instance, when you say: There is no God but God and Muhammad is the Messenger of God, will there be a day when this statement changes or is replaced by something else? We will keep on fighting until we enforce God's Law. We will not change as long as we live. We may adopt few tactical changes regarding certain battles or other matters relating to certain events according to prevailing realities, but we will never undergo fundamental changes."

Al-Golāni continued to refute the notion that his organization's international affiliation tarnishes the image of the Syrian rebels, who are claim to be, by and large, local jihadi fighters and do not want to be tainted with the perception that they are aided by an international organization such as al-Qaeda. He said:

> "As Muslims we have a right to depend on our Muslim peoples. The Muslim world cannot be divided by mountains or rivers, or by other Muslim states. That division is an injustice perpetrated a century ago [i.e., after the fall of the Ottoman Caliphate]. We [al-Qaeda] only recognize one Muslim nation imposed upon all states."

The substance of al-Golāni's responses is no different from those of any devout Muslim who is frank about seeking the imposition of Muslim Law in the Land of Islam (*Dar al-Islam*). For instance, as a political representative of the Muslim Brothers and in response to demonstrators' demanding "the people want imposing God's Law," the deposed former elected president of Egypt Muhammad Morsi also publicly announced that his ultimate aim was the imposition of Muslim Law.[54] This implies that Al-Qaeda, ISIS, or any force that intends to revive the era of the ancestors (*al-Salaf*) of the first Muslim caliphate must seek to "cleanse the Land of Islam from apostates,"[55] subdue the infidels living in conquered territories by having them pay the infidel tax (Quran 9:29), and then take the battle to the Land of War (*Dar al-Harb*)[56] until the Day of Judgment is called by the Lord of the Universe (*Rab al-'Alamīn*).

The popular Muslim belief that God populated earth to enforce His law upon His creation is the religious basis of the notion that Holy War must persist against "apostates" in the Land of Islam and against non-Muslims in the Land of War until conformity to Muslim scriptures is universal or until the Day of Judgment. This belief is so fundamental to most Muslims' collective understanding of Islam that when authors trained in religious discourse write to fellow Muslims, they refer to it in a casual manner that requires no further justification.[57] Yet, successive Muslim rulers were not always persistent, strict, and systematic in enforcing Muslim Law in the Land of Islam, or in waging war against the inhabitants of the Land of War. Historically, Muslim rulers displayed a variety of attitudes towards non-conformists within conquered territories and sometimes struck peace agreements with non-Muslim political dominions and referred to them as the Land of Truce (*Dar al-Sulh*) that were contingent upon payments to exclude them from the Land of War.[58]

However, as Tables 6.1 and 6.2 show, the Wahhābī attitude, singularly adopted in territories controlled by the Saudi-Wahhābī alliance, ISIS, al-Qaeda, and the Taliban continues to be meticulous in enforcing Muslim Law. In contrast, territories controlled by the governments of Syria and Iraq (among other predominantly Muslim states) allowed the coexistence of various theological and legal traditions. Because of the plurality of those religious traditions, coupled with the non-enforcement of Muslim Law, many Levantines (those living in the "Levant," or in the lands of the Eastern Mediterranean) and Iraqis, who are Muslims by birth, are able to live thoroughly secular lifestyles that can hardly be distinguished from their non-Muslim compatriots.

Table 6.1a Comparative practice of Islam

Sentences under Muslim Criminal Law				The Pillars of Islam					Territories Where Enforced or Practiced
Flogging	Stoning	Amputation	Beheading	Pilgrimage	Fasting	Charity Tax	Regular Prayer Regime	Declaration of Faith	
				Practiced	Practiced	Practiced	Practiced	Practiced	Government-Controlled Syria
				Practiced	Practiced	Practiced	Practiced	Practiced	Government-Controlled Iraq
Enforced		Enforced	Enforced	Practiced	Enforced	Enforced	Enforced	Enforced	Wahhābī Saudi Arabia
Enforced	Enforced	Enforced	Enforced	Practiced	Enforced	Enforced	Enforced	Enforced	Wahhābī ISIS
Enforced	Enforced	Enforced	Enforced	Practiced	Enforced	Enforced	Enforced	Enforced	Wahhābī al-Qaeda

Table 6.1b Comparative practice of Islam

Muslim Civil Law						Women's appearance	
Slavery	Holy War	Infidel Tax	Gender & Religious Inequality	Polygamy/Inheritance	Killing Apostates	Shapeless Clothes, Headscarf, or Face Cover	Territories Where Practiced or Enforced
	Practiced		Practiced	Practiced/Enforced		Practiced	Government-Controlled Syria
	Practiced		Practiced	Practiced/Enforced		Practiced	Government-Controlled Iraq
Practiced until 1961	Practiced		Enforced	Practiced/Enforced	Practiced	Enforced	Wahhābī Saudi Arabia
Enforced	Enforced	Enforced	Enforced	Practiced/Enforced	Enforced	Enforced	Wahhābī ISIS
Enforced	Enforced	Enforced	Enforced	Practiced/Enforced	Practiced	Enforced	Wahhābī al-Qaeda

In a recent interview, the former chief cleric of the Grand Mosque of Mecca, Adel al-Kalbani, candidly admitted that ISIS's Salafi-Wahhābī ideology is also adhered to in Saudi Arabia, and he pointed out the prevailing misguided emphasis on its televised executions of apostates instead of a discussion of the putative religious basis of these executions:

> ISIS is a Salafi offshoot. Some allege that intelligence agencies created ISIS, but an intelligence agency cannot create something new; it only exploits that which exists. They [intelligence agencies] exploited those who carry that [Salafi] ideology; ISIS's ideology is Salafi; it is not based on the Muslim Brothers' ideology; it is not based on [Sayed] Qutb's [work]; it is not Sufi; it is not Ash'ari [one of the four legal schools]; it [ISIS] makes inferences from our [Wahhābī] books and principles. For that reason, most of those who criticize it do not criticize its ideology but its actions. For example, consider the case of the apostate. Why don't we discuss who should execute him? We only discuss the method of killing him and say that it is monstrous and hurts our image in the eyes of the world. Does this mean if we only kill him in a manner that does not hurt our image then it would be fine?... No doubt ISIS was given weapons and ammunition and was allowed to expand and grow. However, those who were behind it benefited [from its rise] by using our principles; those principles are in our books, and [their promoters] are among us. We have those who have the same ideology, but who apply it in a modified manner. You know of many cases when a few journalists were killed [in Saudi Arabia] because of certain religious judgments [issued against them], even a few religious scholars were rebuked and their blood was shed, all of which were based on Salafi religious judgments, not on judgments from outside the Salafi tradition.[59]

If we were to take al-Kalbani's assessment of ISIS's ideology to its logical conclusion, then our understanding of the brutal images of mass or individual executions broadcast by ISIS as a criterion for defining terrorism should be the same for non-broadcast images of mass beheadings carried out in Saudi Arabia.[60] Moreover, almost all of what seemed to be appalling actions of ISIS in the eyes of the world community, such as raids into neighboring territories, killing of captured adult males, enslaving women and children, and confiscating their belongings and real estate, were practiced in the period of the formation of the first Saudi state,[61] and in turn were also justified by Quranic verses and the anti-apostasy wars (*hroub al-ridda*) led by his first successor Abu Bakr.[62] For that reason, al-Kalbani is asking us not to focus on the actions but on the ideology that inspires and justifies them. That ideology is Wahhābī religious doctrine based on enforcing the rules laid out in the Quran and on the imitation of the actions of the Prophet Muhammad and of his companions. If we were to consider ISIS or al-Qaeda's killing of infidels and apostates,[63] enslaving their women and children,[64] and confiscating their belongings and real estate[65] to be a form of terrorism that ought to be included in the War on Terror, then we need to focus on the religious basis of that terror.

ISIS was not born in vacuum; it is only boldly enforcing widely accepted beliefs in the Arab and Muslim world. For instance, "The Consolidated Arab Penal Law" adopted by the Arab League in 1996 defines apostasy and its punishments in a manner similar to the Wahhābī doctrine. Below is an extract from chapter seven of that penal code:

> Chapter 7
> Apostasy
> Articles 162–165
> Article 162: The apostate is a male or female Muslim who forsakes the Islamic religion by uttering clear words to that effect, committing acts that demonstrate such intent, or one who insults God, his Messengers, or the Islamic religion, or purposefully changes any letter in the *Quran*.
>
> Article 163: An apostate is punished by execution when intent is proven and when he insists on his apostasy after given three days to repent.
>
> Article 164: The apostate's repentance is accepted after he reverses his infidelity and does not repeat it more than twice.
>
> Article 165: All the apostate's actions after he is declared an apostate are considered absolutely void and all of the wealth he gained from those actions shall be transferred to the state's coffers.
>
> This section dealt with apostasy based on God's saying (who wishes a religion other than Islam, it will not be accepted from him).
>
> The above Articles were based on Quran 2:285…, Quran 4:152…, and on the Prophet's (God's prayer and peace be upon him) saying: "If one changes his religion, kill him" and his other saying "a Muslim's blood can be shed only under three conditions: Infidelity after belief, adultery after marriage, and killing without right." … There is disagreement [among the four legal schools] on whether all of the apostate's wealth is confiscated, or only what he earns after apostasy…. The Shafi'i, Maliki, and Hanbali schools rule that the apostate's entire wealth should be confiscated, while the Hanafi rules that only the wealth earned after apostasy can be confiscated…[66]

From the above extract, one may conclude that apostasy from Islam is a major crime that amounts to grand treason. It is an act similar to defection to enemy ranks in time of war. The notion that apostates ought to be punished by death is ingrained in many Muslims from childhood and is why the notion found its way to the Arab League's constitution. The fear of being accused of apostasy explains why many Muslims are reluctant to criticize religious authority and why they tend to side with co-religionists on religious or benign secular disputes. Given the high cost of defection, many Muslims tend to conform in public, even if few privately are not fully convinced of the justness of their cause. For them, solidarity with a fellow Muslim takes precedence over all other considerations, assuming of course that both belong to the same sect.

al-Qaeda's user guide for transformation into ISIS

In 2004, a 112-page document appeared on the World Wide Web in the Arabic language in which one of al-Qaeda's ideologues writing under the assumed name of Abu Bakr Naji elaborated on the process by which "the Muslim Community (*al-Umma*) can be delivered from servility and lead humanity toward the path of divine guidance and salvation."[67] It is a "Salafi Jihadi" project, which Naji believes is the most effective one compared to rival projects declared by various brands of the Muslim Brothers.[68] According to Naji, the establishment of the Islamic State must proceed through three stages. In the first stage, holy warriors activate "the thorn of spite and exhaustion (*shawkat al-nikāya wa al-inhāk*)," whereby they undertake intensive terrorist operations for an extensive period to exhaust the "apostate regimes" and ultimately paralyze their abilities to control the societies upon which they preside. The weakening of the regimes and their eventual fall is bound to result in savage chaos. The second stage is that of "the management of savagery (*idarat al-tawahush*)," when the Jihadi organizations present themselves as new authorities that manage that savagery of that chaos by offering themselves as enforces of a much needed order to people who are desperate to have any kind of order. The holy warriors' administration would take place at the beginning on small local scales where they will provide essential goods and services, maintain order, provide Islamic education, raid adjacent territories, plunder their wealth, and then gradually consolidate those territories until in the third "thorn of empowerment (*shawkat al-tamkīn*)" stage when they declare an Islamic State.

An intervention by imperialist powers will not help the collapse of the apostate regimes because that intervention will clearly demonstrate to the Muslim masses that the imperial powers are the enemies of Muslims. As hostilities against such intervention intensifies, any invading force will eventually withdraw in utter defeat, for modern Western societies live a life of luxury and will not tolerate the sacrifices necessary for them to prevail in an extended war. During this process:

> spite attacks against the Crusader and Zionist enemy must be varied in kind and broadened not only in the entire Muslim world, but also outside it, if possible, to distract the enemy alliance and drain it as much as possible.... [Moreover] as we confront the people of the cross and their apostate helpers and their soldiers, we have no objections to shed the blood of the latter; indeed we believe it is an utmost duty to do so unless they repent, perform prayers, and pay the charity tax, and devote all religion to God only.[69]

Those measures are necessary because the times that Muslim world is presently going through resembles the period immediately after the death of the Prophet

Muhammad, where "the weak believers thought that the blade of the sword of Islam had been withdrawn after the Messenger's death, God's prayers and peace be on him. They grasped the opportunity to abandon this religion" and the majority of the Arabian Peninsula fell into apostasy.[70] The conditions of the Muslim community also "resembles the period of the beginning of the holy war at the time of the prophet. We therefore need to massacre and take actions like those that were undertaken against Bani Qurayza and others."[71] For, "we do not engage in truce with the apostate enemy, even if that may be possible with the original infidel."[72] Finally, "we affirm that our battle is a battle of unification against infidelity and of belief against polytheism; it is not an economic, political, or social battle."[73]

The War on Terror: what is to be done?

It is misleading to believe that terrorist groups everywhere and at all times are born out of marginalization, unemployment, and poverty. Since the beginning of the Arab Muslim conquest of the Fertile Crescent, its native inhabitants were dispossessed, impoverished, marginalized, murdered, or deported in mass by regimes whose aim was to enforce a rigid interpretation of Muslim Law.[74] Yet, throughout centuries of that unjust process, most of those victims did not produce terrorist groups in reaction to their ill treatment. Moreover, none of the regions currently occupied by ISIS are inhabited by destitute people. The Arab and non-Arab Muslim fighters flocking into Syria since the rebellion of the Sunna commenced in late 2011 are not coming in from poor regions. None of their leaders are from socially disadvantaged backgrounds. A few of the youth who came from Western Europe to participate in the holy war against those they were told were apostates and infidels may have indeed been from places in the Muslim diaspora where they were not able to assimilate. Whether they were marginalized by the host European societies or were self-marginalized by failing to assimilate is worthy of investigation by other scholars.[75]

The Muslim diaspora is not the only diaspora in the Western world. Non-Muslims from the Middle East or elsewhere in Asia have flourished and continue to flourish in the West. The influx of jihadi fighters into Syria and Iraq from Europe came not to seek employment but a share of the glory promised to them for "cleansing" the Land of Islam from "apostates and infidels" and also to create a caliphate of which the communities they grew up in only dreamed.

The organization that has currently crystallized itself as ISIS is a religious movement par excellence. It has been in the making in the Arabian Peninsula for more than two centuries, but has turned outward toward the Fertile Crescent in the past half century and toward the rest of the world in the last two decades. Today, it has culminated in a revolutionary force that uses Wahhābī ideology as a political and military tool to gain power in a manner similar to the way the Saudi–Wahhābī alliance used it in the eighteenth century to unify and rule the Arabian Peninsula. While various regional and international powers used ISIS's territorial expansion to attack their enemies or advance their strategic interests,

The ideological origins of ISIS 127

none of them created ISIS. The U.S. allowed ISIS to grow and was reluctant to stem its advance possibly so its ferocity would help to carve out a Sunni Muslim region from the Black Sea in the north to the Red Sea in the south that separates Shia Iran and Iraq from Lebanon's Hezbollah and their Syrian allies, an attempt to redraw new maps that will presumably provide more security to Israel.[76] In their effort to create an independent state, the Iraqi Kurds used ISIS to attack the Shia militia and Iraqi army that represented the Iraqi central authority.[77] The Turkish government, in turn, used ISIS to simultaneously fight the Syrian Kurds and the Syrian government.[78]

As was the case with the Wahhābī expansion in the Arabian Peninsula of the eighteenth century, today ISIS and its allies' path to real power in the Fertile Crescent were paved by brute human force, not by divine intervention. Therefore, the arming of the militant evangelical Muslim fundamentalists, not only ISIS and al-Qaeda, must be stopped and their urban concentrations must one by one be placed under siege and subsequently taken over and the militants disarmed. Policy makers in the United States must swallow their pride, stop arming the Islamist rebels in Syria, and help with rebuilding the Syrian and Iraqi armies. This is a necessary short-term step if any long-term process of rebuilding a potentially peaceful Middle East is to be considered. While there is sufficient reason to believe that their disarming will eventually succeed,[79] their ideological foundation will remain intact and will reemerge unless it is taken seriously, instead of issuing the apologetic reactions we often hear.[80] These armed groups represent the same dark forces that terrorized the inhabitants of the Muslim world lest they question prevailing religious dogmas and that have maintained their dominance since the decline of Arab–Islamic civilization centuries ago.[81]

The dominant Western perspective on the War on Terror cannot be separated from the historical and religious contexts that frame that conflict for Muslims and Westerners alike. Mitigating religiously-inspired terrorist activities in the Middle East or against Western targets cannot succeed without the Muslim community's curbing of Wahhābī expansionism and then reversing it. The movement to return to the era of the Devout Ancestors has proven to be catastrophic for the Muslim world. Its outward direction toward the West is testing the patience of Western societies. Russia, as evidenced by its controversial intervention in the Syrian conflict, has already shown its resolve, while China is still quietly watching from a distance and has not entered the fray. The form of a Chinese reaction to a future Wahhābī expansion within the Chinese Muslim regions is difficult to predict, but the Uighurs in those regions have long chafed under the rule of the dominant Han population and some have engaged in what the Chinese government deems terrorist activities.

The secular Middle Eastern perspective

Claims such as Islam is a religion of "equality and freedom,"[82] or that the atrocious violent acts seen in the Middle East are being committed by "adherents to such faith that has been created out of a person's own ideology" that are unrelated to "the true teachings of Islam"[83] because "Islam is a religion of peace"[84] are brushed aside by thorough readers of Muslim scriptures, whether they are Islamists or secular, as apologetic and accommodating to Western pressure. While Islamists are adamant in their rejection of secular ideology, there is a general consensus among secular Middle Easterners that a reversal of Wahhābī expansionism requires devout Muslims and prudent Western policy makers to reassess an ostrich-like attitude that denies the religious basis of the rise of Salafi-Jihadi groups and admit to the following:[85]

1. The ideologies of al-Qaeda, ISIS, the Muslim Brothers, and rival jihadi groups are derived from a fundamentalist interpretation of Muslim scriptures. These groups are not "twisting" contents of religious scriptures, or forming extreme interpretations of them. They are applying them verbatim. If we care to hear, they are telling us that the Prophet Muhammad was also a statesman, who established a state that they want to restore by imitating his actions. He was guided by revelation to use violence to establish and maintain that state and that is why ISIS calls its state "a caliphate by the way of the prophecy."[86] The leaders of those groups are clerics and experts in Muslim scriptures. Recently, Yusuf al-Qaradawi, the de facto grand mufti of the Muslim Brothers, said to a would-be suicide bomber on al-Jazeera's program "Muslim Law and Life" that "you cannot blow yourself up amidst people whenever you want; you can only do it when the group asks you to blow yourself up. You do it for the group; not for yourself."[87]
2. The state that Salafi-Jihadi groups seek to establish treats non-conformists in a manner similar to that of other totalitarian states.
3. The return of Islam to the era of the Devout Ancestors does not provide solutions to contemporary social problems, let alone solutions to the phenomenon of terrorism. Nor does it stop the Western violent reaction known as the "War on Terror."
4. Islam is a religion and as such should not be enforced by the power of any state.
5. The terrorism committed against Western targets is usually not a reaction to poverty; the perpetrators of 9/11 were not poor nor did they grow up in poor neighborhoods. Al-Qaeda's former leader was born to a billionaire Saudi family. The present al-Qaeda leader is a medical doctor from a privileged Egyptian family.
6. Terrorist groups do not necessarily arise because of repressive governments. Using relative standards, the French, Belgian, and U.S. governments are hardly repressive when compared to many Asian and African states, yet their jihadi citizens have targeted fellow citizens based mainly on their religious identities.
7. The Islam we currently know through the text of the Quran and the biography of the Prophet Muhammad is mediated through at least 150 years of oral transmission and therefore was not only subject to human error and inconsistencies, but was also not intended to be taken as a universal moral

system valid for all times.[88] Many of the Quran's verses were religious judgments that were considered just in seventh century standards, but they are not just in modern standards. In his lecture on "Rationality in Jurisprudence" on October 13, 2012, the religious scholar Ahmad al-Qabanji, who also claims to be a descendent of the Prophet Muhammad, said:

> You ask, How did [modern] terrorists become terrorists? Have you seen what their Prophet did [in reference to mass beheadings and assassinations]?!... The rule of the Prophet was in keeping with the reason of his time. If the Prophet were here today, he would absolutely not do what he did when he was a ruler—or else he would be like Osama bin Laden.[89]

The Western perspective

Since 9/11, much has been said from Western perspectives about the ethics and efficacy of anti-terrorism strategies.[90] Casualties from Iraq, Afghanistan, and Pakistan resulting from the "War on Terror" since the 9/11 attacks amounted by 2012 to a minimum of 1.3 million. That figure today is likely to be around two million, the vast majority of whom were non-combatants.[91] Such high death toll has deepened and broadened a sense of injustice perpetrated by the West upon Muslims, the fact which provided Salafi Jihadi groups reason to prove the "evilness of the West" and to mobilize Muslims to fight it at all cost.

A moral question keeps on presenting itself. If human life has value in the West within constitutional limits, then what is the moral base that permits Western authorities to take the lives of those who do not fall under their political authority? Moreover, what is the moral base by which Western electorates give their representative authorities the discretionary power to kill non-combatant foreign nationals beyond their political domains?[92] Such ethical problems have prompted few Western intellectuals re-examine the moral basis of the War on Terror; others, such as Scott Atran, went on further to understand the motivation for young people, especially Europeans, to join terrorist organizations, such as al-Qaeda and its daughter ISIS.

Conclusion

This secular Middle Eastern assessment of the War on Terror for reversing the spread of the Wahhābī version of a militant evangelical Muslim fundamentalism in the Middle East recommends a persistent effort to re-educate many future generations. The process has to begin by recognizing that many religious institutions in the Middle East are deeply rooted in dogmatic thinking and deference to religious authority, which often disguise power relationships that reproduce despotic hierarchies. People's understanding of religion as a set of dogmas and commandments inherited from their ancestors will not change without the activation of critical thinking. For critical thinking to be revived, people need to

130 M. Tomass

acquire logical skills and apply them to the study of their intellectual past and the history of their religions in a relatively secure environment. Without an intellectual revolution to dismantle the prevailing religious institutions' dominance over intellectual activities, we are bound to see a resurgence of terrorist organizations that feed upon the aliments of modern societies and give its adherents the false hope of acquiring eternal pleasure in the afterlife by taking the lives of their fellow humans who do not accept their narrative or do not conform to their ethical standards. Because security is a pre-requisite for education, today's militant evangelical Muslim fundamentalists must be disarmed as a first step in any attempt to reverse their expansion.

Notes

1 See a Syrian rebel leader, the highest-ranking defector from the Syrian army, Abd al-Jabbar al-Ukaidy (around minute 11:00 of the below-mentioned video), speaking in reference to the new regional Sunni military alliance led by Saudi Arabia: "everyone who is not Sunni is an infidel," only the Sunna are Muslims. "الملف ـ التحالف الإسلامي الذي أعلنت عنه السعودية," YouTube Video, December 17, 2015, posted by "HalabToday Fm," 11:00/34:30, www.youtube.com/watch?list=PLd 6zytedotWrmXDCTdp4av0_HCVhRBWfW&v=D3fOuLfoiA4.
2 See a list of recent items sent to the Syrian rebels in Jeremy Binnie and Neil Gibson, "Infantry Weapons, US arms shipment to Syrian rebels detailed," *IHS Jane's Defence Weekly*, April 8, 2016, www.janes.com/article/59374/us-arms-shipment-to-syrian-rebels-detailed.
3   Through its Conflict and Stability Fund the [British] government is spending £2.4 million on private contractors working from Istanbul to deliver "strategic communications and media operations support to the Syrian moderate armed opposition [to the Syrian government]" (MAO), while the British government claims it has set up media operations for moderate fighters.
         (Ian Cobain, Alice Ross, Rob Evans, and Mona Mahmood, "How Britain funds the 'propaganda war' against Isis in Syria," *Guardian*, May 3, 2016, www.theguardian.com/world/2016/may/03/how-britain-funds-the-propaganda-war-against-isis-in-syria)
4 For alternative definitions, see Charles Webel, *Terror, Terrorism, and the Human Condition* (New York: Palgrave Macmillan, 2004), 5–13.
5 See John Bingham, "ISIS attacks on Christians and Yazidis 'genocide' say peers," *Telegraph*, February 23, 2016, www.telegraph.co.uk/news/religion/12169130/ISIS-attacks-on-Christians-and-Yazidis-genocide-say-peers.html.
6 After the Syrian Army took back the town of al-Qaryatayn from ISIS, Nabil Fayad, a native of the town retells in painful details the process through which it was re-Islamized by ISIS. Nabil Fayad, "وعادت القريتين... حرّة حزينة" [And al-Qaryatayn Is Back… Free and Sad]," April 4, 2016, www.nabilfayad.com.
7 Most of the foreign fighters have joined ISIS or al-Nusra, which by definition are Salafi-Jihadi, but few formed their own organizations, such as the Army of the Mujahidin and al-Ansar, an umbrella group for those arriving from the Caucuses with the aim of establishing an Islamic State.
8 The most comprehensive list of the Syrian anti-government fighting groups according to the BBC's sources comprises about 1,000 groups and total about 100,000 fighters. They commonly have names with a religious significance, such as al-Farouq [a title given to the second caliph] Brigades, the Monotheistic Brigade [the Muslim Brothers'

The ideological origins of ISIS 131

armed wing], the Conquest Brigade, the Army of Islam, the Islamic Brigade, the Islamic Free Levant, the Brigades of the Grandsons of the Messenger [the Prophet Muhammad] and many other groups. Those groups form "fronts" and also label them with a religious name, such as the Front for the Liberation of Islamic Syria, The Syrian Islamic Front (both labeled in the West as "moderate"), al-Nusra Front (the Syrian al-Qaeda), and the Islamic State of Iraq and Syria. For a complete list of the names of the subgroups, see "الأزمة السورية: دليل الجماعات المسلحة في سوريا," January 21, 2014, www.bbc.com/arabic/middleeast/2014/01/131213_syria_rebels_background. The anatomy of the Syrian rebel groups according to a London-based Saudi-owned, anti-Syrian regime source is composed of entirely Salafi-Jihadi groups, including the Muslim Brothers' al-Tawhid Brigade which is classified as moderate. See Ashraf Abu Jalala, "هذه أبرز الجماعات المُقاتلة في سوريا," Elaph, December 2, 2013, http://elaph.com/Web/news/2013/12/853070.html.
9 Muhammad ibn Abd al-Wahhāb, *Mu'allafāt al-Shaykh al-Imām Muhammad ibn 'Abd al-Wahhāb*, 5 vols. (al-Riyād: al-Mamlakah al-'Arabīyah al-Sa'ūdīyah, Jāmi'at al-Imām Muhammad ibn Sa'ūd al-Islāmīyah, Usbū' al-Shaykh Muḥammad ibn 'Abd al-Wahhāb, 1983); and 'Abd Allāh al-Sālih 'Uthaymīn, *Muhammad ibn 'Abd al-Wahhab: the man and his works* (London: I. B. Tauris, 2009), 77–108.
10 Ahmad ibn Taymiyya, "al-Hisba fi al-Islam," in *Isa ibn Rumayh, Majmu'* (Cairo: n.p., 1921), 232, 277, 281–282.
11 Husayn ibn Ghannam, *Ta'rikh Najd al-Musamma: Radat al-Afkar wa al-Afham li Murad Hal al-Imām wa Ta'dad Ghazawat Dhawi al-Islam*, vol. I (Cairo: n.p., 1949), 107, 150.
12 Ibid., 143.
13 Muhammad ibn 'Abd al-Wahhab, *Kitāb al-Tawhīd alladhi huwa Haq Allah ala al-Abīd* (Cairo: n.p., 1927), 59.
14 Sulayman ibn Suhman, *Kashf Ghayaheb al-Zalam an Awham Jala' al-Awaham* (Riyad: n.p., 1956), 274.
15 Muhammad ibn Abd al-Wahhab, *Kitāb al-Tawhīd alladhi huwa Haq Allah ala al-Abīd*, 42–44, 46, 50–53.
16 Husayn ibn Ghannam, *Ta'rikh Najd al-Musamma*, 52–55.
17 'Abd Allāh al-Sālih 'Uthaymīn, *Muhammad ibn 'Abd al-Wahhab*, 56.
18 Muhammad bin Abd al-Wahhab, *Fatawa wa Masael al-Imam al-Sahykh Muhammad ibn Abd al-Wahhab*, collected, edited, and verified by al-Sahykh Saleh bin Abd al-Rahman al-Atram and Muhammad bin Abd al-Razzaq al-Darwish (n.p., n.d.), 9–10, http://ia800206.us.archive.org/16/items/waq50041/04-2_50044.pdf.
19 M. Lecker, "al-Ridda," in *Encyclopaedia of Islam*, Second Edition, eds. P. Bearman, Th. Bianquis, C. E. Bosworth, E. van Donzel, W.P. Heinrichs, Brill Online, 2016, Reference, Harvard University, http://referenceworks.brillonline.com.ezp-prod1.hul.harvard.edu/entries/encyclopaedia-of-islam-2/al-ridda-SIM_8870.
20 Hasan al-Rubki, *Lam' al-Shihab fi Sirat Muhammad ibn Abd al-Wahhab*, ed. Ahmad Abū Hakima (Beirut: n.p., 1967), 112.
21 'Uthmān ibn Bishr, *Unwan al-Majd fi Tarikh Najd* (Beirut: n.p., 1967), 169.
22 Jamāl al-Dīn al-Afghānī, *al-Radd alā al-Dahriyyīn* (Cairo: n.p., 1925).
23 D. D. Commins, *Islamic Reform: Politics and Social Change in Late Ottoman Syria* (New York: Oxford University Press, 1990).
24 Israel Gershoni, "Arabization of Islam: The Egyptian Salafiyya and the rise of Arabism in pre-revolutionary Egypt," *Asian and African Studies* 13 (1979): 22–57.
25 Qusayy Muhibb al-Dīn al-Khatīb, *Fihrist al-Maktaba al-Salafiyya* (Cairo: n.p., 1978).
26 Z. S. Bayyūmī, *al-Ikhwān al-muslimūn wa al-djamāāt al-islāmiyya fi al-ḥayāt al-siyāsiyya, 1928–1948* (Cairo: n.p., 1979).
27 Hasan al-Bannā, *Madjmūat rasāil al-imām al-shahīd Hasan al-Bannā* (Beirut: Dār al-Andalus, 1956).

28 Mustafā al-Sibāī, *al-Sunna wa-makānatuhā fi al-tashrī al-islāmī* (Cairo: Dār al-Urūba, 1961).
29 Salāh Abd al-Fattāh al-Khālidī, *Sayyid Qutb: min al-mīlād ilā al-istishhād* (Damascus: n.p., 1991).
30 Sayyid Qutb, *Maālim fi al-Tarīq* (Cairo: n.p., 1964).
31 Danny Orbach, "Tyrannicide in Radical Islam: The Case of Sayyid Qutb and Abd al-Salam Faraj," *Middle Eastern Studies* 48:6 (2012): 961–972.
32 Sayyid Qutb, *al-Adāla al-ijtimāiyya fi al-Islām* [*Social Justice in Islam*] (Cairo: n.p., 1952).
33 Sayyid Qutb, *Fī Zilāl al-Qurān* [*In the shadows of the Qurān*], 30 vols. (Cairo: n.p., 1953–1959).
34 "Wahhābī ideology penetrates the basis of Hamas," *al-Akhbar*, April 8, 2016, www.al-akhbar.com/node/255571.
35 Cinar Kiper, "Sultan Erdogan: Turkey's Rebranding into the New, Old Ottoman Empire," *The Atlantic*, April 5, 2013, www.theatlantic.com/international/archive/2013/04/sultan-erdogan-turkeys-rebranding-into-the-new-old-ottoman-empire/274724.
36 "الجربا يطلب من السعودية زيادة الدعم للجيش الحر" Aljazeera.net, April 23, 2014; "والسعودية وراء تقدّم الجيش السوري الحر في الشمال والجنوب خالد خوجة: دعم تركياً" *Turk Press*, May 7, 2015, www.turkpress.co/node/8214.
37 See a Muslim scholar's definition of infidelity and apostasy in Munqidh bin Mahmoud al-Saqar, *Al-Takfir wa Dawabitahu* (Rabitat al-cAlam al-Islami [World Muslim League], n.d.), 9–11, https://ia800302.us.archive.org/2/items/waq116931/116931.pdf. See also an English translation of a recent effort to explain the proliferation of declaring the apostasy of Muslims by fellow Muslims in Taha Jabir al-Alwani, *Apostasy in Islam: A Historical and Scriptural Analysis*, trans. Nancy Roberts, abridged by Alison Lake (International Institute of Islamic Thought, 2012), http://iiit.org/iiitftp/publications/Bibs/Books-in-Brief%20Apostasy%20in%20Islam%20A%20Historical%20and%20Scriptural%20Analysis.pdf.
38 Jean-Charles Brisard and Damien Martinez, *Zarqāwi: The New Face of al-Qaeda* (Cambridge, UK: Polity Press, 2005), 3–13.
39 Ibid., 15.
40 Colin Powell's famous 2003 UN speech claiming that al-Zarqāwi was already in Iraq coordinating along with Saddam Hussein planned terrorist attacks against Western targets was one of the long list of fabrications that the U.S. Secretary of the State uttered that day. Prior to the U.S. invasion of Iraq, Al-Zarqāwi was a minor and largely unknown figure outside Jordan. وثائقي ابو مصعب الزرقاوي الجزء 1, YouTube Video, July 1, 2010, posted by "WWW.TA3NA.COM," www.youtube.com/watch?v=i2po2jgWI_c.
41 See footage of the blowing up of the Imam Ali Mosque in al-Najaf where worshipers lost their lives including Ayatollah al-'Uzma Muhammad Baqer al-Hakim, "السلام تفجير مرقد الإمام علي عليه," YouTube Video, May 8, 2011, posted by "قناة مزارات," www.youtube.com/watch?v=lhK6NZeQg3o.
42 See "The New Media and the Islamic Awakening" in Mark Tomass, *The Religious Roots of the Syrian Conflict: The Remaking of the Fertile Crescent* (New York: Palgrave Macmillan, 2016).
43 In a 2007 audio tape, Bin Laden defends the Islamic State of Iraq against all those fighting it: أسامة بن لادن يتحدث عن الدولة الإسلامية والأحداث الجارية, YouTube Video, March 25, 2015, posted by "ISIS HMH," www.youtube.com/watch?v=VZ35oLfujRE.
44 Ruth Sherlock, "How a talented footballer became world's most wanted man, Abu Bakr al-Baghdadi," *Telegraph*, November 11, 2014, www.telegraph.co.uk/news/worldnews/middleeast/iraq/10948846/How-a-talented-footballer-became-worlds-most-wanted-man-Abu-Bakr-al-Baghdadi.html.
45 الظواهري يأمر دولة العراق والشام بالإنسحاب من سوريا, YouTube Video, November 8, 2013, posted by "Aljadeedonline," www.youtube.com/watch?v=mTP_lfV1foU.

46 داعش ترد على الظواهري وتؤكد بقائها في العراق وسوريا, YouTube Video, November 8, 2013, posted by "Aljadeedonline," www.youtube.com/watch?v=9JzT9c9fW0M.

47 مبايعة أبي محمد الجولاني قائد جبهة النصرة للشيخ الظواهري القائد العام للمجاهدين, YouTube Video, May 26, 2013, posted by "mohamed sayed," www.youtube.com/watch?v= USkf0fa9Vm8.

48 See Zahran Alloush, the Commander of the Army of Islam, reassuring people of the closeness of his organization to al-Nusra Front, to the extent that he is willing to trade his religious authorities with theirs to serve as judges: "مع جبهة النصرة وعلاقة قائد جيش, النصرة أبي محمد الجولاني الإسلام بقائد جبهة قنبلة قائد جيش الإسلام," YouTube Video, November 21, 2013, posted by "ArourSwords," www.youtube.com/watch?v= -aEoXOfot-k&ebc=ANyPxKrAgDRUFdSBomIhV7qR1KL9s_fhpl_aCXxCfmS8QI3 HMgxQKVDkcivQh3Wi9jjJR23QWpL8cYzNSug0RLflxvBy0voc6A&spfreload=1.

49 See the first army defector and self-declared "Free Syrian Army" leader's reaction to the praise of al-Nusra Front, "قائد الجيش الحر رياض الأسعد يتحدث عن جبهة النصرة," YouTube Video, March 20, 2013, posted by "Free Syria 201," www.youtube.com/ watch?v=clpDKTEXiDc.

50 "فصائل عسكرية في حلب تعلن اندماجها باسم حركة نور الدين الزنكي", posted September 16, http://all4syria.info/Archive/251877; and see al-Jazeera's interview with the leader of al-Tawhid Brigade Abd al-Qader Saleh, where he claims that "al-Nusra Front are our brothers": Al-Jazeera, December 12, 2012, www.aljazeera.net/news/reportsand interviews/2012/12/21; Ernesto Londoño and Greg Miller, "CIA begins weapons delivery to Syrian rebels," Washington Post, September 11, 2013, www.washington-post.com/world/national-security/cia-begins-weapons-delivery-to-syrian-rebels/ 2013/09/11/9fcf2ed8-1b0c-11e3-a628-7e6dde8f889d_story.html; Barbara Starr, "U.S. delivers 50 tons of ammunition to Syria rebel groups," CNN, October 12, 2015, www. cnn.com/2015/10/12/politics/syria-rebel-groups-ammunition-50-tons/; Adam Entous, "U.S., Allies to Boost Aid to Syria Rebels," The Wall Street Journal, November 4, 2015, www.wsj.com/articles/u-s-allies-to-boost-aid-to-syria-rebels-1446682624.

51 See an interview with a "Free Syrian Army" commander about his arrest and torture by al-Nusra Front: YouTube Video, posted by "AlAanTV," August 19, 2015, "في الجيش الحر عن أسباب قتاله لداعش جبهة النصرة تستجوب قياديا," www.youtube.com/ watch?v=6wDNb2dvkCw. See also an earlier al-Nusra arrest of a "Free Syrian Army" commander in the city of Daraa: "جبهة النصرة الحر في مدينة درعا جنوب سوريا تعتقل أحد قادة الجيش," YouTube Video, posted by "AlAnTV," May 5, 2014, www. youtube.com/watch?v=Xzx0NikOF6U; and see a graphic description of a "Free Syrian Army" commander of his arrest and torture by al-Nusra: "بتعذيب وإهانة العقيد في الجيش الحر أيسر خطبا في درعا جبهة النصرة تقوم," YouTube Video, posted by "AlAnTV," May 7, 2014, www.youtube.com/watch?v=khJyzKCnzhg.

52 Three months after this meeting, the Islamic Ahrar al-Sham, one of the components of the U.S.-sponsored Army of Conquest assassinated al-Nusra Front's commander, apparently in an effort to pressure it to disassociate itself from al-Qaeda. See Abd Allah al-Umari, "عناصرها على يد «أحرار الشام» والتوتر يخيم على إدلب جبهة النصر تعلن الاستنفار العام بعد مقتل أحد," April 13, 2016, al-Quds al-Arabi, www.alquds.co.uk/?p= 515700.

53 "لأول مرة على شاشة أورينت نيوز .. تصريحات قائد جبهة النصرة أبو محمد الجولاني," You Tube Video, posted by "Orient News", December 12, 2015, www.youtube.com/ watch?v=xXgeoFIUY8Y, my translation.

54 See "وجهة نظر الرئيس محمد مرسي في تطبيق الشريعة الإسلامية," YouTube Video, posted by "7yatELsalaf," December 1, 2012, www.youtube.com/watch?v=DKoL1xMIabo.

55 See a justification for the religious judgment to kill apostates based on the sayings of the Prophet Muhammad in Fatwa No. 68357, "شبهة وجوابها حول قتل المرتد والزاني المحصن," October 20, 2005, http://fatwa.islamweb.net/fatwa/index.php?page=showfatwa& Option=FatwaId&Id=68357.

56 A. Abel, "Dār al-Harb," in *Encyclopaedia of Islam*, April 2, 2016, http://reference works.brillonline.com.ezp-prod1.hul.harvard.edu/entries/encyclopaedia-of-islam-2/dar-al-harb-SIM_1700.

57 See an author's casual reference to "the Land of War" as a commonly agreed upon term in the London-based, pro-Saudi electronic newspaper *Elaph*: Hamza bin Muhammad al-Salem, "Syaset al-Qaradawi ka Fiqh [the policy of al-Qaradawi as Islamic Jurisprudence]," June 28, 2013, www.elaph.com/Web/NewsPapers/2013/6/820970.html.

58 D. B. MacDonald; A. Abel, "Dar al-Ṣulḥ." *Encyclopaedia of Islam*, Second Edition. Edited by: P. Bearman, Th. Bianquis, C. E. Bosworth, E. van Donzel, W. P. Heinrichs. Brill Online, 2016. Reference. Harvard University. May 27, 2016, http://referenceworks.brillonline.com.ezp-prod1.hul.harvard.edu/entries/encyclopaedia-of-islam-2/dar-al-sulh-SIM_1708.

59 "Leading Saudi cleric says IS and Saudi Arabia 'follow the same thought,'" *Middle East Eye*, January 28, 2016, www.middleeasteye.net/news/top-saudi-cleric-says-and-saudi-arabia-follow-same-thought-626782255.

60 Kim Bellware, "Mass Execution Is Part Of Saudi Arabia's Long History of Horrors," *The Huffington Post*, January 6, 2016, www.huffingtonpost.com/entry/saudi-arabia-mass-execution-history_us_568c43e1e4b0cad15e625f74.

61 Elizabeth M. Sirriyeh, "Suʿūd, Āl," in *Encyclopaedia of Islam*, May 5, 2016, http://referenceworks.brillonline.com.ezp-prod1.hul.harvard.edu/entries/encyclopaedia-of-islam-2/suud-al-SIM_7215.

62 M. Lecker, "al-Ridda," in *Encyclopaedia of Islam*, May 5, 2016, http://reference works.brillonline.com.ezp-prod1.hul.harvard.edu/entries/encyclopaedia-of-islam-2/al-ridda-SIM_8870.

63 See footage of al-Nusra Front slaughtering Syrians for being apostates: YouTube Video, posted by "EyeOHawk," June 28, 2013, "النصرة» الإجرامية الوهابية بإدلب يَذبحونَ», «جبهة مُرتزقة عصابات مذهبية لأسباب سوريين مُواطنين ",www.youtube.com/watch?v=Ku UcMrKtweM&list=PLltntqUQr3xEnkWLGYMdYvjNb9GzA2r8Q.

64 See a prominent Egyptian cleric teaching in a sermon that when Muslims invade a territory, all of the conquered people, their property, and real estate become the property of the Islamic State and are distributed to the holy warriors, including the women, who have to be their sex slaves: "الحويني : احكام الاسلام بخصوص السبايا والغنائم بعد الحرب", YouTube Video, posted by "Heba Ezzat," September 27, 2015, www.youtube.com/watch?v=fej0sah-SrQ. See a woman Professor, Suad Saleh, of Al-Azhar University of Cairo, Egypt, issuing a religious judgment that Muslim fighters can enslave their enemies' women that are captured in war and use them as sexual surrogates because according to Muslim Law, "an enemy that had captured Muslim land, attacked Muslims, or attacks Muslim beliefs, then it would be legitimate to wage war on them and enslave their women and have the Muslim leaders, army, or any Muslim enjoy having sex with the slaves in the same manner that he enjoys having his wives": "مفكر حر" by posted "شاهد استاذة ازهرية تفتي لداعش بالتمتع بسبايا الحروب ملك يمين", January 9, 2016, http://mufakerhur.org/?p=46907. See also Julian Robinson, "ISIS execute 250 women in Mosul for refusing to become sex slaves under the group's 'sexual jihad,'" *Mail Online*, April 20, 2016, www.dailymail.co.uk/news/article-3549668/ISIS-execute-250-women-Mosul-refusing-sex-slaves-group-s-sexual-jihad.html#ixzz46TsilOfR.

65 Elisa Griswold, "Is This the End of Christianity in the Middle East? ISIS and other extremist movements across the region are enslaving, killing, and uprooting Christians, with no aid in sight, the *New York Times*, July 22, 2015, www.nytimes.com/2015/07/26/magazine/is-this-the-end-of-christianity-in-the-middle-east.html?_r=0. Nina Shea, "ISIS Genocide against 'People of the Book'—How Long Will Kerry Continue to Talk around It?" National Review, March 16, 2016, www.nationalreview.com/article/432884/isis-genocide-christians-middle-east-iraq-syria-john-kerry-state-department.

The ideological origins of ISIS   135

66 The Arab League, The Council of Justice Ministers, 128–129, posted by The Arab Center for Legal and Juridical Research, a sub-organ of the Arab League, http://carjj.org/node/237, My translation.
67 Abu Bakr Naji, "إدارة التوحش : أخطر مرحلة ستمر بها الأمة" [*Idaret al-Tawahush: Akhtar Marhala Satamur biha al-Ummah* (Markaz al-Dirasat wa al-Buhouth al-Islamyya, n.d.) The management of savagery: The Most Critical Stage the Muslim Community Will Pass Through, (Center for Islamic Studies and Research, [2004]), 3. See a 2005 English translation by William MaCants, https://azelin.files.wordpress.com/2010/08/abu-bakr-naji-the-management-of-savagery-the-most-critical-stage-through-which-the-umma-will-pass.pdf https://pietervanostaeyen.files.wordpress.com/2015/02/idarat_al-tawahhush_-_abu_bakr_naji.pdf. Elsewhere, the book is by published by (Dar al-Tamarud [House of Rebellion], Syria, n.d.), http://almenhag.blogspot.com/2015/06/idarat-altawahhush-abubakr-naji-pdf.html.
68 A rival author, presumably presenting the Muslim Brothers' program, disapproves of the tactics presented in al-Qaeda's manifesto, but accepts its ultimate objectives. See Ghazi al-Tawba, "قراءة في كتاب القاعدة عن ادارة التوحش" [A Reading in al-Qaeda's Book on the Management of Savagery]," January 29, 2015, www.aljazeera.net.
69 Ibid., 31. My translation.
70 Ibid., 32. My translation.
71 Ibid., My translation.
72 Ibid., 33. My translation.
73 Ibid., 112. My translation.
74 See chapters 2 and 6 in Mark Tomass, *The Religious Roots of the Syrian Conflict*.
75 William McCants and Christopher Meserole, "Explaining Sunni Militancy Around the World," *Foreign Affairs*, March 24, 2016, www.foreignaffairs.com/articles/2016-03-24/french-connection.
76 Mark Tomass, *The Religious Roots of the Syrian Conflict*, 206–209.
77 Michael Rubin, "Kurdish official calls defeating ISIS 'a huge mistake,'" April 26, 2016, American Enterprise Institute, www.aei.org/publication/kurdish-official-calls-defeating-isis-a-huge-mistake; and ibid., "On Kurds, Kornets, and criticisms," April 27, 2016, www.aei.org/publication/on-kurds-kornets-and-criticisms.
78 Steven Lendman, "More Evidence of Turkey's Support of the Islamic State (ISIS), in Liaison with US and NATO," *Global Research*, January 12, 2016, www.globalresearch.ca/more-evidence-of-turkeys-support-of-the-islamic-state-isis-in-liaison-with-us-and-nato/5500916; David Graeber, "Turkey could cut off Islamic State's supply lines. So why doesn't it?" *Guardian*, November 18, 2015, www.theguardian.com/commentisfree/2015/nov/18/turkey-cut-islamic-state-supply-lines-erdogan-isis; Barney Guiton, "'ISIS Sees Turkey as Its Ally': Former Islamic State Member Reveals Turkish Army Cooperation," *Newsweek Magazine*, November 7, 2014, www.newsweek.com/isis-and-turkey-cooperate-destroy-kurds-former-isis-member-reveals-turkish-282920.
79 Barak Mendelsohn and William McCants, "Experts Weigh In: What is the future of al-Qaeda and the Islamic State?" *Brookings*, January 7, 2016, www.brookings.edu/blogs/markaz/posts/2016/01/07-future-of-al-qaida-and-isis-mendelsohn-mccants.
80 See for instance, the 27-page letter endorsed by 126 Muslim scholars to ISIS entitled: "Open Letter to Dr. Ibrahim Awwad Al-Badri, alias 'Abu Bakr Al-Baghdadi,' To the fighters and followers of the self-declared 'Islamic State', Peace and the mercy of God be upon you," September 19, 2014, www.lettertobaghdadi.com/pdf/Booklet-English.pdf.
81 See Mark Tomass, *The Religious Roots of the Syrian Conflict*, 103–106.
82 See the essay by a former Secretary General of the Organization of Islamic Cooperation, Iyad Amin Madani, "We Must Understand Why Some Muslims Turn Radical," *Time*, December 1, 2015, http://time.com/4128647/radicalization-of-muslims/.

83 This sample was taken from a multi-faith public gathering at which Imam Abd al-Hakim of the Muslim Community of Palm Beach County defended the religion he promotes. See George Bennet, "Parties Seem to Diverge on Muslims," *Palm Beach Post,* May 26, 2015.
84 Manal Omar, "Islam Is a Religion of Peace," *Foreign Policy,* November 9, 2015, http://foreignpolicy.com/2015/11/09/islam-is-a-religion-of-peace-manal-omar-debate-islamic-state/.
85 The conclusions I list below are based on my reading of unofficial and often anonymous opinions published in social media by either secular authors, or genuine Islamist revisionists.
86 An Arabic sign posted at the entrances of cities, towns, and villages: "على منهاج النبوة خلافة," see a sample in Haytham Mannaʿ, "داعش من هجرات الوهم إلى بحيرات الدم خلافة," *Al-Arab,* July 30, 2014, www.alarab.co.uk/?id=29105.
87 Author's recollection of a live interview in late November 2015.
88 Ahmad al-Qabbanji is a leading Shia religious scholar who is attempting to revive the Muʿtazila school of philosophy that accompanied the rise of Arab Muslim civilization. Among other things, he argues that the Quran cannot be treated as a verbal expression of God's will. See Yotam Feldner, "Liberal Iraqi Shi'ite Scholar Sayyed Ahmad Al-Qabbanji Calls For Reason In Islamic Discourse and Jurisprudence," Inquiry and Analysis Series Report No. 937, February 21, 2013, www.memri.org/report/en/print7015.htm.
89 Ibid., Alqabnji's public lectures are videotaped and posted on YouTube www.youtube.com/watch?v=rcT8EZSVfSo&list=PL59cEV8Fl3aPV3-bfQ3qlJK7LM9Iye 033. A summary of his background and views are posted in the Arabic language on his website www.facebook.com/DoYouEvenKnowLB/photos/pcb.532684270252803/532683840252846/?type=3&theater.
90 Charles Webel and John Arnaldi (ed.), *The Ethics and Efficacy of the Global War on Terrorism: Fighting Terror with Terror* (London, UK: Palgrave Macmillan, 2011).
91 See the complete report of Physicians for Social Responsibility, "Body Count: Casualty Figures after 10 Years of the "War on Terror," March 2015, www.psr.org/assets/pdfs/body-count.pdf.
92 In April 2016, a US air strike directed at an ISIS storage facility in Iraq allegedly killed 36 civilians belonging to the extended Zeidan family in a housing complex in the yabisat area near Mosul among whom were 17 women and 11 children. See Ali al-Saqa, "الغرباء فقط سيُقتلون" [only strangers shall be killed]," *al-Mayadeen,* May 26, 2016. See also Paul Wood, "The US is killing more civilians in Iraq and Syria than it acknowledges," *Guardian,* February 1, 2016, www.pri.org/stories/2016–02–01/us-killing-more-civilians-iraq-and-syria-it-acknowledges.

7 Winning the hearts and minds of the Pukhtuns of Afghanistan and Northwest Pakistan with altruism, public health and development, not by terrorism and counterterrorism

Sher Mohammed Khan

Introduction

The region of Afghanistan and Pakistan between the Oxus and Indus Rivers was in the news before 9/11 and continues to be in the news. Known as Waziristan ("land of the Wazir"), this region, comprising northwest Pakistan and Afghanistan as a whole, is very interesting because of its scenic beauty, history, archaeology, and culture.

The people living in Waziristan are called Pukhtuns, or Pushtuns or Pathans. Historically, it is said that people in this region, especially the Pukhtuns, belong to the lost tribe of Israelites. They have their own code of conduct called "Pushtunwali," which compels them to provide unquestioning "protection" to anyone asking for it.[1]

According to the Pukhtun "Hujra" (men's place), persons on the run who have committed some crime are to be given protection ("Panah"). During the Taliban rule in Afghanistan from the 1990s until the American invasion and occupation of Afghanistan shortly after 9/11, "terrorists" were given "Panah." For example, a special delegation went from Pakistan to Mullah Omar, former leader of the Taliban, to hand over Osama Bin Laden, but he refused because of "Pushtunwali." Today, the region and its borderlands are famous (or infamous) because of their seemingly never-ending catastrophes and are chiefly known in the West as the training ground for the 9/11 tragedy as well as for harboring and exporting "terrorists." Is this because of external factors, internal factors, or both nature or nurture? To address this question, an excursion through the region's history and geography is necessary.

The region's geography and history

The Hindu Kush Mountains and the world's largest mass of high, snow-capped mountains, including K2, are not very far from Waziristan. The region was part of the Persian Empire, established by Cyrus the Great in 559 BCE. Cyrus the

Great was not only a benevolent emperor, but there was progress and peace in the area during his time.

The region was controlled by the Achaemenian Empire (530–331 BCE) for almost 200 years, until Alexander the Great entered the scene. Alexander had a hard time when he entered this region and crossed with his army over the Khyber Pass to India. Alexander was injured in fighting in Massage, near Malakand, which was much later the scene of battles during the "Forward Policy" of the British. So the region has been subjected to wars for many years, which is probably no fault of the people living in the region.

Buddhism spread to South East Asia from this region. The silk route from China passed through this area. During the 1960s and early 1970s, this route was known as the "Hashish route," or "Hippy Route," because young Westerners traveled to Kabul, Peshawar, India, and Nepal. At that time, one could see young people on the roadsides, in the streets, in the villages, and in the cafes, puffing their cigarettes (joints) filled with "Charas," cannabis, and without any fear of suicide bombers. Prior to the 1980s, violence in any form towards travelers, or Westerners, was unheard of, presumably because of the built-in Pukhtun culture of hospitality and protection of strangers. These days, the route is known as the "Terrorist Route" in some circles.

However, prior to its settlement by today's well-known terrorists, the region has produced people like Sher Khan, aka Sher Shah Suri (1539–1554), who ruled for five years as King of India and was considered to be one of the "greatest [rulers] the world ever has produced and will produce" (according to a personal communication by S. A. Khan in 2009, when he visited the India office library for a presentation of his books). Ahmad Shah Abdali (1747–1773), for example, was another Pukhtun King. He came from Kandahar, the current base of the Afghan Taliban. Ahmad Shah Abdali ruled Afghanistan and Northern India and was one of the greatest conquerors who have ever appeared in Asia. His chief contribution lies in the fact that he was the creator of an independent Afghanistan.

In his dealings with the Afghans and Baluchis, Ahmad Shah Abdali pursued the principle of reconciliation. He tried to please and win over the people first, and the local chiefs who could not be reconciled were initially defeated and then treated kindly. Ahmad Shah Abdali won over the people by giving equal consideration to the many tribes of Afghans. In addition, he enforced many humane reforms in order to win their goodwill and cooperation. He stopped the form of punishment requiring the loss of limbs, nose or ears, and forbade his successors to revive this cruel practice.

The present political leaders in Afghanistan and Pakistan can and should emulate the character and habits of successful past rulers like Sher Shah Suri and Ahmad Shah Abdali, who put the welfare of their people first and acted without arrogance. Winning the hearts and minds of people in this region would be conducive to lasting peace, which in turn will lead to progress and prosperity.

In contrast, the first (1840–1842) and the second British Afghan Wars (1878–1880) are cited by historians as examples of misguided foreign policies leading to atrocities, deaths, and destruction, as usually happens when terrorism is met by counter terrorism. More recently, the region has become known for giving sanctuary to terrorists and exporting terrorism, which on the whole are due to external factors.

In the early 1970s, the route from Khyber Pass to Herat, a border town between Afghanistan and Iran, was peaceful and was well built. During this time I traveled on it several times to Herat and three times to London. One section of this highway was by constructed by the Russians, another section by the Americans, and the third by the Japanese.

At that time, Russia wanted to extend its influence over the region and so it trained Afghan soldiers, both in Kabul and Russia. Afghan students were also encouraged to seek higher education in Russian universities. Afghan King Zahir Shah (1914–2007) was removed by Muhammad Daud Khan (1909–1978), followed by an internal power struggle, mainly by left-leaning but inexperienced political parties.

Afghanistan had not learnt from its past. For example, during Britain's rule over India, King Amir Amanullah of Afghanistan was a modernizer and wanted to bring such modern transportation facilities as railways in the late 1930s. But British-controlled India did not want a hostile government on its northwest, one that was near Russia. The result was that religion was invoked, and, with the connivance of religious leaders and the British intelligence, the forward-looking King was replaced.

In the 1970s, the internal struggle continued, until Najibullah Ahmadzai (1947–1996) a medical doctor, trained and educated in Russia, took over. This time, instead of the British, it was the United States that did not want Russian influences in Kabul. So the U.S. found a willing partner in the person of Pakistan Military Strongman Zia-ul-Haq (1924–1988), a "religious bigot" and strong believer in "Strategic Depth."

The rest is history: During the 1980s, billions of dollars were funneled by the U.S. and Saudi Arabia through Pakistan to the mujahedeen resistance against the Soviet Union. Jihad was invoked, and the "warriors of god" were armed and trained. The CIA worked in cahoots with the ISI (Inter-Services Intelligence agency) of Pakistan. Osama Bin Laden was the product of these policies, and he lived in Peshawar, Pakistan, along with his Al-Qaeda followers, near where I lived. I had no idea of this at the time, but I came to know it when CNN was filming a documentary, "In the Shadow of Bin Laden."

During the decade-long Afghanistan War following the Russian invasion in 1979, for many Pukhtuns in Pakistan and Afghanistan the "infidel" was Russia, largely because of the preaching by radical Islamist mullahs to young Muslim boys in the religious seminaries funded by the ISI. Both local and foreign people encouraged, funded, trained, and fought the Soviet forces in Afghanistan.

The region was abandoned by the West after the defeat and withdrawal of the Russians in 1989, which culminated in the breakup two years later of the only superpower rival to the U.S., the Soviet Union. The victorious mujahedeen then treated the mosques in which they preached as disposable objects—to be used and discarded. Al-Qaeda organizers probably also felt that way. The consequences were summarized by Hillary Clinton, who in her book *Hard Choices* mentions the price paid by the West in general and the U.S. in particular for abandoning Afghanistan, "[in] 1989 the Soviets withdrew [and] we paid a grievous price for allowing the country to become a safe haven for terrorists."[2]

Today, the "infidel" is the "West"—because of the never-ending "War on Terror."

The "disease" of terrorism

Terrorism has been likened to a "disease." In contrast, health is defined by the World Health Organization (WHO) in 1948 as "physical, mental, social and spiritual wellbeing and not only absence of disease." Accordingly the perpetrators of *both* terrorism and counter terrorism can spread "disease."

Bee stings can be very painful. Similarly, both "terrorism and counter terrorism" are very painful. The old medical adage is that "prevention is better than cure." But when it comes to the application of this adage to terrorism in general and to Afghanistan/Pakistan region in particular, it is, "prevention is not only better, it is cheaper" than the "cure" of counter terrorism.

Terrorism is also likened to cancer, which according to Siddhartha Mukherjee, is the "emperor" of all maladies.[3] Cancer can be prevented and detected early. Most, if not all cancer-causing agents are known. One is atmospheric pollution, and bombing from the air, sea and land does cause pollution. When it comes to treatment, such aggressive and potentially mutilating measures as surgery and nuclear radiation work, but some cancerous tissues lurking in the background may grow and cause havoc. Cancer starts in individual cells, which proliferate, grow and invade—just like terrorism. But the human body has built-in defense mechanisms to combat disease. In the case of terrorism in this region, quality education—I repeat, quality education—and poverty alleviation will self-treat the "disease" of terrorism.

"Manmade" catastrophes, and such natural disasters as earthquakes, as well as the cultural tradition of retaliation, have done immeasurable devastation to the local environment and innocent people. Millions of people, especially children and women, have been displaced, their health has been damaged, and many have psychological problems. Currently, gastroenteritis has reached epidemic proportions. More than 100 polio cases were reported in 2014.

Women and children are by and large not harmed by the Pukhtuns, unlike terrorism and counter terrorism, whose victims are primarily children and women. The West's indiscriminate bombing from the air and shelling from the ground, during the so called "War on Terror," have maimed and killed children and women as they stay in their mud houses.

It is high time that the root causes of militancy and terrorism are identified and addressed, some of which are poverty, social injustices, unemployment, and poor governance. Prevention and early detection of maladies are not only more effective, but are cheaper, than waging an unending "war on terrorism." Consequently, the region is in turmoil both from internal as well as external factors, leading to the displacement of millions of people seeking refuge in Europe and elsewhere.

An unending war, or a Global Village?

It is 25 years since American military forces swept into Kuwait by air and sea (1991) to end Saddam Hussein's occupation of that country. But the entire region still "reels from Gulf War effects."

Daesh, aka ISIS or the Islamic State, has emerged and has taken control of about a third of Iraq and Syria. Today, the United States finds itself in a quandary, which it had probably hoped to avoid in 1991—stay in the region and fight a seemingly endless war "on terrorism," or leave and risk the "spread of the terrorist disease" both locally and globally.

In contrast to an unending War on Terror, it should not take many years during this century to develop the infrastructure for building the educational institutions necessary to impart quality education with an emphasis on "global citizenship," to create adequate healthcare facilities, and to provide the local people with proper political governance in the so-called "tribal belt" straddling the boundary between Pakistan and Afghanistan, from which millions have been displaced and thousands have been killed, especially children and women. But as they say, "Where there is a will, there is a way" and the best way is an altruistic approach to win the hearts and minds of even the so-called "terrorists." One does not have to "reinvent the wheel" because nations have done it in the past.

Will peace, progress and prosperity come to the region? The late James W. Spain an American diplomat and writer, dedicated his last book about the Pukhtuns "To my grandchildren, Jeanie Sikandra and James Stephen, may they one day come to know and love the Frontier as their parents, grandparents and great-grandparents did."[4] At the time of this writing in early 2016, there is continuing resentment by the Pukhtuns and many others in the region of the only super power, the U.S. But winning the "Hearts and Minds" of the Pukhtuns of Afghanistan and North West Pakistan will fulfill the dreams of not only James Spain, who died in 2008, but many others.

In contrast to some American presidential candidates during their 2016 campaigns who claimed that "Islam hates us," the reality is that Islam teaches peace and humanitarian values and does not teach hatred. The reasons given by these candidates for the Muslims' "hatred" of the West in general, or America in particular, include the West's high standard of living.

But 99 percent of the people living in the so called "terrorist areas" have never visited the West or America. However, they do hear the terrifying noises of the bomb blasts from the air and shelling from the ground, and the survivors then take part in the funerals and mourning of their near and dear ones and see the devastation around them, which is exploited by vested interests. Charles

Lindholm has written about how the "Generosity and Jealousy" in Pukhtun culture have been exploited by the rulers of this region in the past, these admirable qualities still being exploited by the military and civilian rulers.[5]

The U.S. spends trillion of dollars for the "protection" of countries from Asia to the Middle East, and even for the "defense" of Europe. In return, "we get peanuts."

If less than 1 percent of that money spent to "fight terrorism" were spent on "altruistic activity," in winning the hearts and minds of the local peoples, and on quality education, healthcare facilities, and infrastructure, rather than on such manmade disasters as "counter terrorism," then terrorism would be minimized if not eliminated. On the other hand, the general public in the West sees and hears only about the devastation caused by the bomb blasts in their midst by radicalized young Muslim "terrorists," who are known as "Islamic Jihadists."

Conclusion

The GWOT has cost trillions of dollars and has brought misery to millions of people locally and globally, notably in terms of the internal displacement and migration to Europe of its victims. Various factors and elements make one leave one's country: including economic reasons and disasters, especially the manmade ones now happening in Afghanistan, Iraq, and Syria. Therefore, instead of an unending War on Terror by bullets and bombs, which has not worked so far, an altruistic approach and finding the root causes of terrorism should be substituted. In the case of North West Pakistan and Afghanistan, these causes are: poverty, social injustices, unemployment, and poor governance. Prevention, according to the old adage, is not only better, it is cheaper.

An altruistic approach needs to be applied by decision makers rather than retaliation and revenge, such as "an eye for an eye," which, according to Martin Luther King Jr., leaves everyone blind. A systematic application to the problem of Rudyard Kipling's "W's" (Why, Which, When, Where, What) can also help address the root causes of the manmade disasters.

Long ago, the Muslim writer Avicenna-Abu Ali Sina (981–1037) was the foremost philosopher and physician of his time. His books (such as *The Canon of Medicine*) were read throughout Europe. But since that time, there have been very few contributions by the Muslim world to science and technology. Why has there been this intellectual deterioration?

Robert R. Reilly has analyzed the so called "ideological radicalization" of the younger generation of Muslims, who should be made aware of the contributions made by Muslims in the past to humanity and should be using their energies for productive humanitarian work instead of for such destructive "manmade disasters" as terrorist acts, which have caused not only local catastrophes to millions but have also led to Islamophobia.[6] On the other hand, the advocates of the War on Terror ought to try and win the hearts and minds of people by helping in the provision of health facilities, quality education, good governance, and poverty alleviation both materially and intellectually. There is Pukhtun proverb that says, "to clap, you need two hands" or in English," it takes two to tango".

In his book, *Pakistan A Hard Country*, Anatol Lieven cites the poetry of the warrior poet Khushal Khan Khattak (1613–1689):[7]

> The every name Pakhtun spells honour and glory,
> Lacking that honour what is the Afghan story?
> In the sword alone lies our deliverance,
> The sword wherein is our predominance,
> Whereby in days long past we ruled in Hind;
> But concord we know not, and we have sinned.

The author continues:

> one way of looking at the Pathans of Pakistan is as eighteenth-century Scots without the alcohol. Equally importantly, the society of the Pathan areas, and the tribal areas in particular, is rougher by far than that of eighteenth-century Scotland, and this in turn produces a much rougher kind of religious radicalism. Alas, there is no great modern Enlightenment culture to produce a contemporary Pathan Adam Smith or David Hume.

And Rehman Baba (1653–1711), the Sufi poet of the region has said:

> Grow flowers that your path may rosy be,
> When you sow thorns, they hurt you instantly,
> If you shoot arrows, you should understand
> That they recoil and cause you tragedy.[8]

Hopefully, the children and grandchildren of those of us living in the region will practice and preserve the "Pukhtunwali" of generosity, hospitality and "honour" wherever they live in the "Global Village." I also hope that they will strive for peace, progress, and prosperity, both individually and collectively, in the land of their ancestors and beyond.[9]

Acknowledgments

Thanks to Charles Webel for giving me the opportunity to learn and work on this chapter. Thanks are also due to Safina Kausar, Atif Rose Yusufzai, and Ali Shah for my literature search, and to Salman Usama (no relationship to Osama bin Laden) for typing.

Notes

1 For details on the Pukhtuns' culture, history, and geography see: Fazal Khaliq, *The Uddiyana Kingdom: The Forgotten Holy Land of Swat* (Swat, Pakistan: Shoab and Sons 2014); Olaf Caroe, *The Pathans 550 B.C.–A.D. 1957* (New York: Macmillan, 1964); and Haroon Rashid, *The History of Pathans* (Islamabad: Printo Graphic, 2002).

2 Hillary Rodham Clinton, *Hard Choices* (New York: Simon and Schuster, 2014).
3 Siddhartha Mukherjee, *The Emperor of All Maladies* (New York: Simon and Schuster 2010.
4 James W. Spain, *Pathans of the Latter Day* (New York: Oxford University Press, 1995).
5 Charles Lindholm, *Generosity and Jealousy: The Swat Pukhtun of North Pakistan* (New York: Columbia University Press, 1982).
6 Robert R. Reilly, *The Closing of the Muslim Mind* (ISI Books: Wilmington, Delaware, 2011.
7 Anatol Lieven, *Pakistan, a Hard Country* (London: Penguin, 2011).
8 Rehman Baba, *The Nightingale of Peshawar*, Second Edition, translated by Jens Enevoldsen (Peshawar: InterLit Foundation, 1993).Sher M. Khan, *In Pursuit of Knowledge* (Cirencester, UK: Mereo Memoir Books, 2016).
9 Sher M. Khan, *In Pursuit of Knowledge* (Cirencester, UK: Mereo Memoir Books, 2016).

Part III
Calculating the costs of the War on Terror

Mark Tomass

What are the costs and benefits of the seemingly unending War on Terror? What are the declared versus actual "successes" and "defeats" incurred by the major antagonists since 9/11? This section addresses in depth these crucial questions.

Charles Webel and John Arnaldi examine critically examine official mainstream constructions of "terrorists," "terrorism" and "counterterrorism" as powerful rhetorical frames used to sell the GWOT and the justifications for initiating and continuing it. They show that these frames underlie attempts to justify the morality of killing in "war." They suggest an alternative construction for understanding the roots of terrorism and for devising "antiterrorism" strategies to replace the largely ineffective "counterterrorism" policies being used to deal with terrifying acts of political violence. This framework is based both on an empirical analysis of how groups labeled "terrorist" end, as well as on a normative assessment of the utility and morality of "fighting terror with terror." The two authors conclude by arguing that antiterrorism strategies consistent with moral and legal norms would lessen if not eliminate attacks on civilians while preserving the human rights of both the victims and alleged perpetrators. Webel and Arnaldi conclude by arguing that antiterrorism is an effective and largely nonviolent, hence ethical alternative to the largely unethical and ineffective "war on terrorism."

William Cohn claims that the chaos in the parts of the Middle East where the U.S.-led forces have most directly intervened was foreseeable because, since 9/11, power has been unhinged from law, and law has been unhinged from morality. Cohn shows how the US-led policies pursued in the name of security have made people globally and locally far less secure. According to Cohn, the War on Terror is not meeting its stated objectives to weaken militant jihadists and to eliminate terrorist groups and acts because of the unethical methods used. Cohn also analyzes why, unlike the Vietnam War, the War on Terror has not come home to America. While most Americans remain largely detached from the wars being waged in the Middle East to defend their "national security," the current refugee crisis may change their obliviousness to political reality, and thus may also provide an opportunity also to change the direction of U.S.-led counterterrorism policies.

In the third chapter in this part, Laurie Calhoun argues that although the terror and anxiety instilled in communities where drone strikes are regularly carried out has been well documented, lethal drones continue to be regarded by Western political leaders as an essential tool in the global War on Terror. The citizens who pay for drone strikes have largely accepted targeted killing as legitimate under the assumptions that this new form of "warfare" eliminates enemies without risking harm to good soldiers, and also allegedly minimizes collateral damage. However, in reality, body count as the sole measure of collateral damage is misleading in the Drone Age, because the most dramatic effects of lethal drones are found among the survivors, some of whom are traumatized and others are "radicalized" by what they have seen.

Calhoun further argues that throughout the War of Terror, terrorists, insurgents, and militants have been conflated, as though these categories were interchangeable. Many of those killed in Afghanistan and Iraq after the US invasions regarded themselves as defending their own land from the occupiers. Calhoun argues that as more and more countries acquire the means to kill by remote-control, the broader cultural and political costs of this technology will finally come to light. The United States, Britain, and Israel have eliminated nationals located abroad. However, other governments, including those of Pakistan and Nigeria, have already begun executing their compatriots within their homelands. The leaders who authorize drone strikes in the future can be expected to follow the lead of the U.S. government by stigmatizing their enemies as terrorists and claiming that capture is infeasible. When drones strikes become commonplace, citizens will come to fear the possibility of being eliminated by their own government for opposing current policies. Lethal drones will serve then to eliminate dissent, making the countries in most need of democratic reform the least likely to achieve it.

8 The global war on terrorism
How ethical and effective?

Charles P. Webel and John A. Arnaldi

Introduction: September 11, 2001 and its aftermath

On September 11, 2001, 19 men hijacked four passenger jets and carried out attacks that killed almost 3,000 people in the United States, demonstrating the vulnerability of powerful nations to massive attacks by small groups of violent extremists. This shocking example of "asymmetric warfare" between powerful nations and sub-national adversaries was an appropriate wake-up call for a nation seemingly inured to its vulnerability to mass political violence within its borders. But rather than waiting for a full accounting of the facts surrounding the attacks and for a debate of all reasonable responses to them, the U.S.-led coalition chose to respond to the violence with more violence—massive military retaliation framed as a "Global War on Terrorism" (GWOT).

Since the beginning of the GWOT, terrorist attacks have increased outside the U.S. The official U.S. government data from the 2010 Report by the National Counterterrorism Center (NCTC) indicate, inter alia, that the worldwide number of U.S.-designated terrorist attacks (excluding Iraq) increased from 7,763 in 2006 to 8,916 in 2010; the number of global deaths (excluding Iraq) attributed to these attacks increased from 7,191 in 2006 to 9,822 in 2010,[1] but that the number of U.S. civilian deaths attributed to these attacks was only 15 out of 13,186 total deaths associated with terrorist attacks, including Iraq.[2] These trends are consistent with data from 2002–2006 and since 2010.[3] The fact that almost 99.9 percent of the victims of global terrorist attacks are *not* Americans may be a significant reason why, in the U.S. at least, there has been, until late 2015, a widespread (mis)perception that terrorism is decreasing.

In addition to the growth and spread of terrorist groups and nascent Islamist "states" such as ISIS/DAESH since 9/11, the freedoms lost to U.S. citizens because of the Patriot Act have not been restored, and U.S.-led wars continue to be waged in many countries. At the same time, amid big increases in military spending and huge revenues for military contractors and armaments manufacturers, the U.S. and Western economies remain shaky, with the middle class shrinking and income/asset inequalities between the top 0.1 percent and everyone else increasing.[4] Based on such circumstances, most Americans and Europeans do not feel more secure now than on September 10, 2001. Instead, "a majority of Americans believes that over the last decade the U.S. overinvested resources in some of the responses to the 9/11 attacks and that this overinvestment has contributed to America's economic problems today," and two in three believe U.S. power and "influence has diminished in the world over the last decade and a half."[5]

A principal aim of our analysis[6] is critically to examine official mainstream constructions of "terrorists," "terrorism" and "counter-terrorism" as powerful rhetorical frames used to sell the GWOT and the justifications for initiating and continuing it. These frames also underlie numerous ethical assumptions—attempts to justify the morality of killing in "war"—which we call into question.

Framing the conflict

> The language of counter-terrorism incorporates a series of assumptions, beliefs and knowledge about the nature of terrorism and terrorists. These beliefs then determine what kinds of counter-terrorism practices are reasonable or unreasonable, appropriate or inappropriate.[7]

The language used to frame a problem also shapes the solution. For example, after the attacks of September 11, the dominant Western narrative for war, promoted by many top U.S., British, and other coalition decision-makers, framed a "war against" terrorism, especially extremist Islamic terrorism, as the front line in a "clash of civilizations"—a new and grave threat to the "civilized" world. The failure of existing national security policies to prevent the attacks of September 11 was cited as evidence that new, tougher methods were urgently needed. This language shaped and focused the range of possible solutions—the methods employed must be on the scale of a "global war against evil."

The frame of a "War on Terror" is a clever piece of political rhetoric, a powerful martial metaphor, and a slogan deployed by political decision makers to generate a rally-round-the-flag effect. Like the similarly ill-fated domestic "Wars" "on Drugs and Poverty," the phrase the "Global War on Terror(ism)" is both a linguistic catalyst for mobilizing a nation against an apparently self-evidently malevolent "enemy," and a tool for generating support on behalf of the "defensive" measures ostensibly needed to rid the world of such a global "evil."

But also like the never-ending "Wars on Drugs and Poverty," which have ended neither of *those* "evils," the "Global War on Terror" has not and probably can never be "won," in the sense in which real wars can be won or lost. Instead, the GWOT has "succeeded" in fattening the pocketbooks of those who benefit from the trillions of dollars invested in it (mostly members of the increasingly global military-industrial-technological-academic-prison complex), while it has brought ineffable agony to its mostly dark-skinned victims in and near the Middle East.

Consistent with the GWOT frame, high-level Bush administration officials claimed that the U.S. and international legal standards of waging a "just war" would handicap counter-terrorism efforts, so they replaced those standards with a preventive war doctrine derived largely from a neoconservative version of realpolitik. This frame has also justified a radical weakening of established legal rights and procedures, such as passage and renewal of the USA Patriot Act, which grants U.S. government agencies greater powers to investigate, prosecute, or detain *potential* terrorists—but at the cost of limiting the civil rights of all citizens. Furthermore, in light of the terrorist attacks perpetrated by the Islamic State and its sympathizers in late 2015 and 2016, many European nations—most notably France and Belgium—are also adopting more stringent and potentially authoritarian counter-terrorism measures, at the risk of weakening some civil rights, including freedom of expression and the right to privacy.

If a different narrative than the frame of a "Global War on Terrorism" had been used, different solutions might have been prescribed. For example, if the attacks of September 11 had been framed as crimes perpetrated by a small group of violent extremists, an international law enforcement narrative would have been more appropriate than global warfare. This narrative would have explained that terrorism is an old problem, not limited to Muslim extremists, and that contemporary terrorism committed by non-state actors (or "Terrorism From Below") is presenting a new ideological face, which might be fought effectively with methods that protect civil and human rights. It would have focused more on dealing with the nature of violent acts than on the clash of ideologies. Most significantly, a law enforcement model might neither have disregarded domestic and international laws nor have conducted the massive bombings and occupations of sovereign nations, which, in disregard for the proportionality of just war, have caused, at a minimum, hundreds of thousands of casualties to date, a toll far exceeding the comparatively small number of suspected terrorists. By combining law enforcement and human security models, strong multilateral anti-terrorism strategies might still be developed and implemented at much lower financial and human costs than required for the seemingly unending and increasingly expanding "GWOT."

What is terrorism? Who are terrorists?

> The enemy is not a single political regime or person or religion or ideology. The enemy is terrorism—premeditated, politically motivated violence perpetrated against innocents.
>
> (*National Security Strategy*, 2002)[8]

> This is terror against terror.... No ideology, no cause, not even the Islamic cause—can account for the energy which fuels terror. The aim is no longer even to transform the world, but ... to radicalize the world by sacrifice.... There is indeed a fundamental antagonism here, but one which points past the spectre of America ... and the spectre of Islam ... to triumphant globalization battling against itself. In this sense, we can speak of a world war—not the Third World War, but the Fourth and the only really global one, since what is at stake is globalization itself.... The repression of terrorism spirals

around us as unpredictably as the terrorist act itself. No one knows where it will stop.... And ... that is terrorism's true victory.... There is no remedy for this extreme situation, and war is certainly not a solution, since it merely offers a rehash of the past...

(Jean Baudrillard, *The Spirit of Terrorism*)[9]

Terrorism ... *is a social construction* ... is not given in the real world but is instead an interpretation of events and their presumed causes.... When people and events come to be regularly described in public as terrorists and terrorism, some governmental or other entity is succeeding in a war of words in which the opponent is promoting alternative designations such as "martyr" and "liberation struggle".

(Austin T. Turk)[10]

Just about everybody claims to be against terrorism—but people disagree about whether some particular political violence amounts to terrorism. The term *terrorism* has a core of descriptive content; but, in addition, it is used to express value judgments—and because people disagree about those value judgments, they apply the term differently. Thus the familiar saying that one person's terrorist is another man's freedom fighter.

(Trudy Govier)[11]

Terrorism is a vexing term because of its historical variability and because its meaning is influenced more by the political agenda and value judgments of those using the term than by any fair-minded description of the violent acts and their perpetrators.[12] Who is or is not a "terrorist" and what may or may not be acts of "terrorism" depend largely on the perspective of the person or group applying these terms. As a *political construct* "terrorism" is an ideologically useful way of branding those who may violently oppose a particular policy or government as beyond the moral pale, and hence "not worthy" of diplomacy and negotiations, or universal human rights protections.

When defined within the narrative of national security, any actual or threatened politically motivated attack by *sub-national* agents on non-combatants, and, arguably, against soldiers, police, and political leaders, has been considered an act of "terrorism." This definition is consistent with Western "orthodox terrorism theory ... [which is] based on the legitimacy/illegitimacy dualism that constructs non-state violence as terrorist while state violence is deemed to be legitimate."[13] The failure of orthodox theory to address attacks by states or state-sponsored agents is a serious limitation that obscures the fact that both state and non-state actors contribute to the perpetuation of political violence.[14] Orthodox terrorism theory has been criticized as "a barrier to resolving terrorism and conflict and therefore needs to be overcome if reconciliation and a lasting peace are to be achieved."[15]

Placing "terrorism" and "terrorist" in quotation marks is done not to excuse culpability or minimize the horror of such acts but to emphasize that often one person's "terrorist" is another's "freedom fighter." In the case of insurgent or guerrilla warfare, sub-national groups who see themselves as freedom fighters may primarily target the leaders and combatants of the ruling elites with the goal of removing them from power. Examples include the anti-colonialist and anti-imperialist struggles for national liberation conducted in North America (e.g., the U.S. War of Independence) and Western Europe during the late eighteenth and early nineteenth centuries and continuing after World War II in Africa and South Asia against such European empires as the British, French, Dutch, and Portuguese. In this sense, "terrorism" is as old as violent human conflict.

Moreover, yesterday's "terrorist" may become today's ally or tomorrow's chief of state—if successful in seizing or otherwise gaining state power. A "positive" example of this is Nelson Mandela, who after 27 years of incarceration for acts of sabotage equivalent to what is now labeled terrorism, was elected president of South Africa and gained such international respect that he was awarded the Nobel Peace Prize. Other leaders who had been considered terrorists by opponents and were awarded the Nobel Peace Prize include Yasser Arafat, Menachem Begin, Yitzhak Rabin, and Henry Kissinger.

History also gives many examples of state-sponsored terrorism when nations used terrifying violence in attempts to control, weaken or eliminate rival political parties or ethnic or other sub-national groups, whether within their own borders or elsewhere. If a fair-minded understanding of terrorism is to be gained, critical examination of state-sponsored terrorism must not only be limited to such notorious cases as Hitler, Stalin, and Saddam Hussein, but must also include all cases of state-sponsored terrifying violence, even when perpetrated or sponsored by Western democracies.

Whether from above (TFA, or state terrorism) or from below (TFB, or non-state terrorism), perpetrators usually claim their actions are legitimate and "ethical" because they are "necessary" for "self-defense" or some other "greater good." For example, governments may apply terrorizing internal measures against their own citizens, which they justify by appeals to national security, while they rationalize their attacks on foreign nationals and the military occupation of other nations by claiming the right of self-defense.

Prime examples of state-sponsored terrorism, justified by the American government as self-defense, were the 2003 U.S. "Shock and Awe" bomb and missile attacks on Baghdad, Iraq, a densely populated city of five million people. These attacks were designed "to frighten, scare, intimidate, and disarm" and to destroy the Iraqis' sources of electrical power and drinking water.[16] Reporting and analysis in the mainstream U.S. press focused on the legitimacy of the attacks while saying very little about the more than 6,700 civilians who were killed in the first three weeks of the massive attacks on Baghdad's infrastructure.[17] While the mass media and domestic press enthusiastically devoted much attention to the details of the high-technology weapons used, they failed to question the possibility that these attacks might meet the criteria for war crimes under the Geneva Conventions, which unequivocally state:[18]

> Article 51.2. The civilian population as such, as well as individual civilians, shall not be the object of attack. Acts or threats of violence the primary purpose of which is to spread terror among the civilian population are prohibited.
>
> Article 54.2. It is prohibited to attack, destroy, remove or render useless objects indispensable to the survival of the civilian population, such as ... drinking water installations and supplies and irrigation works.[19]

Likewise, non-state perpetrators of terrifying political violence may claim they're acting in self-defense against state oppression or foreign occupation, or are retaliating for violence perpetrated by states against their people. Many attacks committed by insurgents against occupying forces in Afghanistan, Iraq, Palestine, and elsewhere are viewed as anti-imperialist, not "terrorist," by their perpetrators, as are acts of political violence against Western and Russian civilians, whose governments are bombing and killing people in Syria, Yemen, and elsewhere. A notorious example of justification for violent attacks by non-state perpetrators is an open letter to the American people from Osama Bin Laden, who claimed that al-Qaeda was fighting the U.S.:

> because you attacked us and continue to attack us.... You attacked us in Palestine.... You attacked us in Somalia; you supported the Russian atrocities against us in Chechnya, the Indian oppression against us in Kashmir, and the Jewish aggression against us in Lebanon. Under your supervision, consent and orders, the governments of our countries which act as your agents, attack us on a daily basis.... You have starved the Muslims of Iraq ... [where] more than 1.5 million Iraqi children have died as a result of your sanctions, and you did not show concern.[20]

Here is a brief overview of this tumultuous period in history: between the first Gulf War (1990–1991) and 9/11, U.S.-led and U.N.-imposed sanctions against Iraq directly or indirectly killed hundreds of thousands, perhaps millions, of civilian non-combatants; on 9/11, al-Qaeda-linked operatives killed nearly 3,000 in New York and Washington, D.C.; the U.S.-led coalition then declared war on terrorism and attacked and occupied Afghanistan and Iraq in late 2001 and early 2003, respectively; and during the GWOT that followed 9/11, hundreds of thousands have died and millions have been wounded and/or displaced from their homes, almost all of them in the combat zones of the Middle East and North Africa. Now there are more terrorists than before 9/11, and they are killing many people in Pakistan, Syria, France, Turkey, Belgium, Iraq, Afghanistan, Yemen, Libya, Nigeria, and elsewhere.

If anything can be said about this litany of terrifying violence, it is that violence begets more violence. Regardless of the actors' affiliations or justifications claimed, for the victims all such acts are prima facie unethical.

The "ethics" of terror and terrorism

> There is no war against terrorism being waged or being prepared for waging. What we have been witnessing since 2001 and what we are going to witness in the near future are not wars against terrorism, but wars, period.
>
> (Rüdiger Bittner, *Ethics of Terrorism and Counterterrorism*)[21]

> One becomes a killer by killing.[22]

The "Global War on Terror" presents special challenges for mainstream and heterodox ethical traditions. Consequentialists, deontologists, and pacifists must all grapple with the dilemmas posed by terrorist violence in general, and by the uncertainties and tensions generated by responding to terrorist attacks, whether from below or from above.

A brief overview of general approaches to ethics may be helpful. Morality is concerned with the customary nature of right and wrong, good and bad actions; and ethics (or moral philosophy) studies the groundwork of morality. Applied ethics seeks an understanding of the moral dimensions of specific, real-life controversies (such as terrorism and the GWOT) and their potential solutions.

Deontology argues that the morality of an act is determined by an actor's goodwill—the *intent* to fulfill a moral duty or obey an applicable moral rule. From a Kantian deontological perspective, a rule is ethical when:

1 it is *categorical*—there are no exceptions to its application;
2 it exhibits *universality*—when the rule is applied to one person or group, the resulting good must equal the good obtained when the same rule is applied to any other persons or groups, and should be generalizable to humanity as a whole; and
3 it does not use persons as the means to gain specific ends—it respects all persons as the specific end.[23]

Utilitarianism is a version of consequentialism in which morality is determined by an act's utility (efficacy) in producing the greatest good for the most people. Good ends justify the means. The efficacy of an act has greater moral significance than the actor's intentions. In theory, this approach seems simple enough, however, in actual application of utilitarian and consequentialist principles, the morality of an act is dependent upon how the outcome criteria are defined and measured, and also by who defines them. For example, a drone attack may be judged a success by the nation that launched it because it met its criterion for killing alleged enemy combatants or those (allegedly) planning terrorist attacks, while the villagers where the attack took place may judge it an immoral act because civilians were killed. The same would be true for judging the ethics of using nuclear weapons and other weapons of mass destruction—the outcome might be judged a success by the attackers, but the survivors and other members of the global community probably won't agree. Additionally, judgment of results often depends upon the length of time between the act and the evaluation of its consequences. For example, in the case of the drone attack, immediately afterward it may be judged a success because it killed the targeted group of alleged terrorists, but over a period of several years it may be judged a failure because many of the family, friends, and community of those killed subsequently supported or joined terrorist groups, or failed to cooperate with the nation that launched the drone.

Specific applications of ethics to war usually encompass three influential Western ethical traditions: realism/realpolitik, just war, and pacifism, each relevant to ethical analysis of the GWOT. All three traditions presume that an individual has a "natural" right to life; however, they differ in the extent to which war is acceptable as a moral means of protecting lives designated as innocent and of preserving "national security" (considered by governments to be the greater good). They also differ in how war should be conducted and how the end of war should be defined.

Realism or Realpolitik argues that the political behavior of nations and their adversaries is based, not on civilian private morality, but on pragmatic considerations of national self-interest and power. The principle of universality is not a consideration, as the overriding moral obligation is to national security—the nation's defense of its own citizens and interests. From this perspective, it makes no sense to fight under rules that might give an advantage to the enemy and thereby prolong the war, when unrestricted military action, even including total war, might end the war more quickly and efficiently.

Some realists claim that "the side that initiates war [or terrorist attacks] commits a criminal act and, in so doing, the members of that side thereby forfeit any right they might have had to protection under the law."[24] This same line of reasoning has been applied to terrorists (and those suspected of being terrorists or supportive of terrorists), who, because they have demonstrated blatant disregard for human life, ethics, and the law, are viewed as having forfeited all moral and legal rights, including the right to life. State authorities are therefore free to use whatever means necessary to prevent potential terrorists from perpetrating acts of violence, even if those means are outside the limits of the law. After 9/11, the Bush administration used this reasoning to justify detention and "enhanced interrogation" of suspected terrorists as "unlawful enemy combatants" without due process or protections of humanitarian or U.S. law (as for example at secret "black sites" and the military prison at Guantanamo Bay, Cuba).

The ethical criteria of the *Just War Tradition* presume that it is in the interests of all nations to restrict war within certain limits that will minimize harm to persons, especially to civilians and other non-combatants. Two phases of warfare are considered: *Jus ad bellum* stipulates the criteria for *initiating* a just war, while *jus in bello* describes just conduct during war. The criteria for initiating a just war are: just cause, legitimate authority, right intention, probability of success, proportionality, and last resort.[25] The requirements for *conducting* a just war are discrimination (protection of non-combatants from harm) and proportionality.[26] Some of the limitations of this approach are that neither the root causes of violent conflict nor the needs for reconciliation between the conflicting parties after the war are addressed. International Humanitarian Law, including the Geneva Conventions, attempts to codify the ethics of just war into law. Unfortunately, the just war criteria and the laws based upon them have failed to reduce the frequency or destructiveness of war, in large part due to the ease with which nations can interpret the criteria in favor of their own interests.

Pacifism is an ethical system that may tend to be absolutist about the universality and inviolability of the sanctity of human life—war is never defensible as a moral exception to society's standard prohibition against killing. For most pacifists, the principle of discrimination—designating groups of persons as innocent or guilty (worthy of protection vs. "legitimate" targets, in contrast to those that are "illegitimate")—is irrelevant because all persons have a natural right to life that is not dependent upon their group affiliation, their citizenship (usually acquired involuntarily by virtue of birthplace), or the fallible determinations made by human authorities. Although pacifism is commonly mischaracterized as a naïve, one-dimensional anti-war perspective, the goals of pacifism extend beyond "negative peace" (the absence of war) to the establishment of a sustainable "positive peace"—"peace by peaceful means" that addresses injustice and other root causes of violent conflict using empirically informed peace-making and peace-building strategies.[27]

The ethical framework one applies to framing "terrorist" acts of political violence, whether from above or from below, significantly influences the actions one takes to "counter" that violence. Hence, realists would initiate and justify "counter"-terrorist operations that result in significant "collateral damage" (civilian casualties) on the grounds that "national security" requires state-sanctioned "force" to "counter" the "illegitimate" violence of "insurgents" and "terrorists." People acting from "just war" and "consequentialist" principles would try to justify the use of state force to counter illegitimate terrorist violence by "balancing" the perceived "benefits" and "costs" of counter-terrorism and by "justifying" a "War on Terror" (Bush) or "global contingency operations" (Obama) as an ethically permissible response to a "greater evil" ("international terrorism"). Most pacifists, in contrast, would consider both terrorist and counter-terrorist violence as unethical and would seek an alternative.

It should be noted, though, that these are "ideal-typical" ethical frameworks and few people fit entirely within one tradition. Accordingly, our own analytic and ethical framework, while leaning toward pacifism, also incorporates appropriate elements of realpolitik, just war principles, and consequentialism. But the burden for pacifists is not merely to decry political violence as "unethical" but also to propose effective alternatives to terrorizing political acts designed to oppose "imperialism" (the frame of many sub-national "terrorists") or to "counter" terrorism (the frame of most governments).

The ethics of the global War on Terror

> The cardinal principles of humanitarian law are aimed at the protection of the civilian and civilian objects. States must never make civilians the objects of attack and must consequently never use weapons that are incapable of distinguishing between civilian and military targets.
>
> (The International Court of Justice, Paragraph 78, Legality of the Threat or Use of Nuclear Weapons, Advisory Opinion, July 8, 1996)[28]

Since the advent of the "Age of Global Terrorism," dating from the early twentieth century, when "total war," "strategic bombing," and weapons of mass destruction became acceptable components of military and diplomatic strategy, many important previously held distinctions of just war have been rendered meaningless. Most notably, there has been a gradual collapse of the distinction between "illegitimate" (i.e., civilian non-combatants) and "legitimate" (i.e., military) "targets," as well as of the distinction between "terrorists" and "the states" (and peoples) that, allegedly, "support them." Accordingly, the very idea of a "just war," must be called into question because of the colossal civilian casualties during virtually every major war since 1939, including the "Global War on Terror." The massive violations of the requirements of "jus in bello" vitiate the "principle of discrimination," aka "non-combatant immunity." As Michael Walzer has stated, "The dualism of *jus ad bellum* and *jus in bello* is at the heart of all that is most problematic in the moral reality of war."[29]

When violations of non-combatant "immunity" become an intrinsic part, and the foreseeable effect, of such strategic policies as the bombing of cities (resulting in hundreds of thousands of casualties during and after World War II) and the occupation of nations "that harbor terrorists" (also resulting in hundreds of thousands of civilian casualties and millions of displaced persons since the U.S.-led invasions of Afghanistan and Iraq and the subsequent civil wars in Libya, Yemen, and Syria), *the theoretical separation of "ends"* ("defeating totalitarianisms" and "vanquishing terrorists") *and "means"* (aerial bombings, "renditions," "targeted assassinations," "enhanced interrogation techniques," drone attacks, etc.) *collapses*, as do claims of proportionality (given the massive destruction of civilian lives and cities as compared to the relatively low losses incurred by the U.S.-led coalition). These failures to meet requirements for non-combatant immunity and proportionality violate the principles of *jus in bello* and both international and U.S. domestic law.

Furthermore, the "Global War on Terror" has *not* been fought "as a last resort," with a realistic "goal of peace" and a "reasonable" chance of success, which are among the necessary conditions required by *jus ad bellum* for the initiation of a "war to be just."[30] The ongoing "just war on terror(ism)," no matter how comprehensible as retaliation for TFB atrocities and mass murders, is *unjust* because the costs to civilians greatly exceed any perceived "benefits" in terms of revenge and "national security." Instead, the conflict endures and escalates, without an endpoint in sight or a clear means of achieving, or recognizing (measuring), either "victory" or "defeat."

Finally, this century-long process is leading to the erosion of the boundary between "terrorism" and "war," to such a degree that, since at least the early days of World War II, for the civilian populations of the affected states, war has, ipso facto, become indistinguishable from terrorism. Terror, or psychological warfare, is not just employed by sub-national extremists, but has also become a predictable tool to be employed by war planners and policymakers. This turn of events is on the one hand a regression to the kind of "barbarism" that preceded the rise of "civilization" about 5,000 years ago in the Ancient Near East, and on the other hand is a seemingly inevitable consequence of technological "progress" unaccompanied by a comparable "moral evolution" on the parts of the proponents, practitioners, and apologists for TFA and TFB alike.

National security, human security, anti-terrorism, and the costs of the GWOT

> Conceptualizations of security as defined by the vital interests of human beings rather than of the state are long overdue—and still virtually absent from mainstream political and media deliberations.[31]

National security and human security are not equivalent terms. Within the traditional paradigm of national security, the nation-state arrogates to itself the principal authority for protecting the collective health and welfare of its citizens. National security is primarily a political-military construct based upon the war narrative asserting that superior military force and weaponry are necessary means to stop and/or destroy enemies. When the "enemy" is framed as "terrorists," national security strategies may be framed as "counter-terrorism."

In contrast, "human security is an emerging paradigm" that challenges "the traditional notion of national security by arguing that *the proper referent for security should be the individual rather than the state*" (emphasis added).[32] Human security is people-centered, congruent with the universality principle of ethics and equity in law as well as evidence that national, regional, and global stability and peace often result from strategies and methods that respect individual humans and their needs for safety and security.

Anti-terrorism is a multilateral strategy congruent with human security. It advocates ethical, legally-sanctioned methods for establishing effective communication and just relations between adversaries, resolving conflicts peacefully, and bringing terrorists to justice. An example of using anti-terrorism methods instead of terrorist attacks on the government is Tunisia, where, in January 2011, many Tunisian citizens successfully employed nonviolent methods to overthrow the repressive, autocratic government. Another outstanding example is the relatively nonviolent dismantling of the apartheid government of South Africa in 1994 after decades of violent, terrorizing attacks by all sides of the conflicts. These cases of successful popular resistance to state terrorism, and the wave of nonviolent revolutions against autocratic regimes in Eastern Europe during the late 1980s, and since then in some parts of Asia and Africa, demonstrate the efficacy of nonviolence from below as an effective anti-terrorist strategy. Regrettably, it is more difficult to think of cases of anti-terrorist nonviolence from above by states threatened by violent insurgencies, however, the "Good Friday Accords" between the British and Irish governments, and the IRA (Irish Republican Army) may be one example.[33]

The war of the world? Is there a viable nonviolent alternative to the global war on terrorism?

> If we assume that humankind has a right to survive, then we must find an alternative to war and destruction.... The choice today is no longer between violence or nonviolence. It is between nonviolence or nonexistence.
> (Martin Luther King, Jr.)[34]

> Only by the elimination of terrorism's root causes can the world hope to succeed in greatly reducing it if not putting an end to it.
> (Haig Khatchadourian, *The Morality of Terrorism*)[35]

With the "Global War on Terror" (GWOT) about halfway through its second decade, the future of life on earth may hinge on the political will, or lack of it, to respond forcefully—but nonviolently—to terror and terrorism. Is the future of the world to include an ever-escalating series of attacks and counterattacks culminating in global annihilation? Or can such hypothetical, but foreseeable, terrors be minimized by the judicious application of self-restraint on the one hand, and of nonviolent means of conflict resolution on the other hand? The answer is "maybe a great deal, maybe very little; it depends on the situation." But to assume, as does the national security paradigm, that the only, or best, "realistic" response to the use of deadly force, or terror, is to reply either "in kind" or with even greater force may guarantee that our common future will be even more terrifying than has been our collective history. Is this the future we wish our descendants to have?

Or is there a less violent, or even a nonviolent, alternative to counter-terrorism (TFA)? One possibility is to replace *counter*-terrorist violence with *anti*-terrorist *prevention and interception measures*. Another is *negotiation* with members or representatives of anti-state terrorist groups. And finally, there are *changes in state political policy*. These include ending the occupation(s) of territories that non-state terrorists are dedicated to "liberating," and incorporating representatives of these groups into the political process (as has been done with Hamas in Palestine and the IRA in Northern Ireland).

Since the 9/11 attacks, the world in general and the American, French, Belgian, Turkish, and British publics in particular have become acutely aware of international terrorism and its devastating effects on the bodies, minds, and hearts of its victims. But while great attention has been paid to the military and geopolitical dimensions of terrorism and counter-terrorism, relatively little effort has been made to understand the historical, cultural, and ideological roots of terrorism. As Bob de Graaff has noted: "there has been a remarkable one-sidedness in American counter-terrorism strategy and that is the dominant use of military means"[36]

Almost no one appearing in Western mass media has proposed a nonviolent, or less violent—*an ethically defensible, sustainable, and effective*—alternative to the current GWOT, and to the "resource wars" over water and energy that are becoming an increasing threat to global and regional peace and security.

What is increasingly becoming a war without end—a conflict with significant potential to escalate to a war of the world involving weapons of mass destruction—must cease. Consequently, it is imperative that we pursue and develop an effective and ethical plan for the prevention of terrorism from above and below, as well as for reconciliation between the adversaries.

While it seems to be a common assumption that the only alternatives are either to "stay the course" until "the terrorists are defeated," or to "cut and run," that is, to withdraw "prematurely" from such "frontlines" of the GWOT as Afghanistan, Syria, and Iraq, it is incumbent on critics of this "war" to pose a viable alternative to this false dilemma. This would achieve such demonstrable results as reducing the incidence and lethality of "terrorist" attacks globally and locally, and minimizing casualties on all sides.[37]

Conclusion

> Whenever the conditions are present that would give what Joan Bondurant calls "the process of creative conflict" a chance of successes, it should be favored. The Gandhian method of winning over one's opponents through nonviolent pressure may well be more effective than violence in undermining people's attachment to mistaken views ... if the massive violence of war can be justified, which is dubious, terrorist acts can also be, if they have certain characteristics ... as limited terrorism is better than war, less violent alternatives to terrorism are better than terrorism, and nonviolent pressures are better than violent ones. It is indeed the case that violence leads to more violence. Rather than trying to "wipe out once and for all the enemies that threaten us," which is impossible, the more successful, as well as more justifiable, approach to violence is to lessen its appeal.
> (Virginia Held, *How Terrorism is Wrong*)[38]

And as Noam Chomsky has recently stated:

> The last 15 years is what's called the "Global War on Terror." The method that has been used in the "Global War On Terror" is violence. That's what we're [the U.S.] good at. Violence. So we invade. We kill people with drones. We have all kinds of ways of killing people. What has been the effect? Take a look. Fifteen years ago terrorist groups were concentrated in a small tribal area in Afghanistan. That was it. Where are the now? All over the world. The worst terrorist crimes are going on in West Africa with Boko

Haram, a lot of which is an offshoot of the bombing in Syria. They're in West Africa, South Asia, Southeast Asia. They carry out attacks in Turkey, in Paris and so on. We've succeeded in spreading it from a little corner of tribal Afghanistan to most of the world. It's a great achievement for the use of violence.[39]

Consequently, it is time to change course. The Global War on Terror has demonstrated the ineffectiveness and immorality of fighting terror with greater terror. A predominantly nonviolent anti-terrorism strategy might be a more effective, and almost certainly a more ethical, alternative.

> Everyone has the right to life, liberty, and security of person.
> (Universal Declaration of Human Rights, Article 3, United Nations)[40]

Notes

1 National Counterterrorism Center (NCTC), *2010 Report*, Chart 17, 27, NCTC Resources and Products. www.nctc.gov/index.html.
2 Ibid., Chart 9, 19.
3 See the conclusion of this book for more data.
4 Jonathan Turley, *Big money behind war: the military-industrial complex*. Opinion 11, January 2014. www.aljazeera.com/indepth/opinion/2014/01/big-money-behind-war-military-industrial-complex-20141473026736533.html. (Last accessed May 30, 2016).
5 Shibley Telhami and Steven Kull, *The American Public on the 9/11 Decade: A Study of American Public Opinion*, The Brookings Institution and Anwar Sadat Chair, University of Maryland Program on International Policy Attitudes (PIPA) (September 8, 2011), 2.
6 See Charles P. Webel and John A. Arnaldi, eds., *The Ethics and Efficacy of the Global War on Terrorism: Fighting Terror with Terror* (New York: Palgrave Macmillan, 2011).
7 Richard Jackson, *Writing the War on Terrorism: Language, Politics and Counterterrorism* (New York: Manchester University Press, 2007), 8–9. For a sophisticated discourse analysis of the rhetorical framing of "The War on Terror," see Stephen D. Reese and Seth C. Lewis, "Framing the War on Terror: The Internalization of Policy in the US. Press," in Webel and Arnaldi, op. cit., 139–150.
8 The National Security Strategy of the United States of America, September 2002, 5.
9 Jean Baudrillard, *The Spirit of Terrorism*, tr. Chris Turner (London: Verso, 2003).
10 Austin T. Turk, "Sociology of Terrorism," *Annual Review of Sociology*, 30 (2004): 273.
11 Trudy Govier, *A Delicate Balance: What Philosophy Can Tell Us About Terrorism* (Boulder, Co: Westview Press, 2002), 87.
12 For contending definitions of "terrorism," see David Barash and Charles P. Webel, *Peace and Conflict Studies*, 3rd ed. (London: SAGE Publications, 2014), chapter 4, esp. 44–47; Charles P. Webel, *Terror, Terrorism and the Human Condition* (New York: Palgrave Macmillan, 2007), chapter 1, esp. 8–10; Trudy Govier, *A Delicate Balance: What Philosophy Can Tell Us About Terrorism* (Boulder, Co: Westview Press, 2002), 86–92, who also focuses on victims while noting the "double standard" and "Our Side Bias" of decrying the "terrorism" of political violence directed against us while exonerating uniformed agents of our state's political violence; Robert F. Goodin, *What's Wrong Terrorism?* (Cambridge: Polity Press, 2006), 36–37, 46–49, and 54–55; J. Angelo Corlett, *Terrorism: A Philosophical Analysis* (Dordrecht: Kluwer Academic Publishers, 2003), 116; Jean Baudrillard, *The Spirit of Terrorism* (London:

Verso, 2003); and Jacques Derrida in Giovanna Borradori, *Philosophy in a Time of Terror* (Chicago: University of Chicago Press, 2003), 102–109. For "The Language Game, Semantics, Theatre, and Western Model of Terrorism," see Edward S. Herman and Gerry O' Sullivan, "'Terrorism' as Ideology and Culture Industry," in *Western State Terrorism*, ed. Alexander George (Cambridge: Polity Press, 1992), 43–52.

13 Jason Franks, "Orthodox terrorism theory and reconciliation: The transition out of terrorism," in Judith Renner and Alexander Spencer, eds., *Reconciliation after terrorism: strategy, possibility or absurdity?* (New York: Routledge, 2012), 28.

14 "Terrorism" is used by most people in a rather unfortunately hypocritical manner. It appears that politicians of various countries condemn as "terrorist" acts of political violence ... against their own countries, or those of their allies, while they fail to admit that their own governments sponsor actual terrorism. The U.S. is a clear instance of this. J. Angelo Corlett, *Terrorism A Philosophical Analysis* (Dordrecht: Kluwer Academic Publishers, 2003), 48.

15 Franks, "Orthodox terrorism theory and reconciliation: The transition out of terrorism," 27–28.

16 Harlan K. Ullman, James P. Wade, L. A. Edney, Frederick Franks, Jr., Charles Horner, Jonathan How, and Keith Brendley, *Shock and Awe: Achieving Rapid Dominance*, Defense Group Inc., 1996, 34. www.dodccrp.org/files/Ullman_Shock.pdf (Last accessed March 26, 2016).

17 "The War in Iraq: 10 Years and Counting." *Iraqbodycount.org.* www.iraqbodycount.org/analysis/numbers/ten-years/ (Last accessed March 27, 2016).

18 John A. Arnaldi, "In Whose Interest? Ethics in Journalism and the War on Terror," in Charles P. Webel and John A. Arnaldi, op. cit., 160.

19 Protocol Additional to the Geneva Conventions of August 12, 1949, and relating to the Protection of Victims of International Armed Conflicts, Protocol I, June 8, 1977, www.icrc.org/ihl.nsf/INTRO/470 (Last accessed March 26, 2016).

20 Osama bin Laden, "Full text: bin Laden's 'letter to America'," *Guardian*, November 24, 2002. www.theguardian.com/world/2002/nov/24/theobserver (Last accessed March 23, 2016).

21 Rüdiger Bittner, "Morals in Terrorist Times," in Georg Meggle, ed., *Ethics of Terrorism and Counterterrorism* (Piscataway, N.J.: Transaction Books, 2005), 207–213.

22 Laurie Calhoun, "Just War? Moral Soldiers?" *The Independent Review* 4.3 (2000): 325.

23 Robert Johnson, "Kant's Moral Philosophy," *Stanford Encyclopedia of Philosophy*, April 2008, http://plato.stanford.edu/entries/kant-moral/.

24 Paul Christopher, *The ethics of war and peace*, (Upper Saddle River, New Jersey: Pearson Education: Pearson Education, 2004), 3.

25 Michael W. Brough, John W. Lango, and Harry van der Linden, eds., *Rethinking the just war tradition* (Albany, New York: State University of New York Press, 2007), 244–246.

26 Ibid., 246–247.

27 Baljit Singh Grewal, "Johan Galtung: Positive and Negative Peace," August 30, 2003, www.activeforpeace.org/no/fred/Positive_Negative_Peace.pdf (Last accessed on March 26, 2016).

28 The International Court of Justice, Paragraph 78, Legality of the Threat or Use of Nuclear Weapons, Advisory Opinion, July 8, 1996. Available at: www.icj-cij.org/docket/index.php?p1=3&p2=4&k=e1&p3=4&case=95.

29 Michael Walzer, *Just and Unjust Wars* (New York: Basic Books, 1977), 21.

30 Barash and Webel, *Peace and Conflict Studies*, ibid.

31 Ross, "Rethinking Human Vulnerability, Security, and Connection Through Relational Theorizing," in *Comparative Education, Terrorism, and Human Security: From Critical Pedagogy to Peacebuilding*, ed. Wayne Nelles (New York: Palgrave Macmillan, 2003), 38–39.

32 "Human Security," *Wikipedia*, https://en.wikipedia.org/wiki/Human_security (Last accessed on March 20, 2016).
33 See Marie Breen-Smyth, "Reconciliation and Paramilitaries in Northern Ireland," in Judith Renner and Alexander Spencer, eds., *Reconciliation after* terrorism: strategy, possibility or absurdity? op. cit.
34 See Martin Luther King, Jr. "A Christmas Sermon on Peace." 1967. www.ecoflourish.com/Primers/education/Christmas_Sermon.html. (Last accessed October 29, 2016) and "Pilgrimage to Nonviolence" Chicago, Illinois. April 13, 1960 http://kingencyclopedia.stanford.edu/encyclopedia/documentsentry/pilgrimage_to_nonviolence/. (Last accessed Oct 29, 2016).
35 Haig Khatchadourian, *The Morality of Terrorism* (New York: Peter Lang, 1998).
36 Bob de Graaff, "There's a good reason they are called al-Qaeda in Iraq. They are al-Qaeda … in … Iraq," in *Critical Perspectives on Counter-Terrorism*, ed. Lee Jarvis and Michael Lister (New York: Routledge, 2015), 28.
37 See the conclusion of this book.
38 Virginia Held, *How Terrorism is Wrong: Morality and Political Violence* (New York: Oxford University Press, 2011).
39 Noam Chomsky, Smashing Interviews. http://smashinginterviews.com/interviews/newsmakers/noam-chomsky-interview-enormous-sense-of-hopelessness-and-anger-reflected-in-appeal-of-trump-and-sanders. (Last Accessed May 27, 2016).
40 Universal Declaration of Human Rights, Article 3, United Nations. Available at: www.un.org/en/udhrbook/pdf/udhr_booklet_en_web.pdf.

9 Led astray
Legal and moral blowback from the global War on Terror

William A. Cohn

Introduction—15 years of fury

The past 15 years add to the great weight of evidence that the militarized response to terrorism is unethical and ineffective, and that law has often been used as an amoral tool in the name of an illogical security paradigm. The so-called European migrant crisis is the foreseeable result of the reckless pursuit of regime-change that has wrought havoc in Iraq and Libya, turning them into failed states and breeding grounds of terror, and Syria made into a new cold war battlefield for weapons and mayhem. The humanitarian disaster caused by the post-9/11 U.S.-led global War on Terror (GWOT) is now more evident than five years ago, and five years from now the resulting ecological and economic disasters will be more evident than they are today.

Over the past 15 years, we have seen a dramatic rise in war casualties,[1] war refugees,[2] the breakdown of states, the rise of a new type of state which preys on things falling apart in those prior states ripped apart by war,[3] and a ratcheting up of old rivalries to supplement the perpetual war paradigm[4] created by war profiteers.[5]

The humanitarian crisis confronting Europe and beyond is largely attributable to the failure of U.S.-led anti-terror policy. As hundreds of thousands of refugees flee lawless Iraq, Syria, Libya, Yemen and Somalia, we see the latest humanitarian disaster of the U.S.-led purported anti-terror policy. Desperate refugees from these countries have been forced to flee their homes, while the people of the U.S. and NATO member states have been led astray by the politicians and propagandists who promised to bring democracy to these states by toppling existing regimes—yet delivered mainly weapons, warfare, and misery.

The ongoing civil war that is destroying Iraq and Syria has caused the largest mass exodus of people from the Middle East ever. More than half of the Syrian population of 23 million has been forced to flee their homes. Four million Syrians and three million Iraqis have fled their home country as of September 20, 2015. That number will surely grow. The Iraq-Syrian war is the main cause of the European refugee crisis, and the misery that both causes and accompanies this mass exodus.[6]

Promotion of regime change in the Middle East was a central tenet of neoconservative policy. While the term blowback refers to unintended consequences, it is hard to argue that the humanitarian disaster we now see was not in fact an entirely foreseeable consequence of the U.S.-led policies of the past 15 years. Indeed, the foolishness of the U.S.-led response to terrorism over the past 15 years is well-documented in the public domain.[7]

Politicians have not learned the obvious lessons from their past failed policy. Just as the lesson hawks learned from the American war in Vietnam was to censor war reporting in order to manufacture domestic support for war, the lesson learned from the debacles in Iraq and Libya is that we must use greater force in Syria.[8] The leading candidates to become the forty-fifth U.S. President have "foreign policy teams dominated by the very people who pushed America into the Iraq debacle, and learned nothing from the experience."[9] Again, ideology and opportunism override rationality and common sense. Our so-called leaders must be made to change course by energized strategic civil society engagement, education and activism. We must be skeptical of all the rationales offered for militarism.[10]

America's longest war has been a disaster. Historian Andrew Bacevich notes:

> The tendency to see the region (the Greater Middle East) and Islamic World primarily as a problem that will yield to an American military solution is, in fact, precisely the problem. To an unseemly and ultimately self-destructive degree, we have endorsed the militarization of U.S. foreign policy.

In his new book, he cogently argues that none of the assumptions underlying U.S. militarism in the region has any empirical basis.[11]

Has the arc of the moral universe bent away from justice post-9/11? Have rule of law principles been replaced by the rule of men fashioning their own perverted version of justice? Can we correct course? Are the winds of change blowing with sufficient strength? These questions remain 15 years on, as do the answers—for those who seek them.

Law and ethics

Law should be a beacon of virtue, but it often falls far short. At its best, law enshrines ideals of fairness, dignity, autonomy, equality and justice. At its worst, law is a tool the rich and powerful use to maintain and further their advantage in society. Law differs from ethics, which is why there exists civil disobedience.[12] Law rooted in sound moral principles commands respect; unprincipled law breeds fear and scorn. Does fear now bind us to law? Has the ideal of a rule of law rooted in universal moral principles been replaced by the rule of men bent on fashioning their own version of justice?

Post-9/11 events in the United States, Guantanamo, Iraq, Afghanistan, Libya, and beyond have raised questions about established law and its applicability. Do we best combat terrorism by military might? law enforcement? intelligence? diplomacy? a combination of these? Does application of the rule of law in response to terrorism enhance or degrade our security?

Some say we are now engaged in a new kind of war where the old rules no longer apply.[13] Some say it is not a war,[14] and that established rules and norms are vital and indispensable—they define who we are and we degrade them at our own peril.[15] GWOT has been reframed by NATO as a worldwide armed conflict with al-Qaeda and its offshoots, including ISIS, and associated forces. Still, the campaign prioritizes military action over law enforcement; thus GWOT remains an apt description of policy.

Fifteen years of trial and error with settled norms of constitutional justice enable us to draw conclusions. GWOT is not meeting its stated objectives (to weaken militant jihadists) because the methods used (kidnapping, assassination, indefinite detention, torture, hyper-secrecy, illegitimate war, indiscriminate killing) are wrong—unethical and ineffective. As shown herein, rather than enhancing security, the misguided policies of GWOT have made us less secure.

Rule of law—help not hindrance

The origins of the rule of law can be found in antiquity, namely the writings of Aristotle and the development of Roman law. Aristotle developed the concept of natural law rooted in universal morality.[16] Natural law theorists use ethical principles to evaluate law. Cicero saw natural law as the necessary foundation for all valid law.

Basic rule of law principles include:

- supremacy of law—all persons are subject to law; no one is above or below it
- limited government power; individual liberties
- due process[17] (basic fairness in legal proceedings)
- presumption of innocence (*writ of habeas corpus*; no coerced confessions)
- separation of powers; checks and balances → oversight
- an independent judiciary
- protection of minority rights against the "tyranny of the majority"/mob rule
- access to information → transparency
- blind justice → accountability
- a concept of justice; an underlying moral basis for all law
- doctrine of judicial precedent; common law methodology
- restrictions on the exercise of discretionary power
- legislation is prospective, not retrospective
- a rational and proportionate approach to punishment.[18]

Post-9/11 responses by Western governments have brought to the fore the relationship between means and ends—can immoral acts be justified in pursuit of ostensibly virtuous aims? Can such acts bring good results? The international legal community has been shaken by state-sanctioned indefinite—and sometimes incommunicado—detention of terror suspects, extrajudicial abductions, secret prisons, indiscriminate killing, and torture.[19]

Indeed, Kafkaesque scenarios have been all-too-frequent in the GWOT. For instance, David Luban writes: " 'no punishment without a crime,' the most basic of all the principles of the rule of law" has been violated in the treatment of the prisoners at Guantanamo. The proposed transfer to a maximum security prison in Illinois would violate this principle by moving "men never convicted of a crime from a prison camp to a punishment facility." Further, "Under the laws of war, among them the Geneva Convention, POW's are to be detained in non-punitive conditions. If these men are truly 'law-of-war detainees', then the same should be true for them."

The International Bar Association issued a resolution in 2005:

> The IBA, the global voice of the legal profession, deplores the increasing erosion around the world of the rule of law [which] is the foundation of a civilized society. It establishes a transparent process equal and accessible to all. It ensures adherence to principles that both liberate and protect.

In 2009, the International Commission of Jurists concluding a three-year study of GWOT policies adopted by the U.S., U.K. and others, stated:

> We have been shocked by the damage done over the past seven years by excessive or abusive counter-terrorism measures in a wide range of countries around the world. Many governments, ignoring the lessons of history, have allowed themselves to be rushed into hasty responses to terrorism that have undermined cherished values and violated human rights.

For a millennium, Western secular rule of law principles have been the guiding light of establishing more just and prosperous communities. Aristotle asserted, "The rule of law is better than that of any individual."[20] Unchecked power corrupts; thus, transparency and accountability are indispensable. Immanuel Kant taught that natural law is international law, which is needed for peace.[21]

War mentality

In the GWOT, the criminal justice response to acts of terrorism has given way to a military approach. The Bush administration's decision to cast 9/11 as an act of war rather than a criminal act has had foreseeable dire consequences.[22] It helped enable the Patriot Act, Homeland Security Act, Military Commissions Act, intelligence and defense authorization acts, the unprecedented use of executive signing statements, a unitary executive theory, and other measures to weaken individual rights and strengthen the powers of the national security state, greatly reducing transparency and accountability. Rampant corruption, ineffective policy, mayhem, massive loss of life, and loss of faith in democratic institutions have ensued.

The past 15 years have seen a major expansion of the concept of armed conflict, stretching it to cover violent criminal acts such as terrorism. The transitory

U.S. military rules of engagement are far more permissive of killing than human rights law or a state's domestic law, providing a rationale for assassinations of alleged terrorists and the killing of civilians in combat zones, and prompting the Director-General of the International Committee of the Red Cross (ICRC) to ask whether international humanitarian law (IHL)—regulating the conduct of hostilities and the protection of persons during armed conflict—was still relevant.[23] The 1907 Hague Convention and the 1949 Geneva Conventions are the main sources of modern IHL. Recent attacks on hospitals, including the killing of 42 people at a hospital in Kunduz, Afghanistan, have been decried as gross violations of IHL.[24]

The Bush administration's GWOT approach was premised on the notion that the U.S. is at war with al-Qaeda and international terrorism in general, rather than targeting the people who commit acts of horrifying political violence as criminals who should be captured and prosecuted. Secret prisons in Romania, renditions to Syria, drone strikes in Yemen, illegal wiretapping, and the indefinite detention of prisoners at places like Guantanamo all rest upon the war construct. The Obama administration has reformed but not rejected this construct.[25] President Obama stated in 2010 "Our nation is at war" and "We are at war."[26] The Authorization for Use of Military Force (AUMF) Against Terrorists basically gave Bush a legal/military blank check in the name of fighting terrorism, subverting constitutional separation of powers. Passed by Congress on September 14, 2001, AUMF gave the President the power to use military force against:

> those nations, organizations, or persons he determines planned, authorized, committed, or aided the terrorist attacks that occurred on September 11, 2001, or harbored such organizations or persons, in order to prevent any future acts of international terrorism against the United States by such nations, organizations or persons.

A recent attempt to repeal the 2001 AUMF failed.[27] The success the legal system has had in dealing with criminal acts of terror has been disregarded.[28]

The construct of a war without end against a nebulous enemy has grave historical implications.[29] Emergency war powers end when the war ends. When do emergency powers end in GWOT? Because terrorism is not aligned with particular states or governments, against which war may be declared, negotiations entered into, or peace accords signed by its representatives after a military outcome, such a "war" can never be won, and therefore carries the very-real prospect of perpetual war.[30] In the words of James Madison:

> Of all the enemies to public liberty war is, perhaps, the most to be dreaded, because it comprises and develops the germs of every other.... In war too, the discretionary power of the executive is extended ... and all the means of seducing the minds, are added to those of subduing the force, of the people. No nation could preserve its freedom in the midst of continual war.[31]

Lawless conduct

The Bush administration violated law governing the legitimate basis for and conduct of war,[32] maintaining that GWOT could not be restrained by international law, portraying the Geneva Conventions as irrelevant and international organizations as appeasers of evil.[33] It also violated the Nuremberg Principles.[34] These violations did not go unnoticed or unchallenged. Of the many voices of protest, one mainstream example was American writer and story-teller Garrison Keillor, who accused Bush of war crimes.[35]

The Bush administration held that "unlawful enemy combatants" are not entitled to the protections of international humanitarian law because they allegedly pose an unconventional threat in an ongoing war—a contention firmly rejected by the U.N., E.U., jurists and legal scholars.[36] The 1949 Geneva Conventions provide for comprehensive categorization and treatment of all actors, even saboteurs. As then-U.N. Secretary General Kofi Annan told the BBC in 2006, by U.S. logic prisoners at Guantanamo could be held in perpetuity without charge. The same "logic" applies to "the battlefield," which in GWOT may be anywhere in the world. The May 31 2010 *New York Times* editorial (Backwards at Bagram) addresses the evisceration of the right of habeas corpus as courts have deferred to excessive claims of executive power in GWOT. The *Times* notes that the creation of law-free zones "was dreamed up by Mr. Bush and subsequently embraced by President Obama." A federal appeals court ruling on the U.S. military prison at Bagram Air Base in Afghanistan overturned a district judge's ruling that a detainee captured outside of Afghanistan, far from any battlefield, and then shipped to Bagram to be held indefinitely, has a right of habeas corpus. The appeals court reasoned that this would "hamper the war effort."

America's leadership has been undermined due to the discrepancy between its words and deeds. America, the moving force for the Nuremberg Trials, assisted emerging democracies to draft constitutions and establish institutions to uphold the rule of law. As noted by human rights attorney-scholar Scott Horton, the consistent application of the Nuremberg rules "seems to have been completely forgotten, and the rule seems to be: Scapegoat a few enlisted men, but no senior official or senior officer will be held to account for anything. It's the total abnegation of the Nuremberg rule."[37]

Impunity for criminal abuses of GWOT prisoners continues under the Obama administration, abetted by the decision not to investigate the history of criminal abuse under his predecessor, and the ongoing use of GWOT policy like the state secrets defense to lawsuits alleging abuse.[38] Obama's Department of Justice announced on November 9, 2010, following a prolonged investigation into the destruction of videotapes of brutal interrogations of terror suspects, that it will not prosecute any of the CIA officers or top-lawyers who were involved in obstructing justice by destroying evidence of torture and other criminality. According to CIA officialdom, the agency withheld the existence of the tapes from the federal courts and the September 11 Commission, which had asked the agency for records of the interrogations, because officials feared the devastating impact of their disclosure.

In other words, the CIA knew that torture was horrifyingly wrong and that its disclosure would mobilize public protest. Thus, in addition to destroying evidence, a war on journalism has been deployed in order to keep the public in the dark.[39] Nonetheless, systemic torture in GWOT is a matter of public record. The fact that criminal proceedings have been brought only against leakers and not torturers is what enables war criminals to appear in the media as influential policy-makers, and allows Donald Trump and other candidates for office to advocate barbaric unlawful policy.[40]

Following 9/11, some U.S. officials cast law as a weapon of the enemy.[41] The U.S. turned the rule of law on its head—linking judicial processes with terrorism, and ignoring its history shaping the norms and institutions it now denigrated.[42] The notion espoused by former attorney general Alberto Gonzalez that the U.S. may disregard law precedent is inimical to its jurisprudence. According to the *New York Times*, "Because Bush does not recognize that American law or international treaties apply to his decisions as commander in chief [hearings afforded Guantanamo detainees] mock any notion of democratic justice."[43] The Nuremberg Principles compel accountability for abuses, whoever bears responsibility. The lack of accountability of U.S. officials for detainee abuses at Abu Ghraib, Bagram and elsewhere is stark.[44]

"Trust us"

GWOT enabled government secrecy and muzzling of dissent. Casting 9/11 as an act of war created a bunker mentality[45]—marked by a series of radical executive orders, and steamrolling legislation through a pliant Congress. GWOT also entailed police harassment and unlawful detention of scores of citizens based merely on their name, national origin and appearance.[46] In the media there was what has been aptly described as a "paralysis of skepticism" on issues such as Iraq's alleged WMD and ties to al-Qaeda.[47] The major media outlets misled their viewers by presenting Pentagon propagandists as independent expert analysts.[48] Those who dissented were demonized. In GWOT, Bush said, "you are either with us or you are with the terrorists." Thus, if you question GWOT tactics you are suspect.

Dissent is a core value guaranteed by the First Amendment. National security and free speech are often in tension, especially during times of armed conflict. National security has afforded policymakers with a long-standing rationale for bending the rules. Long before 9/11 officials deviated from norms of fairness and decency in fighting enemies: The Alien and Sedition Acts of 1798 criminalized speech critical of the government; Abraham Lincoln suspended habeas corpus; Red scares followed both world wars; more than 100,000 Japanese-Americans were imprisoned without charge during WWII; in the 1950s anti-communist crusaders discarded the presumption of innocence. Tactics placing expediency over principle were also employed against witches and anarchists. In this regard, GWOT is not at all a different kind of war, but a continuation of long-standing anti-democratic practices.

GWOT tactics have deep roots which transcend party lines and administrations. Bush-Cheney's bravado in going to "the dark side" was stylistically deviant, but the policy of kidnapping suspected terrorists was enabled by executive orders from the Clinton Presidency. Today, Obama's crackdown on whistleblowers and condemnation of Ed Snowden and WikiLeaks furthers executive secrecy, and secrecy abets the lawless use of force. As noted in the October 9, 2010 *New York Times* editorial (Lethal Force Under Law), "The Obama administration has sharply expanded the shadow war against [alleged] terrorists, using both the military and the CIA to track down and kill hundreds of them, in a dozen countries, on and off the battlefield."[49]

Former U.S. Supreme Court Justices Goldberg ("Power not ruled by law is a menace.") and Brandeis ("Sunlight is the best disinfectant.") sought to prevent abuse of power. Indeed, democracy rests upon mistrust by the people of the government at least as much as trust—that is why we have the Bill of Rights, and law mandating open government, record keeping requirements, access to information, and public disclosures.

Dark times

Following the 9/11 attacks, Vice-president Cheney said of the U.S.: "We have to work the dark side, if you will. Spend time in the shadows of the intelligence world."[50] In November 2005, the *Washington Post* broke the story of CIA-run secret prisons in Europe.[51] The "black sites" (the term used in classified U.S. documents) revelations led to an outcry in Europe with governments accused of consenting to American political prisons on their soil. The Council of Europe, which oversees compliance with the European Convention on Human Rights, found violations of international and European law "concerning the transfer and temporary detention of individuals, without any judicial involvement ... individuals had been abducted and transferred to other countries without respect for any legal standards."[52]

Kidnappings of individuals suspected of having committed acts of terrorism were carried out by the CIA's counterterrorist center rendition group—whose agents wore black masks while abducting suspects—rather than by law enforcement officials making arrests and bringing indictments.[53] So-called extraordinary rendition bears no resemblance to extradition, the transfer of criminal suspects through proper legal channels. The rendered suspect is denied legal protections that accompany physical presence in a territory which respects the rule of law. With no criminal charges pending, suspects are abducted, hidden and, according to Amnesty International and others, brutalized. Extrajudicial action, widely used by Bush and continued by Obama,[54] is neither founded upon nor connected with any court of law.

The *New York Times* commented upon the case of Maher Arar, a Canadian citizen rendered to Syria:

> There, he was held for 10 months in an underground rat-infested dungeon and brutally tortured because officials suspected that he was a member of

al-Qaeda. All this was part of a morally and legally unsupportable United States practice known as "extraordinary rendition," in which the federal government outsources interrogations to regimes known to use torture and lacking fundamental human rights protections.[55]

The Canadian government apologized to Mr. Arar and paid him financial compensation for its role in his abduction. The U.S. government has neither apologized nor acknowledged any wrongdoing—an all-too-familiar result for those who have suffered abuse in the War on Terror. Another example is Khaled el-Masri, a German citizen who alleged he was kidnapped and tortured by U.S. officials, had his claims verified by German state investigators but, as other like-victims, was denied his day in court when the U.S. government said that to defend against the case would require the disclosure of state secrets.[56]

Abductees merely suspected of wrongdoing have been routinely locked up indefinitely and incommunicado and sent to countries known for human rights abuses, such as Jordan, Morocco, Syria and Egypt.[57] With no judicial oversight, the same operatives who capture a suspect oversee their own actions. U.N. Commission on Human Rights Special Rapporteur Manfred Novak says extraordinary rendition is arbitrary detention and "a complete repudiation of the law."

The U.S. rendered terror suspects to Syria and Egypt while its own State Department Human Rights Report condemned these countries' use of torture. Former CIA director Porter Goss called waterboarding [holding a prisoner's head under water until near drowning] a "professional interrogation technique," and when asked to define torture said it is "in the eye of the beholder." A U.N. Report concluded that U.S. attempts to redefine torture in order to allow conduct "that would not be permitted under the internationally accepted definition of torture are of utmost concern."[58]

In December 2005, the House of Lords ruled that evidence obtained through torture is inadmissible in British courts regardless of who did the torturing. Britain's highest court noted the more than 500 years of English law and the moral weight of international treaties and obligations, adding:

> The principles of the common law, standing alone ... compel the exclusion of third party torture evidence as unreliable, unfair, offensive to ordinary standards of humanity and decency and incompatible with the principles which should animate a tribunal seeking to administer justice.[59]

The 1984 UN Convention Against Torture, signed by the United States and 158 other states, establishes torture as unjustifiable and intolerable. The ticking-bomb scenario is oft-employed by those condoning torture via a cost-benefit approach. This scenario, whereby a terrorist in custody won't tell how to defuse the bomb which will kill many innocents in a matter of minutes, is a fanciful tailor-made scenario used to justify torture. Nearly all experienced interrogators assert that torture does not produce useful information (since a person will say anything to stop the torture), but rather wastes precious law enforcement resources in a wild-goose chase.[60]

Torture soils the torturer, degrading the principles which were its greatest strength.[61] Torture leads to a no-win Catch-22. Having acted outside the bounds of law and decency, those who obtain information by torture find it inadmissible in a court of law, making the prosecutions of those tortured and many other criminals near-impossible. And so, indefinite unlawful detention continues and places like Guantanamo become their custodians' prisons too.[62] Obama's inability to fulfill his pledge to close Guantanamo is one more sign that U.S. officials have become prisoners of their unethical and unlawful practices.

An August 2010 report by *ProPublica* and *The National Law Journal* states that only 24 of the 779 men who have been held at Guantanamo have even been charged with a crime, and following the 2008 Supreme Court ruling that prisoners at Guantanamo can challenge their detention as enemy combatants under the constitutional right of habeas corpus the U.S. lost 37 of the 53 such cases brought in federal court.[63] These cases largely turned on the inability to prove terrorist acts because the evidence was tainted by torture. Thus, torture is a bad act which brings bad results.

Secret government

In his 1961 farewell address, President Eisenhower warned of the growing influence of the "military-industrial complex"—an alliance of military, economic and political interests with "unwarranted influence" on American government.[64] GWOT has enabled a military-security contractor complex. The rise of private contractors and their influence on public officials comprises a government within the government—one shrouded in secrecy, which is beginning to come to light.[65]

In July 2010 the *Washington Post* reported on the vastly expanded and transformed American national security operations post-9/11.[66] Top Secret America documents the existence of more than 1,250 government agencies and 1,930 private companies working on security-oriented programs at some 10,000 sites throughout the U.S. An estimated 854,000 people have top-secret security clearance, 265,000 of whom are employees not of the government but of private, profit-making businesses. Then-defense secretary Robert Gates and then-CIA director Leon Panetta told the *Post* they worry "whether the federal workforce includes too many people obligated to shareholders rather than the public interest—and whether the government is still in control of its most sensitive activities."[67]

Glenn Greenwald writes, "Most of what the U.S. government does of any significance—literally—occurs behind a vast wall of secrecy, completely unknown to the citizenry."[68] Greenwald notes that close to 50 percent of all U.S. tax revenue now goes to military and intelligence spending.[69] According to the *Post*:

> The top-secret world the government created in response to the terrorist attacks of September 11, 2001, has become so large, so unwieldy and so secretive that no one knows how much money it costs, how many people it

employs, how many programs exist within it or exactly how many agencies do the same work.[70]

Within nine years, the U.S. intelligence budget grew to two-and-a-half times its size on September 10, 2001.[71] $75 billion was spent in 2009.[72] Intelligence and other security agencies were given "more money than they were capable of responsibly spending."[73] The *Post*'s two-year investigation found U.S. national security operations thoroughly lacking in oversight, with contractors playing an ever more important role.[74]

> To have the country's most sensitive duties carried out only by people loyal above all to the nation's interest, federal rules say contractors may not perform what are called "inherently governmental functions." But they do, all the time in every intelligence and counterterrorism agency.[75]

Then-defense secretary Gates confessed, "I can't even get a number on how many contractors work for the Office of the Secretary of Defense."[76]

The *Post* reports, "Most [contractors] are thriving even as the rest of the United States struggles with bankruptcies, unemployment and foreclosures. The privatization of national security work has been made possible by a nine-year 'gusher' of money."[77] According to Professor Alison Stanger, this has helped the enemy by blurring the line between the legitimate and illegitimate use of force in war zones.[78] Military contractors in Afghanistan now outnumber U.S. troops three to one, the highest ratio of contractors to military personnel in U.S. history.[79] Naomi Klein describes the trend of privatizing core public functions as the outsourcing of the government's brain. Has sovereignty been outsourced?

The Snowden leaks enable us to see the architecture made by our shadow government, exposing the magnitude of the national security state's manipulation of institutions and law in order to maintain and extend power and control over the people.[80] Once again, we see that leaks are healthy for the democratic ecosystem—enabling a much needed corrective to the political tendency toward excessive secrecy.[81] We also see that Obama's unprecedented crackdown on leakers is harmful to our democracy. Ultimately, in our digital age, secrecy can only be maintained by intimidating the people to not use their freedoms. The greatest harm of the vast state surveillance system, involving a murky alliance between Silicon Valley and the national security state, is the chilling effect it has on the people, knowing that big brother is always watching.[82]

Fear factory: for war and stupidity

While war profiteers are building "smart bombs" and other new means of killing, they are using both new and old methods to keep the public dumb enough to consent to senseless pro-war policy. In addition to intimidation by the surveillance state, this involves corruption, coercion, influence-peddling, fear-mongering, and all sorts of propaganda to manufacture consent for militarism.

Propaganda has infiltrated culture to keep terror omnipresent. It has also been used as a tool to legitimize immoral ineffective policy. For instance, the well-marketed film *Zero Dark Thirty* depicts torture as providing useful intelligence which led to the capture of Osama bin Laden. The CIA was involved in every stage of the film-making process, leaking classified information with impunity in order to create the false impression for moviegoers around the world that torture works.[83] Likewise, the Emmy Award winning Fox television show "24" leads viewers to believe fiction, not reality, when each weekly episode presents the fanciful ticking bomb scenario used to justify torture.[84] The message of the show's protagonist is taken as gospel: "Whatever it takes" in fighting Islamic extremism—but the portrayal of the utility of torture is directly at odds with reality, as noted by real interrogators like Ali Soufan.

Television, Radio and Web commercials also invoke patriotic jingoism supporting GWOT. For instance, McDonald's uses post-9/11 patriotism in a widely run commercial.[85] Numerous other companies invoke support our troops as part of their marketing campaigns. Myriad entertainment forms have been propagandized to support war, sometimes involving secret cash payments, such as the Pentagon paying professional sports teams and leagues to honor the troops during their contests and broadcasts.[86] In post-9/11 major league baseball, the seventh inning stretch was changed from the singing of *Take Me Out to the Ballgame* to the singing of *God Bless America* and a tribute to the troops. Carlos Delgado was denied his deserved place in the baseball hall of fame seemingly in retribution for his moral courage in being the only player who did not participate in these daily displays of pro-military patriotism. Professional sports entertainment is a major part of the lives of Americans. Fifteen years on, this mindless shameless display of pro-military propaganda continues daily.

Mainstream media institutionally serves the war mentality through its business practices, and biases in reporting "news". This involves corporate ownership, advertising revenues, and the atrophied "journalism" it practices. As Glenn Greenwald argues, most people who call themselves journalists aren't. As the Fourth Estate, journalists should be challenging the official story, not parroting it. David Barstow won a Pulitzer Prize for his investigative reporting showing how CNN, Fox, CBS, and NBC misled their viewers in airing propaganda orchestrated by Donald Rumsfeld's Pentagon in support of the U.S. war in Iraq.[87] Scholar Lance Bennett's Indexing Theory posits four media biases which serve to keep viewers lost in the spin cycle.[88] This serves to keep the public from focusing on the need to hold torturers accountable for their crimes against humanity.[89]

Specifically on GWOT, consider the following: According to FBI data, 94 percent of the terrorist attacks carried out in the U.S. between 1985 and 2005 were by non-Muslims, yet the media portrays acts of terror as almost exclusively carried out by Muslims.[90] White gun violence accounts for more terror crimes in the U.S. than Muslim terror acts, yet media coverage given to Muslim terror is more than 20 times that given to white gun terror.[91] Fairness and Accuracy in Reporting (fair.org) has documented gross anti-Muslim media bias in reporting terror perpetrators and victims.[92]

However, despite efforts to manufacture consent for barbarism and to make war without end the new normal, as the costs and wrongfulness come to the surface[93] dissent spreads. So, new enemies and conflicts (even recycled ones) play a useful role for merchants of death, and so Putin and the Russian bear are called in from stage left as a (old) new threat to security.

Tortured and wounded—one and all

If the root of terror is fear, humiliation, anger, desperation and hopelessness,[94] then U.S. foreign policy is obviously counter-productive in meeting its stated aims.

Fifteen years after 9/11, the facts are clear:

1. Tortured is clearly defined under international and state law
2. The U.S. response to 9/11 involved practices which constitute torture under the law—these practices were systemic, ongoing over years, widespread, and approved by the highest levels of the U.S. government
3. The CIA destroyed evidence in a futile effort to cover-up its atrocities
4. Torture and other atrocity is shroud in the flag
5. Although individuals who tortured and sanctioned torture are known, nobody has been punished for torture
6. With respect to the U.S. government involvement in torture, the only people who were prosecuted for crimes are the people of conscience in government who sought to get the facts out regarding torture and other human rights violations
7. Torture is classed along with genocide and other crimes against humanity under international law, as the worst possible violations of humanity and nature

What has happened since September 2001 is remarkable. Our professed values and heritage have been shelved for false security.[95] War profiteers have warped democracy. Professionals in law,[96] psychology,[97] and medicine[98] have acted as tools of torturers. Dissent has been criminalized.[99] Free speech and protest are now viewed with suspicion—children have been imprisoned for tweeting about ISIS,[100] animal rights and environmental activists have been classed as terrorists for peaceful protest,[101] efforts have been made to criminalize aggressive investigative journalism. Language has been degraded and logic mocked. The public sphere has been ceded—now even the area in front of the Supreme Court is off limits to the public.[102] The propaganda of American exceptionalism and killing has bled deeply into the culture and psychology of the country, making all people less free and less secure.

Evidence of the failure of the GWOT

Have kidnapping, torture, secrecy and war brought about a better or safer world? Kishore Mahbubani argues that unethical and unlawful GWOT practices like torture and Guantanamo have brought America into disrepute—and serve as powerful recruiting tools for terrorists.[103] A comprehensive study by the Rand Corporation provides evidence supporting this claim.[104]

As for the avowed goal of GWOT (to weaken militant jihadists), the military approach is in disarray. 2010 became the deadliest year for NATO forces in the then nine-year Afghan war.[105] Wars have failed to establish stable governance in Iraq or Afghanistan. The *International Herald Tribune* reported that the trend is further deterioration: "Even as more U.S. troops flow into Afghanistan, the country is more dangerous than it has ever been during the war.... The number of insurgent attacks has increased significantly."[106]

This fits with the findings of the key intelligence bodies of the U.S. government (the CIA and the NIE) that the presence of U.S. armed forces in foreign land is a magnet for insurgents, and the findings of leading scholars.[107] Former-CIA anti-terror expert Michael Scheuer writes, "U.S. forces and policies are completing the radicalization of the Islamic world ... it is fair to conclude that the United States of America remains bin Laden's only indispensable ally."[108] Noam Chomsky argues that if we apply the law approach of relying on predictable outcomes as evidence of intent, we may conclude that the declared goals of GWOT are not the real ones.[109]

The 2006 National Intelligence Estimate (NIE), the cumulative assessment of all U.S. intelligence agencies, concluded that rather than improving its national security, the tactics used in GWOT, especially in the war in Iraq, worsened the U.S. position by creating a recruitment vehicle for violent Islamic extremists and motivating a new generation of potential terrorists.[110] The Rand Corporation reached similar conclusions in 2008.[111] The Iraqi government is now weak and the Taliban strong. Iran is stronger. Al-Qaeda now has roots in Iraq, which it did not have before GWOT. GWOT has been a boon to rather than a deterrent to terrorism.[112] Over the past 15 years, there has been a steady and dramatic rise in the incidence of terror attacks by non-state actors and the fatalities caused by such terror attacks.[113]

On September 22, 2010, three key Obama administration officials testified to Congress that the threat of terrorism is spreading. Homeland Security Secretary Janet Napolitano said the U.S. was confronting "more diverse activity" as al-Qaeda had inspired a more diverse array of terror groups.[114] This follows the trend in U.S. government reports of an ever-increasing terrorist threat since 2001, especially since the 2003 invasion of Iraq.[115] A 2005 Chatham House study concluded "there is no doubt that the invasion of Iraq has given a boost to the al-Qaeda network in propaganda, recruitment and fundraising, while providing an ideal training area for terrorists."[116] The presence of U.S. forces in Afghanistan strengthens the Taliban and jihadists, just as the U.S. military presence in the Islamic holy lands of Saudi Arabia feeds militant jihadism throughout the Islamic world. As the Rand Corporation 2008 study concludes, "making a world of enemies is never a winning strategy."[117]

War is costly—in many ways. The secret war documents published in 2010 by WikiLeaks provide first-hand accounts painting a grim portrait of the wars in

Afghanistan and Iraq. These documents inject a dose of reality, countering the sanitized narrative used by officials and parroted by the media. They cut through euphemisms like "collateral damage," revealing the carnage of these wars. The October 24, 2010 U.K. *Sunday Observer* editorial (A Moral Catastrophe: The Final Reasons for Going to War are Being Swept Away) says the WikiLeaks files:

> reveal how allied forces turned a blind eye to torture and murder of prisoners held by the Iraqi army. Reports of appalling treatment of detainees were verified by the US army and deemed unworthy of further investigation ... build[ing] a portrait of a military occupation deeply implicated in practices that were illegal under international law and unconscionable in the eyes of any reasonable observer.[118]

Lawless amoral conduct also makes the chicken come home to roost as Malcolm X put it. There were more terrorism arrests in the U.S. in 2015 than in any other year since 2001, and so-called homegrown terror attacks are rising. William Finnegan reports:

> Hundreds of Americans—and thousands of Europeans—have made their way to Syria and Iraq to join the fighting for the so-called caliphate. But now ISIS is asking its supporters, as Al Qaeda did before it, to stay home and stage attacks where they are, particularly in Dar Al-Kufr (non-Muslim lands). The goal is to provoke crackdowns and divisions—within the West, between Muslims and the West, between different groups of Muslims. The strategy is working.[119]

The costs of the GWOT are myriad and staggering. In their joint report called *Body Count: Casualty Figures after 10 Years of the War on Terror*, Physicians for Social Responsibility, Physicians for Global Survival, and the Nobel Prize-winning International Physicians for the Prevention of Nuclear War concluded that at least 1.3 million lives lost in Iraq, Afghanistan, and Pakistan alone since the onset of the war following September 11, 2001. As the report notes, this is a conservative estimate, and the total number killed in the three countries "could also be in excess of two million, whereas a figure below one million is extremely unlikely."[120] According to a 2013 report of Harvard University's Kennedy School of Government, the monetary cost of the GWOT from 9/11 until early 2013 was approximately $6 trillion.[121] Great portions of the Middle East and Asia have been thrown into further chaos and suffering.[122] War refugees have made a desperate exodus to Europe, polarizing politics on the continent.[123] Trillions of dollars have been spent and the result is more war, inequality, debt, poverty, pain, suffering, fear, polarization, and desperation.[124]

The wars helped to sink the American economy into its worst recession since the 1930s. President Bush inherited a $281 billion federal budget surplus, the largest surplus in American history, when he took power in 2001. When he left office, the U.S. had record current account and trade deficits. Liberty has been eroded as privacy has given way to surveillance. The social contract has been ruptured, as hope and prosperity have given way to fear and poverty.[125] Military Keynesianism is America's time-tested response to economic hard times. In whose interest? Perhaps the mission has actually been accomplished. Perpetual war and the disintegration of order abroad are hugely profitable for those in the obsolete "war masquerading as security" industry.

A better approach: prevent terrorist attacks legally and ethically

Clearly, the unethical, illegal and anti-democratic tactics used in GWOT have not made the world better or safer. The rule of law safeguards liberty, security and justice. Policies rooted in abuse, illegality and deception are doomed to fail because they degrade the very principles we strive towards. What can be done?

Take practical steps, don't over-react, and think through the consequences of policies. The sealing of the cockpits on airplanes was a sensible and effective remedy to the threat of terrorists hijacking planes to use as missiles. If we look at the means by which terror attacks are being carried out today we can see that in the U.S. guns are used, and in Europe chemicals are being used to make explosives. So, gun control laws will help reduce terror in the U.S., and wider use of police dogs to detect the malodorous chemicals being used to make bombs in Europe will help to stop terror attacks there.[126]

The war in Iraq was disastrous because ideology trumped common sense. It was entirely foreseeable that occupying Iraq would incite terror attacks. Shifting Justice Department lawyers from white collar crime to terror-funding prevention was likewise overzealous and senseless. It doesn't require much money to get a desperate enraged person to become a suicide bomber. Again, unforeseen consequences ensued, abetting financial recklessness, impunity and our ongoing Great Recession.

As well, corruption has been abetted, leading to foolish policy such as the military transfer program to local law enforcement, which has foreseeably undermined relations between police and the public they are supposed to serve and protect, creating a culture of mistrust, brutality and hatred.[127] The streets in America now resemble a war zone in a growing number of communities.

The 2008 Rand study of terror groups since 1968 found they ended because they joined the political process or because local police and intelligence agencies arrested or killed key members. "Military force has rarely been the primary reason for the end of terrorist groups.... [This] suggests fundamentally rethinking post-9/11 U.S. counterterrorism strategy."[128] The report criticizes the U.S. for making military force its primary policy instrument, arguing that police and intelligence work should be the backbone of U.S. efforts.[129]

Officials should better coordinate law enforcement and intelligence activities both domestically (local law enforcement, FBI and CIA coordination is needed, not turf wars) and internationally. The Christmas day 2009 failed bombing attempt by the troubled young Nigerian man who tried to ignite explosives in his underwear is a cautionary tale exposing the failings of GWOT.[130] This was the very type of act GWOT was supposed to prevent, all the warnings were there, and the would-be-bomber never should have been allowed to board the Northwest Airlines flight. The same can be said of the 2013 Boston Marathon bombing. The multiple systemic failings show that throwing money at the problem doesn't fix it. The bloated national security bureaucracy described in the *Washington Post*'s Top Secret America is a system which compiles so much information in such an uncoordinated manner that it cannot connect the dots even when they are laid out in a clear way, which is to say that the post-9/11 intelligence community can neither think nor see straight.[131]

Use the criminal justice system to investigate and prosecute terror acts, not the Pentagon and CIA. Use proven methods of law enforcement, not extrajudicial means—the British police apparently foiled a plot to blow-up transatlantic airplanes by dogged police work using lawful surveillance and international cooperation. Europe's law enforcement approach has been relatively successful combating terrorism. There is no admissible evidence against the vast majority of the prisoners held at Guantanamo. That no charges have been brought against these people held for more than a decade proves the failure of the lawless U.S. dark-side approach.[132]

Use the institutions and agencies established for collective defense and development, allowing them to do their jobs, rather than, e.g., pressuring scientists and intelligence officials to distort their findings to fit some preconceived political agenda, or preventing the International Atomic Energy Agency (IAEA) from completing its inspections. Stop demonizing opponents; maintain channels of communication, even with perceived enemies, because "rogue states" are better than failed states—at least there is someone to negotiate with.[133] At home, keep secrecy and censorship to a bare minimum. Dissent and open debate are vital for democracy, as are transparency and accountability.[134] "Trust us" prevents us from knowing whether government claims of foiled terror attacks and new threats are legitimate. Impunity assures that war crimes and other immoral and unlawful acts will continue; lawbreakers must be punished.

Fund the UN Millennium Development Goals. Suicide bombers are borne mainly out of desperation; fighting dire poverty will reduce terror. This implies that the U.S. government should no longer support corrupt oppressive regimes in Egypt, Saudi Arabia and elsewhere that use their countries' oil wealth primarily to further their own privileged position in society and to promote hatred and terror abroad—but rather should use development aid to reduce poverty and inequity.[135] This further implies that spending for U.S. military and arms trafficking should be redirected towards economic and social development.[136]

With so much media focus on terrorism following the attacks in San Bernardino, Copenhagen, Paris and Brussels, seldom if ever does the most obvious question get asked: Why? What led these human beings to commit such monstrous acts? We cannot rationally address the problem if we do not understand its causes. In *What Terrorists Want*, Louise Richardson claims that terrorists are largely driven by a sense of moral righteousness in combatting perceived injustice. In *Talking to the Enemy*, the anthropologist Scott Atran examines the social context of militancy, claiming that more than dying for a cause terrorists die for those in their social networks. Atran reveals terrorism as social, decentralized and rather anarchic.[137]

Deterrence of terrorist attacks should be the goal of a well-coordinated anti-terrorism policy. Indeed, an ounce of prevention is worth a pound of cure. *The Economist* reports:

> Does it matter to the United States that Somalia is becoming a hotbed of global jihad? The answer most often heard in Washington is impenetrable. "Somalia is not important until it launches a terrorist attack which makes it important," explains a Pentagon official.[138]

This is like a doctor telling a healthy patient, "I'll give you an examination when you're in the ICU." The U.S. Constitution establishes civilian command of the military, yet policy often reflects the Pentagon's priorities. This must change if we are to de-escalate GWOT and reduce terrorism.

Live and learn

Philosopher George Santayana warned "Those who do not remember the past are condemned to repeat it." A level-headed analysis of the challenge of defeating terror makes clear what works and what doesn't.

At the Nuremberg Trials, U.S. Chief Counsel Robert Jackson stated:

> If certain acts of violations of treaties are crimes, they are crimes whether the United States does them or whether Germany does them, and we are not prepared to lay down a rule of criminal conduct against others which we would not be willing to have invoked against us.... We must never forget the record on which we judge these defendants is the record on which history will judge us tomorrow. To pass these defendants a poisoned chalice is to put it to our own lips as well.[139]

Kant wrote, "a violation of rights in one part of the world is felt everywhere."[140] That is most true today—and the consequences of injustice include terrorism. GWOT marks a low-point in American history for the gravity, scope and impact of its immoral practices. Making enemies is never a winning strategy. Hypocrisy is unethical, and weak.

Treating the globe as a battlefield is certainly not the way to reduce terror or terrorism.[141] We can apply simple logic to the past 15 years (but for A, no B; but for B, no C. Thus, no A, no C): Al-Qaeda did not exist in Iraq prior to the U.S. military misadventure there. ISIS did not exist, but for the rise of Al-Qaeda in Iraq. Thus, ISIS would not exist but for U.S. militarism and war mentality. Further, Libya now affords safe haven to all terror groups today, following the NATO military misadventure there.

FDR wisely said, "the only thing we have to fear is fear itself." Stopping the war-machine will not be easy—powerful industries and policymakers are profiting by spreading fear and war. It will require an actively engaged civil society to counter the fear-mongering and carnage of the GWOT. Building peace requires greater strength than waging war. The U.S. government must be made to stop acting in ways that—predictably—enhance the threat of terrorism.[142]

In order to do this, we must educate people about the corruption of politics and the public sphere caused by the deep state in the U.S.A. Let's be frank, GWOT is a symptom of deeply embedded distortion—reflected by money in politics and its manifestations.[143] Business will seek profit, government is to safeguard. Since 1980, free market follies have reigned.[144] The media serves to manufacture consent for destructive policy, spinning a tale told to us as idiots, full of sound and fury, leading to misery. Absent energized and organized dissent, those who profit from GWOT will lead us further down a path of barbarism and decay. We must use all the tools and imagination we can muster in order to forge new paths toward justice.

At present, there has been no official reckoning, no truth and reconciliation commission, only denial and deceit. We must demand that there be an official record of war crimes committed in GWOT and that those responsible are punished.[145] Otherwise, we will be led like sheep into the abyss.

Changing course

Every action brings a reaction. Terror from above brings terror from below.[146] Ongoing extreme abuse of power brings protest and dissent. Perhaps we are ascending from the depths to which we have sunk. Ed Snowden, Bernie Sanders, and yes, even Donald Trump, are marking some change. Level-headed energized dissent will make that change one which brings greater decency, and which better safeguards the future of humans and the natural world which enables our existence.

New opportunities for progress arise constantly. The Panama Papers revelations[147] offer one recent example of how technology and investigative journalism offer powerful tools for teaching.[148] Education and digital activism must be accompanied by direct action[149]—which is indispensable in the struggle for social justice. We have the means and capacity to catalyze an uprising against myopic policy based on greed and corruption.

We can change course—to align law and policy with ethics, and bend the arc of our moral universe toward justice. Perhaps we are nearing a peak. We find strength in our moral heroes. Emma Goldman for her free-thinking and life. Rosa Parks for saying NO! Dr. King for his eloquent moral clarity and vision. Muhammad Ali for his principled courage. Nelson Mandela for his strength, grace, and generosity of spirit. Vaclav Havel for his wisdom in living in truth and showing the power of the powerless. And the list goes on. We can be sure that ending the war mentality which has fed the immoral and ineffective GWOT policies will be a struggle. It is a struggle we must engage so long as we hold any capacity for love. Perhaps we are cohering around moral principles that bind all people, forging policy that is sane, and will give actual meaning to security.[150]

Notes

1 Physicians for Social Responsibility (PSR), International Physicians for the Prevention of Nuclear War (IIPNW) and Physicians for Global Survival (PGS), "Body Count: Casualty Figures After 10 Years of the "War on Terror": Iraq, Afghanistan, Pakistan", March 2015, www.psr.org/assets/pdfs/body-count.pdf; Neta C. Crawford, "Death Toll: Will The U.S. Tolerate More Civilian Casualties In Its Bid To Vanquish ISIS?", January 21, 2016, http://cognoscenti.wbur.org/2016/01/21/civilian-casualties-iraq-syria-us-war-on-isis-neta-c-crawford; Barry S. Levy and Victor W. Sidel, "Adverse health consequences of the Iraq War", March 16, 2013, www.thelancet.com/pdfs/journals/lancet/PIIS0140–6736(13)60254-8.pdf.
2 See the reporting of Patrick Cockburn, e.g.: Patrick Cockburn; *Independent*, "Refugee crisis was caused by a careless West that allowed anarchy and fear to take root in the Middle East: The war in Syria and Iraq has gone on as long as the First World War", September 19, 2015, www.independent.co.uk/news/world/middle-east/refugee-crisis-was-caused-by-a-careless-west-that-allowed-anarchy-and-fear-to-take-root-in-the-10509173.html; the UNHCR, e.g., Jonathan Clayton and Hereward Holland; ed. Tim Gaynor, *United Nations High Commissioner for Refugees (UNHCR)*, "Over one million sea arrivals reach Europe in 2015: UNHCR figures show over one million refugees and migrants reach Europe by sea in 2015, with almost 4,000 feared drowned", December 30, 2015, www.unhcr.org/5683d0b56.html; Stefan Lenhe, Marwan Muasher, Marc Pierini, Jan Techau, Pierre Vimont, and Maha Yanya, *Carnegie Europe*; October 1, 2015, http://carnegieeurope.eu/2015/10/01/roots-of-europe-s-refugee-crisis/iie3; Amnesty International, "Annual Report 2015/2016", 2016, www.amnesty.org/en/latest/research/2016/02/annual-report-201516/; Thalif Deen, *Inter Press Service (IPS)*, "Europe Invaded Mostly by "Regime Change" Refugees", September, 2015, www.ipsnews.net/2015/09/europe-invaded-mostly-by-regime-change-refugees/.
3 Martin Smith, *Frontline*, "Rise of ISIS", October 28, 2014, www.pbs.org/wgbh/frontline/film/rise-of-isis/.
4 Mary Ellen O Connell, When Is War Not a War? The Myth of the Global War on Terror, *ILSA Journal of International and Comparative Law*, 12(2), (2005).
5 Andrew Rettman, "US to quadruple military spending in Europe", Febrary 2, 2016, https://euobserver.com/foreign/132101; Rick Lyman, "Eastern Europe Cautiously Welcomes Larger U.S. Military Presence", February 2, 2016, www.nytimes.com/2016/02/03/world/europe/eastern-europe-us-military.html?_r=0.
6 Patrick Cockburn, *Independent*, "Refugee crisis was caused by a careless West that allowed anarchy and fear to take root in the Middle East." September 20, 2015, http://timesofindia.indiatimes.com/world/middle-east/Refugee-crisis-was-caused-by-a-careless-West-that-allowed-anarchy-and-fear-to-take-root-in-the-Middle-East/articleshow/49033416.cms.
7 William A. Cohn, "The Security Trap", www.informationclearinghouse.info/article37911.htm; William A. Cohn, "Another Terror Trap", September 29, 2014, www.counterpunch.org/2014/09/29/another-terror-trap/.
8 Jo Becker and Scott Shane, "Hillary Clinton, 'Smart Power' and a Dictator's Fall", February 27, 2016, www.nytimes.com/2016/02/28/us/politics/hillary-clinton-libya.html?hp&action=click&pgtype=Homepage&clickSource=story-heading&module=span-ab-top-region&region=top-news&WT.nav=top-news.
9 Paul Krugman, "Crazy about money," *New York Times*, March 26–27, 2016, 7.

10 Jeff Bachman, *Common Dreams*, "Revisiting the 'Humanitarian' Intervention in Libya", March 15, 2016, www.commondreams.org/views/2016/03/15/revisiting-humanitarian-intervention-libya.
11 Andrew J. Bacevich, *America's War for the Greater Middle East: A Military History*, (New York: Random House, 2016); Andrew J. Bacevich, *Politico Magazine*, "Let's End America's Hopeless War for the Middle East", April 3, 2016, www.politico.com/magazine/story/2016/04/middle-east-foreign-policy-afghanistan-unwinnable-213778.
12 Civil disobedience is an act of individual conscience to deliberately violate a law seen as unethical based on the principle that one has a moral right to disobey an immoral law. See Henry David Thoreau's *Civil Disobedience* (Massachusetts: Elizabeth Peabody, 1849); Rev. Martin Luther King Jr. "Letter from a Birmingham Jail," (1963), available at http://abacus.bates.edu/admin/offices/dos/mlk/letter.html, in which Dr. King writes that "one has a moral responsibility to disobey unjust laws" and "Injustice anywhere is a threat to justice everywhere.".
13 See John C. Yoo, "War, Responsibility, and the Age of Terrorism," *Stanford Law Review*, 57 (2004): 793; See also the legal opinions rendered by Bush administration lawyers Mr. Yoo, Jay Bybee and Alberto Gonzalez, available at The National Security Archive, "The Interrogation Documents: Debating U.S. Policy and Methods", July 13, 2004, www.gwu.edu/~nsarchiv/NSAEBB/NSAEBB127/.
14 Mary Ellen O Connell, When Is War Not a War? The Myth of the Global War on Terror, *ILSA Journal of International and Comparative Law*, 12 (2), (2005).
15 See: David Cole, *What Bush Wants to Hear*, (New York; Rev. Books), November 17, 2005; Ronald Dworkin, "Terror and the Attack on Civil Liberties," *The New York Review of Books*, November 6, 2003, available at www.nybooks.com/articles/archives/2003/nov/06/terror-the-attack-on-civil-liberties/; Ronald Dworkin, Rights and Terror, 2003, available at www.law.nyu.edu/clppt/program2003/readings/dworkin.pdf; Laurence H. Tribe, *The Tanner Lectures on Human Values*, delivered at Oxford University, May 20 and 21, 2002, transcript available at www.tannerlectures.utah.edu/lectures/documents/volume24/tribe_2002.pdf.
16 Aristotle, *Nicomachean Ethics*, Book V – On Justice and Fairness (350 BC).
17 There is a common misconception that the due process clause of the Fifth and Fourteenth Amendments of the Bill of Rights (protection against government action depriving an individual of life, liberty or property without due process of law) applies only to U.S. citizens. The Framers of these amendments regarded life, liberty and property as basic human or natural rights that do not depend upon citizenship, which is why these amendments refer not to citizens but to persons.
18 David Luban, "Has Obama Upheld the Law?" *The New York Review of Books*, April 21, 2016.
19 Scott Horton, "Jurists: War on Terror Tactics Have Undermined Basic Values", February 17, 2009, www.harpers.org/archive/2009/02/hbc-90004415. See also International Commission of Jurists (ICJ), www.icj.org; International Bar Association (IBA), http://ibanet.org; William A. Cohn: As Blackwater Rises the Rule of Law Recedes, *The DePaul Rule of Law Journal* (Fall 2010); *Definitions of Convenience*, 8 The New Presence: Prague J. Cent. Eur. Aff. 28 (2006).
20 Aristotle, *Politics*, 51.
21 Immanuel Kant, *Perpetual Peace: A Philosophical Essay* (1795). Translation available at http://oll.libertyfund.org/index.php?option=com_staticxt&staticfile=show.php%3Ftitle=357&Itemid=27.
22 See President Bush's address to a joint session of Congress on September 20, 2001, available at www.americanrhetoric.com/speeches/gwbush911jointsessionspeech.htm.
23 Angelo Gnaedinger, "Is IHL still relevant in a post-9/11 world?", www.icrc.org/web/eng/siteeng0.nsf/html/ihl-article-300906.

24 Médecins Sans Frontières (MSF), "Kunduz Hospital Airstrike", April 29, 2016, www.msf.org/en/topics/kunduz-hospital-airstrike.
25 The Center for Constitutional Rights conducted an April 1, 2010 assessment of Obama's record on GWOT issues (http://ccrjustice.org/obamas-record) taking issue with ongoing: abuse of executive authority; ghost detentions; material support convictions; indefinite detention of suspects at Guantanamo and elsewhere; habeas corpus denial; renditions; violation of individual civil liberties; lack of accountability for past crimes; abuse of the state secrets privilege; and human rights abuse by military contractors. See also the writings of Joanne Mariner at findlaw.com, including at http://writ.news.findlaw.com/mariner/20090630.html. See also, Charlie Savage, *Power Wars: Inside Obama's Post-9/11 Presidency* (New York: Little, Brown, & Co., 2015). See also, supra note 18.
26 Quoted in Peter Baker's "Obama's War Over Terror" available at www.nytimes.com/2010/01/17/magazine/17Terror-t.html?scp=1&sq=Peter%20Baker%20on%20Obama&st=cse; which concludes, "much of the Bush security architecture is almost certain to remain part of the national fabric for some time to come, thanks to Obama." See also: Jennifer Daskal, "Obama's Last Chance to End the 'Forever War'," April 27, 2016, www.nytimes.com/2016/04/27/opinion/obamas-last-chance-to-end-the-forever-war.html?ref=opinion&_r=0.
27 McCauley, Lauren, "Thanks to U.S. Congress, Endless War Will … Not End," *Common Dreams*, May 18, 2016, http://commondreams.org/news/2016/05/18/thanks-us-congress-endless-war-will-not-end.
28 See *In Pursuit of Justice: Prosecuting Terrorism Cases in the Federal Courts*, A White Paper prepared by a team of experienced law enforcement lawyers headed by two former U.S. Attorneys on behalf of Human Rights First in 2008. They conclude that:

> the existing criminal justice system is an established institution that has generally done a good job in handling international terrorism cases … it has proved to be adaptable and has successfully handled a large number of important and challenging terrorism prosecutions over the past 15 years without sacrificing national security interests or rigorous standards of fairness and due process.
>
> p. 129 of the Report, available in its entirety at www.humanrightsfirst.org/pdf/080521-USLS-pursuit-justice.pdf

See also "The memory hole" by Dahlia Latwick, at www.slate.com/id/2263793/; "Invisible Men," available at www.slate.com/?id=3944&qp=26373; and Jennifer Daskal, "Obama's Last Chance to End the 'Forever War'," April 27, 2016, www.nytimes.com/interactive/2016/04/07/us/terrorists-in-us-prisons.html.
29 Hilary Benn, a senior aide to Tony Blair, said in 2007 that the phrase "War on Terror" strengthens extremists: "In the U.K. we don't use the phrase 'War on Terror' because we can't win by military means alone and because this isn't one organized enemy with a coherent set of objectives."
30 See David Barash and Charles Webel, *Peace and Conflict Studies*, 2nd ed. (Thousand Oaks, Ca.: Sage Publications, 2009), p. 62. The authors present a compelling argument that terrorism has always and will always exist which makes GWOT most threatening. As well, GWOT professes to wage war against terror, a noun (thing), which is in itself fallacious. Although war has also been declared against poverty and drugs, this is using war in the broader meaning of battle or struggle. War in its traditional legal meaning of armed conflict may only be logically applied against an identifiable enemy.
31 Quoted in "What America Lost," by Fareed Zakaria, *Newsweek*, September 13, 2010, p. 8. On "seducing the minds" see David Barstow's Pulitzer Prize report "Behind TV Analysts, Pentagon's Hidden Hand," New York Times, April 20, 2008. See, more recently, "Guantanamo Censors," The *International Herald Tribune*, September 22, 2010, p. 6. On the implications of the endless war paradigm see the

writings of Andrew Bacevich, including *Washington Rules: America's Path to Permanent War* (New York: Metropolitan Books, 2010).

32 The Bush Doctrine, used in Iraq, of "taking the battle to the enemy" is a direct repudiation to the UN Charter which prohibits the use of international force unless in self-defense or *via* Security Council authorization. It would enable China to invade Taiwan and India to invade Kashmir. See Scott Horton, "Kriegsraison or Military Necessity? The Bush Administration's Wilhelmine Attitude Towards the Conduct of War," 30 *Fordham Int'l L.J.* 576 (2006–2007).

33 The U.S. attorney general's January 25, 2002 memo to the President refers to the Geneva Conventions as "quaint" and "obsolete". The ICRC found the U.S. guilty of systematic and serious violations of the Geneva Conventions of 1949 (e.g., Convention III governing the treatment of prisoners of war and Convention IV on protecting civilians in times of war). International law prohibits incommunicado detention. The Geneva Conventions require that prisoners whereabouts be documented and made available to family and governments, and that the ICRC have access to all detainees and places of detention. Violations have occurred in Iraq, Guantanamo, Afghanistan, and the secret CIA prisons.

34 War crimes, "punishable as crimes under international law" under the Principles, encompass "Violations of the laws or customs of war which include … murder or ill-treatment of prisoners of war." The Center for Constitutional Rights filed charges seeking war crimes indictments against U.S. officials including former CIA chief George Tenet and former defense secretary Donald Rumsfeld. Together, the first four Nuremberg Principles establish personal responsibility and accountability for violations of law. See Committee of the Red Cross (ICRC); February 2004, "Report on the Treatment by the Coalition Forces of Prisoners of War and other protected persons in Iraq", http://cryptome.org/icrc-report.htm. Human Rights Watch issued a report (available at www.hrw.org and at www.washingtonpost.com/wp-dyn/articles/A33349-2005Jan24.html) which led to the *New York Times* January 27, 2006 editorial "An Indictment of America": "When Human Rights Watch … focuses its annual review on America's use of torture and inhumane treatment … everyone who believed in the United States as the staunchest protector of human rights in history should be worried."

35 Garrison Keillor, "When the emperor has no clothes," *International Herald Tribune*, March 3, 2006.

36 See, e.g.: David Cole, "What Bush Wants to Hear", *The New York Review of Books*, November 17, 2005; Ronald Dworkin, "The Threat To Patriotism," *The New York Review of Books*, February 28, 2002; Justice Richard Goldstone, "U.S. Antagonism Toward the International Rule of Law: The View of a Concerned 'Outsider'" *Washington Univ. Global Studies Law Review*, 4 (2), 205 (2005); Michael Ratner, "Moving Away From the Rule of Law: Military Tribunals, Executive Detentions and Torture," 24 Cardozo L. Rev. 1513 (2002–2003) and Michael Ratner and Ellen Ray, Guantanamo: What the World Should Know (2004, White River Junction, Vermont: Chelsea Green Pub. Co.); Kenneth Roth, "Human Rights as a Response to Terrorism," *Oregon Review of International Law* (2004). See also International Commission of Jurists (ICJ), icj.org; International Bar Association (IBA), http://ibanet.org and American Bar Association, http://americanbar.org.

37 Interview with Scott Horton in the January 28, 2005 issue of *Executive Intelligence Review*, available at www.larouchepub.com/other/interviews/2005/3204scott_horton.html.

38 The Obama administration has used the state secrets defense in cases on: Bush-era warrantless wiretapping; surveillance of an Islamic charity; its assassination program; and, the torture and rendition of CIA prisoners. See the *New York Times* editorials of October 1 (Shady Secrets) and October 26, 2010 (Indefensible Defense).

39 See: William Cohn, "Fighting the Sunlight: The James Risen Case in Context", June 8, 2014, www.commondreams.org/views/2014/06/08/fighting-sunlight-james-risen-case-context; David Sirota, "Obama's war on journalism", June 28, 2013, www.salon.com/2013/06/28/obamas_war_on_journalism/; James Risen, *Pay Any Price: Greed, Power, and Endless War* (Houghton, Mifflin, Harcourt, 2014).

40 See, e.g., "Candidates and Counterterrorism," Editorial, *New York Times*, March 25, 2016 (print edition, p. 7), on statements made following the Brussels attack: "Predictably, the two leading Republicans called for severe measures against Muslims. Donald Trump also reiterated his faith in waterboarding suspected terrorists and Senator Ted Cruz said the police must 'patrol and secure' Muslim neighborhoods."

41 Former U.S. Homeland Security Secretary Michael Chertoff accused IGO's of using international law (IL) "as a rhetorical weapon against us." The Pentagon's 2005 National Defense Strategy also views IL as a threat to the US: "Our strength as a nation will continue to be challenged by those who employ *a strategy of the weak using international fora, judicial processes and terrorism.*"

42 According to the annual report of Amnesty International:

> Governments collectively and individually paralyzed international institutions and squandered public resources in pursuit of narrow security interests, sacrificed principles in the name of the "War on Terror" and turned a blind eye to massive human rights violations. As a result, the world has paid a heavy price, in terms of erosion of fundamental principles and in the enormous damage done to the lives and livelihoods of ordinary people. The War on Terrorism is failing and will continue to fail until human rights and human security are given precedence over narrow national security interests.

43 "They Came for the Chicken Farmer," March 8, 2006, available at www.nytimes.com/2006/03/08/opinion/08wed1.html?scp=1&sq=%22mock%20any%20notion%22&st=cse.

44 See: Sandra Coliver, "Bring Human Rights Abusers to Justice in U.S. Courts: Carrying Forward the Legacy of the Nuremberg Trials," 27 Cardozo L. Rev. 1689 (2005–2006); Mark Danner, "Torture and Truth," *The New York Review of Books*, June 10, 2004; Kenneth Roth, *Getting Away with Torture? Command Responsibility for the U.S. Abuse of Detainees* (New York: Human Rights Watch, 2005).

45 The noun bunker mentality is defined by *The Merriam-Webster Dictionary* as "a state of mind especially among members of a group that is characterized by chauvinistic defensiveness and self-righteous intolerance of criticism.".

46 See the Human Rights Watch and ACLU report *Witness to Abuse: Human Rights Abuses Under the Material Witness Law Since September 11, 2001*, available at www.aclu.org/national-security/us-scores-muslim-men-jailed-without-charge. See also "Indefensible Defense," Editorial, *New York Times*, October 26, 2010 discussing *Ashcroft v. al-Kidd*: "It turns on a sacrosanct principle: The government cannot arrest you without evidence that you committed a crime."

47 Ian Buruma, "Theater of War," *New York Times Sunday Book Review*, September 17, 2006, Reviewing *The Greatest Story Ever Sold: The Decline and Fall of Truth from 9/11 to Katrina* by Frank Rich (Penguin Books, 2006).

48 See David Barstow report, supra at note 31.

49 New York Times, "Lethal Force Under Law", October 9, 2010, www.nytimes.com/2010/10/10/opinion/10sun1.html.

50 Cheney made this statement on NBC's *Meet the Press* on September 16, 2001, adding "A lot of what needs to be done will need to be done quietly, without any discussion…" Quote available at www.pbs.org/wgbh/pages/frontline/darkside/themes/darkside.html.

51 See the Pulitzer Prize winning reporting of Dana Priest at www.washingtonpost.com/wp-dyn/content/article/2005/11/01/AR2005110101644.html and www.washingtonpost.com/wp-dyn/content/linkset/2006/04/17/LI2006041700530.html.
52 Report available at http://assembly.coe.int/CommitteeDocs/2006/20060606_Ejdoc162006PartII-FINAL.pdf and further Council findings at www.coe.int/T/E/Com/Files/Events/2006-cia/.
53 Cohn, *Definitions of Convenience*, noted supra at note 19.
54 David Johnston, "U.S. Says Rendition to Continue, but With More Oversight", August 24, 2009, www.nytimes.com/2009/08/25/us/politics/25rendition.html.
55 A Judicial Green Light for Torture," February 26, 2006, available at http://query.nytimes.com/gst/fullpage.html?res=980CE5D81F3EF935A15751C0A9609C8B63&scp=1&sq=%22rat-infested%20dungeon%22&st=cse.
56 On September 7, 2010 a federal appeals court ruled that former prisoners of the CIA cannot bring lawsuits over their alleged torture in overseas prisons because such suits might expose secret government information. ACLU lawyer Ben Wizner commented:

> To this date, not a single victim of the Bush administration's torture program has had his day in court. That makes this a sad day not only for the torture survivors who are seeking justice in this case, but for all Americans who care about the rule of law and our nation's reputation in the world. If this decision stands, the United States will have closed its courts to torture victims while providing complete immunity to their torturers.

Quoted in Charlie Savage, "Court Dismisses a Case Asserting Torture by CIA," *New York Times*, September 8, 2010. In his 2015 book *Power Wars* (New York: Little Brown & Co.), Savage reports that Obama was never informed by the Dept. of Justice when it initially used the state secrets defense under his watch, was livid, but then acquiesced to its continued use.
57 See "Outsourcing Torture," by Jane Mayer in the February 14, 2005 *New Yorker*. See also her *The Dark Side: The inside story on how the war on terror turned into a war on American ideals* (New York: Doubleday, 2008).
58 See the February 16, 2006 UN Report, available at www.unhchr.ch/huricane/huricane.nsf/0/52E94FB9CBC7DA10C1257117003517B3?opendocument.
59 Sarah Lyall, "Britain's Top Court Rules Information Gotten by Torture Is Never Admissible Evidence", December 9, 2005, www.nytimes.com/2005/12/09/international/europe/09britain.html; *Guardian*, "Torture evidence inadmissible in UK courts, Lords rules", December 8, 2005, www.guardian.co.uk/world/2005/dec/08/terrorism.uk.
60 Robert Fisk, "Torture does not work, as history shows", February 2, 2008, www.independent.co.uk/opinion/commentators/fisk/robert-fisk-torture-does-not-work-as-history-shows-777213.html; Newsweek Stuff, *Newsweek Magazine*, "Neuroscience: Torture Doesn't Work and Here's Why", September 21, 2009, www.newsweek.com/2009/09/21/the-tortured-brain.html; Bobby Ghosh, "A Top Interrogator Who's Against Torture", April 24, 2009, www.time.com/time/nation/article/0,8599,1893679,00.html?cnn=yes; Robert W. Thurston, "The History of Torture Shows It Does Not Work", May 31, 2009, http://hnn.us/articles/88225.html; David Rose, "Tortured Reasoning", December 2008, www.vanityfair.com/magazine/2008/12/torture200812; *National Journal*; November 29, 2005, "CIA Veterans Condemn Torture", www.nationaljournal.com/about/njweekly/stories/2005/1119nj1.htm.
61 See the writings of Mark Danner, including his 2004 book *Torture and Truth* (New York: The New York Review of Books) and "US Torture: Voices from the Black Sites," *The New York Review of Books*, March 2009.
62 At his 2009 inauguration President Obama declared, "As for our common defense, we reject as false the choice between our safety and our ideals." Upon taking office

his first act was to sign an executive order to close Guantanamo prison. His subsequent GWOT policies and inability to close Guantanamo is testament to the U.S. govt. being trapped by its unlawful GWOT policies which placed expediency over principle.

63. See New York Times, "Legacy of Torture", August 26, 2010, www.nytimes.com/2010/08/27/opinion/27fri1.html; Chisun Lee, *The National Law Journal*, "Judges reject evidence in Gitmo cases", August 16, 2010, www.law.com/jsp/nlj/PubArticleNLJ.jsp?id=1202466489442&Judges_reject_evidence_in_Gitmo_cases&slreturn=1&hbxlogin=1.

64. Eisenhower warned the American people, "We have been compelled to create a permanent armaments industry of vast proportions.... The potential for the disastrous rise of misplaced power exists and will persist."

65. Jody Freeman and Martha Minow (eds.) *Government by Contract: Outsourcing and American Democracy* (Cambridge, MA: Harvard University Press, 2009); Scott Shane and Ron Nixon, "US Contractors Becoming a Fourth Branch of Government," *International Herald Tribune*, February 4, 2007, available at www.nytimes.com/2007/02/04/world/americas/04iht-web.0204contract.4460796.html.

66. Washington Post; "Top Secret America", http://projects.washingtonpost.com/top-secret-america/.

67. Ibid.

68. Glenn Greenwald, "A Democratic insider's call for a new presidential secrecy power", December 7, 2008, www.salon.com/news/opinion/glenn_greenwald/2010/07/19/secrecy.

69. Ibid; See also Brandy Zadrozny, "Read the Pentagon's $59 Billion 'Black Budget'", June 3, 2014, www.thedailybeast.com/articles/2014/03/06/inside-the-pentagon-s-59-billion-black-budget.html.

70. Washington Post; "Top Secret America", http://projects.washingtonpost.com/top-secret-america/.

71. Ibid.

72. The $75 billion figure does not include many military or domestic counterterrorism activities and programs. Ibid.

73. Ibid.

74. Ibid; See David Rose, "The People vs. The Profiteers," *Vanity Fair*, November 2007, available at www.vanityfair.com/politics/features/2007/11/halliburton200711. See also: "Billions Over Baghdad," *Vanity Fair*, October 2007, available at www.vanityfair.com/politics/features/2007/10/iraq_billions200710; Gary Shteyngart, *Absurdistan* (Random House: New York, 2006), for a sardonic fictionalized depiction of corrupt wasteful war culture; and William A. Cohn: "As Blackwater rises the rule of law recedes," *DePaul University Rule of Law Journal*, Fall 2010; "Democracy Devolved: shrinking the public sphere" *The New Presence (TNP)*, 12 (4), Fall 2009; "Government Inc.," *TNP*, Vol. 11, No. 1, Winter 2008. On the failure to punish contractors for their crimes, see James Risen, "U.S. falters in punishing Blackwater personnel," *International Herald Tribune*, October 22, 2010, p. 5.

75. http://projects.washingtonpost.com/top-secret-america/.

76. Ibid.

77. Ibid.

78. Alison Stanger, *One Nation Under Contract: The Outsourcing of American Power and the Future of Foreign Policy* (New Haven: Yale University Press, 2009). The U.S. rationale for declaring enemy fighters in Afghanistan "unlawful enemy combatants" was that they did not wear uniforms, carry their arms openly or follow a recognized chain of command. But of course the same is true for the contractors who comprise an ever-larger portion of the U.S. fighting force throughout the world.

79 Micah Zenko, "The New Unknown Soldiers of Afghanistan and Iraq", May 29, 2015, http://foreignpolicy.com/2015/05/29/the-new-unknown-soldiers-of-afghanistan-and-iraq/; Jeremy Scahill, "Stunning Statistics About the War in Afghanistan Every American Should Know", December 20, 2009, www.alternet.org/story/144694/. See also the writings of Jeremy Scahill, including *Blackwater: The Rise of the World's Most Powerful Mercenary Army* (New York: Nation Books, 2007), *Dirty Wars* (New York: Nation Books, 2013), and *The Assassination Complex* (New York: Simon & Schuster, 2016).
80 See Glenn Greenwald, *No Place to Hide: Edward Snowden, the N.S.A., and the U.S. Surveillance State* (New York: Metropolitan Books, 2014).
81 See Jack Shafer, "Live and Let Leak: State Secrets in the Snowden Era," *Foreign Affairs*, March/April 2014.
82 See: William A. Cohn; "Who's Zooming Who? The Real Story of the Prism Program", www.pritomnost.cz/en/world-politics/395-who-s-zooming-who-the-real-story-of-the-prism-program; William A. Cohn; "Fooled Again? False security premised on less democracy and more war", www.pritomnost.cz/en/component/content/article/19-world-politics/449-fooled-again-false-security-premised-on-less-democracy-and-more-war; William A. Cohn; "Europe Leads on Rights, Part I.", www.pritomnost.cz/en/component/content/article/19-world-politics/374-europe-leads-on-rights-part-i; Bill Cohn, "NSA Surveillance is Not Securing Anybody," *The Prague Post*, January 3, 2014.
83 Jack Mirkinson, "The CIA's insidious Hollywood propaganda: New report highlights alarming details about "Zero Dark Thirty", September 11, 2015, www.salon.com/2015/09/11/the_cias_insidious_hollywood_propaganda_new_report_highlights_alarming_details_about_zero_dark_thirty/; Patrice Taddonio, "WATCH: How the CIA Helped Make "Zero Dark Thirty", May 15, 2015, www.pbs.org/wgbh/frontline/article/watch-how-the-cia-helped-make-zero-dark-thirty/.
84 Jane Mayer, "WHATEVER IT TAKES. The politics of the man behind "24", February 19, 2007, www.newyorker.com/magazine/2007/02/19/whatever-it-takes.
85 Hayley Peterson, "McDonald's Slammed For Using 9/11 To Sell Burgers", January 13, 2015, www.businessinsider.com/mcdonalds-slammed-for-invoking-911-2015-1.
86 Laura Barron-Lopez, Travis Waldron, "Pentagon Paid Up To $6.8 Million Of Taxpayer Money To Pro Sports Teams For Military Tributes," November 4, 2015, www.huffingtonpost.com/entry/defense-military-tributes-professional-sports_us_5639a04ce4b0411d306eda5e; Christian Davenport, "The Pentagon paid lucrative sports franchises millions to honor troops," November 4, 2015, www.washingtonpost.com/business/economy/the-pentagon-paid-lucrative-sports-franchises-millions-to-honor-troops/2015/11/04/4d39c50c-8324-11e5-9afb-0c971f713d0c_story.html.
87 David Barstow, "Behind TV Analysts, Pentagon's Hidden Hand," April 20, 2008, www.nytimes.com/2008/04/20/us/20generals.html.
88 University of Chicago Press, http://press.uchicago.edu/ucp/books/book/chicago/N/bo22679593.html.
89 William Cohn, "Insult to Injury: A Tortuous Spin Cycle on US Torture," January 17, 2015, www.commondreams.org/views/2015/01/17/insult-injury-tortuous-spin-cycle-us-torture.
90 Omar Alnatour, "Muslims Are Not Terrorists: A Factual Look at Terrorism and Islam," December 9, 2015, www.huffingtonpost.com/omar-alnatour/muslims-are-not-terrorist_b_8718000.html.
91 Democracy Now!, "Does U.S. Ignore Right-Wing Terror? More Killed by White Extremists Than Jihadists Since 9/11," June 25, 2015, www.democracynow.org/2015/6/25/does_us_ignore_right_wing_terror.
92 FAIR, "Remembering Victims of Terror–and Forgetting Some Others", January 7, 2015, http://fair.org/international/europe-international/remembering-victims-of-terror-and-forgetting-some-others/; Jim Naureckas, "Why Are Persons Unknown More

Likely to Be Called 'Terrorist' Than a Known White Supremacist?", June 19, 2015, http://fair.org/home/why-are-persons-unknown-more-likely-to-be-called-terrorist-than-a-known-white-supremacist/ See also: Margaret Sullivan, "Are Some Terrorism Deaths More Equal Than Others?," April 2, 2016, www.nytimes.com/2016/04/03/public-editor/terrorism-victim-coverage-new-york-times-public-editor.html?ref=opinion&_r=1.

93 Technology has been a great help in exposing abuses of power, with WikiLeaks, Chelsea Manning and the Snowden leaks being a few of the well-known examples. As well, the digital revolution has catalyzed the Arab Spring, the Black Lives Matter movement and so much more. As technology makes secrecy and censorship near-impossible over time, fear and intimidation take on a vital role in the efforts of those in power to control the public.

94 Democracy Now!, "Abdel Bari Atwan: Inside How the U.S. & Saudi Arabia Aided Growth of the Islamic State", November 17, 2015, www.democracynow.org/2015/11/17/abdel_bari_atwan_inside_how_the.

95 Nadia Prupis, "Federal Court Blocks 'Truth About Torture' in Ruling on Senate Report," May 13, 2016, http://commondreams.org/news/2016/05/13/federal-court-blocks-truth-about-torture-ruling-senate-report; Raphael Minder, "Crackdowns on Free Speech Rise Across a Europe Wary of Terror," February 24, 2016, www.nytimes.com/2016/02/25/world/europe/spain-europe-protest-free-speech.html?hp&action=click&pgtype=Homepage&clickSource=story-heading&module=second-column-region&region=top-news&WT.nav=top-news. See also, David Cole, "Chewing Gum for Terrorists," *New York Times*, January 2, 2011.

96 In addition to the known long list of government officials who sanctioned torture, and those who did the torturing, including private military contractors, professions have been perverted as hired guns to assist in torture rather than using the intrinsic value of their training and knowledge to say NO to such obvious wrongdoing. See: Marjorie Cohn, "Advising Clients to Commit War Crimes with Impunity: An Unethical Practice," 2011, www.law.seattleu.edu/Documents/sjsj/2012fall/Cohn.pdf; Alan Bock, "Underlying Problems in South Asia," June 4, 2002, www.antiwar.com/lobe/?articleid=326; Martha F. Davis, "Learning From the Torture Memos," January 26, 2016, http://rwi.lu.se/2016/01/learning-from-the-torture-memos/. In his 2016 book *Power Wars*, Charlie Savage reports that John Yoo was known, not flatteringly, as Dr. Yes, for his willingness to twist the law to get the results wanted by his superiors.

97 In Psychology, the American Psychology Association has had a long shameful hidden role in the story of American torture, acting in collusion with the CIA and Pentagon. See: Katherine Eban, "Torture, American-Style: The Role of Money in Interrogations," July 14, 2015, www.vanityfair.com/news/2015/07/torture-american-style-hoffman-report; John Bohannon, "APA hit with new torture allegations," April 30, 2015, www.sciencemag.org/news/2015/04/apa-hit-new-torture-allegations; Adam Zagorin, "Yes, America's Psychologists Abetted Torture Interrogations," August 7, 2015, www.pogo.org/blog/2015/08/yes-americas-psychologists-abetted-torture-interrogations.html?referrer=https://www.google.cz/.

98 In medicine, physicians assisted in torture and were condemned by the American Medical Association. See: Elise Viebeck, "AMA rebukes doctors for role in CIA 'torture'," December 12, 2014, http://thehill.com/policy/healthcare/227005-ama-rebukes-doctors-for-role-in-cia-torture; Xeni Jardin, "AMA report on CIA physicians' role in torture," August 4, 2010, http://boingboing.net/2010/08/04/ama-report-on-cia-ph.html.

99 Chris Hedges, "Criminalizing Dissent," August 13, 2012, www.truthdig.com/report/item/criminalizing_dissent_20120813.

100 Julian Hattem, "Virginia teen gets 11 years for aiding ISIS," August 28, 2015, http://thehill.com/policy/national-security/252172-virginia-teen-gets-11-years-for-tweeting-support-for-isis.

101 Steve Cooke, "Animal Rights and Environmental Terrorism," 2013, jtr.st-andrews.ac.uk/articles/10.15664/jtr.532/galley/597/download/; Green is the New Red, "About," no date, www.greenisthenewred.com/blog/about/. Santamaria, Cara E., "The Criminalization of Dissent: The Evolution from Activism to Domestic Terror." Ethics of Business and Government term paper, University of New York in Prague, Spring 2016.
102 Robert Barnes, "Supreme Court closes its front doors to the public," May 4, 2010, www.washingtonpost.com/wp-dyn/content/article/2010/05/03/AR2010050302081.html.
103 Mahbubani, Dean of the School of Public Policy at the National University of Singapore, writes of Asia's loss of respect for Western practices:

> Few in the West understand how much shock Guantanamo has caused in non-Western minds. Hence, many are puzzled that Western intellectuals continue to assume that they can portray themselves and their countries as models to follow when they speak to the rest of the world on human rights.
> (End of Whose History? *IHT*, November 12, 2009)

104 *How Terrorists Groups End: Lessons for countering al Qaida* (The Rand Corporation/Rand.org, 2008) by Seth Jones and Martin Libicki, drew its conclusion that GWOT was failing by means of an examination of 648 terror groups that existed between 1968 and 2006. In conclusion at p. 139 the authors note that "making a world of enemies is never a winning strategy."
105 "2010 is deadliest year for NATO in Afghan war," *New York Times*, September 21, 2002, available at www.nytimes.com/2010/09/22/world/asia/22afghan.html?emc=eta1.
106 "Afghanistan growing more dangerous" *IHT*, September 13, 2010, p. 1, continues: "In August 2009, insurgents carried out 630 attacks. This August, they initiated at least 1,353…. 'The humanitarian space is shrinking day by day' said Abdul Kebar, a CARE Afghanistan official."
107 University of Chicago political scientist Robert Pape has spent years conducting research on terror and suicide bombing. Pape finds that al-Qaeda style terror is "less a product of Islamic fundamentalism than of a simple strategic goal: to compel the U.S. and its Western allies to withdraw combat forces from the Arabian Peninsula and other Muslim countries." Pape and others note that Osama bin Laden turned against the U.S. in 1991 because he saw it as occupying the holiest Arab land in Saudi Arabia.
108 Cited in Noam Chomsky's "War on Terror," Amnesty International Annual Lecture on January 18, 2006 at Trinity College in Dublin, Ireland, available at www.brianmay.com/experts/waronterror.pdf.
109 Available at www.erich-fromm.de/biophil/joomla/images/stories/pdf-Dateien/Preis_2010_031.pdf.
110 See Rami Khouri, "A Bad Decade," *New York Times*, December 30, 2009 on the negative impacts of the past decade on the Middle East, and the rising clout of Iran, and his article in *New York Times*, June 30, 2010, op. ed.
111 *How Terrorists Groups End: Lessons for countering al Qaida* (2008) by Seth Jones and Martin Libicki, supra note 104.
112 Further empirical support can be found in the article by Webel and Arnaldi in this book.
113 Ibid.
114 National Counterterrorism Center (NCC) Director Michael Leiter, and FBI Director Robert Mueller told the Senate Homeland Security and Governmental Affairs Committee that the threat of al-Qaeda using Americans and other Western nationals to attack the US has grown, noting that at least 63 US citizens have been charged or convicted of terrorist acts or related crimes since 2009. Home grown plots have reached their highest level since 9/11 according to NCC. See: BBC News,

"US Congress warned of home-grown terrorism threat," September 22, 2002, www.bbc.co.uk/news/world-us-canada-11392083.

115 According to U.S. officials quoted in the *New York Times*, in May 2005, the CIA reported that "Iraq has become a magnet for Islamic militants similar to Soviet-occupied Afghanistan two decades ago and Bosnia in the 1990s." The CIA concluded that "Iraq may prove to be an even more effective training ground for Islamic extremists than Afghanistan was in al-Qaeda's early days."

116 Quotes cited in Noam Chomsky's "War on Terror," Lecture noted supra at note 108.

117 *How Terrorists Groups End: Lessons for countering al Qaida* (2008) by Seth Jones and Martin Libicki, p. 139, cited supra note 103. See also "War and Consequences" available at www.comw.org/pda/0609bm38.html.

118 The War Logs are available at http://warlogs.wikileaks.org/, and reporting on them is available in the *New York Times* of October 23–25, 2010. On the information contained in the War Logs which suggests that the sectarian bloodbath in Iraq has been part of an unofficial U.S. policy, see: Martin Chulov, "Iraq war logs: 'The US was part of the Wolf Brigade operation against us'," October 28, 2010, www.guardian.co.uk/world/2010/oct/28/iraq-war-logs-iraq; and Gareth Porter, "Torture Orders Were Part of US Sectarian War Strategy," November 1, 2010, www.commondreams.org/headline/2010/11/01-6. On the attacks against Wikileaks, see: William A. Cohn, "A Tri-partite Ruse to Confuse," at www.informationclearinghouse.info/article26747.htm and "Shooting the Messenger," *The Prague Post*, November 3, 2010.

119 William Finnegan, "Last Days: Preparing for the apocalypse in San Bernardino," *The New Yorker*, February 22, 2016.

120 Sarah Lazare, "Body Count Report Reveals At Least 1.3 Million Lives Lost to US-Led War on Terror," March 26, 2015, www.commondreams.org/news/2015/03/26/body-count-report-reveals-least-13-million-lives-lost-us-led-war-terror.

121 See Sabir Shah, "US Wars in Afghanistan, Iraq to Cost $6 trillion," September 20, 2013, www.globalresearch.ca/us-wars-in-afghanistan-iraq-to-cost-6-trillion/5350789.

122 For instance, Pakistan. Imtiaz Gul, author of *The Most Dangerous Place: Pakistan's Lawless Frontier*, writes that Jihadist forces are strengthening in Pakistan in 2010. See Imtiaz Gul, "Pakistan's New Networks of Terror," June 10, 2010, www.foreignpolicy.com/articles/2010/06/10/pakistans_new_networks_of_terror.

123 As well, the cycle of violence which breeds acts of terror fuels extremist right-wing political forces. After the Brussels attack extreme right parties surged in Germany and Austria, while in France the far right National Front "seized issues ready-made for its base, calling for France Frist, or a France for the French, in elliptical anti-immigrant, anti-Muslim language. Such appeals have resonated more broadly with a public worried about security, immigration and economic stagnation." "Europe: A Terror Attack, Then Far Right Moves In," *New York Times*, April 1, 2016.

124 Supra note 112.

125 In 2014, the poverty rate was 14.8 percent: United States Census Bureau, "Poverty," May 12, 2016, www.census.gov/hhes/www/poverty/about/overview/. In 2010, one in seven Americans lived in poverty, a 15-year high according to "Recession Raises Poverty Rate to a 15-Year High", *New York Times,* September 17, 2010, www.nytimes.com/2010/09/17/us/17poverty.html?_r=1&scp=1&sq=Poverty%20Census&st=cse.

126 Following the Brussels attack, *The New York Times* reports:

> Among the clearest signs of the Islamic State's growing capacity for terrorist attacks is its progress for making and deploying bombs containing triacetone triperoxide, or TATP. The white explosive powder was found in the suicide belts of the Paris attackers and in the suitcases of the Brussels bombers, as well as in two other ISIS-led plots in 2014 and 2015. TATP has become terrorists go-to explosive in Europe.... The overpowering odor that comes with refining and

Led astray: legal and moral blowback 193

storing TATP was noticed by the building's owner weeks before the bombings, Belgian officials said but he did not report it until after the attacks. (Rukmini Callimachi, "Building the machinery of terror," *New York Times*, March 30, 2016, p. 5)

127 Dexter Filkins, "'Do Not Resist' and the Crisis of Police Militarization," May 13, 2016, www.newyorker.com/news/news-desk/do-not-resist-and-the-crisis-of-police-militarization; Glenn Greenwald, "The Militarization of U.S. Police: Finally Dragged into the Light by the Horrors of Ferguson," August 14, 2014, https://theintercept.com/2014/08/14/militarization-u-s-police-dragged-light-horrors-ferguson/; Michael Shank and Elizabeth Beavers, "America's police are looking more and more like the military," October 7, 2013, www.theguardian.com/commentisfree/2013/oct/07/militarization-local-police-america.
128 Rand report, p. xiii, cited supra note 104.
129 Our analysis suggests that there is no battlefield solution to terrorism. Military force usually has the opposite effect from what is intended: It is often overused, alienates the local population by its heavy-handed nature, and provides a window of opportunity for terrorist-group recruitment.
130 Nick Allen, "Barack Obama admits 'unacceptable systemic failure' in Detroit plane attack," December 29, 2009, www.telegraph.co.uk/news/worldnews/northamerica/usa/barackobama/6908709/Barack-Obama-admits-unacceptable-systemic-failure-in-Detroit-plane-attack.html; Jack Kelly, "Blowing Up Obama's Naive Approach to Terrorism," January 3, 2010, www.realclearpolitics.com/articles/2010/01/03/obamas_approach_to_terrorism_blows_up_99755.html. Red flags included: The would be bomber's father had warned U.S. authorities about his son's radicalism a month earlier; Britain had banned him from entry; and, he had paid for his ticket in cash and had no luggage. Only a faulty detonator and quick action by the passenger sitting next to him saved the 278 passengers.
131 Mattathias Schwartz, "The Whole Haystack," January 26, 2015, www.newyorker.com/magazine/2015/01/26/whole-haystack.
132 Human Rights Watch, "Guantanamo: Facts and Figures," April 18, 2016, www.hrw.org/video-photos/interactive/2016/03/10/guantanamo-facts-and-figures; Andy Worthington, "Prisoners: Who's Still Held," www.closeguantanamo.org/Prisoners; Therese Postel, "How Guantanamo Bay's Existence Helps Al-Qaeda Recruit More Terrorists," April 12, 2013, www.theatlantic.com/international/archive/2013/04/how-guantanamo-bays-existence-helps-al-qaeda-recruit-more-terrorists/274956/; Charlie Savage, "No Terror Evidence Against Some Detainees," May 28, 2010, www.nytimes.com/2010/05/29/us/politics/29gitmo.html?_r=1.
133 See, e.g., "Face Reality: Talk to the Taliban" by Gilles Dorronsoro of the Carnegie Endowment for International Peace, *International Herald Tribune*, September 15, 2010, p. 6. On the challenges of fostering dialogue, *Holder* v. *Humanitarian Law Project* was the first Supreme Court case of the post-9/11 era to pit free speech rights against national security. The Court held that the government's compelling interest in preventing terrorism outweighed the plaintiff's free speech claims. In a 6–3 ruling the Court said that even advice on peaceful conflict resolution may be prosecuted under a law banning material support of terrorists. Attorney David Cole of the Center for Constitutional Rights says "When the Court allows unsupported speculation about 'terrorism' and disapproval of a speaker's viewpoint to justify making advocacy of human rights a crime, the First Amendment as we know it is in serious jeopardy." Human rights lawyer Scott Horton writes that after *Citizens United* v. *FEC*, the case in which the Court struck down campaign finance restrictions as violating the free speech protections of corporations, "America stands alone as the only country in the world which grants human rights to corporations, just as it is curtailing human rights to humans. It's a curious sign of the times."

134 Former U.S. Supreme Court Justice Potter Stewart noted, "Censorship reflects a society's lack of confidence in itself."
135 See the documentary "Black Money" at pbs.org/frontline. The US Pentagon budget increased each year of the first decade of the twenty-first century, an unprecedented run in the country's history, and under the government's current budget plans this steady rise will last for at least another decade. Is this a permanent war budget? Is the U.S. department of defense more aptly, as it was called until 1947, the department of war? "The Pentagon dodges the bullet: Barack Obama is spending more on defence than his predecessors," *The Economist*, February 6, 2010, p. 45; William A. Cohn, "De-based," *The New Presence*, Winter 2010.
136 The U.S., while preaching peace, has long held first place in the global arms race: SIPRI, April 2016, www.sipri.org/media/pressreleases/2016/milex-apr-2016. It spends as much as the next 14 countries combined, and maintains more than 700 military bases around the world. UC Professor Emeritus Chalmers Johnson dates back to 1949 what he calls the U.S. "military Keynesianism – the determination to maintain a permanent war economy and to treat military output as an ordinary economic product even though it makes no contribution to either production or consumption." See his Trilogy: *Blowback* (2000); *The Sorrows of Empire* (2004); *Nemesis* (2006).
137 See the interview with Scott Atran in this book.
138 "What's to be done?" *The Economist*, September 18, 2010, p. 47.
139 Quoted in "Justice Jackson at Nuremberg," by Whitney R. Harris, in *The International Lawyer* 20 Int'l L. 867 (1986).
140 Immanuel Kant, *Perpetual Peace: A Philosophical Essay* (1795).
141 David Luban describes the escalation of U.S. intervention of Libya as "a de facto (even if unacknowledged) war to bring about regime change. This was surely one of the biggest blunders of Obama's foreign policy: the campaign left Libya a fractured and chaotic haven for terrorists, and the escalation probably doomed any future UN-backed humanitarian interventions." "Has Obama Upheld the Law?" *The New York Review of Books*, April 21, 2016.
142 Albert Einstein defined insanity as "doing the same thing over and over again and expecting different results."
143 See Jane Meyer, *Dark Money* (New York: Penguin Random House, 2016).
144 William A. Cohn, "As Blackwater Rises, the Rule of Law Recedes," 2010, www.yumpu.com/en/document/view/29591001/depaul-rule-of-law-journal-college-of-law-organizations-amp-journals; Tortured Profits of Doom: Legal Loopholes, Ethics of Convenience, and Pretzel Logic. *The New Presence*: The Prague Journal of Central European Affairs; Spring 2010, Vol. 12 Issue 1.
145 On April 22, 2016, a U.S. judge allowed the first case against U.S. torturers to proceed in federal court since 9/11, 2001. See Deirdre Fulton, "Landmark Ruling Will Finally Allow Victims to Hold CIA 'Torturers to Account'," April 22, 2016, http://commondreams.org/news/2016/04/22/landmark-ruling-will-finally-allow-victims-hold-cia-torturers-account As well, other countries courts are rejecting CIA impunity: Barry Hatton, "Ex-CIA agent loses appeal against extradition to Italy," April 26, 2016, http://news.findlaw.com/apnews/eb1299b2a9cd436393146ab8ca576ab4.
146 On drone warfare, see the article by Laurie Calhoun in this book. On America's new global covert wars and for more on drone strike killings, see Jeremy Scahill's books, supra note 79.
147 The International Consortium of Investigative Journalists (ICIJ), "The Panama Papers", https://panamapapers.icij.org/.
148 Glenn Greenwald, "A Key Similarity Between Snowden Leak and Panama Papers: Scandal Is What's Been Legalized," April 4, 2016, https://theintercept.com/2016/04/04/a-key-similarity-between-snowden-leak-and-panamapapers-scandal-is-whats-been-legalized/.

149 Direct action means going beyond working within the confines of the conventions set forth by law and institutions. Power concedes nothing. Limits must be tested in the struggle for social justice. But for the anti-apartheid divestment movement there would be no economic sanctions legislation to help South Africans bring down the apartheid regime. Likewise, the fossil fuel divestment movement on campuses today is affecting share prices of oil companies and energy policy. Recall, the first thing Bush 43 did as President was to appoint Dick Cheney to head a commission to direct U.S. energy policy. But for U.S. energy policy being fixed on fossil fuel there may not have been the military misadventure in Iraq, and thus no al-Qaeda in Iraq, and thus no ISIS. Direct action can take many forms, not just civil disobedience and bodies on the streets, but any strategic use of moral imagination to go beyond convention in order to bring change in accordance with one's values. See, for instance, Terry Tempest Williams, "No drilling on our land," *New York Times*, March 30, 2016, p. 7.

150 Henry A. Giroux, "The National Insecurity State: America's Addiction to Terrorism," *Monthly Review Press,* February 26, 2016; www.truth-out.org/progressive picks/item/34979-the-national-insecurity-state; Henry A. Giroux, "America's Addiction to Terrorism: The National Insecurity State," 2016, www.information clearinghouse.info/article44322.htm.

10 Terror from above and within

The hidden cultural and political costs of lethal drones

Laurie Calhoun

Introduction: the normalization of drone killing

In the early years of the Global War on Terror (GWOT), undertaken by the George W. Bush administration in response to the terrorist attacks of September 11, 2001, the targeted killing of terrorist suspects in unoccupied lands using unmanned combat aerial vehicles (UCAVs), or lethal drones, was a covert and exceptional practice. Bush's successor, President Barack Obama, dramatically expanded the targeted killing program, authorizing hundreds of strikes in several different Muslim lands: Iraq, Afghanistan, Pakistan, Yemen, Somalia, Libya and Syria.[1] Under a pretext of national security, most drone strikes and their outcomes were not publicly acknowledged by the US government for more than a decade, as a result of which debate about the wisdom and efficacy of drone killing was suppressed. Over the course of the first 15 years of GWOT, the secretive use of lethal drones to dispatch suspects was normalized, having come to be viewed by the US military and the Central Intelligence Agency (CIA) as a standard operating procedure.

During a Democratic presidential candidate debate on October 14, 2015, former Secretary of State Hillary Clinton gushed that the 2011 US intervention in Libya was an example of "smart power at its best."[2] Muammar Gaddafi had been removed from power and killed after hundreds of US missiles were fired on Libya from drones, but no US troops were killed during the mission. Rival candidate Bernie Sanders, a self-declared progressive and Democratic socialist, told audiences on the campaign trail that, if elected president, he would continue Obama's "assassination drone program," because it seemed to be effective.[3] The very fact that Sanders, a death-penalty opponent, should use the word "assassination" in discussing Obama's foreign policy illustrates how the former taboo against the premeditated, intentional hunting down and killing of specific persons has been lifted. After the hundreds of drone strikes authorized by Obama in the name of national defense, the formerly controversial practice of assassination seems perfectly permissible even to some self-styled progressives.

Most people, including politicians, derive their views on the "effectiveness" of the drone program from sources such as the *New York Times* headlines, which invariably replicate administration soundbites such as "Four Suspected Militants

Slain." After seeing dozens, if not hundreds, of such headlines, readers may come to elide the word "suspected" and immediately conclude that yet another group of "bad guys" has been eradicated from the face of the earth. Civilian casualties have nearly always been omitted from US government drone strike reports, suggesting that the technology is exceptionally precise and minimizes collateral damage.

One of the reasons why so little has been reported in the mainstream Western press about the innocent civilians harmed in the remote tribal regions where most drone strikes are carried out is because it is too difficult and dangerous for reporters to fact check in such contexts.[4] Western news outlets therefore depend on the official statements of administration spokespersons as the best available source of information. By uncritically parroting and replicating the official reports prepared by drone program administrators, the mainstream media have bolstered the impression that many more terrorists than civilians have been harmed in the drone campaigns, and that targeted killing is indeed a form of "smart war."

By early 2016, the governments of nearly 90 countries had UAVs (unmanned aerial vehicles), and at least 19 countries had or were about to obtain UCAVs.[5] The dissemination of remote-control killing technology all over the world is attributable to not only the lucrative economics of military industry more generally, but also the precedent set by the US government. The swift spread of lethal drones to the farthest reaches of the planet has been further propelled by the self-evident "rationality" of using the latest and greatest military technology to spare the lives of soldiers wherever and whenever possible. If the purpose of having a military is to be able to win wars, and if most other countries have or are about to acquire lethal drones, then any military made to forego the technological breakthrough would seem to be at a decided disadvantage. Even worse, come wartime, a nation's own soldiers may die needlessly. Given such considerations, it may not be clear why any citizen would oppose his or her government's decision to acquire lethal drones.

Collateral damage and its consequences

It is not always possible to ignore or deny that innocent persons were killed by drone strikes, particularly when the victims are Westerners. Italian citizen Giovanni Lo Porto and US citizen Warren Weinstein were two hostages killed by a drone in Pakistan along with a group of suspected al-Qaeda members in January 2015. Even on the rare occasion when the deaths of innocent people are acknowledged, the ratio of "good guys" to "bad guys" purportedly killed is thought by many to be acceptably small.[6] Comparisons of even the worst projections of the civilian body count of the drone campaigns—whether hundreds or thousands of victims—with the tolls of conventional wars such as those in Iraq, Afghanistan and Vietnam, lead many people to conclude that the use of lethal drones is preferable to full-scale invasions.

The false dichotomy that either UCAVs must be deployed in lands such as Yemen, Pakistan, and Somalia, or else invasions by ground troops will be necessary, has been successfully promulgated by the drone program executors. The "no boots on the ground" trope was used repeatedly by President Obama, who in promoting his campaigns capitalized on risk aversion among politicians and the populace after the disastrous 2003 invasion of Iraq and its aftermath, during which thousands of US troops perished. In fact, the domain of military action has been enlarged by the advent of remote-control killing technology, for missiles are fired on lands where combat soldiers would arguably never have been sent. Nonetheless persuaded to believe that US soldiers' lives are being spared, taxpayers have tended to ignore the subtler and more insidious effects of the drone killing of persons pegged as "suspicious" in lands far away.

Even granting for the sake of argument that more "terrorist suspects" than civilians have been slain, advocates of drone warfare have been working with a simplistic and misleading concept of collateral damage as exhausted by body count. However, there are three distinct forms of collateral damage: first-, second-, and third-order. First-order collateral damage, the innocent civilians killed, is both tragic and lamentable, but second- and third-order collateral damage are far more strategically, morally, and politically significant in the Drone Age.

The persons who survive but are deprived by drone strikes of their family members and property—their homes, workplaces, cars, etc.—are the victims of second-order collateral damage.[7] One of the little-discussed implications of the thousands of military-age males incinerated in the various US drone campaigns is that thousands of fatherless children and husbandless wives have been left bereft and further impoverished. In the remote territories where strikes tend to be carried out, the husband is often the breadwinner or provider. In some of these societies, a widow cannot easily remarry. A drone strike against her husband and the father of her children will dramatically alter the course of all of their lives.

Several studies by NGOs and human rights groups, including Amnesty International and Human Rights Watch, have documented the fear and anxiety induced by the hovering above in the sky of lethal drones.[8] This is where the simplistic measure of collateral damage as body count completely misleads people about the wisdom of drone killing. What I term "third-order collateral damage" includes the psychological effects on community members who may not have lost a family member to a missile strike—yet. Some of the people living under lethal drones are left not bereft but in a psychologically fragile state. They no longer feel safe. Their sense of equanimity and security has been shattered.

Alkarama, an organization based in Switzerland, conducted interviews in the fall of 2014 with residents of communities in Yemen where drone strikes had been repeatedly carried out.[9] The human rights group discovered that even people who have not lost any family members to drone strikes exhibit psychological afflictions—anxiety, fear and paranoia—on a par with bereft survivors. Some of these people find it difficult to plan for the future and lose interest in former sources of joy. When missiles are fired from drones, no matter who is killed, and even when they are terrorist suspects rather than obvious cases of collateral damage (children and women), the entire community may become plagued by the fear of their own imminent destruction. Because these shadowy "wars" are never declared, they also have no ceasefire. The terror caused by lethal drones can be chronic, for survivors never know whether they will be next in line to die. Do people have the right to live in peace and with a sense of security? If so, then the lurking above of drones known to emit deadly missiles constitutes a violation of those rights.[10]

The "smart war" argument for remote-control killing is impugned by the reality of second- and third-order collateral damage, for in addition to fear and anxiety, extreme levels of anger are found among people in communities living under lethal drones. This anger is especially marked in young boys, who may vow to retaliate by joining militant groups in response. Some of the victims destroyed by drones have relatives or friends who will seek revenge and undertake jihad in the name of the innocent victims killed. Orphans may end up as new recruits to extremist groups. Even if their father was associated in some way with a violent faction, his children have known him as their father and may feel the need to defend his honor. Given these dynamics, the very drone strikes intended to keep terrorism in check may well have the opposite effect, causing the ranks of the radical Islamic jihadists to swell.

More than 15 years into GWOT, the counterproductive nature of drone warfare is in full evidence throughout the Middle East. Many young Muslim men have reacted with righteous indignation to US military initiatives abroad, denouncing them as war crimes committed by the Western infidels. Most obviously, outrage at the comportment of the occupiers gave rise to the virulent insurgency in both Afghanistan and Iraq, among not only native inhabitants but also militants who traveled abroad to fight alongside their Muslim brethren.[11]

Beyond the declared war zones of Afghanistan and Iraq, lethal drones were used repeatedly by the CIA in Yemen, with the permission of the central government authority. Militants mobilized in response, eventually deposing President Abd Rabu Mansour Hadi in early 2015.[12] Yemen has been embroiled in a vicious civil war ever since.[13]

"Kill don't capture" policy

During the US occupations of Afghanistan and Iraq, *insurgents* and *militants* who posed a threat to the occupiers were regarded as *unlawful combatants* and legitimate targets for military attack.[14] From there, the *unlawful combatant* label and similar rules of engagement (ROE) came to be applied to terrorist suspects in unoccupied lands, even in places where the targets could not threaten to harm any allied soldier, given that there were none around.

Barack Obama made the closure of the Guantánamo Bay prison in Cuba, where many men were held for years without charges, a central plank of his successful 2008 election campaign. Upon assuming the presidency, he adopted a "kill don't capture" approach to counterterrorism. The administration claimed that they only killed suspected terrorists when capture was "infeasible," but a close look at the data—the near absence of suspects apprehended abroad under

Obama—suggests that the capture of drone strike targets in remote-tribal regions was perfunctorily defined as "infeasible." "Infeasibility of capture" did not denote the physical inability of a team of Navy SEALS to descend from the sky and encircle a suspect. Rather, "infeasibility of capture" connoted for the most part an unwillingness to expend resources and risk US lives. The political difficulty of housing a prisoner, should he in fact be captured rather than killed, appears to have figured importantly in the drone warriors' decisions to fire missiles wherever and whenever suspects were identified.[15]

The case of Shaker Aamer, a former British resident incarcerated at Guantánamo Bay for 14 years, serves as a cautionary tale. The detainees, including Aamer, were denigrated by then-Secretary of Defense Donald Rumsfeld and other Bush administration officials as "the worst of the worst." Years later, it emerged that most of the prisoners were innocent and had no connections whatsoever to any terrorist organization. How and why were so many innocent men mistakenly swept up and locked away in the prison at Guantánamo Bay? In large part because generous bribes were offered to bounty hunters. Aamer was finally released in 2015 after years of assiduous efforts on the part of human rights groups and attorneys.[16]

The use of paid informants has been every bit as integral to the drone program as it was in the taking of prisoners under Bush, which implies that many of the people intentionally destroyed by drones may have been wrongly executed. In other words, even the already misleading figures on first-order collateral damage (ignoring second- and third-order effects) may grossly underestimate the sheer toll of innocent life and helps to explain the extreme anger found among survivors of drone strikes. If Shaker Aamer had been identified as a terrorist suspect in 2011, rather than 2001, he would now, in all likelihood, be dead, filed away in the official story as yet another "suspected militant killed."

According to classified US government documents made public by *The Intercept* in 2015, the unnamed adult male victims of drone strikes are written off as "Enemy Killed in Action" (EKIA) in the official story of what has been done.[17] Along with HUMINT, human intelligence derived from persons who provide information about prospective targets in exchange for money, SIGINT, or signals intelligence, is often used to finger suspects. These electronic sources include video footage taken by drones, and data derived from cell phones and SIM cards. The potential for error is obvious. The wife of a jihadist may be mistaken for her husband if she shares a cellphone with him. But the suspected jihadi himself may have been pegged because his name was found among the contacts of someone already identified as a "bad guy." From there, more people may be deemed fair game for execution because they have somehow "associated" with another person identified as a terrorist suspect. That is how kill lists are compiled: data from known terrorist suspects (who, it is important to underscore, are *suspected* of complicity in terrorism) is mined to find the names of more persons to be hunted down and killed. The process can continue on like this endlessly, generating longer and longer kill lists in a disturbing conflation of serial homicide with national defense.

Drone strike targets have been pegged for death on the basis of hearsay and circumstantial evidence, which would not hold up in a court of law. Yet there is no way to contest the killers' version of the story, for they act simultaneously as the judge, the jury, the executioner, and the writers of the history of what has transpired. Under Obama's watch, innocent men not unlike Shaker Aamer, who was released after years of deprivation and torture, are not imprisoned but summarily executed. In reply to criticisms that unnamed men of military age have been indiscriminately targeted, former CIA Director Michael Hayden has objected: "They were not. Intelligence for signature strikes always had multiple threads and deep history. The data was near encyclopedic."[18] But if the people being killed are of unknown identity, then how could knowledge of them be *encyclopedic*?

The apparently sincere testimony of administration figures continues to be taken at face value to imply that more and more drones and missiles should be produced, and more and more operators trained to fire them. Which means that more and more analysis will be needed to locate suitable targets, if the "killing machine" is to be kept up and running.[19] With the toll of dead "terrorist suspects" taken as the sole measure of success, program administrators and analysts naturally aim at the highest possible number.

In March 2016, reports surfaced of a US air attack in Somalia, which culminated in the deaths of an estimated 150+ persons identified as Al Shabaab terrorists said to be preparing for an "imminent" attack. The targets were destroyed by a combination of unmanned and manned bomber strikes.[20] The use of manned bombers along with drones in Somalia to wipe out a large group of human beings claimed to have been on the verge of perpetrating evil against the people of the United States represents a further progression down a continuum of evermore lethal US foreign policy.

Initially, shortly after September 11, 2001, drone strikes were used against named, "high-value" targets believed to have already engaged in terrorist attacks culminating in the deaths of innocent people. Next, "medium-value" targets were hunted down and killed. Eventually, foot soldiers became the primary targets, and drone strikes began to be used against unnamed suspects, whose "patterns of behavior" or "disposition matrix" matched those of known terrorists.[21] The military-age men destroyed by drones in such "signature strikes" are presumed guilty until proven innocent of future potential nefarious schemes said to justify their annihilation.[22] The citizens paying for the strikes are never permitted to assess the evidence because, they are told, it would jeopardize national security. But defining all military-age male suspects in so-called hostile areas as guilty until proven innocent does not mean that they are. It just makes the executions easier for the citizens paying for the deaths—and for everyone involved at every level of the "kill chain"—to accept.

The targets of the March 2016 air raid in Somalia were said to be assembled for some form of ceremony. Both the use of manned bombers in a country with which the United States was not officially at war and the magnitude of the carnage were noteworthy. Where it used to be that individual people believed to be guilty of specific crimes were hunted down and slain, this Somalia mission illustrated the broadening of killing campaigns to include amorphous groups of unidentified men gathering for unknown reasons. Based on the government's post-strike report, US officials appear not to have known what the "ceremony" was about, suggesting that their intelligence was not very fine-grained. Nonetheless, the 150+ persons present were deemed legitimate targets and massacred.

Two weeks after the mass killing in Somalia, also in March 2016 but this time in Yemen, another large-scale US attack was reported, with the death toll estimated at greater than 50 persons.[23] Once again, and as is customary, all of the victims were identified post-mortem as "imminent threats" to US forces and allies. All told, 200+ persons were destroyed in only two attacks over the course of two weeks, with many others harmed. None of the dead were civilians, according to US officials.

"None of the dead were civilians" is a familiar refrain among drone program administrators. John Brennan, the director of the CIA since 2013, avowed in June 2011, while serving as Obama's top counterterrorism advisor, that there had been no collateral deaths caused by the targeted killing program during the previous year in Pakistan.[24] In March 2011, US officials had claimed that a series of coordinated airstrikes in Datta Khel (Pakistan) killed no civilians. Locals later revealed that the missile strikes had wiped out the community's tribal elders as they were meeting peacefully for a *jirga* (traditional assembly) to settle a dispute over a chromite mine.[25] The wide disparity in damage reports on Datta Khel and elsewhere was a straightforward consequence of the fact that the US administration had redefined the concept of "civilian" so as to exclude male persons of military age.[26]

The news of the slaughter of 150+ men in Somalia and the 50 more in Yemen only two weeks later hardly registered on the major news networks broadcasting in the United States. We do not know whether any wives and children were in attendance at the March 2016 "ceremony" in Somalia. If so, they will be written off as "collateral damage." In all of the ongoing uncertainty and vagueness about the conduct and aims of US drone policy, one thing is fairly certain: nearly all of the victims have been brown skinned. In arguably one of the worst examples of racial profiling in human history, able-bodied males in remote territories are simply assumed by the drone warriors to be terrorists and worthy of execution until proven otherwise.

When mistakes are made, and children and nonthreatening men and women are slain, it may be that persons on the ground who provided information culminating in strikes were themselves shameless mercenaries or "bad guys," whose aim was to earn some money or to shore up their power and eliminate rivals in their domain. In other cases, analysts keen to find "opportunities" to kill, and laboring under a confirmation bias (former US Secretary of Defense Leon Panetta was once described as seeing a terrorist training camp wherever he saw a group of men doing jumping jacks) decide to launch drone attacks based on their hunches. What have they got to lose? The perpetrators can always cover their tracks by invoking State Secrets Privilege.

Disturbingly, some of the most outspoken proponents of targeted killing have stood to gain financially from the practice as a result of their connections to companies working in collaboration with the US government to prosecute the drone campaigns. The more missiles fired, the more will be produced, generating a profit-based motive for killing more and more. Because private companies are also involved in the analysis leading up to strikes, they, too, are rewarded for identifying as many targets as possible.[27] The unbridled enthusiasm for targeted killing on the part of persons with direct connections to the drone industry warrants special scrutiny, and former CIA director and NSA director Michael Hayden is a case in point. Not only is Hayden a principal of the Cherthoff Group, he also serves on the board of directors at Alion Science and Technology, Motorola Solutions, and Mike Baker International, all of which enjoy Pentagon contracts relating to drone warfare.[28]

Ongoing public complacency conjoined with groupthink among administrators in an institution homogenized over the years since the War on Terror began ensure that the killers will continue to up the ante. The very reasoning used to rationalize drone strikes could eventually lead to genocide. Eliminating suspects along with their families would be one way of preventing the creation of terrorists out of children incensed at having been rendered orphans by war makers. Logically speaking, it's not all that different from defining all military-age males as "unlawful combatants" and fair game for execution. The precedent for such policy has already been set: Abdulrahman al-Awlaki, the son of Anwar al-Awlaki, was "taken out" by a US missile strike in Yemen shortly after having celebrated his sixteenth birthday.[29]

Drone-enhanced executive power

The popular arguments for using lethal drones as a primary counterterrorism tool shroud the truth about what political leaders are likely to do once they have gained access to remote-control killing machines. Lethal drones not only provide militaries with the means to fight wars without sacrificing soldiers, they also empower leaders to be able to wage what are characterized as "wars" in countries which otherwise would not have been invaded. Suddenly, missiles can be fired any- and everywhere, because the entire world has become a battlefield.[30] The mere possession of lethal drones transforms what were previously the remote tribal regions of sovereign nations into places where a seemingly endless list of "unlawful combatants" are waiting quietly, like animals in the wilderness, to be hunted down and killed.

When soldiers' lives are not at risk, there is much less, if any, political pressure to seek out and secure the support of the populace before wielding the weapons of war. The mere possession of lethal drones may therefore serve to enlarge the domain of state-inflicted homicide carried out at the sole discretion of the executive. The bolstering of executive power brought about by the development of drone technology is, needless to say, appealing to leaders themselves. In purely political terms, the ability to appear strong by wielding deadly force can cause a leader's popularity to surge—provided that he or she is not sacrificing soldiers abroad. Lethal drones therefore offer a win-win arrangement for politicians: they can wage and fight unilateral wars without having to write condolence letters to the families of fallen soldiers.[31]

Once remote-control killing machines are at arm's length, and intentional, premeditated homicide is but a push-button away, the political argument for using lethal drones is strengthened in the minds of government administrators by the need to demonstrate to the populace that taxpayers' money has not been squandered. The guiding logic becomes: "What's the point of having X, if you're not going to use X?" Former US Secretary of State Madeleine Albright posed a variant of this question to Colin Powell: "What's the point of having this superb military you're always talking about, if we can't use it?"[32]

It may sound repulsive to peace-loving people for government officials to be shopping around for opportunities to wage war, but that is precisely what has happened with lethal drones—albeit one act of homicide at a time. Case in point: Britain.

Before the Drone Age, British Prime Minister David Cameron would likely never have entertained the possibility of dispatching his compatriots without indicting much less trying them for crimes. Capital punishment is prohibited by both British law and the EU Charter. But with a large fleet of Reaper drones and missiles at his disposal, Cameron awakened to the possibility of executing suspects using the weapons of war. Because he used missiles, rather than pistols, poisons or strangulation wires, to destroy British citizens Reyaad Khan and Ruhul Amin in Syria in August 2015, Cameron was able to characterize the assassinations as acts of national self-defense.[33] Who could object to that depiction, when it had already been accepted with open arms by the American public for years, in hundreds of drone strikes authorized by US leaders?

The pro-assassination norm arose only as a result of the development of remote-control killing technology and the willingness of government officials to use it in the wake of the terrorist attacks of September 11, 2001. The same norm continues to be absorbed and perpetuated by politicians with the power to wield the weapons of war long after the perpetrators of the crimes of 9/11 have disappeared. In the absence of a rigorous public debate about the morality of drone killing, leaders who suddenly acquire the means to stalk, hunt down, and slaughter targets suspected of complicity in terrorism can be expected to continue to follow the examples of the early drone warriors. Claiming to be "tough on terrorism," such leaders will be keen to exercise their authority and avail themselves of their new-found capacity to kill by remote control.

President Obama asked the American people to "trust" him about his administration's use of lethal drones, which they did, as did the many Western political leaders both at home and abroad who have condoned the drone campaigns. The barrier to state homicide was lowered significantly by Obama through his signature policy, "kill don't capture." Even worse, justice has been doubly perverted through a linguistic sleight of hand: "suspected terrorists" are not charged with crimes but rebranded as "unlawful combatants" and slaughtered in the manner of armed enemy soldiers on a battlefield. Even in "personality strikes," when targets are named individuals believed to be associated with extremist groups, the missiles which aim to kill them often destroy others in their stead.[34]

As a result of the drone industry boom, Obama's "strike first, suppress questions later" targeted-killing policy will likely be one of his most enduring legacies, to be taken up by future leaders, both in the United States and beyond. We have no idea who those leaders will be, nor whether they will be of good judgment and worthy of the same broad blanket of trust which Obama's cool demeanor managed to inspire. Whatever care US administrators may have taken to avoid collateral damage in their own precedent-setting drone campaigns, they have no power over the use of this technology by their successors or by leaders in lands far away. They, too, will meet behind closed doors to decide whom to kill, when and why, on the basis of secretive criteria to which only the drone warriors themselves are privy.

Both modern and medieval

The US government has done a splendid job of persuading citizens to believe that they are being protected by drone strikes, but an abysmal job of making the world a safer place, as evidenced by the ongoing chaos and carnage throughout the Middle East. Rather than attempt to understand the proliferation of terrorist franchises over 15 years of GWOT, Western media outlets continue to grant the US administration the benefit of the doubt, just as they have in the past, and all the more since the 9/11 attacks. However, drone assassination is not merely war business as usual. There is something sinister at play: the very psyches of Western people are being transformed by this use of remote-control killing technology. People are becoming more and more inured, even numb, to the reality of state-inflicted homicide and what it means to exterminate their fellow human beings, tellingly referred to by the killers themselves as "bug splat."[35]

During the twentieth century, people who repeatedly and premeditatedly stalked and hunted down human beings with the intention of ending their lives were commonly referred to as sociopathic or psychopathic serial killers. In the Drone Age, uniformed soldiers are being asked to do the very same thing, even while knowing that their own lives are not in any danger when they annihilate targets after having spied on them and their families in the manner of voyeuristic peeping Toms.[36] Enticed by generous salaries and benefits packages, young persons are being lured to become professional assassins who spend their workdays tracking and killing human beings who were never indicted, much less tried, for their allegedly capital crimes.

The use of lethal drones to dispatch persons suspected of complicity in terrorism represents a major rupture in modern Western people's thinking about when homicide is supposed to be justified. Bureaucratic targeted killing diverges dramatically from the concept of legitimate self-defense familiar to combat soldiers on the ground, which helps to explain the incidence of PTSD among drone operators who have realized their mistake only too late.[37] Along with former drone operators, many activists, academics, and other military veterans have repeatedly expressed grave concerns about remote-control killing, including the blowback likely to ensue from the drone campaigns.[38]

Even setting to one side the problem of blowback, the use of lethal drones to terminate targets' lives on "battlefields" stipulated as such by the killers themselves represents an abandonment of many modern democratic triumphs, not only human rights, but also transparency and due process, which took centuries to be developed and codified in Western institutions. The legality of the targeted killing of unarmed suspects in unoccupied lands who are not actively engaged in combat has been scrupulously examined and called into question by a number of scholars, including two successive UN Special Rapporteurs on Extrajudicial Execution, Philip Alston and Christof Heyns.[39] Among other problems, if the persons being killed were truly *soldiers*, then they would need to be provided with the opportunity to surrender in accordance with the Geneva Conventions. If, on the other hand, the targets were truly *suspects*, then they would be covered by Article 11 of the Universal Declaration of Human Rights, the "innocent until proven guilty" clause.

US government officials and other drone program supporters have responded to such complaints by reiterating that the targeted suspects are *unlawful combatants* and therefore not protected by military protocols and international law. In 2010, the US Department of Justice issued a White Paper asserting that the targeted killing, even of US citizens, was legal under some circumstances. The argument rests on a contentious redefinition of "imminent threat" as not requiring immediacy. It also trades on the drone warriors' flexible and contestable concept of "infeasibility of capture."[40]

There have never been any international norms governing the use specifically of lethal drones, which became available to leaders only in the twenty-first century. However, protocols covering assassination, to which drone-delivered missiles are a means, are already enshrined in the UN Charter, the Universal Declaration of Human Rights, and the Geneva Conventions. These documents have been reinterpreted creatively by the US government so as to rationalize the practice of targeted killing even in lands where there are no US soldiers on the ground who could be said to be directly protected by drone strikes. Armed with UCAVs, the executives of ostensibly democratic governments have acquired a Godfather-like capacity to order summary executions at their caprice. Remote-control killing may be the result of an ultramodern technology, but "Off with their heads!" predates the 1215 Magna Carta.

Even the most atrocious of practices have always been legal until they were made illegal through the concerted efforts of legislators. As a result most obviously of geopolitics, the leaders of other nations have docilely condoned the precedent-setting use of drones by the US government and are in the process of being coopted, thanks to the drone industry boom and the global spread of the new technology. Based on the comportment of the lethal drone-armed political leaders to date, it would seem to be only a matter of time before the government officials of many other states will seek to locate and eliminate some of their compatriots in war zones far away—or at home, as was done in 2015 by the central governments of Iraq, Nigeria, Afghanistan, and Pakistan.[41] The logic is seductive but corruptive, and many political leaders will succumb, having been lured down the path to drone killing as a result of the example set by the US government during the first two decades of the twenty-first century.

Some of the men being killed may well be militants, but given the origins of Western democratic states, the question must be posed: what is supposed to be wrong with opposing the government, if one lives under authoritarian or tyrannical rule? Modern democracies emerged in human history as a result of the efforts of dissidents—often militants—who believed fervently in human liberty and were willing to fight and die to wrest control of their lives from monarchs.

Long range effects of drone killing on Western civilization

The secrecy of the early drone warriors and the willingness of the mainstream media to parrot official reports have together served to minimize dissent to targeted killing. The long-range, global implications of drone warfare have never been addressed publicly by policymakers. In its ever-more lethal campaigns, the US government has been systematically destroying human beings abroad using UCAVs but without sacrificing US personnel. One surmises that if the leader of any other nation in the world had been the first to execute thousands of people abroad on mere suspicion of their possible association with extremist groups, he or she might have been indicted for war crimes at the International Criminal Court (ICC) in The Hague. More than 15 years since the War on Terror began, the US lethal drone precedent remains largely unchallenged by Western political elites. As more and more leaders get in on the drone killing game, it will become progressively more difficult for diplomats to air complaints without implicating their compatriots.

Targeted killing is politically palatable at the launching end of missiles because leaders are able to fight what are labeled "wars" without risking their fellow citizens' lives—at least in the short term. Blowback to military killing emerges later on down the line and can be expected to destroy more innocent people in the West, thereby provoking a vicious vortex of retaliatory violence. What is regarded by some as the war on Muslims in the Middle East will continue to inspire persons residing in the West to carry out retaliatory attacks, as in Paris and San Bernardino in 2015, and in Brussels in 2016. Beyond the inevitable blowback, humanity itself is being degraded, and not only because young people in the West are being lured to work as assassins.

Some of the bravest and brightest young people of the Muslim communities under siege are being eliminated for protesting what they themselves take to be moral atrocities and gross injustices perpetrated by the US government and its current allies. Consider the case of Junaid Hussain, a 21-year-old British national who was hunted down and killed in Syria by a US drone in August 2015. As in many other cases, this young man was killed in a strike after a previous missile had hit other, untargeted people. The toll of collateral damage in these communities—the civilians either killed or left bereft and traumatized—is itself a grave wrong, but there are broader implications as well. Junaid Hussain may have been a hacker for ISIS, but in order to appreciate the long-range effects of the drone campaigns, it is necessary to pause the killing machine, step back and ask: *Why was he collaborating with ISIS?*

Recall that Osama bin Laden explicitly stated that he had supported the attacks of September 11, 2001 (probably orchestrated by Khalid Sheikh Mohammed and executed by Mohamed Atta), in retaliation to the 1991 Gulf War and the establishment of US military bases in Muslim lands such as Saudi Arabia. The US government's response was to attack Iraq again, killing even more innocent people than they had already destroyed, and establishing even more military bases abroad than there were before. Lethal drones are now operating out of bases dotting the globe and hovering above more and more Muslim lands. Under the circumstances, it is hardly surprising that new extremists continue to arise in protest to the ever-proliferating drone campaigns.

British national Junaid Hussain was a mere child when the US government invaded Iraq in 2003 with the blessing of then-British Prime Minister Tony Blair. As a result of that arguably illegal invasion, the group of fundamentalists now known as ISIS joined forces with al-Qaeda in efforts to repel the occupiers. Over the course of the short lifetime of many of the young people targeted for obliteration in recent years, hundreds of thousands of Muslims were killed directly by Western governments, led by the United States. In view of that history, it seems quite likely that Junaid Hussain became sympathetic with anti-Western terrorists because he was outraged by the slaughter of so many Muslim people in Iraq, Afghanistan, Pakistan, Yemen, Somalia, Libya, Syria, and beyond. Before finding himself at the receiving end of a Hellfire missile, Hussain had already been convicted and imprisoned for six months in Britain for having hacked into Tony Blair's email account.[42] Upon relocating to Syria, this ISIS sympathizer was hunted down and killed—executed without trial by lethal drone—using intelligence provided in part by the British government.

Terrorists, insurgents, dissidents, and militants have long been conflated, as though these categories were interchangeable. But many of the men killed in Afghanistan and Iraq after the US invasions regarded themselves as defending their homeland from the foreign occupiers. Moreover, in places such as Yemen, it seems likely that at least some of the militants who oppose the authority of their central government are attempting to change their society for the good: "One man's terrorist, is another man's freedom fighter."

Named, "high-value" targets have been systematically culled from Muslim communities, leaving younger and younger suspects to be dispatched as the new "No. 2" evil terrorist leader. Who were these young men? What would they have done, who might they have become, had they not perceived their communities to be under attack and decided to fight back? We will never know. Throughout the Middle East, brown-skinned people have been categorically denied human rights through summary strikes based on racial profiling. Scores of young people with great potential have been and continue to be slain on the mere suspicion that they might at some unknown time in the future attempt to carry out terrorist attacks.

Remote-control killing is new in history, but terrorism is not new to the Drone Age. It is a tactic often taken up by dissidents in desperate times, such as Nelson Mandela, who eventually became the first black president of South Africa. As a young man, Mandela was regarded by the South African government as a dangerous terrorist. He was apprehended and thrown into prison, where he stayed for 27 years before emerging as a champion of peace.[43] As disturbing as this suggestion will seem to some readers—and no doubt difficult for many to believe— at least some of the many men killed by lethal drones have been ideologically closer to Nelson Mandela than to Osama bin Laden, despite their physical similarity to the latter.

Can persons who attempt to fight back against gross institutional injustice, as did Nelson Mandela, possibly emerge in the Drone Age? It is becoming less and less likely that they will survive, for lethal drones are spreading all over the globe and being used already by some governments to kill their own citizens in the homeland. "Kill don't capture" policy would have terminally silenced the future president of South Africa, if only lethal drones had existed at that time.

Conclusion

The US government's ambitious agenda to rid the world of suspects who might possibly be thinking about possibly planning to attempt to carry out possible future acts of potential terror against the people of the United States is a vain and Sisyphean quest. Any rational consideration of the prevailing quagmire in the Middle East by persons who do not stand to profit from drone killing can only conclude that the range of covert operations instigated under Presidents George W. Bush and Barack Obama have failed miserably, not only morally, but also tactically and strategically. Mired in lethal centrism, the drone warriors appear altogether incapable of facing up to the truth, that lethal drones have not stemmed the tide of terrorists. Instead, career administrators take the recent attacks in the West as evidence of the need to kill even more so-called terrorists, under the obtuse assumption that angry Muslim men "wherever they may hide" are the equivalents of Osama bin Laden.

In truth, the notorious al-Qaeda leader, and the operatives and fellow travelers who masterminded and conducted the terrorist attacks of September 11, 2001, were unique in history. Most drone strike targets have shared these genuine terrorists' skin color and may have dressed similarly. Many no doubt despised the US government, given its endless incursions into Muslim lands and its blanket assertion of the right to kill anyone anywhere at any time and for any reason. But the bulk of the people annihilated by lethal drones to date have been poor tribesmen living in remote regions of Third World countries. They have been very unlike the clever and wealthy mastermind and the educated foot soldiers behind the attacks of September 11, 2001. One wonders whether some of the many victims of the drone campaigns in recent years have even had passports. Yet somehow the guiding sophism that every brown-skinned adult male located in a remote tribal region is an existential threat to Western civilization continues to serve as the basis for US policy.

Leaders of all stripes, republicans and monarchs alike, who authorize targeted killing in the future can be expected to follow the example of the US government by stigmatizing their enemies as terrorists and claiming that capture is infeasible. The unfettered expansion of executive power suggests that nihilistic lethal centrism, which denies the intrinsic value of human beings, will continue to dominate policy, leading eventually to the same treatment of suspects at home as abroad. Can anyone reasonably deny that US citizen Anwar Al-Awlaki would have been more dangerous to the people of the United States in Manhattan than he was in Yemen? Or that British citizens Reyaad Khan and Ruhul Amin would have been more dangerous to the people of Britain in London than they were in Syria? Once leaders have already decided to kill their own citizens—even hackers such as Junaid Hussain—without trial, why should it matter whether they are located at home or abroad?

As more and more countries acquire the means to dispatch human beings by remote-control, and elect to do so in the homeland, the broader cultural and political costs of this technology may finally come to light. When drone strikes become commonplace, citizens may come to fear the possibility of being annihilated by their own government for opposing—or for being thought to oppose—its policies. Unless the precedents set by the first drone warriors are reversed, institutionalized targeted killing will serve to minimize dissent, freezing political reality in place, and making the countries in most need of democratic reform the least likely to achieve it. Along with persons decried as the "worst of the worst," the "best of the best" may gradually be culled from human societies over time as dissidents are crushed and criticism silenced. Great forces for moral and political change such as Nelson Mandela may eventually become extinct.

Notes

1 The Bureau of Investigative Journalism has compiled a complete data set of strikes in Pakistan, Yemen and Somalia. The data for Afghanistan, Libya, Syria, and Iraq is less complete because of the covert and collaborative nature of most operations in those war zones. However, in Pakistan alone, Obama had conducted 373 confirmed strikes by May 16, 2016. See: "Get the data: Drone Wars", *The Bureau of Investigative Journalism*, www.thebureauinvestigates.com/category/projects/drones/drones-graphs/.
2 Conor Friedersdorf, "Hillary Defends Her Failed War in Libya," *The Atlantic*, October 14, 2015. www.theatlantic.com/politics/archive/2015/10/hillary-clinton-debate-libya/410437/.
3 "Bernie Sanders: I would continue assassination drone program," *Novanews*, August 31, 2015. www.shoah.org.uk/2015/08/31/bernie-sanders-i-would-continue-assassination-drone-program.
4 In the PBS documentary film *Rise of the Drones* (2013), directed by Peter Yost, Shuja Nawaz of the Atlantic Council explains: "We know fairly well how many strikes are occurring. What we don't know is the details, who the targets were, whether they were actually eliminated, or whether some other people were killed, because verification is very difficult."

5 Data on countries' drone possession and acquisition can be found at the New America website "World of Drones:" http://securitydata.newamerica.net/world-drones.html.
6 Declan Walsh, "Drone Strikes in Pakistan are Said to Take Toll on Leadership in Pakistan," *New York Times*, April 24, 2015. www.nytimes.com/2015/04/25/world/asia/cia-qaeda-drone-strikes-warren-weinstein-giovanni-lo-porto-deaths.html?_r=0.
7 The second-order consequences of first-order collateral damage are discussed in Chapter 3, "Truth and Consequences," of Laurie Calhoun, *War and Delusion: A Critical Examination* (New York: Palgrave Macmillan, 2013), pp. 47–66.
8 Human Rights Watch, "Between a Drone and Al Qaeda: The Civilian Cost of US Targeted Killings in Yemen," October 2013; Amnesty International, "'Will I Be Next?' US Drone Strikes in Pakistan," October 2013; International Human Rights and Conflict Resolution Clinic at Stanford Law School and Global Justice Clinic at NYU School of Law, "Living Under Drones: Death, Injury, and Trauma to Civilians from US Drone Practices in Pakistan," September 2012; and Center for Civilians in Conflict (CIVIC), "Civilians in Armed Conflict: Civilian Harm and Conflict in Northwest Pakistan," October 2010.
9 Alkarama, "Traumatising Skies: U.S. Drone Operations and Post-Traumatic Stress Disorder (PTSD) Among Civilians in Yemen," June 24, 2015. http://en.alkarama.org/component/k2/1764-yemen-alkarama-s-report-2015-traumatising-skies-u-s-drone-operations-and-post-traumatic-stress-disorder-ptsd-among-civilians-in-yemen?Itemid=.
10 The question whether living in peace is a human right being violated by the use of lethal drones is scrupulously examined by a variety of authors in a special issue of the journal *Peace Review*: Volume 27, no 4, 2015.
11 Gregory D. Johnsen, *The Last Refuge: Yemen, Al-Qaeda, and America's War in Arabia* (New York, NY: W. W. Norton & Company, 2013), p. 143.
12 Hakim Almasmari and Martin Chulov, "Houthi rebels seize Yemen president's palace and shell home," *Guardian*, January 20, 2015.
13 Wikipedia, "Yemeni Civil War," November 1, 2016. https://en.wikipedia.org/wiki/Yemeni_Civil_War_(2015%E2%80%93present).
14 Wikipedia. "Unlawful Combatant," November 1, 2016. https://en.wikipedia.org/wiki/Unlawful_combatant.
15 Daniel Klaidman, *Kill or Capture: The War on Terror and the Soul of the Obama Presidency* (New York, NY: Houghton Mifflin, 2012).
16 Adam Goldman and Missy Ryan, "Shaker Aamer, longtime Guantanamo detainee, to be freed to Britain," *Washington Post*, September 25, 2015. www.washingtonpost.com/world/national-security/british-resident-held-at-guantanamo-bay-to-be-sent-to-the-united-kingdom/2015/09/25/716dced2-62ea-11e5-b38e-06883aacba64_story.html.
17 See: "The Drone Papers" at *The Intercept*: https://theintercept.com/drone-papers/.
18 Michael V. Hayden, "To Keep America Safe, Embrace Drone Warfare," *New York Times*, February 19, 2016. www.nytimes.com/2016/02/21/opinion/sunday/drone-warfare-precise-effective-imperfect.html.
19 Greg Miller and Julie Tate, "CIA Shifts Focus to Killing Targets," *Washington Post*, September 1, 2011. www.washingtonpost.com/world/national-security/cia-shifts-focus-to-killing-targets/2011/08/30/gIQA7MZGvJ_story.html.
20 Helene Cooper, "U.S. Strikes in Somalia Kill 150 Shabab Fighters," *New York Times*, March 7, 2016. www.nytimes.com/2016/03/08/world/africa/us-airstrikes-somalia.html?rref=collection%2Ftimestopic%2FSomalia&action=click&contentCollection=world&region=stream&module=stream_unit&version=latest&contentPlacement=13&pgtype=collection&_r=0.
21 Greg Miller, "Plan for Hunting Terrorists Signals US Intends to Keep Adding Names to Kill Lists," *Washington Post*, October 23, 2012. www.washingtonpost.com/world/national-security/plan-for-hunting-terrorists-signals-us-intends-to-keep-adding-names-to-kill-lists/2012/10/23/4789b2ae-18b3-11e2-a55c-39408fbe6a4b_story.html.

22. Spencer Ackerman, "Inside Obama's drone panopticon: a secret machine with no accountability," *Guardian*, April 25, 2015. www.theguardian.com/us-news/2015/apr/25/us-drone-program-secrecy-scrutiny-signature-strikes.
23. Spencer Ackerman, "Massive US airstrike in Yemen kills 'dozens' of people, Pentagon says," *Guardian*, March 22, 2016. www.theguardian.com/world/2016/mar/22/us-airstrike-yemen-dozens-dead-al-qaida-terrorism-training-camp.
24. Scott Shane, "CIA is Disputed on Civilian Toll in Drone Strikes," *New York Times*, August 11, 2011. www.nytimes.com/2011/08/12/world/asia/12drones.html.
25. Salman Masood and Pir Zubair Shah, "C.I.A. Drones Kill Civilians in Pakistan," *New York Times*, March 17, 2011. www.nytimes.com/2011/08/12/world/asia/12drones.html.
26. Jo Becker and Scott Shane, "Secret 'Kill List' Proves a Test of Obama's Principles and Will," *New York Times*, May 29, 2012. www.nytimes.com/2012/05/29/world/obamas-leadership-in-war-on-al-qaeda.html?pagewanted%3Dall.
27. David S. Cloud, "Civilian Contractors Playing Key Roles in U.S. Drone Operations," *Los Angeles Times*, December 29, 2011. http://articles.latimes.com/2011/dec/29/world/la-fg-drones-civilians-20111230.
28. Micah Zenko, "Evaluating Michael Hayden's Defense of Drone Strikes," *Politics, Power, and Preventive Action, the Council on Foreign Relations Blog*, February 20, 2016. http://blogs.cfr.org/zenko/2016/02/20/evaluating-michael-haydens-defense-of-cia-drone-strikes/.
29. Craig Whitlock, "U.S. airstrike that killed American teen in Yemen raises legal, ethical questions," *Washington Post*, October 22, 2011. www.washingtonpost.com/world/national-security/us-airstrike-that-killed-american-teen-in-yemen-raises-legal-ethical-questions/2011/10/20/gIQAdvUY7L_story.html.
30. Jeremy Scahill, *Dirty Wars: The World is a Battlefield*, (New York, NY: Nation Books, 2013).
31. See Chapter 9, "Death and Politics," of Laurie Calhoun, *We Kill Because We Can: From Soldiering to Assassination in the Drone Age* (London: Zed Books, 2015), pp. 199–222.
32. Colin L. Powell and Joseph E. Persico, *My American Journey*, (New York, NY: Random House, 1995), p. 576.
33. Patrick Wintour and Nicholas Watt, "UK forces kill British Isis fighters in targeted drone strike on Syrian city," *Guardian*, September 7, 2015. www.theguardian.com/uk-news/2015/sep/07/uk-forces-airstrike-killed-isis-briton-reyaad-khan-syria.
34. Spencer Ackerman, "41 Men Targeted but 1147 Killed: US Drone Strikes – the Facts on the Ground," *Guardian*, November 24, 2014. www.theguardian.com/us-news/2014/nov/24/-sp-us-drone-strikes-kill-1147.
35. Chris Cole, Mary Dobbing and Amy Hailwood, *Convenient Killing: Armed Drones and the 'Playstation' Mentality*, (Oxford: The Fellowship of Reconciliation, 2010).
36. Former drone sensor operator Brandon Bryant describes the role as "the ultimate peeping Tom" in *Drone*, a 2014 documentary film directed by Tonje Hessen Schei.
37. Pratap Chaterjee, "Drone Whistleblowers Step Out of the Shadows," *Huffington Post* blog, April 21, 2016. www.huffingtonpost.com/pratap-chatterjee/drone-whistleblowers-step-out-of-the-shadows_b_9748958.html.
38. For expressions of concern in filmed interviews, see: *Unmanned: America's Drone Wars*, a 2013 documentary film directed by Robert Greenwald.
39. Philip Alston, "Report of the Special Rapporteur on extrajudicial, summary or arbitrary executions," United Nations General Assembly Human Rights Council, May 18, 2010; Christof Heyns, "Report of the Special Rapporteur on extrajudicial, summary or arbitrary executions," UN General Assembly Human Rights Council, September 13, 2013.
40. "Department of Justice White Paper: Lawfulness of a Lethal Operation Directed Against a U.S. Citizen Who is a Senior Operational Leader of Al-Qa'ida or An

Associated Force," Department of Justice, Washington, D.C, June 2010. www.fas.org/irp/eprint/doj-lethal.pdf.
41 Tim Craig, "Pakistani military says it drone killed 3 suspected militants," *Washington Post*, September 7, 2015. www.washingtonpost.com/world/pakistan-begins-drone-warfare-on-its-own-soil/2015/09/07/b7c56858-553a-11e5-8bb1-b488d231bba2_story.html; Siobhan O'Grady, "The U.S. and Israel aren't the only countries killing people with drones," September 8, 2015. http://foreignpolicy.com/2015/09/08/the-u-s-and-israel-arent-the-only-countries-killing-people-with-drones/.
42 Stephen Swinford, "British ISIL Fighters: Everything we know about the three dead Britons," *Telegraph*, September 8, 2015. www.telegraph.co.uk/news/uknews/terrorism-in-the-uk/11850076/British-isil-fighters-profiles-Ruhul-Amin-Reyaad-Khan-Junaid-Hussain.html.
43 The story of Nelson Mandela is portrayed in the 2013 film directed by Justin Chadwick, *Mandela: Long Walk to Freedom*.

Part IV

Analyzing, negotiating with, and ending terrorist groups

Mark Tomass

To what extent are the counterterrorist wars in the Middle East and, increasingly, Western Europe being waged on the basis of empirical and related accounts of the costs and benefits of negotiating with state-designated terrorist groups, and how have these groups historically come to an end? The contributions in this section discuss what it means to "win," "lose," and reach a "stalemate" when confronting terrorist groups, and which circumstances may facilitate negotiations toward the ending of hostilities.

In a dialogue with Mark Tomass, Scott Atran reflects on his fieldwork with members of ISIS and with those who were candidates to join them. Atran considers ISIS to be the most influential and politically novel countercultural force in the world today. His goal is to figure out what appeals to those who are joining it "in order to tame the beast within us before it kills us." With that aim in mind, Atran discusses a range of topics pertaining to the War on Terror, beginning with the aims of the terrorists, their motivations, their recruitment patterns, their typical profiles, and the difficulties a researcher faces in making a scientific study of them. Atran believes that the reckless, violent approach pursued by America and Britain has transformed al-Qaeda from a small band of fairly well-educated, violent extremists into a youthful social movement that appeals to thousands of disaffected Muslim immigrants in the Western diaspora, as well as to millions who are economically and politically frustrated in the Middle East. Volunteers for ISIS seek all that is lacking in the jaded, tired world of democratic liberalism, especially on the margins where Europe's immigrants mostly live. Therefore, to stop the spread of this trend in the West, the challenge for democracies is to provide an alternative means of satisfying the quest for glory and meaning that motivates many of those who join ISIS. One of Atran's insights with the most practical applications is for academics and law enforcement to focus more on personalized "counter-engagement," as opposed to providing counter-narratives. Atran suggests that these actors should work to address and harness the fellowship, passion, and purpose of individuals, as ISIS does.

In the next chapter, Johan Galtung proposes that the West try listening to what "terrorists," such as many Taliban and even a few from al-Qaeda, are saying. He believes that if one listens patiently to them in their own cultural and geographical contexts, what they say is often not unreasonable. The unreasonable position is not knowing what they say. Galtung claims that he does not know of a case where there is no basis for a reasonable, sustainable solution. According to Galtung, the "state terrorists" in Washington seem so dedicated to military planning and execution that there is little time or manpower left for any Plan B; alternative views and plans receive either no resources at all, or they are not thought through. He claims that the Washington establishment's remarkable insensitivity to cultural and structural factors reveals that they either don't understand, or don't want to understand, the context in which the "terrorists" are committing their horrific acts. And yet it is Washington and al-Qaeda, not 1.4 billion Christians and 1.3 billion Muslims, who will have no choice but to start a dialogue, in secret and in public. They cannot go on eliminating each other in the search for the elusive "roots" of the evil on the other side that would make them victorious. Galtung suggests focusing on elements of the conflict deeper than both sides' violent strategies, such as identifying incompatibilities and compatibilities between the parties and exploring possibilities for turning conflict into cooperation through dialogue toward a solution.

In his "Tale of Two Counter-Terrorisms," Douglas Carr, a military veteran and conflict researcher, provides a glance at the parallel vectors of terrorism between victim and perpetrator, offers reactions to the Paris and Brussels attacks, and makes an assessment of Belgian counterterrorism and counterinsurgency efforts. Carr introduces the essay with a personal account of the March 22, 2016, bombings in Brussels. He opens with the Belgian government's knee-jerk reaction, summarizing leading academics' statements, and analyzing the escalation of the current threat and its consequences. Tracing the discourse of terrorism to the "contested concept" of radicalization as it surfaced in European security circles after the 2004 Madrid bombings, Carr describes the current scholarly debate across France and Belgium. Since 2004, radicalization has been used more and more to denote Islamic-leaning, wayward youth traveling to fight in Iraq and Syria or committing irreversible acts of domestic terrorism on European soil. He concludes with his own and other veterans' experience in counterinsurgency, exploring how both the military and the police learn from each other, as roles begin to shift between the two in counterterrorism, and emphasizing the development of trust on the ground between the indigenous communities and the police and civic authorities.

Finally, Audrey Kurth Cronin analyzes the US response to the 9/11 attacks in historical context. She reveals four patterns common to all prolonged wars, where means become ends, tactics become strategy, boundaries are blurred, and the search for a perfect peace replaces reality. Because Cronin believes that ending the state of war against al-Qaeda will have an influence upon the US public psychologically and will shift the American narrative in ways that help the US government better adapt to ongoing global changes, she lays out a four-stage strategy for ending terror and the War on Terror. First, she suggests the revocation or revision of the 2001 Authorization for the Use of Military Force. Second, she recommends that the role of armed drones be scrutinized in terms of their impact on long-term American interests and the global implications of the precedent being set. Third, as the United States ends the War on Terror, it must also rebalance US counterterrorism policy. Being at war, the United States has overemphasized and over-resourced the military response to al-Qaeda at the expense of nonmilitary means. Finally, Cronin suggests that the US government must bring its own costs and risks into sharper alignment in order to portray to the American public a more realistic image of the War on Terror.

11 A dialogue on why Western youth are attracted to ISIS

Scott Atran and Mark Tomass

Mark Tomass: Scott Atran is an anthropologist who emphasizes direct observation of human behavior and the interpretation of the meanings that people give to their experiences. His approach is based on the belief that all human beings have common experiences to which they can relate and are therefore capable of understanding the feelings of others. With this approach, he tries to see reality through another person's eyes.[1] That is why Atran believes that the key to understanding why people are attracted to terrorist organizations as ISIS is to empathize with them, but without necessarily sympathizing with them. Accordingly, Atran is a participant observer of ISIS members' lives to the extent he feels it is morally permissible, and then he writes about his experiences with them.

Due to his years of fieldwork with members of Salafi Jihadi groups, their affiliates, and supporting communities, Atran has gained insights into the modes of thinking of Jihadists and would-be jihadists which he shared with the world on April 23, 2015 from the podium of United Nations Security Council.[2] In that speech, Atran told us that what inspires the most lethal terrorists in the world today is an exciting cause and call for action that promises glory and esteem in the eyes of peers, not the Muslim scriptures themselves. Therefore, he suggested that for the West to prevent further terrorist attacks in its territories, it must offer those would-be jihadists alternative paths, where they could realize their dreams of a positive meaningful life and which they would be able to have an opportunity to achieve through struggle and sacrifice in comradeship through their own initiatives.

Since his speech to the UN, Scott Atran acquired new findings about the ways in which Muslim youths are joining ISIS that show some markedly different recruitment patterns. He shared those new findings with me in May and June of 2016 as we corresponded about his perspectives on various topics pertaining to my book with Charles Webel. Below, I break down our correspondences by specific topics which he addressed:

MT: Do ISIS fighters from Europe and elsewhere in the Muslim diaspora have the same enlistment and recruitment patterns as past groups of jihadi fighters?

SA: In some respects yes, but in others no. About three out of every four people who join Al-Qaeda or ISIS in the diaspora do so through groups of peers, in search of a meaningful path in life. It is rare that parents are ever aware that their children desire to join the movement: in diaspora homes, Muslim parents are reluctant to talk about the failings of Western foreign policy and ISIL, whereas their children often want desperately to understand. These tendencies were similar for those diaspora enlistments to al-Qaeda after 9/11. But there are some important changes with recruitment patterns today, at least for Europe and North America:

1   Although about three out of four travel to their destination in peer groups, often with people they already know from preexisting social networks, including friends and family, now close friends and family, which were responsible for the lion's share of prior recruitment and radicalization, are directly responsible for only one out of five who join militant organizations.
2   A bit more than half are recruited via direct personal contact with members of a militant organization such as ISIL and Nusra (Al-Qaeda's Syrian affiliate).
3   One in four recruitments involve a religious mentor.
4   Slightly more than one in ten occurs solely via the internet.
5   Recruitment of women has become significant, up to more than one in four in some countries, like France.

MT: What is the typical profile of volunteers and supporters of ISIS who join from outside the Middle East?
SA: A summer 2014 ICM poll revealed that more than one in four French youth—of all creeds—between the ages of 18 and 24 had a favorable attitude towards ISIL; and. Even if this figure proves too high, support and or tolerance for the Islamic State among disaffected Western youth is worrisome. In Barcelona, five of 11 captured ISIS sympathizers who planned to blow up parts of the city were recent converts from atheism or Christianity. In France, one in four are converts and tend to be the most difficult to dissuade from the path of jihad. They tend to become some of the most fearsome foreign fighters.
MT: Is scientific research able to predict with any accuracy the person who is likely to engage in violent terrorist acts?
SA: For various reasons pertaining to the nature of the research sample, a researcher working with armed groups, such as ISIS, does not have the luxury of meeting the standards of human subjects and scientific protocols enforced by universities or governmental institutions. For example, standard informed consent would, as a practical matter, require providing the names and addresses of researchers, and IRB (Institutional Review Board) personnel of the researchers' institution, to members of ISIS; and that is a violation of federal law given that the stated goal of ISIS is to kill Americans whenever and wherever it can locate them. For example, the fourth issue of the ISIS English language publication Dabiq calls on supporters of ISIS to

"follow the fatwa to kill any American, Canadian or French person in their own lands ... civilians and military alike," with instructions on how to carry out such attacks on the streets with easily available everyday objects. Nevertheless, even with avowed members of murderous organizations we try to provide human subjects protection, including complete anonymity and procedures that ensure that the research involves no greater than minimal risk for persons being interviewed or studied, including prisoners.

As far as scientific controls are concerned, sometimes we interview and test whoever we can get to, so we often use opportunity samples rather than randomized samples. Also, for many questions we aren't particularly interested in nonviolent control populations, although for some we are: for example, if we want to understand how otherwise normal people become violent actors then we need non-violent control group comparisons. But if we want to understand better how to deal with violent actors who are already active, and to help prevent terrorist attacks or manage to survive on the battlefield, then we only need to know something directly about the violent actors we may face.

Dealing with the issue is difficult in part because of an established gap between expressed willingness and actual willingness; that is, between what people promise to do and, when it comes down to it, whether they pick up the gun or strap on the vest. Nearly all academic studies of support for terrorism or the allure of ISIS and its ilk extrapolate from expressed willingness to say and do things stated in surveys, interviews and the like. More often than not, it is not even the expressed willingness of violent actors and fighters themselves, but attitudes extrapolated from studies of the general population. So what I do with my research team is to actually go to the battlefield and interview and run controlled experiments with fighters on the frontlines, which has the advantage of eliminating the gap between expressed and actual willingness to make costly sacrifices, including fighting and dying, because you can monitor hours spent in combat, numbers of times wounded and gravity of wounds before re-engagement, group casualty rates, and so forth.

Over the last two years we have been trying to scientifically deal with a critical problem first publicly raised by President Barack Obama in September 2014, when he endorsed the judgment of his Director of National Intelligence: "We underestimated the Viet Cong ... we underestimated ISIS and overestimated the fighting capability of the Iraqi army.... It boils down to predicting the will to fight, which is an imponderable."

Our research suggests quite the opposite: predicting who is willing to fight and who isn't, and why, is quite ponderable and amenable to scientific study. In our recent interviews and psychological experiments on the frontlines in northern Iraq with Kurdish fighters of the Peshmerga and the PKK (Kurdistan Workers' Party), with captured ISIS fighters, and with Jabhat al-Nusra (al-Qaeda) fighters from Syria, we have a good initial indication of willingness to fight. Two principal factors interact to predict readiness to make costly sacrifices (go to prison, lose one's life, have one's family suffer, die, etc.).

The first factor is perception of relative commitment of one's own group versus those of the enemy to a sacred cause. This can be measured through behavioral experiments and tracked via neural imaging to show four elements.

1. Disregard for material incentives or disincentives: attempts to buy people off ("carrots") from their cause or punish them for embracing it through sanctions ("sticks") don't work, and even tend to backfire.
2. Blindness to exit strategies: people cannot even conceive of the possibility of abandoning their sacred values or relaxing their commitment to the cause.
3. Immunity to social pressure: it matters not how many people oppose your sacred values, or how close to you they are in other matters.
4. Insensitivity to discounting: in most everyday affairs, distant events and objects have less significance for people than things in the here and now; but matters associated with sacred values, regardless of how far removed in time or space, are more important and motivating than mundane concerns, however immediate.

The second factor in predicting willingness to fight is the degree of fusion with one's comrades. Consider, by way of illustration, a pair of circles where one circle represents "me" and a larger circle represents "the group". In one set of experiments, we asked participants to consider five possible pairings: in the first pairing, the "me" circle and "the group" circle don't touch; in the second pairing, the circles touch; in the third they slightly overlap; in the fourth they half overlap; and in the fifth pairing, the "me" circle is entirely contained within "the group" circle. People who choose the last pairing think and behave in ways entirely different from those who choose any of the other pairings. They experience what social psychologists call "identity fusion," wedding their personal identity ("who I am") to a unique collective identity ("who we are"). Such total fusion demonstrably leads to a sense of group invincibility and a willingness of each and every individual in the group to sacrifice for each and every other.

Only among the Kurds do we find commitment to the sacred cause of "Kurdeity" (their own term) and fusion with fellow Kurdish fighters comparable to commitment to cause and comrade among fighters of the Islamic State.

To be sure, not all who fight with the Islamic State are committed zealots. When we asked captured Islamic State fighters in Iraq: "What is Islam?" they answered: "My life," but they had little knowledge of the Quran or hadith, and none of Muslim history. Their sense of religion was fused with the vision of a caliphate that kills or subjugates any nonbeliever, but their conversion was not complete. In the face of almost sure execution by the Kurds, most were ready to recant. In one conversation picked up by a Kurdish walkie-talkie, a fighter with a local accent asked for help: "My brother has been killed. I am surrounded. Help me take his body away." The reply: "Perfect, you will join him soon in Paradise". The fighter retorted: "Come for me. This Paradise, I don't want." But foreign fighters are a different matter: Kurds and others perceive them as their fiercest and most dedicated adversaries, willing to die almost to a man.

Recently we monitored a small but telling battle, the first engagement of the initial push of the Iraqi army (trained and actually led by American "advisors") to retake Mosul. Fierce combat erupted on February 1 at a northern Iraqi village called Kudilah. A Western-backed coalition of several hundred Arab Sunni tribesman, Kurdish soldiers in the Iraqi army and forces of the Kurdish Peshmerga advanced on about 90 ISIS fighters who occupied the outpost. ISIS combatants counterattacked, led by young men wearing explosive vests. These well-trained warriors scurried through battle lines until they reached the enemy. Seventeen blew up themselves. Members of these suicide squadrons are called *inghimasi*, meaning "those who dive in deep." Another handful of *inghimasi* blew up themselves to cover the retreat of their comrades. All in all, more than half of the ISIS fighters died that day.

The *inghimasi's* determination and self-sacrifice inspires their comrades to fight to the death. Islamic State fighters retained control of Kudilah after two days of heavy fighting, despite being outnumbered. Waning morale and an unwillingness to lose more men led coalition forces to retreat.

Willingness to fight and make costly sacrifices is also strongly associated with perceptions of physical formidability on the battlefield and, even more importantly, with spiritual strength. ISIS and Kurdish fighters both tend to rate America's physical force at the maximum on both fixed and continuous measurement scales, but they rate America's spiritual force as middling. By contrast, both ISIS and Kurdish fighters rate ISIS's physical force as meager or middling, but it's spiritual strength at the maximum. Most fighters on all sides think that material prowess and interest drive the US, whereas spiritual belief and commitment drive ISIS.

In other tests, we find that the more people believe in the other's spiritual force, the less they believe in their own spiritual force (prevalent in the regular Iraqi army), and the less they are inclined to make costly material sacrifices against the enemy. The Islamic State's perceived spiritual force seems to intimidate, even paralyze some of its adversaries.

These findings give sense to the actual course of fighting and suggest that the effort to retake Mosul and degrade the Islamic State may require planning and action in a very different way than imagined.

MT: How then can the question of who joins the jihadi movement be investigated? How do you figure out what motivates people to join brutal organizations such as ISIS and the personal transformations that lead folks with unremarkable backgrounds to commit acts of incredible violence and self-destruction?

SA: Asking "why" people join the jihad has been rather an unproductive exercise and no interesting science has come out of it, or out of the kitchen-sink notion of "terrorism" as a field of study, for terrorism is a means for vastly different political actors and agendas. Rather, the science is best focused on the process of "how" people join different violent movements, of which the jihadi movement is a particular kind and worthy of study in its own right.

One interesting aspect of the jihadi movement, unlike other movements, such as contemporary white supremacists, is that it appeals to people who span the normal distribution and to a diversity of populations. So the interesting question to ask is: "How can and do otherwise perfectly normal people become violent jihadis?"

MT: Is the West misunderstanding the root causes of jihad and its attraction for young people?

SA: Much of the discussion and research on counter-radicalization and countering violent extremism has focused on understanding "root causes" and developing "counternarratives." I think such a focus has been, and will likely continue to be, a massive waste of time.

Talk of "religion," or "marginalization," or "search for significance" or any other "root cause" of a general nature is pretty worthless because these terms vastly overspecify. If indeed we're trying to address something that applies to, say, between 0.03 percent (of Muslims in France) or 0.14 percent (of Muslims in Belgium) of the eligible populations, then we can be guaranteed, on statistical grounds, that any explanation based on general ideological, socioeconomic, or psychological conditions will massively overpredict (i.e., around 99.9 percent of people who fit the conditions that fit most jihadis and jihadi-wannabes, e.g., religious fervor, marginalization in host societies, youth in transitional stages of life) and likely fail, leading to enormous waste of treasure and time and lives lost waiting for solutions that never come. And if the percentages are as low as that, then the true causes must be a complex interaction among heterogeneous person- and situation-specific factors, including close or chance proximity to those already in the jihad or moving towards it.

In other words, the locus of attention, whether academic or law enforcement, should be based on knowledge of the specific networks and contexts that produce recruits, not macro-factors like religious belief or marginalization or yearning of youth. We may find broad demographic, cultural, political, and socioeconomic factors that significantly reduce the potential pool of susceptible recruits, but any such reduction still wildly over predicts. However, once we have the detail of the networks involved, then we can isolate more relevant structural aspects of individual pathways into (and out of) jihadi networks and perhaps also more general structural aspects of the growth and evolution of these networks over time (something which does not now exist).

MT: What do you think of attempts to challenge the jihadi narrative that is attracting Muslim youth with counter-narratives?

SA: As far as counter-narratives and counter-messaging are concerned, these are basically worthless (or if worthwhile, then there is as yet no evidence of it). Counter-narrative and counter-messaging (even if they were "on target" and not, as now, mostly negative mass messages that lecture rather than engage) are mostly about "ideology," that is, ideas disembodied from the social networks in which ideas are embedded and given life, and which in turn animate and give life to social networks. Rather than "counter-narratives," again, academics and law enforcement would better focus on personalized "counter-engagement," addressing and harnessing the fellowship, passion, and purpose of particular people, as ISIS does, rather than shot gunning cookie-cutter ideas.[3]

MT: Are there certain preconditions or certain environments that encourage jihadi and ISIS recruitment?

SA: To be sure, there are privileged zones of recruitment in different regions: the petty criminal world of France, universities in the UK, professional associations in North Africa, former anti-Russian guerillas in the Caucasus and Central Asia, and so on. And there are particular reasons for each of these.

Let's take France, for example, and the involvement of petty criminals. As far as the jihad is concerned, serious involvement with criminal networks began after 9/11 as an unintended consequence of the ability of the USA to stop major financial aid to suspect groups, especially through charities. So al-Qaeda and others began looking for funding and arms in those clandestine networks best able to provide those services, namely criminal networks. And in the petty criminal networks were lots of marginal youth, because of opportunity costs. In France, 7–8 percent of the population is Muslim, but the majority of the country's prison population is young Muslim males. Yet most of them really don't want to be criminals, and then the jihad comes along and says to them:

> Look what this sick, immoral, and nihilist society has done to you, but you can turn the tables in following God, redeem yourselves, save others; and you can do this best by using the savoir-faire of the underworld, its skills and knowledge, against the society that forced you to suffer there.

A very powerful and persuasive message, that.

Today—and this is new in the jihad—about one-fourth of ISIS recruits from France are converts, and now nearly one-third are women. Converts, in their born-again fervor to become mujahedin (becoming Muslim per se is really only a secondary aspect) are among the hardest to dissuade from continuing along the path to radicalization and tend to become some of fiercest fighters. The girls who join tend to be younger, better educated, and from a higher socioeconomic bracket than the boys. They reject the gendered, sexless, multicultural norms of their host societies as evidence of a lack of moral principles and right conduct. They want red lines, where women are women and men are men, save for the one dimension where women and men share equal and novel status—that of revolutionary violence as a rite of passage to break the chains of the present order, to liberate them personally from (as they often put it) a "transgendered" identity neither Arab nor French, to liberate their Muslim brothers and sisters from oppression, and to inaugurate a new-old world order, even if they have to destroy the present world to do it. That, of course, is the essence of an apocalyptic mindset, and it is more apparent with the Islamic State Caliphate than with al-Qaeda. (Bin Laden opposed any declaration of a Caliphate as long as the US was a hegemon powerful enough to defeat or contain it and so delegitimize it for future generations; whereas Zarqawi and his successors, Omar al-Baghdadi and Abu Bakr al-Baghdadi, believed that declaring a Caliphate would draw the US into a bottomless quagmire and thereby legitimize and globally empower the Caliphate sooner rather than later.)

MT: How do you see the future of jihad, given the current policies of law enforcement and national security organizations?

SA: It is important to realize that the violent jihadi movement is only the tip of an iceberg that extends across the fragmented Arab Sunni nations and diaspora communities: For every one violent radical there are many nonviolent and non-radicals who are helping this person, wittingly or not. Without these tacit support networks, the movement could not be sustained. But dealing with the diversity of these support networks or even understanding their structures and dispositions, is not currently a priority for law enforcement or national security, and so the creative processes that lead to radicalization and violence may remain no matter how many violent radicals are captured or killed.

MT: In your UN speech you underplayed the role of religion in inspiring Muslim youths to join ISIS. In fact your experience with them had shown that many of them had no religious education. Then the question that poses itself is why Western hedonistic and liberal values have not reached those would-be terrorists and what does that say about the future of those traditional values?

SA: For the future of democracy and human rights, the core existential issue may be: How comes it that values of liberal and open democracy increasingly appear to be losing ground to those of narrow ethno-nationalisms and radical Islam in a tacit alliance that is tearing the European middle class (the mainstay of European democracy) in ways similar to the undermining of republican values by fascists and communists in the 1920s and 30s? Consider:

"Mr. Hitler," wrote George Orwell (1940/1968) in his review of Mein Kampf, "has grasped the falsity of the hedonistic attitude to life. Nearly all western thought ... certainly all 'progressive' thought, has assumed tacitly that human beings desire nothing beyond ease, security and avoidance of pain." In such a view of life there is no room for greatness and glory, which as Darwin noted motivates heroes and martyrs to motivate others to survive and even triumph against great material odds. "Hitler knows ... that human beings don't only want comfort, safety, short working-hours, hygiene, birth-control and, in general, common sense; they also, at least intermittently, want struggle and self-sacrifice."[4]

MT: If the present Salafi Jihadi groups provide the opportunity for struggle and self-sacrifice, while Western liberalism is losing grounds, then what could possibly defeat ISIS?

SA: Military defeat of ISIS in the ISIS heartland of Syria and Iraq would probably help take the wind out its sails, and lessen its recruiting allure in the West and elsewhere. In fact we are starting to see a significant drop in foreign fighter volunteers as ISIS is being degraded by Russian-backed Syrian army forces, US-backed Iraqi army forces, and the Kurds. But it's likely going to be a long, hard slog. Current estimates for retaking Mosul involve something like 12 coalition brigades, about 50,000 soldiers, against some 8,000 entrenched ISIS fighters. And even this plan is probably wishful thinking (ISIS originally took Mosul with a few hundred combatants, routing an Iraqi army of 18,000).

Soldier for soldier the German army outfought all others by any measure. German armies were destroyed only by the massive production and firepower superiority of the United States and by the massive manpower sacrifice of more than 20 million Russians. Perhaps it will come to that in the struggle against IS, but for now the means arrayed against this dynamic revolutionary movement seem feeble. A political entity preaching and practicing wildly different ideas than other nations and mass movements, holding no appreciable territory only two years ago, still boasts the largest extraterritorial volunteer fighting force since World War II, with enlistees from nearly 100 nations. ISIS still controls hundreds of thousands of square kilometers and millions of people, and has defended unto death a 3,000 km military front against a multinational coalition of armies in ways reminiscent of the French Revolution.[5] In the history of modern insurgencies, there are also important parallels between: the collapse and reaction to the Arab Spring and the pan-European popular uprisings of 1848 and their aftermath, the rise of al-Qaeda in the late twentieth century and that of anarchism in the late nineteenth century, and the present weakening of al-Qaeda relative to the ISIS and the co-opting and near annihilation of the anarchists by the Bolshevists who knew better how to manage their political ambition through military and territorial management and, perhaps most critically, a positive, proactive, coherent and compelling moral and spiritual vision (a sentiment even expressed by some from al-Qaeda's Jabhat an-Nusra fighting ISIS in Syria whom I interviewed, although most still believe that Nusra's version of a *salaf jihad*—offensive Jihad—"tolerant" of others will win the day).[6]

MT: It has become common for elite politicians, including the US Secretary of State and the leaders of the European Union, Russia and the Arab nations, to refer to ISIS as "nihilist" and to call ISIS by its Arabic acronym Daesh, in the hope of depriving the organization a legitimate religion and statehood and acknowledge it only as a "violent extremist group" hell bent on wanton destruction. Does this attitude help in the fight against it, even at the symbolic level?

SA: To dismiss the Islamic State as just another form of "terrorism" or "violent extremism," to insist that it's brutality is simply "immoral," "nihilistic" or "apocalyptic" and therefore inevitably self-destructive, or to refuse to call it by the name it calls itself in the vain hope that by so doing will somehow undermine it, is counterproductive and deluding. From an evolutionary and historical vantage, no developments are really deviant or extreme unless they quickly die; for, those developments that continue to survive are the very stuff of historical change and evolution. From this perspective—and in the light of interviewing and running psychological experiments with ISIS and Nusra fighters on the ground, and with volunteers from Europe and North Africa as well as those who oppose and fight them—the rise of ISIS is arguably the most influential and politically novel countercultural force in the world today even despite its recent setbacks in Syria and Iraq. What propels people from 100 countries to come to this place to blow themselves up? There's got to be something in human beings that this appeals to; otherwise it wouldn't work. And my goal is to figure out what that is in order to tame the beast within us before it kills us.

MT: That leaves us with the inevitable question that is on everyone's mind. What can be done about ISIS?

SA: Short of a massive military onslaught against the Islamic State, whose downstream consequences are likely to be as uncontrollable as they may be undesirable, what else to be done? What dreams may come from current government policies that offer little beyond promises of comfort and security? People who are willing to sacrifice everything, including their lives—the totality of their self-interests—will not be lured away just by material incentives or disincentives. The science suggests that sacred values are best opposed with other sacred values that inspire devotion, or by sundering the fused social networks that embed those values.[7]

Notes

1 H. Russell Bernard, *Research Methods in Anthropology: Qualitative and Quantitative Approaches* (New York: Altamira Press, 2006), 24.
2 For the full text of the speech, see "Scott Atran on Youth, Violent Extremism and Promoting Peace," posted by "gregdowney," April 25, 2015, http://blogs.plos.org/neuro anthropology/2015/04/25/scott-atran-on-youth-violent-extremism-and-promoting-peace/.
3 Tom Bartlett, "The Road to ISIS: An unorthodox anthropologist goes face to face with ISIS. Is the payoff worth the peril?" *The Chronicle of Higher Education*, May 20, 2016, http://chronicle.com/article/The-Scientist-Who-Talks-to/236521.
4 Orwell, G., "Review of Mein Kampf," in *The Collected Essays, Journalism, and Letters of George Orwell*, Vol. 2. Edited by S. Orwell and I. Angus (New York, NY: Harcourt, Brace Jovanovich, 1940/1968).
5 Atran, S., "On the Frontline Against ISIS: Who Fights, Who Doesn't, and Why," *The Daily Beast*, April 19, 2015, www.thedailybeast.com/articles/2016/04/19/on-the-front-line-against-isis-who-fights-who-doesn-t-and-why.html.
6 Atran, S., "ISIS is a revolution," *AEON*, December 2015, https://aeon.co/essays/why-isis-has-the-potential-to-be-a-world-altering-revolution.
7 Atran, S., "The Devoted Actor: Unconditional Commitment and Intractable Conflict across Cultures," *Current Anthropology* 57 (13), June 2016, www.journals.uchicago.edu/doi/full/10.1086/685495.

12 Negotiating with the Taliban
Not war on terrorism, but dialogue for solutions

Johan Galtung

I am sitting somewhere in Afghanistan. Across the table are three Taliban; Pashtuns like most Taliban. My opening question is standard: "What does the Afghanistan look like where you would like to live?", with some equally standard follow-up questions: "What is the worst that happened to you?", and "Was there a good period in the past?"

And they talk, and talk, and talk; it sounds like no Westerner ever asked them questions about what they think. For them the answers were obvious, and they were very eager to explain the obvious:

- The worst that happened to them was the (Sir Mortimer) Durand line in 1893, the 2,250 km border between Afghanistan and at the time the British Empire, today Pakistan, that cut the Pashtun and Baluchi nations in two. Today the Pashtuns, 50 million, are the largest nation in the world without their own state, so their first priority is to undo that line defining them as smugglers, "terrorists" escaping to safety "on the other side".
- Then the Western habit of invading, the UK three times, the USSR once, now the USA and the "coalition of the willing"-still going on.
- What does it look like? Afghanistan-Pakistan without a border.

And then: Afghanistan is not a Western unitary state with capital in Kabul, that is a Western illusion. Afghanistan is a co-existence of eight nations—seven of them also in neighboring countries—and 25,000 villages, very poor, very autonomous. And invincible: there is no central point from which an invader can conquer the whole country. Maybe a loose federation with villages as the basic unit and a small capital; maybe a community with the neighbors in spirit, Islam and language; the economic priority being the positive, not punitive aspect of sharia, basic needs for all, all nations, both genders.

And there we have made terrible mistakes, now learning from more advanced brothers and sisters in Muslim countries. We are improving.

We are very violent so we need some peacekeeping by our more advanced brother and sister countries, Tunisia, Turkey, Indonesia. And then, West of whatever type, will you please stop invading us! Nobody has defeated us, but it has cost us millions of lives.

Yes, it was better before Durand and in the periods between the invasions. What we need now is a coalition government, a loose federation, a community with the neighbors, basic needs priorities for all, peacekeeping by brothers and sisters. The Afghanistan we want.

I remember during my first visit to Afghanistan in January 1968 asking myself my standard question, what does this country remind me of? The answer was, of course, Switzerland; not eight nations, but four (one only Swiss); not 25,000 villages, but 2,300 local communities, a federation with no nations running the country alone, permanent coalition government, neutrality since taking a stand in favor of one or the other neighbor would tear Switzerland apart. A Swiss model?

I am sitting in the office of Dennis Kucinich before they managed to gerrymander the major peace spokesman out of the US Congress, with 8 of his fellow representatives: "Professor Galtung is back from Afghanistan and talks with the Taliban; up came a possible solution".

The reaction in the major "state terrorist" country in the world?

> Very interesting. But we are elected representatives of the US people and they are not interested in solutions. They have elected us for this, V for victory, then we will tell them what the solution is.

I said that victory would elude the USA given their devotion, and unlimited time perspective as opposed to an "administration" or two; that retreat with honor leaving behind a regime to the US taste would also elude them; why not help with a federal constitution and Central Asian Community, becoming their friends? Answer: not our mandate. Me: then you are heading for something worse than defeat and retreat. They: What? Me: Becoming irrelevant. The ball is in other courts.

I am sitting in a State Department office asking my standard question: "What does the Afghanistan look like that you would like to see?" And the answer, predictable since it is US world policy: "with democracy in the sense of fair and free multi-party national elections, and a free market." And an Afghanistan that cannot attack us–9/11.

ME: But that style democracy presupposes an I-culture, the individual as his-her own decision-maker. Afghanistan is 98 percent Muslim, more we-culture, for them voting cuts something organic in winners and losers, for them dialogue to consensus makes more sense. No answer.

ME: And the free market leads to increasing inequality; no problem for Islam. The problem would be misery at the bottom, basic needs not met. How do you handle that? Answer: trickling down. My answer: Pumping up seems to be stronger. Laughter. Problem unsolved.

I am sitting somewhere in Southeast Asia, in front of me are al-Qaeda followers.

ME: What does the world look like you would like to see?
THEY: A world that respects, does not trample upon, Islam.

ME: But don't you trample upon women? And the fourth stage of jihad—exerting yourselves for the faith—is very violent.
THEY: Violence against women is not Qur'anic but tribal traditions not yet overcome. And the fourth stage of jihad is self-defense, legitimate in international law. Against the Crusades, against Zionism, now also against the invasion of Afghanistan.
ME: But there is much jihadism not legitimately declared?
THEY: A problem. But moderate retribution is Islamic.

I am in Madrid at a Dialogue of Civilizations conference; in front of me is a member of Hamas with a tape-recording of Bush saying that God has chosen him to bring democracy to the Middle East. Bush? A blasphemy.

ME: Is there an Israel you can recognize?
THEY: Of course.
ME: Like June 4, 1967?
THEY: Yes, with some modifications, we'll tell in due time when there are real negotiations.

I am sitting in a Pentagon adjoining office with a two-star general, charming and well informed: it costs them $10 to make an IED, a bomb—they can go on forever. Our problem: no Plan B.

He was forbidden by a higher level Pentagon official from talking more with me.

A conference at a think tank in Washington. An excellent talk by a State Department consultant on the history of Israel-Palestine-USA talks. Question from the moderator: "And the solution?" "No idea."

So I am brought in to present the Transcend 1–2–6–20 plan—Palestine recognized also by Israel, with some Israeli cantons on the West bank and some Palestinian cantons in Northwest Israel; cooperation between the two; inside a six state community of Israel with its five Arab neighbors; surrounded by an Organization for Security and Cooperation in West Asia, adding neighbors' neighbors and some of their neighbors—about 20. Silence. No alternative Plan B.

Up come two State Department experts, the task of one being to disseminate US style democracy, of the other a federation. The former got the I-culture/we-culture answer and in addition that you may need a federation first and then democracy in each part to prevent the most numerous nations from dominating all. And for the latter: for a federation they must also identify something that binds them together, not only what divides them. Maybe they want independence, ask them.

Conclusion I. What the "terrorists" say is not unreasonable; what is unreasonable is not knowing what they say. I know no case where there is not a basis for a reasonable—accepted, sustainable—solution. The "state terrorists" in Washington seem so dedicated to military planning and execution that there is little time or manpower left for any Plan B; either nothing at all, or not thought through. The insensitivity to cultural and structural factors is remarkable.

Conclusion II. This has to change for the sake of all involved. *And all it takes are dialogues, preferably public, with all parties.*

Let me now get into more detail about the nexus Afghanistan–Pakistan–USA. *Washington, Carnegie Endowment,* April 18, 2012:

Ladies and gentlemen, first, thanks to The American Muslim Association Foundation for organizing a forum on this controversial topic in the heart of Washington!

You have given me the global perspective on this panel, taking into account much space and time; kind of Einsteinian. Seeing the world from above I sense five grand trends as a backdrop, a context, for the theme: the fall of the US empire; the de-development of the West; the decline of the state system to nationalisms from below and regionalisms from above; the rise of the Rest; and the rise of China.

And then, spiraling down toward the ground, we see those three actors and the countless sub-actors in deadly embraces, so well described by Ahmed Rashid in his *Pakistan on the Brink: The Future of America, Pakistan, and Afghanistan.* Let us highlight some aspects.

We see a wound, a 1,400 mile border dividing Pashtuns, today 50 million, carved in 1893 by Durand—an English foreign secretary of "British India"—between the Empire, today Pakistan, and Afghanistan. Thus, Pashtuns crossing the line are not entering a "safe haven," but are at home. The "treaty" was in English, which Afghanistan's emir did not know. Another signatory was sovereign Baluchistan, later invaded by and incorporated in Pakistan. The Pashtuns were not included.

We sense the US reification of conventional world maps of *states,* like the two mentioned. Yes, they have governments, more or less of, by and for the people, not only for 1 percent, and they have more, or less, or not at all failed states, presidents or prime ministers. But they throw a veil over more important maps of nations, more informative today given the decline of the states. And maps of civilizations, like Arabs, Muslim, Christians, Jews. Not only Muslims have the dilemma of who am I, a citizen of a secular state member of the state system, or a believer in a faith, the *ummah* for the Muslims.

We sense Pakistan's concerns: internal divisions among nations, and the conflict with India, above all, but not only, over Kashmir.

We sense Afghanistan's concerns: others invading, occupying, conquering, from Alexander the Great via the Mongols and three English invasions, one Soviet, and now USA-NATO in a US-led coalition; with varying pretexts. Like hiding the search for a base close to China (Bagram), and for oil from the Caspian to the Indian Ocean, under a pretext of 9/11 coming from Afghanistan in general, and bin Laden in particular; without delivering any public proof of that assertion.

We sense the USA committing the same elementary mistake again and again: the enemy of my enemy is my friend; working well for some issues, but that friend may also have some other points on their agenda. Use bin Laden to beat the Soviets, but maybe he is against secularism in general, not only the Soviet variety? Use Pakistan to beat Islamists on their own ground, but maybe on top of their agenda is to prevent India from having influence in Afghanistan, and hence protecting Pashtuns, Taliban, and housing the key enemy bin Laden? Leading to a de facto war, the Pakistani secret service, ISI, taken by surprise(?) by Obama ordering a US SEAL extra-judicial execution on their lands.

And in the background Ali Bhutto's Islamic bomb, adding to the evangelical, Anglican, catholic-secular, orthodox, Confucian, Judaic and Hindu bombs, competing for god-like omnipotence. Israel's goals, to eliminate that bomb, and stop one in Iran, become US goals. The tail wagging the dog? Partly, but even more important is how the two countries came into being, taking over somebody else's land in the name of their faith, killing, pushing inhabitants into exile, or into reservations. The much longer history of India can also be read in such terms. Maybe a basis for the USA–Israel–India alliance in the area: if one of us falls so does the other, from illegitimacy? Well, they are not the only ones, look at much of Latin America.

How about US–Pakistan relations? Agendas that coincide only on some points and diverge wildly on others will drive them from one conflict to the next as they have for a decade or two. But Afghanistan, and Pakistan in general and ISI and the Army in particular, also use the USA as a milking cow—Pakistan to the tune of $3 billion a year or so.

Some cow. These are the meager, not the fat, cow years. Milk is printed, comes as vouchers, old arms. Not a lasting relation anyhow, and even less so in an Afghanistan where they have to create army and police for the milk transfer. Not strange that the more or less willing partners and US civilians cooperate to have dialogues with the Taliban to get off the hook, the US military saying "give us only X years more and we'll beat them." With drones and SEALs.

USA and NATO will withdraw and bones of the US empire will be buried on Afghan soil. Maybe NATO too. That game offers no solution.

We are back to the grand trends of the opening: power moving to the south and the east, states yielding to federations and regions. Pakistan can probably only survive as a federation with much autonomy for the parts, and as part of a Central Asian community with eight Muslim neighbors including Afghanistan. The more open the border, the more will the Durand wound heal, not by Pakistan or Afghanistan yielding territory to the other, or as a new Pashtunistan. And that region will be more interested in good relations with China—already owner of enormous resources in Afghanistan—than with the USA.

And the USA? Hopefully withdrawing before the war with Pakistan becomes hotter. Or a USA–Israel Judeo-Christian civilization, with all the problems that will imply? A true federation for WASPs and for nations by the USA? A conference with Pakistan to exchange experiences, compare notes from the period 2001–2012?

Where love is missing, separation may be better. Even divorce.

In conclusion some words, maybe guesses, about 9/11 2001.

The Arab/Wahhabite goal was probably *justice,* by executing two people in a public space for alleged sins against Alla'h and lack of *respect* for Islam. The US goal was and is status quo, with *free trade*. Even to talk about bridging the gap is today taboo.

And yet the key parties, let us call them Washington and al-Qaeda, not 1.4 billion Christians and 1.3 billion Muslims, will have to start doing exactly that, through dialogues, secret and public. They cannot go on eliminating each other in the search for the elusive "roots" of the Evil on the other side that would make them victorious. Wiser people on either side—probably some steps removed from the two over-focused, and very similar, top figures—Obama and Osama—may already have started feeling their way into dialogue processes.

"No attack on the USA in exchange for US military withdrawal from Muslim countries that so want" could serve as an example of a possible deal. Another would be to explore the concept of "globalization-free zones"; like no US economic penetration in the Muslim *ummah*.

But the basic approach would be mutual exploration to identify the legitimate elements in such goals as "free trade" and "respect."

Cultural violence stands massively in the way of positive structural peace and in the case of 9/11 even in the way of negative direct peace, simple absence of violence. In the case of 9/11 the culture of violence goes beyond racial prejudice, bringing in such premodern, pre-Enlightenment Puritan and Wahhabite figures of thought as "Chosenness," by God for Self and by Satan for Other, with visions of glory as God's reward and trauma as punishment, and of the final battle, Armageddon, where whoever is not with us is against us. Maybe one day Enlightenment will take root in both cultures.

And one day, even reconciliation.

In the meantime let us drop the terms "terrorist" and "state terrorist"; as a beginning put them in "," quote unquote. Of course they stand for something: very often killing defenseless people not in uniform, from the ground or the air. People in uniform attacking each other, also known as inter-state wars, are dwindling with the state system, and also because the wars are too risky for the combatants, they prefer defenseless victims. Up came the "terrorisms".

However, more basic than their violent strategies of various kinds is something deeper: conflicts, contradictions between parties, incompatibilities. Name the parties, identify their goals, explore incompatibilities and compatibilities for conflict and cooperation, and turn the former into the latter: through dialogues for solution.

13 A tale of two CTs

A ground-level counterinsurgency perspective on Belgian counter-terrorism measures

Casey Douglas Carr

> Crush humanity out of shape once more, under similar hammers, and it will twist itself into the same tortured forms. Sow the same seeds of rapacious licence and oppression over again, and it will surely yield the same fruit according to its kind.
> Charles Dickens, from *A Tale of Two Cities*, Book III, Chapter 15[1]

Introduction: the day of the 2016 Brussels attacks

It was 8:55 am in the morning of March 22, 2016, when I looked up at the big modern clock of the Aloft Hotel at Place Jean Rey, only 300 meters from the Maelbeek metro stop near the center of Brussels. I was late, choosing to bike instead of metro, I was pedaling up to quartier de la Chasse, Etterbeek, when the metro explosion went off. Salah Abdeslam, the only publicly-known living suspect from the November 13 attacks in Paris, had been apprehended on March 18 in Molenbeek, following a shootout in the commune Forest three days prior. I brushed off the noise as there was constant construction in the EU district. From her own office near Parliament, my wife texted me about an explosion at the airport, then Maelbeek. The police barracks in Etterbeek pushed out a long convoy, all sirens blazing. We were used to sirens since the Paris attacks. I continued toward the Vrije Universiteit Brussel (VUB) campus, where students were being told to stay indoors.

If Brussels residents' reaction were to be anything like our reaction to the Paris attacks, which took place during a weekend night rather than during Tuesday morning rush hour, I knew we had some time before we'd be put on lockdown. Even the first emergency vehicles weren't at Maelbeek until well after the metro explosions. Most of us continued our work at the University of Kent in Brussels, where I was currently pursuing a Master's in International Conflict and Security. I met a friend at the Université Libre de Bruxelles (ULB) for lunch and study, discussing the events unfolding. The STIB transportation hub was just behind Cimetière, swamped with plainclothes police carrying UZI and MP5 submachine guns. The metro had been closed since 9:27 am and trains were returning to the hub. My friend and I came across two female plainclothes police officers. As they stopped a BMW, both reached for their beltlines, drawing concealed pistols on the driver; we hastened our pace to ULB. Later, we learned police had been searching for a similar BMW Series 5 in Ixelles two days later.[2] Operations were ongoing and affected the entire city.

The university campuses started being evacuated just after noon. My wife had been let out of lockdown around 10:30 am to go home, while some of those in the European Commission and other buildings closer to Maelbeek remained indoors longer in case of shooters. Children at schools, the closest at Parc Leopold, were being kept indoors for hours with little information, thus leaving parents out of the loop as well. Cell service had been suspended for emergency responders, making SMS and internet the only way to communicate. With no public place open any longer, I decided it would be ok to go home, 500 m from Maelbeek, into the heart of the security lockdown. Before doing so, I bought last-minute groceries to last the lockdown if Brussels' officials would decide to close down for a week as was done after the Paris terrorist attacks.

On my way to the Schuman area, traffic getting out of the city was jammed and police were cordoning off areas. Passing by VUB, another explosion went off to my left. I was the only one walking on that street at the moment, and again I wasn't so alarmed. Other passersby asked me about the blast, and perhaps due to my military past, I understood and suggested it was a controlled detonation with all of the police presence. During the day, many false threats were being tweeted by Islamic State supporters saying "Plusieurs bombes placée à l'Université libre de #Bruxelles #ULB en vengeance pour l'Université de #Mosul"[3] ("more bombs placed at the Free University of Brussels in retaliation for the University of Mosul" [in ISIS-controlled Iraq]), and the police reacted to a specific threat just by my campus. I had been following the current Iraqi Army siege of Mosul, starting with airstrikes the same morning on the University of Mosul according to Mosul Eye,[4] a known hotbed for jihadi bomb-makers since I had been there in 2009.

I made my way home through the deserted streets, police tape funneling any lost passersby around ground zero. Survivors were evacuated out of the metro lines at Schuman, but those unfortunate enough not to have a pick-up at the airport were stuck in facilities with little communication from police or airport authority, other than "stay calm." Lockdown was in full effect. Many of us would spend the rest of the day scanning Twitter for the most up-to-date news. Thirty-two people were reported killed by three suicide bombers, one suspect still on the loose. Many of us had friends stuck, those at the airport or in the EU Institutions, while police activity went on all around for hours. At least it was a sunny day. Brussels was ready, but this time more reluctant for a lockdown. Following the Paris attacks, six days of lockdown cost the city of Brussels an estimated €51.7 million a day for businesses.[5] This time Interior Minister of Belgium, Jan Jambon, declared three days of mourning and things would get back on schedule after, with the exception of Maelbeek and the Brussels Zaventem Airport, a critical airline stopover for many transatlantic flights.

A thousand plots

> I'd hold half a guinea that he don't get no lawwork to do. Don't look like the sort of one to get any, do he?
> (Mr Cruncher, in Charles Dickens' *A Tale of Two Cities*, Book I. Chapter 3)

More information surfaced in the following days, arrests and raids continued throughout the city. From my perspective, the Belgians, and more specifically the Bruxellois, reacted very differently than Parisians, both exaggerated by media coverage. The entire weekend in Paris after the November 13 attacks, a strange feeling hovered in the minds of those who attended the squares in memorial throughout the weekend. Panic and skittish behavior ensued, in reaction to any sound resembling gunfire: foreign media rushed to the scene when a pigeon exploded by exposed electrical wire at Paris' train station Gare du Nord.[6] The media largely portrayed Paris in this light of panic, while on the other hand, it portrayed a very angry Brussels.[7] The best example of this anger is the Twitter hashtag #JeSuisSickofThisShit, with a meme already prepared in January 2016.[8] Although there had been an escalating number of incidents between Paris and Brussels from 2014 to 2015, including the May 24 Jewish Museum shooting, the August 21 Thalys train incident, the January 7–8 Charlie Hebdo shootings, and the January 15 Verviers raids following, in contrast to the subdued response of most Parisians, the March 22 Brussels bombings in 2016 rallied the masses in defiance of hate and fear. People were angry, we had been fooled twice and caught unprepared, but in full knowledge that Brussels should expect an attack.

As an illustration of the massive display of the citizens of Brussels' collective rage, there was a series of demonstrations in the streets following the attacks. Not even the day had passed that, on the steps of the old Brussels Stock Exchange, the Bourse, candles and chalk graffiti started appearing.[9] Hundreds of people gathered over Belgian beers, tweeting #beerNotFear, and speculating about what may have been going on in the minds of the bombers. People started putting up the flags of Belgium, soon followed by others. Many flags of Turkey were put up in memorial for the March 19 bombing in Istanbul. In response, as March 21 was *Newroz* for Persians and Kurds, the latter having declared a federal autonomous region in Syria two days before, the Kurdish People's Protection Unit (YPG) and Kobanî flags draped over the lion statues. It was apparent that multiple parties were riding the solidarity for their own political purposes. On Easter Sunday, a big peace rally was planned at the Bourse, but the night before was cancelled. People still flocked to the Bourse, when a group of 400–500 "casuals against terrorism," men dressed in mostly black sweatshirts and shaved heads, some masked, descended from the Brussels Gare du Nord. The Mayor of Vilvoorde, a town to the north, had warned Brussels police of this group boarding the trains to disrupt the peace rally. Despite ongoing terrorism investigations, the police en masse were able to muster riot control in time to push the "casuals" back north, something they were more prepared for. Six days later, however, a veiled woman was deliberately hit by a car during a Molenbeek protest while the passenger filmed.[10]

To make matters worse, the police and intelligence services were embarrassed at having let so many threats slip through their fingers following the Paris attacks. Police realized the connection of Brussels-native Salah Abdeslam with the Paris attacks only after they had stopped him on the French-Belgian border.[11] In hindsight, the well-known journal Politico succinctly outlined the shortcomings by authorities leading to the Brussels attacks:

1 Belgium didn't act on warnings from Turkey.
2 Too few resources were available to track foreign fighters.
3 House searches were banned between 9pm and 5am.
4 Information and data were not shared.
5 Abdeslam was not interrogated about imminent threats.
6 The Metro continued to run, despite apparent orders to shut down.
7 The police got the wrong "missing bomber."
8 There was confusion about the suspects' previous links to terrorism.
9 There is limited CCTV in Brussels.
10 Border bungle between France and Belgium, and the Schengen area.
11 There is a lack of police accountability and funding.
12 Molenbeek mayors ignored warnings of imminent terrorist attacks.[12]

If one is to follow the timeline of operations tracking Salah Abdeslam, all 12 of these mishaps are manifested in the failure of Belgian officials to act critically in time. From my own experience in counterinsurgency,[13] I disagree with some of the allegations made about these flaws and pinning the weight of the attacks on single individuals, such as Abdeslam, Abdelhamid Abaaoud, and recently captured Mohamed Abrini, all three of whom had been known to authorities for minor criminal offenses prior to the attacks, and were radicalized by veteran *mujahid* Khalid Zerkani. Salah Abdeslam and his brother Brahim, were even reported to authorities on multiple occasions, according to leaked documents.[14]

Since November, Politico has been quite realistic, though harsh on mounting its critique against host city Brussels, declaring Belgium a failed state two weeks after the Paris attacks due to a majority of the attackers and foreign fighters hailing from Brussels' commune Molenbeek of 100,000 residents.[15] In the Westphalian sense of national sovereignty, this notion may be plausible, as Belgium is divided into three semi-autonomous federal regions: the Dutch-speaking (or Flemish) Flanders in the north, the French-speaking Wallonia in the south, and the 1.3 million inhabitants of the 19 Brussels' communes in the central region with predominantly Francophones, but also several non-Belgians gravitating toward the EU institutions as the de facto capital of Europe. A small German-speaking population exists in the east. The Brussels enclave and Wallonia–Flanders divide is one reason Politico claims failed statehood, where the north, south, and central regions are starkly contrasted.[16] To complicate matters, Belgium as a loose federation of these three regions, is ruled by a king whose predecessor was invited to the throne in 1831. Other points in Tim King's Politico article, are decades of failed reforms, which have left Belgian cities hollowed-out socio-economically, extensive political patronage and parochialism, a post-industrialist mire which has made many North African labor migrants now jobless with the decline of coal and steel industry, and what Belgium suffers from most of all is a decentralized and fragmented police force whose separate units rarely communicate.[17] All of these conditions have created an underground ghetto of Molenbeek, home to a concentration of second and third generation Belgians of Moroccan-descent, as well as a large, contemporary artist community.

More diplomatic about his critique of the structural inequalities of Belgium, Rik Coolsaet assesses the reasons for the departure of many Europeans to the Syrian frontlines.[18] Coolsaet draws many of the same conclusions from Belgian youth as radicalization experts Olivier Roy and Scott Atran from French and Moroccan youth. In his assessment of foreign fighters, Coolsaet also recognizes *radicalization* as a contested concept dating from EU policy circles during the 2004 Madrid bombings.[19] Despite becoming a catch-all phrase for profiling wayward Muslim youth, it still holds academic value if understood as a "socialization process in which group dynamics (kinship and friendship)" play a more integral role in drawing an individual to violent extremism than ideology.[20] Following 9/11, radicalization has been used all too often to specify Islamic-related terrorism suspects who have dabbled in literalist Salafi teachings on their path to committing acts of extremist violence in the name of Allah. At a public debate on radicalization hosted by the Flemish Socialist Party following the Brussels attacks, one speaker declared that the problem is not enough radicalization, meaning politically rather than religiously. This debate featured charismatic speaker Dyab Abou Jahjah, who was dubbed by the BBC as "Belgium's Malcolm X" in 2003 for his stance fighting for immigrant-background[21] rights in Antwerp.[22] Abou Jahjah founded the Arab-European League in 2000, of which secular, pan-Arabist ideology and confrontational activism became a backbone for extremist groups in Brussels and Antwerp.[23]

Among the reasons why foreign fighters from Belgium join ISIS, Coolsaet notes Belgian pessimism and nihilism as an increasingly contributing trend.[24] The structural inequalities in Molenbeek were well-known by 1990, when the Flemish right-wing party leader of Vlaams Blok, Filip Dewinter (with whom Abou Jahjah continuously butted heads), made several marginalizing statements regarding the Moroccan Belgians' poverty gap, leading to demonstrations and protests.[25] In Brussels, Coolsaet acknowledges that the "the Belgian-Moroccan community is much more fragmented and individualized" than the well-organized, integrated Belgian-Turkish community. Olivier Roy's main recommendation for countering radicalization is integration; his model compares the French approach of *"assimilationnisme"* (i.e., civic nationalism) to the British "multiculturalism."[26] Coolsaet argues that while "society cannot be blamed for radicalization,"[27] it does create an environment conducive to it. For Coolsaet and Roy, the Islamic State is only a globalized "super-gang," absorbing the delinquent, fringed, Muslim youth subculture,[28] whereas Atran goes further to describe it as revolutionary.[29]

Belgian academics, many of whom hold key positions in such international organizations and think-tanks as the International Crisis Group (ICG) and the Egmont Institute, also describe the failures of Belgium to control its rampant "radicalization" problems. ICG's MENA program director Joost Hiltermann published an interview with terrorism expert Didier Leroy titled *Why Belgium?*[30] Leroy outlines the reasons that ISIS would target Brussels in the first place, at a time when links between the Brussels attackers, Paris attackers, and the Islamic State of Iraq and Sham (ISIS) were still fuzzy. The deployment of many military in the streets following the Brussels attacks freed up the police to do police work. As Coolsaet, Leroy remarks that Belgium has the highest number per capita in Europe of its citizens joining ISIS.[31]

In response to the constant Belgium-bashing since the Paris attacks,[32] Thomas Renard wrote in Politico *Why Belgium is not Europe's jihadi base*.[33] It was not a question of "if" but "when" Brussels would be attacked,[34] rocked by twin suicide bombings the morning of March 22. However great the failure of the state of Belgium and its security forces to prevent the attacks, according to Renard there is little value in pointing fingers. Prevention of the attacks was a collective European—not just a Belgian—responsibility; accordingly the attacks themselves were a European Community failure.[35]

The security forces (see special unit *Groep Diane*[36]) have a successful track record of taking down terrorist networks during the 1970s and 1980s, when nationalist and leftist extremist violence thrived.[37] According to Koutroubas et al. (2009)[38], a bigger perceived threat in Belgium during the 1990s was Turkish–Kurdish tension in Brussels. Due to the collaboration between French and Belgian security forces, the Algerian Armed Islamic Group (GIA) was successfully deoperationalized in 2004.

Dutch historian Ian Buruma also describes Brussels as not a dangerous city (in contrast to Donald Trump, who calls it a "hellhole").[39] He also exalts the interesting, integrative phenomenon of Molenbeek, where immigrant-background Muslims live side-by-side with "non-Muslim hipsters"[40] and for those living there between these categories, such as Salah Abdeslam, I use the term *hipslims*. Buruma accurately describes two differing St. Josse cityscapes of the Art Nouveau family apartment complexes in the shadow of the colossal EU structures, which seemed to have sprung up in the gap between Etterbeek and Schaerbeek. Now all the communes are tightly merged together. Chaotic differences bring the Bruxellois, or *Zinneke*,[41] together.

Following the 2015 and 2016 attacks, Molenbeek had become the place for most police raids, but nearly all communities were affected, from Schaerbeek to Etterbeek. Najim Laachraoui, the university-educated bomb-maker for both the Paris and Brussels attacks, who also blew himself up at the Brussels airport, grew up in Schaerbeek.[42] A suspect, identified as Abderamane Ameroud, was shot in the leg (also Salah Abdeslam was shot in the leg on capture, following Belgian police protocol) at a tram stop in Schaerbeek on March 25, followed by a controlled detonation. Ameroud was already wanted in 2003 for complicity in the assassination of Western-backed Afghan *mujahideen* hero and Taliban opponent, Ahmed Shah Massoud, an operation also planned from Belgium and executed on September 9, 2001.[43] The CBS News article *"Molenbeek and Schaerbeek: A Tale of Two Tragedies"* is rife with speculations about the causes of social inequalities and structural gaps in those communities, asserting that the biggest issue for policing them is a language gap between police and locals.[44] I find this claim hard to support, since a majority of the police are at least bilingual, speaking French, Dutch, and/or English. Many Moroccan-born Molenbeekois (residents of the commune Molenbeek) also speak French.

I have been confronted a couple of times by Molenbeekois when we talk about social inequality-related issues. People like myself and Ian Buruma, now a resident of St. Josse, Brussels' poorest, most ethnically-diverse, and dense commune, disagree with the claim of the ghetto-ization of Molenbeek, but those who grew up there know it best for its "shoes on the wire" and general police neglect, being on the west bank of the River Senne with Brussels proper on the east. In Molenbeek, residents are constantly checked and under assault by police "raids," which before the Brussels and Paris attacks were simply called "warranted arrests." Following the attacks in Brussels, the arrests increased dramatically, spreading throughout the city; and since the bombings, I have witnessed some form of "raid" every week or two.

The level of alleged police brutality, harkening back to the activism of Belgium's "Malcolm X," is also a major issue, though there has been little research on it. Whether these arrests are terrorism-related or not, the general perception, as well as my own, is that when suspects who are apprehended appear to be from immigrant backgrounds, they are swamped by perhaps a dozen or so balaclava-wearing military and police, and nearby onlookers begin texting while closely monitoring the arrests (it was common in Iraq that when a convoy rolls in for an arrest, all the neighbors begin texting). For example during an arrest at the Gare Centrale (main rail station) in Brussels, what started with a two-man military control at the entrance soon escalated into 20 police and military physically pinning the single suspect to the ground, while customers at a nearby brasserie less than five-meters away tried to ignore what was happening and went about their socializing. Another series of raids took place in Molenbeek on the morning of February 16, where I had been in the aftermath of which, nine or 10 individuals were apprehended for terrorist activity, supposedly unrelated to the Paris attacks.[45]

The peak tipping point giving rise to the Islamic confrontational activist group Sharia4Belgium was the passing of a face covering prohibition in 2011 in Belgium,[46] following French legislation the same year.[47] According to an article in *Quartz*, France and Belgium are the only two European countries to install a nation-wide ban on face concealment, including ski masks or balaclavas, whereas in other nations the veil-ban is driven by local politics alone.[48] The fine for wearing a face cover in Belgium was €197. The Sharia4Belgium (S4B) confrontation escalated on May 31 2012, when a woman wearing the *niqab*[49] in Molenbeek was approached by a policewoman requesting identification. She refused to show her face. The confrontation became physical, and after the veiled woman may have headbutted the policewoman, she was arrested. SMS messages shot across the well-networked community of Molenbeek, and within hours 150 demonstrators, including S4B members, were at the police station demanding the woman's release.[50] Following up, the veiled woman, Stéphanie Djato, was later apprehended at the Brussels Zaventem airport in March 2016 (prior to the bombings) on her return from Turkey and was sentenced to 18 months in prison for not presenting her identification during the 2012 incident.[51]

Sharia4Belgium has been instrumental for luring foreign fighters to Syria.[52] Even though its founder, Fouad Belkacem, was imprisoned in February 2012, the May 2012 niqab incident and subsequent protest still succeeded in showing S4B's presence in the community. Members of S4B had travelled to Lebanon "as early as 2010 for ideological and physical training, according to the verdict in the subsequent February 2015" trial and had spent time with Hizb ut-Tahrir (HT, Liberation Party, a more confrontational spin-off of the Muslim Brotherhood) leader Omar Bakri Mohammed.[53] Italian terrorism expert Lorenzo Vidino goes further to point out how S4B, like HT, focused on "winning hearts and minds[54] and mobilizing popular support" through provocative media campaigns, especially depicting immigrant-background Muslims being "unfairly" imprisoned.[55] Vidino states that "the first to leave for Syria were many of the core Sharia4Belgium members who had not been detained by Belgian authorities."[56] Coolsaet's *Fourth Wave*[57] includes 470 residents of Belgium who left for Syria as of January 2016, with a third of whom having returned, some of whom having been imprisoned, another quarter presumably dead in Syria.[58] He estimates that approximately 190 of them are "still active in Syria or Iraq"[59] or, worse, back in Belgium without anyone's knowledge. Both Vidino and Coolsaet reference a Dutch intelligence report from 2014 on similar trends in the Netherlands, which refers to the new jihadism wave and radicalization process as *swarm dynamics*.[60] Swarming, in this case, occurs when youths from all walks of life, with little-to-no communication outside their immediate network, and coming from nearly every city in the Netherlands, Belgium, and France, spontaneously travel to fight in Syria or are encouraged to execute similar operations on European soil. In a military context, swarming may refer to multiple units focusing in on an open-source target, like the children's game "King of the Hill."

The atomized community

> In such risings of fire and risings of sea—the firm earth shaken by the rushes of an angry ocean which had now no ebb, but was always on the flow, higher and higher, to the terror and wonder of the beholders on the shore— three years of tempest were consumed.
> (Charles Dickens, from *A Tale of Two Cities*, Book II. Chapter 24)

There may or may not have also been a potential plot by the Brussels attackers to target the nuclear reactors in Belgium, either by attacking them directly or by trying to obtain nuclear materials for the creation of a dirty bomb. The El

Bakraoui Brothers had been monitoring a top researcher at the SCKCEN nuclear research facility in Mol, not far from the Doel reactors outside Antwerp.[61] The surveillance video was retrieved during a raid in November 2015. On March 26, four days after the attacks, a security guard for the Tihange reactor was shot dead in his bathroom, along with his dog, and while Western media reported his security badge having been stolen, the newspaper Le Soir quickly replied that the badge was secure and that this event had nothing to do with terrorism.[62]

Belgium has seven nuclear reactors, which generate 54 percent of its energy,[63] and another research reactor at Mol. These seven reactors are situated at the Doel facility outside Antwerp and Tihange near Liege. It's unlikely that attackers would be able to generate an explosion large enough to cause a meltdown, but the reactors could be susceptible to a "9/11-style jumbo jet crash."[64] An inside job is much more likely, especially since two employees from the Doel facility left to fight in Syria.[65] Even more harrowing is that an "unknown saboteur tampered with a turbine's lubricant, causing the Belgian plant to shut down for five months" in 2014.[66] Sabotage is a very real threat, and the risk increases dramatically since those structures are becoming out-of-date, with appeals to Belgium by both Germany and Luxembourg to shut down the nuclear reactors as they're falling apart. On November 1, 2015, for example, a small explosion, unrelated to terrorism, erupted in the Doel 3 reactor.[67]

A show of good faith or not, during the last week of April, 2016, the Doel 3 nuclear reactor automatically shut down during a turbine test.[68] Even though Belgium has initiated a plan to reduce nuclear power dependence by 2025, the current malfunctions are being swept under the rug. A recent report by Foreign Affairs reporter Olivia Ward, *The dirty truth about nuclear terrorism,*[69] focuses on several Belgian nuclear-power-related cases. In January 2010, for example, peace activists scaled the chain link fence protecting old stockpiles of Cold War nukes. The same group got even further on a second trip, to demonstrate to officials of how feeble security is in these nuclear facilities.

Nuclear facility personnel were evacuated following the Brussels attacks. Although dirty bombs have never been used in Europe, the vulnerability of the Belgian reactors presents the same structural threat as the fracturing Mosul dam in Iraq, which Kurdish forces were keen to take control shortly after the fall of Mosul to ISIS in 2014. To add to the media-induced mass hysteria, it was announced on April 28, 2016, that Belgium would be issuing iodine tablets to everyone within 100 km of a reactor, which is nearly the entire country, despite claims by government officials that this had already been done following the 2011 Fukushima radiation leak in Japan.[70]

A tale of two counterterrorisms

> It was the best of times, it was the worst of times, it was the age of wisdom, it was the age of foolishness, it was the epoch of belief, it was the epoch of incredulity, it was the season of Light, it was the season of Darkness, it was the spring of hope, it was the winter of despair, we had everything before

us, we had nothing before us, we were all going direct to Heaven, we were all going direct the other way...
(Charles Dickens in *A Tale of Two Cities*, Book I. Chapter 1)

I have been researching radicalization trends in Belgium for a year now with these threats in mind. This was the context from which I perceived the March 22 bombings of the Brussels airport and Maelbeek metro station. The international community, as in the interview between ICG's Joost Hiltermann and ULB's Didier Leroy, asks *Why Belgium?* Why is it that Belgium is the main identified node in the intricate net of global terrorism threats following both the Brussels 2016 and Paris 2015 attacks, when ISIS-inspired terrorist attacks are taking place in major cities across the globe? It might be the tendency of those in the EU Institution bubble to be Brussels-centric, even further instigating anger by victims of ISIS attacks in the Middle East. But to comprehend the rise in terrorist attacks and how to deal effectively with them requires a complex approach. There is no simple answer, as understanding Belgium as a hub for security threats presumes a vast array of system interactions and disjuncture, leading to a vacuum in the European Union infrastructure.

Immediately following the Paris attacks, French President Hollande declared a "state of emergency" and invoked Article 42.7 of the Lisbon Treaty, for the first time calling for a common European defense,[71] reminiscent of George W. Bush's speech following 9/11. Article 42.7 sidesteps the North Atlantic Treaty Organization (NATO), stating "if a member of the European Union is the victim of armed aggression on its territory other states have an obligation of aid and assistance by all the means in their power."[72] Since the 2015 Paris attacks, and accelerated on by the Brussels attacks, the EU, mainly through Germany's efforts, has put proposals for a common European military structure, or a European Defense Union, back on the table.[73]

Full-capacity European battlegroups (EUBGs) have existed since 2007, with multinational forces having carried out the EU missions in Chad and the Central African Union in 2008, as well as its anti-piracy mission Operation Atalanta in the same year.[74] Each battlegroup consists of roughly 1,500-personnel rotating forces from each European country or region, such as the Visegrád Group. Furthermore, legislative proposals for a CIA or FBI-equivalent in Europe to increase critical intelligence-sharing, which have been stalled for so long allegedly due to officials' concerns about compromising sources, are also being pushed through, under pressure from Belgian Prime Minister Charles Michel.[75] Chaillot Paper No. 137, published in March 2016 by the EU Institute for Security Studies (ISS), outlines five possible futures for European defense, starting from the current (1) *bonsai armies*, (2) Defense clusters, (3) Peace operations, (4) European NATO, and the optimal (5) European army.[76]

We've seen it all before: The hysterical ramp-up in security, information centralization, and the deployment of troops on foreign soil to remove an external terrorist threat. These were all the knee-jerk reactions leading to the Bush-era quagmires in Afghanistan and Iraq, commencing in 2001 and 2003, respectively.

I joined the U.S. military in 2006, thinking Operation Iraqi Freedom (OIF) would soon be over, yet the worst battles hadn't even begun. My first trip to Iraq was in 2008, following the General Petraeus-led "Iraqi Surge," in which the U.S. dropped an additional 20,000 boots on the ground in 2007 to supplement the 120,000 forces already there. By the time I was in parachutist school at Fort Benning, Georgia in February 2007, President George W. Bush announced the Surge, and from that speech I prepared my mind for the possibility of an Iraq or Afghanistan deployment. I remember looking forward to it.

From a mainstream American point of view, 2007 was widely deemed a "successful" year in the Iraq conflict, if a reported decrease in violence is regarded as a success. Optimistic scholars, such as Stephen Biddle, Jeffrey Friedman, and Jacob Shapiro, who in 2012 released the report *Testing the Surge: Why Did Violence Decline in Iraq in 2007?*,[77] accounted for the success by noting that the Iraqi Surge was launched in conjunction with the "Sunni Awakening" (*Sahwa*) movement, or the related "Sons of Iraq" program. The *Sahwa*, originally a local, community defense initiative by sheikhs in Anbar province to push out al-Qaeda, was successfully absorbed into U.S. defense planning for the Second Battle of Ramadi toward the end of 2006, though the movement started in 2005. According to Biddle, Friedman, and Shapiro (2012)[78] neither the Surge nor the Sahwa would have functioned well without the other. With roughly 100,000 militia members at its peak, who mostly functioned as neighborhood watch, the Sahwa constituted a significant factor in the war, as well as a significant expenditure of American taxpayer dollars. My team assisted the Military Police in Bayji in late 2008 when the transfer of costs for the Sahwa from the U.S. to Iraq was underway. It was a mess. One fighter from Dora, expressed "the transfer an act of betrayal by the U.S. Army," in a USA Today report,[79] which is a view I heard from many of Iraqi Sunnis. At the same time, rumors spread that the U.S. was planting IEDs against itself to justify its security presence.

Empowering the Sahwa and building trust with the locals were key elements in counterinsurgency operations in Iraq. Petraeus' doctrine, Field Manual 3–24[80] on Counterinsurgency, included elements of empowering local forces and building trust relationships to develop a credible information flow necessary to co-opt an insurgency.

Insurgencies seek to undermine the government or state's ability to provide support to local populations, often by destabilizing government logistics and providing an alternative source, usually with a competing ideology. We rarely, if ever, referred to insurgents as terrorists, even though both insurgents and "terrorists" may target civilian populations to persuade them to call into question their government's ability to protect them. From my perspective the difference between them lies in whether a terrorist or insurgent is a priori domestic—(i.e., Tamil Tigers) or foreign-based (i.e., al-Qaeda), and also whether the frame being used is either domestic or foreign. Accordingly, for me, "homegrown terrorists" are actually insurgents. However, there will never be a domestic counterinsurgency[81] unit, unless a country is in a civil war. Specialized police units are called counter- or anti-terrorist (CT), while military units are called counterinsurgent

(COIN). This line becomes blurred when the police or military play both roles, training each other, where COIN sometimes specifies non-lethal soft power and CT as lethal direct action.[82] In the U.S., citizens are rightly worried about the excessive militarization of police forces, but is anyone complaining about U.S. military taking up police tactics?

From my perspective, the actions of Belgian security before and during the March 2016 attacks indicate a failure on many levels in both counter-terrorism and -insurgency. Intelligence units failed to communicate with each other at crucial points, across and within borders. It is not that they lack sources of information; in counterinsurgency this is referred to as human (HUMINT) or signal intelligence (SIGINT). The failures highlight some of the main paradoxes of counterinsurgency, which are:

1 Sometimes the more you protect your force, the less secure you may be.
2 Sometimes the more force is used, the less effective it is.
3 The more successful a counterinsurgency is, less force can be used and more risk must be accepted.
4 Sometimes doing nothing is the best reaction (probably the only one followed in Belgium).
5 Some of the best weapons for counterinsurgents do not shoot.[83]

These may sound like something out of Sun Tzu, but they became a mantra for me throughout my training. Building trust and credibility with the local communities are the most important aspects of COIN, and Belgium has a long way to go in this regard.

Building trust was how two reservist State Troopers, who were formerly deployed with a Special Forces unit in Afghanistan, turned their hometown, Springfield, Massachusetts, away from gang violence in 2012.[84] Raids and "whack-a-mole"[85] operations targeting key leaders in a criminal or terrorist network can often be unproductive in counterinsurgency. Iraq veteran Alex Horton experienced the butt-end of excessive force and over-proportionate police tactics in a Virginia house raid and wrote about the perversion of military tactics by police units.[86] He had been lawfully sleeping in an apartment next to his own, when he woke up surrounded by a SWAT team with fingers on their triggers ready to fire, mistaking him for a squatter.

For me, experiencing Brussels after the attacks was a similarly enlightening moment, fortunately not as personal. At least I have trust that Belgian police aim for the leg, rather than to kill, and when in doubt about whether a mysterious package contains explosive material, under supervision they blow it up themselves. Two days after the 2015 Paris attacks, just around the corner from my house in Brussels, the police cordoned off an area and dismantled with a robot an anonymous vehicle with French plates. They found a briefcase full of documents in the back seat, instead of bombs.

Reflexes, reflections, and conclusion

> It is a far, far better thing that I do, than I have ever done; it is a far, far better rest that I go to than I have ever known.
> (Sydney Barton, in Charles Dickens' *A Tale of Two Cities*, Book III. Chapter 15)

We did make mistakes in Iraq during my tours of duty there, but more than that, we communicated our mistakes and had counted on the possibility of mistakes (former U.S. Defense Secretary Donald Rumsfeld's "unknown unknowns"). Having participated in over 250 counterinsurgency operations, with an 85 percent success rate of arrests, I had my role down to muscle memory, most of which was spent driving or gunning. Building trust comes at high risk, but to highlight Alex Horton's point,[87] it involves police understanding that wearing a uniform categorically puts the value of their own life below that of the civilian. Like Belgium, where police units are fragmented, in Iraq a platoon could be working with, paying and sharing information with an individual for whom at the same time another platoon was constructing a case that might lead to his eventual arrest.

In Charles Dickens' *A Tale of Two Cities*, the Marquis St. Evrémonde compensates a father with a coin for having run over his son in the crowded streets of Paris. All too often this gesture occurred in Iraq in "collateral damage" cases involving coalition forces' unintended killing or injuring of Iraqi civilians, and even property damage. International humanitarian law, or the law of armed conflict, allows for a certain degree of proportionality so long as the military force is pursuing a clearly distinguishable target with a perceived military advantage. In case that accidents happen—and they do happen—money is usually proffered to the victims' survivors. According to Jason Lyall and Isaiah Wilson's study *Rage against the Machines* (2009),[88] foot patrols were more successful than mounted forces in counterinsurgency operations, as it is necessary to engage in face-to-face interactions with local populations to gather information (whether that information is processed into useful "intelligence" is debatable). Empowering the smallest unit is a principle of COIN, and in so doing, this may also limit collateral damage.

Even if the law forbids it, a majority of those Belgian security forces conducting raids on suspected terrorist hideouts insist on wearing balaclavas in order to hide their identities. These operations may also be conducted only from 5 am to 9 pm (this law may change soon). Accordingly, one should question the ability of such a force to generate popular trust and ability to protect the local citizenry. *A Tale of Two Cities* is all about the construction and reinforcement of the "us-and-them" narrative across cities, neighborhoods, and continents, which is so often perpetuated by violent extremist groups, and we should take this lesson from Dickens.

In Iraq, we would target suspects if we already had warrants, sometimes building a case for years, and typically we needed a visual confirmation of the suspects before entering a house. In contrast, where is Belgian HUMINT during their raids? The security forces have all the equipment, "intelligence," and manpower they need, but like Verviers, St. Denis (it's even been reported that French RAID shot their own dog after police emptied 5,000 rounds only receiving 11 from assailants),[89] and Forest, they all seem surprised and came up short in determining an appropriate use of force. More important than our nighttime raids were our follow-up efforts the day after, which usually involved talking with community leaders about their grievances.

Belgium wants to celebrate its fragmented, decentralized system of doing things, but when it fails to take responsibility for information flows at the bottom levels, this system heightens local distrust of police and government officials, and thus de facto leads to centralization of authority. When many scholars and politicians are calling for a consolidation of European defense and intelligence, they fail to see how the U.S. succumbed to the same fallacious, state-centered logic.

It's true that information needs to be shared more often, even if it's open-sourced, though from the ground and not hoarded in state secrecy. It requires more porous, horizontal unity than rigid, vertical one-way traffic. In times of trouble, it's our natural tendency to look up, to a leader, to a supernatural (super, as in "above") entity. However, the structural inadequacies between Belgium's knee-jerk security reactions, sometimes lack thereof, and the often ignored immigrant-background European identity that has given birth to environments where multiple threats are cultivated[90] need not be overlooked. To address the roots of terrorism, we must look to local actors and avoid creating extra levels at the top, i.e., centralized nodes, which create a false sense of security and increase our vulnerabilities to simultaneous, coordinated terrorist attacks. Radicalization is a spontaneous bottom-up process, and will not be resolved through governmental top-down approaches alone. Trust starts at the local level, and the primary role of the police should be to build trust within local communities. Perhaps hiring a police force that is representative of the population and who live in the very neighborhoods the police are meant to protect is a step to addressing Belgium's, and the West's, terrorism-related security dilemma.

Notes

1 Dickens, Charles. A Tale of Two Cities. Kindle ed., Public Domain, 2010: 1–77.
2 "Des opérations de police ont eu lieu à proximité de la chaussée d'Ixelles." *Le Soir*. March 24, 2016. www.lesoir.be/1161285/article/actualite/regions/bruxelles/2016-03-24/des-operations-police-ont-eu-lieu-proximite-chaussee-d-ixelles.
3 "Responses To Brussels Attacks: ISIS Supporters On Social Media React With Threats, Glee." *MEMRI JTTM*. March 22, 2016. www.memrijttm.org/responses-to-brussels-attacks-isis-supporters-on-social-media-react-with-threats-glee.html.
4 Webber, Rod. "University of Mosul bombing preceded Brussels attack. Why no coverage?" *Daily* Kos. March 23, 2016. www.dailykos.com/story/2016/3/23/1505193/-University-of-Mosul-bombing-preceded-Brussels-attack-Why-no-coverage.
5 Laurens Cerulus. "The Cost of the Brussels Lockdown: €51.7 Million a Day." *POLITICO Europe*. March 8, 2016. www.politico.eu/article/brussels-lockdown-financial-damage-52-million-vrt-terrorism-business.

6 "Comment 'l'explosion' d'un pigeon a semé la panique Gare du Nord." *Huffington Post.* November 22, 2015. www.huffingtonpost.fr/2015/11/22/comment-lexplosion-dun-pigeon-a-seme-la-panique-gare-du-nord.
7 It was French President Hollande who overreacted by ordering airstrikes on Syria the day after the Paris attacks, while Belgian Prime Minister Charles Michel was left dumbfounded and without a viable means of political reaction. Both the NATO and EU defense clauses were invoked, terrorism levels were still elevated. Michel hit a glass ceiling for declaring yet again a war on terrorism. He was caught with the GWOT "hot potato" and all fingers pointed to Belgium as the chink in the fantasized Schengen armor, with Molenbeek now a ghetto-ized jihadist hotbed.
8 Willett, Megan. "The meme #JeSuisSickofThisSh-t makes a major statement about public outcry after terrorist attacks." Business Insider UK. March 22, 2016. www.businessinsider.com/je-suis-sick-of-this-shit-viral-terrorism-2016-3.
9 Spillane, Chris. "Brussels vigil: we don't want to live in fear." POLITICO Europe. March 22, 2016. www.politico.eu/article/brussels-vigil-we-dont-want-to-live-in-fear-terror-attacks-airport-metro-isil-place-bourse-tribute.
10 Porter, Tom. "Brussels: Muslim woman knocked down in Molenbeek hit and run during far-right protest." International Business Times. April 3, 2016. www.ibtimes.co.uk/brussels-muslim-woman-knocked-down-molenbeek-hit-run-during-far-right-protest-1552892.
11 "Paris attacks: manhunt for Salah Abdeslam and accomplices." *BBC News.* November 16, 2015. www.bbc.com/news/world-europe-34826117.
12 Heath, Ryan, Zoya Sheftalovich, Chris Spillane. "Belgium's 12 worst terror misses, mistakes, and misunderstandings." *POLITICO Europe.* March 29, 2016. www.politico.eu/article/the-dirty-dozen-12-mistakes-that-condemned-brussels-to-terror-attacks-isil.
13 The author served as a corporal in the U.S. Army for two deployments to North Iraq from 2008–2010, at the height of counterinsurgency operations and in transition from an occupied to sovereign Iraq under the 2008 Status of Forces Agreement (SOFA).
14 Paravicini, Giulia and Laurens Cerulus. "Belgian police knew since 2014 that Abdeslam brothers planned 'irreversible act'." *POLITICO Europe.* April 28, 2016. www.politico.eu/article/belgian-police-knew-since-2014-that-abdeslam-brothers-planned-irreversible-act.
15 King, Tim. "Belgium is a failed state." *POLITICO Europe.* December 2, 2015. www.politico.eu/article/belgium-failed-state-security-services-molenbeek-terrorism.
16 Ibid.
17 Ibid.
18 Coolsaet, Rik. "Facing the Fourth Foreign Fighters Wave: What Drives Europeans to Syria, and to Islamic State? Insights from the Belgian Case." *Egmont Royal Institute for International Relations.* Paper 81 (March 2016): 1–52. Olivier Roy also remarks on the "case of Muriel Degauque (a Belgian woman who killed herself in Iraq in 2005)" as being one of the first from this "new generation of al Qaeda activists recruiting far beyond the usual pool of second-generation Muslims and numbering people who, 40 years ago would have joined ultra-leftist groups, like the Red Army Faction." Roy, Olivier. "Islamic Terrorist Radicalisation in Europe" in Amghar, Samir, Amel Boubekeur, and Michael Emerson "European Islam – Challenges for Society and Public Policy." Brussels: Centre for European Policy Studies (2007): p. 53.
19 Coolsaet 2016, p. 11.
20 Ibid., p. 12.
21 I hesitate in using the term "immigrant-background" especially in Brussels, where nearly everyone is from outside the city. However, Europeans generally use the politically correct term denoting second, third, or even fourth generation migrants. In the case for Belgium, I'll use "immigrant-background" if referring to those traditionally

assumed Moroccan, Congolese, and Turkish labor migrant families until the 1970s. Another conundrum is referring to French citizens with Algerian roots, especially before Algeria's independence from France in 1962.
22 "Belgium's Malcolm X." *BBC News.* April 3, 2003 as cited in Koutroubas, Theodoros, Ward Vloeberghs, and Zeynep Yanasmayan. "Political, Religious and Ethnic Radicalisation Among Muslims in Belgium". Ethno-Religious Conflict in Europe, *Centre for European Policy Studies* (2009): 51–80.
23 Koutroubas et al. 2009, pp. 61–67.
24 Coolsaet 2016, p. 30.
25 Ibid., p. 31.
26 Roy (2007): 52–60.
27 Coolsaet 2016, p. 35.
28 Coolsaet 2016, p. 21.
29 Atran, Scott. "Why ISIS Has the Potential to Be a World-altering Revolution" *Aeon.* December 15, 2015. https://aeon.co/essays/why-isis-has-the-potential-to-be-a-world-altering-revolution.
30 Leroy, Didier, and Joost Hiltermann. "Why Belgium?" *The New York Review of Books.* March 24, 2016. www.nybooks.com/daily/2016/03/24/brussels-attacks-isis-why-belgium.
31 Leroy and Hiltermann 2016.
32 See Weiss, Michael, Nancy A. Youssef, and Nadette De Visser. "U.S. Officials Bash 'Shitty' Belgian Security Forces." *The Daily Beast.* March 22, 2016. www.thedailybeast.com/articles/2016/03/22/u-s-officials-bash-shitty-belgian-security-forces.html.
33 Renard, Thomas. "Why Belgium is not Europe's jihadi base." POLITICO Europe. March 31, 2016. www.politico.eu/article/belgium-is-not-europe-jihadi-base-terrorism-threat-molenbeek.
34 Ibid.
35 Ibid.
36 *Groep Diane* was the predecessor to elite Federal Police Special Unit or Commissariat Général Special Units (CGSU), similar to American SWAT or French RAID units, formed in response to the terrorist attacks during the 1972 Olympic Games in Munich. This unit of 500 came out of the woodwork for the January 2015 Verviers raid, when two armed suspects were killed. The hunter-goddess Diana, or Artemis, is their unit patch. Coincidentally, the Etterbeek area just north of Brussels police barracks is called La Chasse, or the Hunt. See Favaro, Yasmina. «Qui sont les policiers des unités spéciales?» *RTBF News.* January 17, 2016. www.rtbf.be/info/belgique/detail_qui-sont-les-policiers-des-unites-speciales?id=8792008.
37 Renard 2016.
38 Koutroubas, Theodoros, Ward Vloeberghs, and Zeynep Yanasmayan. "Political, Religious and Ethnic Radicalisation Among Muslims in Belgium". Ethno-Religious Conflict in Europe, Centre for European Policy Studies (2009): 51–80.
39 Buruma, Ian. "In the Capital of Europe." *The New York Review of Books.* April 7, 2016. www.nybooks.com/articles/2016/04/07/brussels-capital-of-europe.
40 Ibid.
41 *Zinneke* refers to the inhabitants (previously to stray dogs) who live around the Senne or Zenne River of Brussels.
42 Capatides, Christina. "Molenbeek and Schaerbeek: a Tale of Two Tragedies." *CBS News.* April 11, 2016. www.cbsnews.com/news/molenbeek-and-schaerbeek-brussels-belgium-a-tale-of-two-terror-tragedies.
43 «Mandat d'arrêt prolongé pour l'homme arrêté et blessé à Schaerbeek.» *Le Soir.* March 26, 2016. www.lesoir.be/1163426/article/actualite/belgique/2016-03-26/mandat-d-arret-prolonge-pour-l-homme-arrete-et-blesse-schaerbeek.
44 Ibid.

45 «Neuf perquisitions menées à Bruxelles ce mardi matin: des personnes rentrées de Syrie et un recruteur arrêtés.» *Le* Capitale (Belgium). February 16, 2016. www.lacapitale.be/1492518/article/2016-02-16/neuf-perquisitions-menees-a-bruxelles-ce-mardi-matin-des-personnes-rentrees-de-s. I was visiting a vegetable market at Place de La Duchesse de Brabant the morning of, while armed military checking IDs at metro stations and sirens were everywhere, I had arrived only in the aftermath of the arrests. About every two weeks following the Paris attacks, similar reports of security forces arresting 10 or so individuals at a time appeared in official Twitter feeds. Some suspects were released within 24 hours, in what counterinsurgency operators call "catch-and-release" when no relevant information is obtained, or "round-up" when multiple individuals are apprehended.
46 Le Cam, Florence, and David Domingo. "Chapter 4: The Plurality of Journalistic Identities in Local Controversies." *Local Journalism: The Decline of Newspapers and the Rise of Digital Media.* Ed. Rasmus Kleis Nielsen. London: I.B. Tauris, 2015. 99–116. E-Book.
47 Kozlowski, Hanna. "The places in the world that have a burqa ban." *Quartz.* January 14, 2015. www.qz.com/326086/the-places-in-the-world-that-have-a-burqa-ban.
48 Kozlowski 2015.
49 Black face-covering veil worn in primarily Arab gulf region.
50 Le Cam and Domingo 2015.
51 «Molenbeek: la femme en niqab interpellée en 2012, arrêtée à Brussels Airport.» *RTBF News.* March 30, 2016. www.rtbf.be/info/regions/bruxelles/detail_la-femme-au-niqab-interpellee-en-2012-a-molenbeek-recemment-arretee-a-brussels-airport?id=9256298.
52 Coolsaet 2016, p. 41.
53 Vidino, Lorenzo. "Sharia4: From Confrontational Activism to Militancy." *Perspectives on Terrorism* 9.2 (April 2015).
54 Winning the Hearts and Minds (WHAM) is also a counterinsurgency slogan.
55 Vidino 2015, p. 11.
56 Ibid., p. 10.
57 Coolsaet's four waves of terrorism correspond approximately to each decade during the past 30 years: (1) 1980s Afghan *mujahideen* of older, high socioeconomic status, such as Bin Laden; (2) 1990s elite expatriates from middle-class in their 30s, typically fighting in Chechnya, Kashmir, Bosnia, or the Philippines; (3) 2000s with homegrown, bottom-up, fluid networks with average age of 27.7 years and criminal records, and finally (4) 2010 generation in their early 20s, nihilists, with little to no future prospects (2006, p. 19).
58 Coolsaet 2016, p. 9.
59 Ibid.
60 "The Transformation of Jihadism in the Netherlands: Swarm Dynamics and New Strength." *AIVD.* September 2014.
61 Ing, Nancy and Alexander Smith. "Brussels Attacks: Bombers filmed nuclear researcher, experts say." *NBC News.* March 24, 2016. www.nbcnews.com/storyline/brussels-attacks/brussels-attacks-bombers-filmed-nuclear-researcher-expert-says-n544776, and «Exclusif: Les Frères El Bakraoui Visaient Nos Centrales Nucléaires!» *La Dernière Heure.* March 24, 2016. www.dhnet.be/actu/belgique/exclusif-les-freres-el-bakraoui-visaient-nos-centrales-nucleaires-56f3778d35702a22d5ad606b.
62 Mainstream media, mostly US and British, still haven't retracted false headlines that the security badge was stolen, despite mass panic about a nuclear threat by terrorists.
63 "Nuclear Power in Belgium." World Nuclear Association, Country Briefings. March 2016. www.world-nuclear.org/information-library/country-profiles/countries-a-f/belgium.aspx.
64 Ward, Olivia. "The dirty truth about nuclear terrorism." *The Star.* April 25, 2016. www.thestar.com/news/world/2016/04/25/the-dirty-truth-about-nuclear-terrorism.html.

65 Ibid.
66 Ibid.
67 "Belgium nuclear power plants 'falling to bits' – German officials." *Reuters*. December 30, 2015. www.rt.com/news/327457-belgium-nuclear-power-hendricks.
68 «Doel 3 à l'arrêt à la suite d'un problème de logiciel lors d'un test de turbine.» *Le Soir*. April 22, 2016. www.lesoir.be/1189298/article/actualite/fil-info/fil-info-economie/2016-04-22/doel-3-l-arret-suite-d-un-probleme-logiciel-lors-d-un-test-turbi
69 Ward 2016.
70 "All Belgians to be given iodine pills for nuclear safety." *BBC News*. April 28, 2016. www.bbc.com/news/world-europe-36157806.
71 Briançon, Pierre and Nicholas Vinocur. "6 Takeaways on Hollande's speech." *POLITICO Europe*. November 16, 2016. www.politico.eu/article/6-takeaways-hollande-speech-parliament-terrorism-syria-jihad-isil/
72 "What is article 42.7 of the Lisbon Treaty?" *POLITICO Europe*. November 18, 2015. www.politico.eu/article/what-is-article-42-7-of-the-lisbon-french-government-terrorist-attacks-paris-treaty.
73 Kiesewetter, Roderich. "Toward a European Defense Union." *Carnegie Europe*. April 29, 2016.
74 Ibid.
75 Barnes, Julian E. and Stephen Fidler. "Brussels attacks give new impetus for more intelligence-sharing in Europe." *The Wall Street Journal*. April 18, 2016. www.wsj.com/articles/brussels-attacks-give-new-impetus-for-more-intelligence-sharing-in-europe-1460952001.
76 Andersson, Jan Joel, Sven Biscop, Bastian Giegerich, Christian Mölling, and Thierry Tardy. "Envisioning European Defence: Five Futures." *European Institute for Security Studies* (ISS). Chaillot Paper No. 137. March 2016.
77 Biddle, Stephen, Jeffrey A. Friedman, and Jacob N. Shapiro. "Testing the Surge: Why Did Violence Decline in Iraq in 2007?" *International Security* 37 (1)(2012): 7–40.
78 Ibid.
79 "Iraq: Govt. takes command of Sons of Iraq." *USA Today*. October 1, 2008. http://usatoday30.usatoday.com/news/world/iraq/2008-10-01-iraq-fighters_N.htm.
80 U.S. Department of the Army. *Counterinsurgency. Field Manual 3–24*. Washington, DC: U.S. Department of the Army, June 16, 2006.
81 see McQuade, Brendan. "The Return of Domestic Counterinsurgency?" *Counterpunch*. April 29, 2011. www.counterpunch.org/2011/04/29/the-return-of-domestic-counterinsurgency.
82 Anderson, Gary. "Counterinsurgency vs. Counterterrorism: A Civilian's View." *Small Wars Journal*. (2010).
83 COIN FM 3–24 2006.
84 Goode, Erica. "With Green Beret tactics, combating gang warfare." *New York Times*. April 30, 2012. www.nytimes.com/2012/05/01/us/springfield-mass-fights-crime-using-green-beret-tactics.html?_r=0.
85 Long, Austin. "Whack-a-Mole or Coup de Grace? Institutionalization and Leadership Targeting in Iraq and Afghanistan." *Security Studies* 23 (3) (2014): 471–512.
86 Horton, Alex. "In Iraq, I raided insurgents; in Virginia, police raided me." *Chicago Tribune*. July 26, 2015. www.chicagotribune.com/news/opinion/commentary/ct-in-iraq-i-raided-insurgents-in-virginia-the-police-raided-me-20150726-story.html.
87 Lyall, Jason, and Isaiah Wilson. "Rage against the Machines: Explaining Outcomes in Counterinsurgency Wars." International Organization 63, no. 1 (2009): 67–106.
88 Horton, Alex. "In Iraq, I raided insurgents; in Virginia, police raided me." Chicago Tribune. Web. July 26, 2015, www.chicagotribune.com/news/opinion/commentary/ct-in-iraq-i-raided-insurgents-in-virginia-the-police-raided-me-20150726-story.html.

89 Allen, Peter. "Diesel the police dog was shot dead by her own side during Paris terror attacks." *Mail Online*. February 15, 2016. www.dailymail.co.uk/news/article-3446511/Confirmed-Diesel-hero-police-dog-Paris-attacks-shot-dead-wounded-innocent-neighbours-reckless-shooting.html.
90 As in the forgotten etymology of the word "radical": *radix* is Latin for "root."

14 The "war on terrorism"
What does it mean to win?*

Audrey Kurth Cronin

> If the decision to end a war were simply to spring from a rational calculation about gains and losses for the nation as a whole, it should be no harder to get out of a war than to get into one.
>
> (Fred Charles Iklé, Every War Must End, 1971/2005)

The war on al-Qaeda appears endless, but every war must end. The US and its allies have made dramatic progress against a once formidable terrorist organization known for its meticulous planning, coordinated attacks, and popular support. Popular support has dropped off, its leader is dead, and developments in the Arab world have shifted its focus back to fighting local enemies and hijacking local insurgencies. Compared to a decade ago, the threat to the United States, the United Kingdom, and Western allies is much reduced. Although it can still inspire small attacks, the organization that attacked the United States in 2001 is marginalized. Research about how terrorism ends has influenced counterterrorism policy decisions.[1] But what about the other side of that coin—the war against al-Qaeda. Recently published books on war termination have ignored it.[2] How exactly will it end?

For Americans, the response to al-Qaeda's 2001 attacks has always been a "war." Against the misgivings of experts and allies, Congress resolved the US debate over "war" or "crime" three days after the 9/11 attacks.[3] With nearly 3,000 dead Americans lying under hot debris, the situation seemed clear: another attack was imminent. Only preventive military force could protect the country from further carnage, delivered either conventionally or with weapons of mass destruction. The 2001 Authorization for the Use of Military Force (AUMF), as robust as any formal war declaration preceding it, bound the bureaucracy to frame the conflict as a "war" rather than a law enforcement problem—and it was a war with no specified end.[4] Even the 1941 war declarations upon Imperial Japan and Nazi Germany had directed the President "to bring the conflict(s) to a successful termination."[5] The boundless 2001 authorization was followed by a series of continuing resolutions providing open-ended funding, 94 percent of which went to the Defense Department.[6] For US policymakers, calling the struggle a "war on terrorism" and then a "war against al-Qaeda and its affiliates" was not just semantics.

Winding down in Afghanistan and Iraq is straightforward compared to ending the war against al-Qaeda.[7] For the United States both of those "overseas contingency operations" conclude when US combat troops are withdrawn and a Status of Forces Agreement enacted to cover postconflict arrangements. Yet planners often forget that both were launched as an integral part of the global response to deadly attacks against the World Trade Centre, the Pentagon, and ultimately a field in Pennsylvania. The end of combat operations in Iraq and Afghanistan is not the end of the war begun in 2001. With smaller ongoing US operations from the Philippines to the Horn of Africa, a sustainable strategy must also weigh means and ends in the ongoing war against al-Qaeda. The alternative is to jerk willy-nilly from overspending to underspending, paranoia to complacency, short-term reaction to long-term decline.

The war on terrorism has remained open-ended in time, geography, and resources—including money, talent, and preemptive lethal force. Ill-defined ends and means are placing US actions outside of familiar strategic, legal, and moral frameworks for evaluating their pros and cons. Military operations and tactics have prevailed, from two massive counterinsurgencies to high-tempo special operations to drone attacks, with a sustainable longer-term approach neglected.[8] Efforts to create a balanced grand strategy across all aspects of US power (military, diplomatic, law enforcement, aid) have failed, unsupported by either the legal or the financial scaffolding of the post-9/11 campaign. Without envisioning an end, policymakers do not calibrate day-to-day plans so that ends and means are aligned. Through its unmatched operational, intelligence, and special operations capabilities, the United States government has made enormous progress, killing bin Laden and crushing the leadership. Yet, even as al-Qaeda is losing, the United States does not seem to be winning. In this war, no one seems to know what "winning" means.

Crime is endless, but wars end. Contrary to popular myth, wars do not all reach closure with surrender ceremonies on battleships, treaty negotiations in French palaces, or even helicopter evacuations from embassy rooftops.[9] Nor do they necessarily return the status quo ante bellum: Going to war irrevocably alters the strategic landscape. The American people will never recapture their pre-9/11 sense of safety, just as the intrusive security procedures and intelligence collection will never disappear. And this is not the first authorization for the use of force against a non-state actor: Native Americans, pirates, and slave traders have all been named in earlier authorizations.[10] But while terrorism itself never ends, wars by their nature demand a distinction between "war" and "peace." So far, the United States government has no idea how to characterize "peace."

This is a serious oversight. All the great strategists agree that war cannot be fought successfully without clear notions of an end state to guide, modulate, and focus operations. More than 2,500 years ago in ancient China, Sun Zi wrote of the chaotic Warring States period that "there has never been a protracted war from which a country has benefited" and "hence what is essential in war is victory, not prolonged operations."[11] Reflecting on the Peloponnesian War, Thucydides wrote in fifth-century BCE, "[i]t is a common mistake in going to war to begin at the wrong end, to act first, and wait for disaster to discuss the matter."[12] In the second book of On War, von Clausewitz observes:

> [y]et insofar as that aim is not the one that will lead directly to peace, it remains subsidiary and is also to be thought of as means.... What remains in the way of ends, then, are only those objects that lead directly to peace.[13]

Fresh out of World War I, Col. J. F. C. Fuller observed, "[p]reparation for war or against war, from the grand strategical aspect, is the main problem of peace, just as the accomplishment of peaceful prosperity is the main problem of war."[14] And, following World War II, British strategist Basil Liddell Hart argued:

> while the horizon of strategy is bounded by the war, grand strategy looks beyond the war to the subsequent peace. It should not only combine the various instruments, but so regulate their use as to avoid damage to the future state of peace—for its security and prosperity.[15]

In the twentieth century, the advent of nuclear weapons meant that American strategic thinking came to be dominated more by economics and engineering than history. But even there the imperative of war termination was brought home in books such as Fred Iklé's 1971 classic, Every War Must End, published during the Vietnam War.[16] No country has ever benefited from an endless war, and the United States is no exception. American policymakers must envision the end of this war or it will further exhaust US forces, distort their strategic planning, and blind them to other threats.

Thinking about how this war will end is crucial to prosecuting it successfully. Yet, the more the United States fights, the longer the war's trajectory seems to grow. Twelve years after 9/11, senior US Defense official Michael Sheehan told Congress that the war with al-Qaeda would continue "for 10 or 20 years' more."[17] How could that be? Clearly Al-Qaeda is not the same organization it was a decade ago. What does "success" mean?[18] The following first evaluates the ongoing US response in historical context, and then suggests how to bring the war against al-Qaeda to an end.

The ongoing US response to al-Qaeda

Through the post-9/11 years, the United States evolved in its answer to al-Qaeda, from major combat operations, counterinsurgency and nation-building in Iraq and Afghanistan, toward juxtaposing the decline of al-Qaeda with the rise of aggressive US special operations and paramilitary intelligence activity globally. Lacking a strong framework for strategy and war termination, the United States replaced the actual threat of al-Qaeda with the possibility of al-Qaeda (or "associates") in a widening range of places.

An unforeseen legacy of defining al-Qaeda as a "global insurgency" in 2005 was the impulse for US action against "transnational violent extremism" universally in 2012.[19] Muslim insurgencies around the world became core US concerns. This was a crucial shifting of American ends, from the protection of the American homeland and the prevention of another attack, to the defense of all parts of the world from the potential for an Islamist extremist entity to hold any piece of territory, anywhere. Former NSC official Mary Habeck put it this way:

> [W]inning against al Qaeda does not depend on body counts, but rather would look very much like victories against other insurgents: the spreading of security for populations in Somalia, Yemen, the Sahel, and elsewhere; the prevention of a return of al-Qaeda to those cleared areas; and the empowerment of legitimate governments that can control and police their own territories. By these standards, we have not yet defeated al Qaeda; in fact, beyond Iraq, Afghanistan, and Somalia, we have hardly engaged the enemy at all.[20]

This implies that the United States should engage in a war on violent extremism anywhere, and thus fight an open-ended global campaign everywhere—a classic recipe for imperial overstretch.

A worldwide perspective also emerged from the unfortunate US tendency to equate failed states with an al-Qaeda threat (or potential al-Qaeda threat), thus pulling many ungoverned corners of the globe into the US sphere of interest.[21] Along with the demand for zero risk at home, such narrow thinking yielded reactionary, expeditionary responses instead of prioritization according to enduring US interests in deciding where to deploy. A light military footprint was not so light when it lacked a strategic framework and global boundaries. In the absence of long-term strategic planning, the United States began to suffer four symptoms common to all prolonged wars: means became ends, tactics became strategy, boundaries were blurred, and the search for a perfect peace replaced reality.[22]

Means become ends

Once any democracy has entered into a war, it is extraordinarily difficult to prosecute that war on the basis of an objective balance of means and ends. After blood has been spilled—especially that of innocent noncombatants, broadcast to the horrified stares of millions throughout the world—it is difficult to take the kind of antiseptic approach to ends, ways, and means that is at the core of strategic thinking. All wars excite emotions such as anger, revenge, retaliation, and protecting sunk costs. One of the three elements of Clausewitz's trinity is "primordial violence, hatred and enmity, which are to be regarded as a blind natural force," after all, and perhaps never more so than when terrorism is involved.[23] The default is to buy, build, organize, and create more means. In the wake of major attacks, the policymaker's natural instinct is to lash out against the enemy and to focus maximal state resources on shoring up the government's primary source of legitimacy, which is the protection of its citizens. As President

Obama's then counterterrorism advisor, John Brennan, stated in April 2012, US counterterrorism strategy is "guided by the President's highest responsibility, to protect the safety and security of the American people."[24]

It follows, then, that in a counterterrorism campaign, keeping means in line with ends becomes extraordinarily difficult, especially if there are no limits placed upon those means from the outset. This was certainly the case in the United States, with the unprecedentedly open-ended 2001 AUMF and the continuing resolutions that followed it. Some of the remarkable successes of the campaign against al-Qaeda have resulted from wise and focused policies: the United State now has better intelligence collection, more cooperation with allies and partners, expanded operational capacity, remarkable technological advances, and much better defenses against the threat. But there is a point at which more means—more operations, more analysts, more data, more reports, more organizations, more operations—become counterproductive. At that point, the marginal benefit no longer exceeds the costs involved, because reducing the risk of terrorism to zero is impossible.

Since 9/11, the United States has built up an enormous edifice of counterterrorism capabilities, especially in intelligence analysis, military operations, and homeland security. In response to 9/11, at least 263 US government organizations have been created or reorganized. There are some 1,271 government organizations and 1,931 private companies that work on programs related to counterterrorism, homeland security, and intelligence, in about 10,000 locations across the United States, and more than two-thirds of that capability resides in the Defense Department.[25] The growth of intelligence capability in particular has been mind-boggling. The system has become redundant, unwieldy, and virtually unmanageable. Individual establishments within this vast new bureaucracy compete for resources, access, and control of information. Intelligence analysts publish some 50,000 intelligence reports each year, often redundant or overlapping. The US Army General responsible for tracking the Pentagon's most sensitive programs observed,

> I'm not aware of any agency with the authority, responsibility or a process in place to coordinate all these interagency and commercial activities.... The complexity of this system defies description.... Because [the system] lacks a synchronizing process, it inevitably results in message dissonance, reduced effectiveness and waste. We consequently can't effectively assess whether it is making us more safe.[26]

In intelligence, the United States could be spending beyond the point of marginal return. Much of the reporting lacks originality, because primary information is finite and analysts are forced to rehash what's already in circulation. As a result, there is more reliance by senior officials upon human briefers to distill and regurgitate what they need to know, drawn and edited from a daily tsunami of information and reports that they cannot reasonably absorb. More information does not necessarily lead to better outcomes, because the human capacity to absorb it is finite: When decision makers have no time to read or even think, considered judgment is replaced by gut reactions. Meanwhile, frustration with the large and unwieldy intelligence bureaucracy leads policymakers to use their discretionary funds to shortcut it: One result is contracts with privateers, who in turn feed specific, rumor-based intelligence directly back to senior leaders. For example, according to the *New York Times*, former CIA operative Duane R. Clarridge ran a private network of spies in Afghanistan and Pakistan. Under investigation for violating regulations, the Department of Defense contract was terminated in May 2011, but Clarridge apparently continued operations with private funding.[27] Big Data in intelligence gathering is likewise overhyped, altering the analyst's focus from causation to correlation—even as savvy terrorists need only unplug from the net or stop using the cell phone. In a decade, the US has gone from having too little understanding of al-Qaeda and too few knowledgeable analysts, to producing overwhelming amounts of data where key nuggets still get lost in the noise.

Meanwhile, spending on defensive measures has also grown dramatically, with annual appropriations for the Department of Homeland Security (DHS) increasing from $29 billion in 2003 to $48 billion in 2012.[28] Obviously, not all of this spending goes toward counterterrorism, with border security, disaster response, and securing cyberspace also looming large; but the department's first strategic goal is "preventing terrorism and enhancing security."[29] Although it has only been in existence since 2003, DHS now has a 192,000-person civilian workforce, making it the third largest US executive department after Defense (771,614 civilians) and Veteran's Affairs (312,878 civilians).[30] Indeed, these three Cabinet Departments now account for about 60 per cent of the total civilian workforce in the Executive branch. Yet DHS funds have often been spent with little or no connection to the level of threat.[31] Shoring up the homeland, especially airline and border security, has been a top priority; but between 2002 and 2010 there was also some $33 billion in grant funding for homeland security assistance to states, specified urban areas, and critical transportation (such as ports and rail systems).[32] The vulnerability of modes of transportation to terrorist attacks, especially airlines, subways, and railways, is well established and important to address. But it must be weighed against glaring inherent weaknesses in the system as a whole, as US infrastructure, including roads, aviation systems, bridges, sewers, public transportation, and the electrical grid (most of which was built in the 1950s and 1960s) is in a serious state of decay.[33] The result is puzzling distortions: Having people almost killed in a New York subway by Najibullah Zazi in September 2009 loomed larger in every respect than actually killing nine people and injuring 80 in a Washington, DC, subway crash three months earlier. The popular psyche is notoriously poor at assessing risk and taking the long view—terrorism is designed to exploit that. Leaders must do better.

Without a strategic framework, US means are becoming ends in themselves. Endlessly expanding means are a problem not just because the American government is spending in an inefficient way, but also because there is a heavy opportunity cost. Policymakers must be prepared for other serious problems such as weapons proliferation, pandemic diseases, deteriorating education systems, transnational criminal networks, and global economic instability. As retired Admiral Dennis Blair, former director of national intelligence, observed, "[a]fter 9/11, when we decided to attack violent extremism, we did as we so often do in this country.... The attitude was, if it's worth doing, it's probably worth overdoing."[34]

Tactics become strategy

A second problem in any endless war is that tactics gradually take the place of strategy.[35] "More absorbing than the final outcome are the perfection of the tools and the mastery of the components and maneuvers that form part of the undertaking," Iklé wrote of the Vietnam War in 1971.[36] With its heavy emphasis upon drone attacks and special operations, the United States government is asking the CIA to fight a war, to be strategic in a way it is not designed to be, while pushing the military Services to become more like the CIA.

The initial response to the 2001 al-Qaeda terrorist attacks was to use military force in major operations on the ground, with invasions and occupations in Afghanistan and then Iraq. Between the Bush and the Obama administrations, there was a shift from emphasizing troops on the ground fighting "al-Qaeda" (which, especially in the beginning, meant virtually anyone shooting at them) to greater reliance on targeting specific enemy leaders. In particular, along with sending more troops to Afghanistan shortly after he took office, President Obama authorized a dramatic expansion of the CIA's program to use drones to target al-Qaeda leaders and other militants on the border between Afghanistan and Pakistan.[37] The administration also greatly increased the role of Special Operations forces within the Afghan theatre and beyond. The logic was to confine the violence to those who were planning to attack the United States and its allies, so as to avoid having to send more blunt, high-casualty large military operations into rough and unfamiliar terrain.

The resulting increase in the use of unmanned aerial vehicles (or drones) by both the US military and the CIA has been unprecedented. From fewer than 50 in 2001, the Pentagon now has some 7,000 aerial drones. The US Air Force trained 350 drone pilots in 2011, which was more than the total number of conventional fighter and bomber pilots being trained (250). There are 16 drone operational and training sites across the United States, from North Dakota, California, New York, and Ohio, and a seventeenth planned.[38] They are needed to support a dramatic ramp up in operations abroad. The number of drone strikes used in the Hindu Kush region of Pakistan over the course of the second Bush administration (2004–2008) was 42. During the Obama administration, the rate of attacks accelerated to 53 in 2009 and peaked at 122 in 2010. Responding in part to hostility toward the program among the Pakistani public, as well as diminishment in potential targets, the number of strikes then began to decline, from 73 in 2011 to 48 in 2012, to 19 thus far in 2013.[39] Meanwhile, drone strikes in Yemen also increased, accelerating after the new Yemeni President, Abdo Rabbo Mansour Hadi, took office in February 2012.[40] While the precise number in Yemen is difficult to determine, the Bureau of Investigative Journalism reported that there had been between 54 and 64 confirmed US drone strikes between 2002 and 2013.[41] In June 2011, the United States also began carrying out drone strikes in Somalia, with the number thus far reported to be fewer than 10.[42] Indeed, US activities in Africa increased, with a significant ramp-up of special operations and CIA paramilitary activities in East Africa, including the capturing or killing of numerous al-Shabaab members in and near Mogadishu, and airstrikes on al-Shabaab training camps.[43] The CIA became as much a paramilitary organization as a spying agency, deploying operatives throughout the world.[44]

One unfortunate result of letting tactics take such a prominent role is that political leaders become unhealthily involved in the details and lose perspective as to the strategic purpose of the war. As Iklé wrote during the Vietnam War, "the senior statesmen may hesitate to insist that these beautifully planned campaigns be linked to some clear ideas for ending the war, while expending their authority and energy to oversee some tactical details of the fighting."[45] This is also happening in the US war against Al-Qaeda. In 2010, President Barack Obama put himself directly in charge of a secret "nominations" process regarding the targeting of senior al-Qaeda operatives whose names appear on a "kill list." By reviewing individual biographies, reportedly personally approving the decision whether or not to take lethal action against individuals, President Obama tried to maintain close control over the use of this new technology. His goal, according to senior aides, was to apply the centuries-old "just war" tradition to each targeting decision, using a rigorous checklist including the imminence of the threat, the reliability of the intelligence, and the infeasibility of capture.[46] Particularly in the wake of near-successful terrorist attempts of 2009, the Obama Administration was determined to mitigate the threat to American civilians on US soil. But in so doing, the president risked becoming "tactician-in-chief," putting aside long-term considerations of US interests in favor of an intense focus on using drones.

Drones and related technologies are necessarily tactical, not strategic. It is not at all clear what the broader plan is for using unmanned aerial vehicles in the context of American interests. An instrument of war seems to have become a policy rather than the other way around. It is not enough to argue that the top priority is to protect American lives, because the extensive use of drones exacts costs in alternate legal, political, and moral dimensions that are not weighed alongside the marginal short-term gain in safety that is sought. For example, one implication of such heavy reliance on drones is that terrorist operatives are almost never captured, a practice that eliminates the intelligence that might be gained by questioning them. This is a serious drawback in view of the vital role such information has played in other successful counterterrorism campaigns. It also risks summary executions of American prisoners in future wars. President Obama has even personally approved drones for use against American citizens in this war, associating the Office of the Presidency with a controversial practice that may undermine Constitutional protections in favor of executions in the name of preemptive self-defense. All of these decisions are made in a perpetual state of wartime urgency against a real threat; yet their legal, ethical, and military implications may some day cost more American lives and treasure than are likely to be suffered in a terrorist attack by today's diminished al-Qaeda.[47]

In short, all of these tactics have important strategic effects; but they do not add up to a strategy. Strategy is not made from the bottom up but from the top down. It is the outcome of this war, not just the tactical victories within it, that will serve the nation's long-term interests.[48] Terrorism sits at the tactical level of warfare. Our response began at the operational level and has now migrated to the tactical level. But American national interests are at the grand strategic level. Currently, tactics are driving US policy, rather than the other way around, and there is no end in sight.

All sense of boundary is lost

The transition from major combat operations in Iraq and Afghanistan to more focused, clandestine operations against specific targets brought with it all the advantages of lower cost and reduced political risk. But the other side of that coin was sharply reduced Congressional oversight, murky local partners, fuzzy legal restrictions, and unlimited geographical scope. Operating without built-in checks and balances has blurred every type of boundary.

Some of those boundaries were built in the wake of misadventures in past clandestine wars. For example, the US prohibition on assassinations, first introduced as a result of the 1975 Church commission investigations into CIA plots against political leaders, has been set aside in this new world. President Gerald Ford's Executive Order 11905 (1976), the first US ban on political assassination, responded to a report entitled "Alleged Assassination Plots Involving Foreign Leaders" by the Senate Select Committee to Study Governmental Operations with Respect to Intelligence Activities, the so-called Church Committee, in the wake of Watergate.[49] The argument now is that the ban pertains only to the killing of political leaders and heads of state, not terrorists. In 2002, with the 2001 AUMF legitimating US military force against "those nations, organizations, or persons he determines planned, authorized, committed or aided" in carrying out the 9/11 attacks, President Bush signed a directive that authorized the targeted killing, not just of Osama bin Laden and senior operational leaders, but of a wide scope of al-Qaeda-associated individuals in a virtually unlimited geographical area.[50] Using CIA drones piloted from remote locations to kill specific individuals who are plotting against the United States is considered different from secretly sending American CIA operatives to assassinate malicious political leaders in person. The killing of American citizens, including Kamel Derwish, Anwar Awlaki, and Samir Khan, then blurred the boundaries even further. One of the reasons for the increased use of drone attacks may be the dilemma of what to do with captives who, if placed on trial, might reveal sources and methods used in their apprehension. The result has been increased reliance upon drone attacks or sometimes rendition to third countries, another clouding of long-standing legal boundaries.[51]

Carrying out covert actions within an open-ended wartime framework is stretching or evading longstanding US measures to bound them. The flow of money and arms in this clandestine war belies the limitations placed upon covert action programs in the wake of the Iran Contra affair of 1985, for example, when money from secret arms dealings with Iran was illegally funneled to US-supported rebels in Nicaragua. Covert actions require presidential notification of Congress. But, in this war, using the military to carry out operations under its so-called Special Access Programs requires no Congressional notification or oversight at all.[52] In US law, Title 50 is the section of the legal code that governs covert intelligence operations, and Title 10 deals with the military, including clandestine military operations. The rules governing Title 10 operations, as in Afghanistan and Iraq, are looser, heightening the incentive to carry on this struggle as a war. In the laudable short-term effort to keep Americans safe from another 9/11, the war on al-Qaeda has demolished legal boundaries designed to ensure balance and oversight for the long term.

Strategic frameworks are likewise being recast in this war. For good or ill, the post-9/11 argument that the United States had to employ preventive attacks in order to protect against attacks by al-Qaeda (especially using weapons of mass destruction) was not new; but the degree to which it has now become widely accepted is. Preventive war has translated into many other areas of national security. Notable among them is cyberspace, where a purely computer-based attack on Libya, without the introduction of combat forces, was recently considered (and rejected) as a form of "active defense."[53] The Stuxnet virus launched against Iran may be another example of preventive attack. Whatever the merits of any of these tactics, the overall strategic picture is worrisome, as the world is now deep into an era of preventive war. In an atmosphere of global instability and hazy boundaries, the domestic and international legal framework for dealing with combat operations is being stretched to allow the US policymaker to accomplish whatever he or she wants to do, rather than to guide his or her choice of actions to begin with—and other leaders are watching.

One additional indicator of both the shift toward tactics and the blurring of boundaries is the dramatically increased role of US Special Forces. The United States has grown the size, role, and prominence of its special operations forces in counterterrorism, giving them responsibility for synchronizing military plans and carrying out operations against global terrorist networks. Spending by US Special Operations Command reportedly quadrupled between 2001 and 2011,[54] and the number of people employed (both military and civilian) doubled.[55] From 2001 to 2011, more than 80 per cent of the US Special Operations forces were deployed to the Middle East but, as the wars in Iraq and Afghanistan wind down, US Special Operations forces are expanding or deepening their global presence to deal with threats in regions such as Asia, Africa, and Latin America. American Special Forces now have a constellation of bases ringing Somalia, in Ethiopia, Djibouti, and Kenya, for example.[56] Commander of US Special Operations

Admiral William McRaven, the brilliant Navy Seal who penned the first post-9/11 counterterrorism strategy and oversaw the raid that killed Osama bin Laden, sought authority to take action outside normal Pentagon channels, developing what he called the "Global SOF Alliance," to enable US forces to be as agile as the enemy. According to ADM McRaven, Special Operations Command would work with diplomats and local security forces whenever possible, but "[t]he exception would be when a local government was unable or unwilling to cooperate with an authorized American mission, or if there was no responsible government in power with whom to work."[57]

The search for a perfect peace replaces reality

It is common for states, once they have embarked upon a war, to seek a level of security that is greater than what existed before the fighting began.[58] For the United States, the classic example was the decision to expand American war aims from July to September 1950 to include crossing the 38th parallel and eliminating the North Korean government in Pyongyang so as to establish a unified Korean state under non-Communist rule. No one wants to risk another 9/11 tragedy. But this war cannot end in total victory, meaning complete military success followed by total elimination of the terrorist threat. That is a fantasy.

The purpose of fighting often changes over the course of a war. Those who argue that the United States is far from defeating al-Qaeda cast US ends in expansive terms. At his July 2011 confirmation hearing before the Senate Intelligence Committee, new National Counterterrorism Center head Matthew Olsen said "he would define the strategic defeat of Al Qaeda as 'ending the threat that Al Qaeda and all of its affiliates pose to the United States and its interests around the world.'"[59] This is a gold standard yet to be met with other dangerous anti-American terrorist groups, including Hezbollah, Revolutionary Armed Forces of Colombia (FARC), and Kahane Chai, yet the United States is not at "war" with them. An open society is never totally invulnerable—another attack will occur, as the 2013 Boston Marathon bombing painfully demonstrated.

Examining the history of terrorism, the United States has been in a relatively safe period. After the tragedy of 9/11, the number of people who died from terrorist attacks in the United States from September 12, 2001 to the end of the decade was only 14 (in 129 incidents, including unsuccessful attempts), a remarkable achievement for American counterterrorism.[60] Each death was regrettable, but this was a tiny figure compared to earlier decades. During the 1970s, 160 people died in terrorist attacks in the United States, in 1,328 terrorist incidents.[61] In the 1980s, there were 44 fatalities (389 incidents), and in the 1990s 202 fatalities (328 incidents). In other words, in the nine years following the 9/11 attacks, the number of people who died from terrorist attacks (and attempted terrorist attacks) in the United States plummeted to the lowest number ever seen since these statistics began to be collected.

Others want a complete end to the threat of attacks anywhere, associated in any way with al-Qaeda. The 2013 Boston bombing, whose connection to al-Qaeda is contested, killed three and injured 264 others. The last major al-Qaeda attack on Western soil occurred in 2005 (the 7/7 London bombings). Completely ending the threat of additional attempts is impossible in the absence of complete annihilation (which would introduce additional ethical and practical problems).[62] The best the US can do is to employ vigilant counterterrorism intelligence, robust international cooperation, effective defense, the participation of a well-informed population, and carefully controlled operations against active, imminent threats.

There are key differences in how counterterrorism analysts define "winning" this war against al-Qaeda, and, to the extent that they guide future policy and determine what it means to achieve "peace," those differences have long-term strategic consequences for the United States. Should winning be defined as no terrorist attacks or attempted attacks on the US and its interests at all? Or no major terrorist attacks on US soil of the kind orchestrated by al-Qaeda on 9/11? If closer to the former, it is a standard that has not existed for the United States since 1970, when it began to keep decent records. If closer to the latter, the US may already be there. Should winning mean that no al-Qaeda "associate" is attacking anyone, anywhere? Or does it mean that the US and its allies have eliminated the al-Qaeda that attacked the United States, and prevented it from resurging? If closer to the former, the US will be forced into a perpetually tactical, reactive mode. If closer to the latter, it may shortly be achieved. Soon all of those directly involved in carrying out the 9/11 attacks will be either in custody or dead. It may be time to broaden the focus to other pressing strategic opportunities and problems—including other states and non-state actors more likely than al-Qaeda is to acquire or use weapons of mass destruction, for example. How the US expends its resources and manages this threat will be an important factor in whether or not it will consign al-Qaeda to the ash heap of history and lead as a great power that inspires others to follow into the twenty-first century. If Americans believe that anybody that calls himself or herself "al-Qaeda" has to be unable to hurt anybody for this war to end, then this war will never end.

Related to "winning" is the glaring need to build psychological resilience among the American people, so that they are less subject to being manipulated by threats of attacks. No campaign works well over the long term without effective defense, meaning not just homeland security but public resilience. American policymakers are human beings responding to widespread political pressure that the United States be kept completely invulnerable on their watch. "Zero risk" assigns them an impossible task while setting the bar for al-Qaeda too low. Al-Qaeda can kill people, yes. But it cannot win this "war" because that is at least partly up to the American people. Overreactions to actual or attempted terrorist attacks are a huge strategic vulnerability, heightening the incentive to orchestrate those attempts to begin with. As tragic as they are, the United States can absorb the kind of smaller attacks that al-Qaeda could now orchestrate (or inspire), and continue to lead the world economically, militarily, and politically in their aftermath.

Finding the exit

Some groups end by denouncing terrorism and going out of business, but that will not happen here. Many in the United States, Europe and elsewhere who believe that this war is endless point to the vicious Salafist ideology that existed before al-Qaeda and will endure long beyond the demise of that organization. Targeting the United States is one way to advance al-Qaeda's goals by damaging what it sees as the underlying support for so-called "infidel" regimes in the Arab World. Violent Salafist ideology and a desire to target the United States and its allies will go on for decades, and other groups will pick up those objectives. Anger at outside interference and intervention will continue long after bin Laden's death.

But al-Qaeda is neither an idea nor an ideology: It's a violent group of terrorists that the United States went to war against and has been pounding very effectively for more than a decade. The 2001 AUMF text (Section 2) reads: "[T]he President is authorized to use all necessary and appropriate force against those nations, organizations or persons he determines planned, authorized, committed or aided the terrorist attacks that occurred on September 11, 2001...." With that organization's defeat in sight, the goal should be to make their twisted ideology as irrelevant as Communism became after the fall of the Soviet Union. There are five things the US must do now to end this war.

First, it is long past time to reassess objectively the longer-term strategic implications of post-9/11 wartime legal measures, including the 2001 Authorization for the Use of Military Force, that are fast in danger of becoming permanent. For the United States, this war began with a remarkably broad authorization for the use of force by the Congress in the aftermath of the 9/11 tragedies. A decade later, a top priority of most Executive Branch officials (in both the Bush and Obama administrations) seems to be to preserve those wartime powers. In the evolving conflicts of the twenty-first century, some of them may be essential and warranted—every serving policymaker's rejoinder is that they are needed to protect American citizens from attack. That may or may not be true: The answer requires judging things that have not happened. Ending this war need not mean a return to the "law enforcement" paradigm that Americans believe made them vulnerable to surprise attacks; but it should restore some degree of peacetime scrutiny of Executive power. In his May 2013 speech on US counterterrorism policy, President Obama recognized the dangers of perpetual war and called for the repeal of the 2001 AUMF.[63] For the sake of the long-term well-being of the United States, it should immediately be reevaluated by a committee of knowledgeable bipartisan experts with no tie to either side of the argument, and then officially revoked or revised by Congress.

Second, policymakers must scrutinize the role of armed drones in our national strategy comprehensively and objectively, especially their impact on long-term American interests and the global implications of the precedent being set. While some argue for a new international legal regime governing drones, the likelihood of achieving meaningful consensus in time to affect ongoing rapid changes is infinitesimal. For the sake of their own national security, Americans must immediately confront the huge implications of the shift toward drones that is well underway in their own military and paramilitary forces, especially the evolving terms of their employment, the legal status both of the targeted and the targeters, the move toward using drones domestically, and the redistribution of resources toward drones and away from other priorities. The Obama Administration has been moving in this direction, particularly following the President's May 2013 speech; however, more must be done to recast the overall policy. The popular demand for perfect security against al-Qaeda terrorist attacks at home without more conventional military engagements abroad is fueling this technology-driven, tactical approach, but the long-term strategic implications are enormous. The US may be a strong enough power to deter the use of drones by other states on its soil, but does it really want to model behavior suggesting vigilante justice internationally? Is the future trademark of US global leadership to be a whining robot circling overhead? Do Americans really want to provide an excuse for Russia or China to name its enemies "terrorists" and then send drones across sovereign borders to kill them? In the United States, the argument has been that targeted killings are legal during wartime. Ending the state of war would bring with it a welcome reconsideration of the circumstances under which the use of lethal force by drones is or is not justified. The short-term benefits of using this tactic must be dispassionately compared against the long-term strategic costs for the United States.

Third, as the United States ends this war, it must also rebalance US counterterrorism policy. Being at war, the United States has naturally overemphasized and overresourced the military response to al-Qaeda at the expense of the non-military means. Decades of international experience with counterterrorism confirm that this emphasis on the use of military force has long-term disadvantages that will not serve American interests or security in the future. As part of its transition toward postwar normality, the United States must focus more energy on diplomacy and building the capacity of partner countries who are dealing with threats that also potentially threaten the US. In particular, enhancing the role of the Department of State in interagency efforts against counterterrorism is extremely important. The formal promotion of the State Department's Office for Combating Terrorism to a full Bureau of Counterterrorism in January 2012 was a step in the right direction toward enhancing its role in building international cooperation against terrorism through diplomatic channels.[64] The Pentagon has vastly overshadowed the State Department's resources and leverage in developing US counterterrorism policy, and this is the time to readjust toward a more viable long-term national strategy. Modeling balanced counterterrorism policies is the best way forward, including not just direct action when required, but also lower profile, longer-term, more prosaic efforts such as prison monitoring, counter-recruitment, countering document fraud, airport security, Internet monitoring, and jihadist chat-room infiltration.

Fourth, and related, the US government must do a better job of bringing its own costs and risks into sharper alignment, synching image and reality in the

What does it mean to win? 267

minds of Americans. Popular resilience is part of a winning strategy against al-Qaeda, and to build it the US government and its people must determine how to go from a state of war to a state of peace, meaning a realistic condition of normality. Ending the state of war against al-Qaeda will have an influence upon the US public psychologically and will shift the American narrative in ways that help the US government better adapt to ongoing global changes. That is not to say that "terrorism" will end. Three weeks after leaving office, outgoing Head of the National Counterterrorism Center Michael Leiter put it this way:

> The American people do need to understand that at least the smaller-scale terrorist attacks are with us for the foreseeable future.... The way that we fundamentally defeat that threat, which is very difficult to stop in its entirety, is to maintain a culture of resilience. Although this threat of terrorism is real and there will be tragic events that lead to the deaths of innocent people, it is not, in my view, an existential threat to our society.[65]

The President must openly and repeatedly say the same thing.

Continued cooperation on counterterrorism is vital. But lastly, the end of this war should bring with it a reassessment of US security commitments globally, with clear prioritization according to national interests. Why, for example, is the United States beefing up its military presence in Africa while simultaneously arguing that the future lies in a rebalancing to Asia? Such a strategic shift is impossible as long as it is willing to get sucked into local insurgencies by carrying out so-called "goodwill" attacks on behalf of governments in Yemen, Somalia, and Pakistan. US forces are reacting to short-term threats against those governments, rather than building a viable global presence to protect the United States and its longstanding allies.

Americans must stop living on adrenaline and build a sustainable future by ending this war and developing some concept of what normality means. The US goal for al-Qaeda must be to transition to where it is a manageable, albeit still dangerous, threat and American policymakers can focus more of their resources and attention on other priorities. Al-Qaeda has not ended. But its ability to launch a major attack against the United States has declined. Critics will argue that the enemy always has a vote. This is true; but does he have a veto? A major coordinated attack from abroad would be catastrophic; however, smaller terrorist attacks on US soil are inevitable and have been the reality for decades. The next time there is a small jihadist attack on American soil—inspired by the legacy of al-Qaeda or even orchestrated by one of its new "associates"—will Americans automatically extend this costly global war for another decade? The United States is not the first great power to meet a serious terrorist threat. Being constantly on the defensive diminishes its global role and stature. While elements of the US government must continue to aggressively counter al-Qaeda, staying on an endless wartime footing is self-defeating.

Notes

* This chapter was first published as Audrey Kurth Cronin (2013) The 'War on Terrorism'. What Does It Mean to Win? *Journal of Strategic Studies*, 37:2, 174–197. Reproduced with permission of Taylor & Francis.
1 See Cronin (2006, 7–48) and Cronin (2009).
2 These include Rose (2010), Reiter (2009) and Moten (2011).
3 Howard (2008) and Heymann (2003). See also Klein (2010), Ackerman (2004) and Manningham-Buller (2011).
4 Bradley and Goldsmith (2005).
5 US Declaration of State of War with Japan (1941) and Declaration of State of War with Germany (1941).
6 Belasco (2011, 5). Of the $1.121 trillion enacted in the "Global War on Terror" by 2010, about $1.1 trillion went to the Department of Defense.
7 The war in Iraq had its own legislation (Authorization for the Use of Military Force Against Iraq Resolution of 2002). Although presented as part of the response to 9/11, the Bush administration realized it was to some degree separate.
8 Cronin (2013).
9 See Strachan and Afflerbach (2012).
10 Bradley and Goldsmith (2005, 2066–2067).
11 See Chapter II, Paragraphs 7 and 21, in Sun Zi (1963, 73 and 76).
12 Speech by the Athenians to the Spartan assembly, 432 BC, The Peloponnesian War, 1.78 [3], translated by Richard Crawley, in Strassler (1996, 44).
13 von Clausewitz (1976, 143). Clausewitz also warns the reader "war is no pastime ... it is a serious means to a serious end" and "[t]he original means of strategy is victory—that is, tactical success; its ends, in the final analysis, are those objects which will lead directly to peace" (Book 1, Section 23, 86).
14 Fuller (1923, 215).
15 Liddell Hart (1954 and 1967, 322).
16 Iklé (2005).
17 Michael Sheehan, Assistant Secretary of Defense for Special Operations, testifying before the Senate Armed Services Committee, May 16, 2013. See "Pentagon: US Still in Armed Conflict with al-Qaeda" (2013).
18 For another perspective on what "winning" means, see Gordon (2007).
19 Kilcullen (2005).
20 Habeck (2012).
21 But not all. The United States seems to be interested only in insurgencies that are linked to al-Qaeda in some way. Kurlantzick (2012).
22 These subheadings are drawn from the arguments in Iklé (2005).
23 von Clausewitz (1976, Book One, Chapter One, 89).
24 Brennan (2012).
25 Priest and Arkin (2010).
26 Ibid.
27 Mazetti (2011).
28 Painter and Lake (2012). See Table 3, DHS Appropriations, FY2003–FY2012, 7.
29 US Department of Homeland Security (2012).
30 Copeland (2011, 21).
31 US General Accountability Office (2012).
32 Reese (2010).
33 Halsey (2011).
34 Ibid.
35 Cronin (2010).
36 Iklé (2005, 14–15).
37 Shane (2009).

38 Bumiller and Shanker (2011) and "'PlayStation pilots' are taking over from the top guns as Air Force switches priorities United States" (2012).
39 New America Foundation (2013). The Bureau of Investigative Journalism (2012) also provides a comparable estimated range of drone strikes.
40 Johnson (2012, 6) and Becker and Shane (2012).
41 The Bureau of Investigative Journalism (2013). Strikes in Yemen have included more traditional cruise missiles and Harrier fighter jets, as well. Shane, Mazzetti, and Worth (2010).
42 The Bureau of Investigative Journalism (2012).
43 Naylor (2011).
44 Shane et al. (2010). See also Mazetti (2013).
45 Iklé (2005, 2).
46 Becker and Shane (2012).
47 Cronin (2013).
48 Iklé (2005, 2).
49 Bazan (2002).
50 Gellman (2001).
51 This was the case, for example, in the secret war in East Africa. Reluctant to put captives on trial, the US reportedly rendered captives to a CIA clandestine prison in Afghanistan. Naylor (2011).
52 Shane et al. (2010).
53 Shanker (2011).
54 The exact figures are in dispute. See Waller (2011).
55 Schmitt, Mazzetti and Shanker (2012).
56 Gettleman et al. (2012).
57 Schmitt et al. (2012).
58 Iklé (2005, 9). Reiter (2009, 66).
59 Schmitt (2011).
60 The Global Terrorism Database (2015).
61 These numbers were reached by searching the database for incidents between 1970 and 1979 (or 1980–1989, 1990–1999, etc.), in the United States, with all criteria for terrorism, and all incidents included regardless of doubt. The post-9/11 search was September 12, 2001–December 31, 2010. The number of fatalities for the decade 2000–2010 (with the 9/11 attacks) was 3011 in 184 incidents.
62 Perhaps not even then. See Cronin (2009), Chapter 5: Repression: Crushing Terrorism with Force.
63 "Remarks by the President at the National Defense University" (2013).
64 Benjamin (2012).
65 Schmitt (2011).

Bibliography

Ackerman, Bruce, "This is Not a War," *Yale Law Journal* 113/8 (June 2004), 1871–1907.
Bazan, Elizabeth B., Assassination Ban and EO 12333: A Brief Summary, CRS Report for Congress RS21037, January 4, 2002, https://archive.org/details/allegedassassina00unit.
Becker, Jo and Scott Shane, "Secret 'kill list' proves a test of Obama's principles and will," *New York Times*, May 29, 2012.
Belasco, Amy, The Cost of Iraq, Afghanistan, and Other Global War on Terror Operations Since 9/11, CRS Report for Congress RL33110, March 29, 2011.
Benjamin, Daniel, "Establishment of the Bureau of Counterterrorism," Special Briefing at the US Department of State, January 4, 2012, www.state.gov/j/ct/rls/rm/2012/180148.htm.

Bradley, Curtis A. and Jack L. Goldsmith, "Congressional Authorization and the War on Terrorism," *Harvard Law Review* 118 (2005), 2047–2133.
Brennan, John O., "The Ethics and Efficacy of the President's Counterterrorism Strategy," April 30, 2012, www.wilsoncenter.org/event/the-efficacy-and-ethics-us-counterterrorism-strategy/#.
Bumiller, Elisabeth and Thom Shanker, "War evolves with drones, some tiny as bugs," *New York Times*, June 20, 2011.
The Bureau of Investigative Journalism, Somalia: Reported US Covert Actions 2001–2012, February 22, 2012, www.thebureauinvestigates.com/2012/02/22/get-the-data-somalias-hidden-war/.
The Bureau of Investigative Journalism, Yemen 2002–2013: US Covert Action, September 26, 2013, www. thebureauinvestigates.com/blog/category/projects/drones/drones-graphs/.
Copeland, Curtis W., The Federal Workforce: Characteristics and Trends, CRS Report for Congress RL34685, April 19, 2011, https://opencrs.com/document/RL34685/.
Cronin, Audrey Kurth, "How Al Qaeda Ends: The Decline and Demise of Terrorist Groups," *International Security* 31/1 (Summer 2006), 7–48.
Cronin, Audrey Kurth, *How Terrorism Ends: Understanding the Decline and Demise of Terrorist Campaigns* (Princeton: Princeton UP 2009).
Cronin, Audrey Kurth, "The Evolution of Counterterrorism: Will Tactics Trump Strategy?," *International Affairs* 86/4 (July 2010), 837–856.
Cronin, Audrey Kurth, "Why Drones Fail," *Foreign Affairs* 91/4 (July/August 2013), 44–54.
Fuller, J. F. C., *The Reformation of War* (New York: E.P. Dutton 1923).
Gellman, Barton, "CIA contemplates assassination jobs," *Washington Post*, October 28, 2001.
Gettleman, Jeffrey, Eric Schmitt and Thom Schranker., "US swoops in and frees two in Somali raid," *New York Times*, January 26, 2012.
The Global Terrorism Database, National Consortium for the Study of Terrorism and Responses to Terrorism (START), University of Maryland, 2015, www.start.umd.edu/gtd/.
Gordon, Philip H., "Can the War on Terror Be Won?," *Foreign Affairs* 86/6 (November/December 2007), 53–66.
Habeck, Mary, "Can We Declare the War on Al Qaeda Over?", Foreign Policy.com, 27 June, 2012, http://shadow.foreignpolicy.com/posts/2012/06/27/can_we_declare_the_war_on_al_qaeda_over.
Halsey, Ashley, "Decaying infrastructure costs US billions each year," *Washington Post*, July 27, 2011.
Heymann, Philip B., *Terrorism, Freedom and Security: Winning Without War* (Cambridge, MA: The MIT Press 2003).
Howard, Michael, "Are We at War?," The 2008 Alastair Buchan Memorial Lecture, London, April 6, 2008; published in Survival 50/4 (August–September 2008), 247–256.
Iklé, Fred Charles, *Every War Must End*, 1971, 2nd revised edition (New York: Columbia UP 2005).
Johnson, Gregory D., "A Profile of AQAP's Upper Echelon," *CTC Sentinel* 5/7 (July 2012).
Kilcullen, David J., "Countering Global Insurgency," *Journal of Strategic Studies* 28/4 (August 2005), 597–617.

Klein, Adam, "The End of Al Qaeda? Rethinking the Legal End of the War on Terror," *Columbia Law Review* 110/7 (November 2010), 1865–1910.

Kurlantzick, Joshua, "Thailand's war without an audience," *Boston Globe*, July 22, 2012.

Liddell Hart, B.H., *Strategy* (London: Faber and Faber 1954 and 1967).

Manningham-Buller, Eliza, "Lecture one: 'Terror,' BBC Reith Lectures 2011: Securing Freedom," September 6, 2011.

Mazetti, Mark, "Former spy with agenda operates a private CIA," *New York Times*, January 22, 2011.

Mazetti, Mark, *The Way of the Knife: The CIA, a Secret Army, and a War at the Ends of the Earth* (New York: Penguin 2013).

Moten, Matthew (ed.), *Between War and Peace: How America Ends its Wars* (New York: Free Press 2011).

Naylor, Sean D., "The Secret War: African Ops May Be Just Starting," *Army Times*, December 5, 2011, www.armytimes.com/news/2011/12/army-africa-mission-may-bejust-starting-120511w/.

New America Foundation, "The Drone War in Pakistan: Analysis," September 26, 2013, http://natsec. newamerica.net/drones/pakistan/analysis.

Painter, William L. and Jennifer E. Lake, Homeland Security Department: FY 2012 Appropriations, CRS Report for Congress R41982, February 21, 2012, http://assets.opencrs.com/rpts/R41982_20120221.pdf

"Pentagon: US Still in Armed Conflict with al-Qaeda," *Military Times*, May 16, 2013, www.militarytimes.com/article/20130516/NEWS/305160010/Pentagon-U-S-still-armed-conflict-al-Qaida.

"'PlayStation pilots' are taking over from the top guns as Air Force switches priorities United States," *The Times* (of London), August 2, 2012.

Priest, Dana and William M. Arkin, "A hidden world, growing beyond control," *Washington Post*, July 19, 2010.

Reese, Shawn, FY 2011 Department of Homeland Security Assistance to States and Localities, CRS Report for Congress R40632, April 26, 2010, www.fas.org/sgp/crs/homesec/R41105.pdf.

Reiter, Dan, *How Wars End* (Princeton: Princeton UP 2009).

"Remarks by the President at the National Defense University," Fort McNair, Washington, DC, May 23, 2013, www.whitehouse.gov.

Rose, Gideon, *How Wars End: Why We Always Fight the Last Battle* (New York: Simon and Schuster 2010).

Ross, Alice K and Jack Serle, "Get the data: What the drones strike," May 23, 2014, www.thebureauinvestigates.com/category/projects/drones/drones-graphs/.

Schmitt, Eric, "Ex-counterterrorism aide warns against complacency on Al Qaeda," *New York Times*, July 28, 2011, www.nytimes.com/2011/07/29/world/29leiter.html.

Schmitt, Eric, Mark Mazzetti and Thom Shanker, "Admiral seeks freer hand in deployment of elite forces," *New York Times*, February 12, 2012.

Shane, Scott, "CIA to expand use of drones in Pakistan," *New York Times*, December 4, 2009.

Shane, Scott, Mark Mazzetti and Robert F. Worth, "Secret assault on terrorism widens on two continents," *New York Times*, August 14, 2010.

Shanker, Thom, "US weighs its strategy on warfare in cyberspace," *New York Times*, October 19, 2011.

Strachan, Hew and Holger Afflerbach (eds), *Why Fighting Ends: A History of Surrender* (Oxford: Oxford UP 2012).

Strassler, Robert B. (ed.), *The Landmark Thucydides: A Comprehensive Guide to the Peloponnesian War*, translated by Richard Crawley (New York: Free Press 1996).

Sun Zi, *The Art of War*, translated by Samuel B. Griffith (Oxford: Oxford UP 1963).

US Congress, Senate Select Committee to Study Governmental Operations with Respect to Intelligence Activities, Alleged Assassination Plots Involving Foreign Leaders, November 20, 1975, https://archive.org/details/allegedassassina00unit.

US Declaration of State of War with Japan, December 8, 1941; and Declaration of State of War with Germany, December 11, 1941, http://avalon.law.yale.edu/subject_menus/decmenu.asp.

US Department of Homeland Security, Department of Homeland Security Strategic Plan: Fiscal Years 2012–2016, Washington, DC, February 2012, 3, www.dhs.gov/xlibrary/assets/dhsstrategic-plan-fy-2012-2016.pdf.

US General Accountability Office, Actions Needed to Reduce Overlap and Potential Unnecessary Duplication, Achieve Cost Savings, and Strengthen Mission Functions, Report GAO-12-464T, March 8, 2012, www.gao.gov/products/GAO-12-464T.

von Clausewitz, Carl, *On War*, edited and translated by Michael Howard and Peter Paret (Princeton: Princeton UP 1976).

Waller, Douglas, "Special Operations Spending Quadruples," Bloomberg, June 7, 2011, www.bloomberg.com/news/2011-06-07/special-operations-spending-quadruples-with-commandodemand.html.

Conclusion

Charles Webel

Ending the war of the world: antiterrorism as a viable alternative to the GWOT

What has happened since 9/11?

Since 9/11, the US-led counterterrorist strategy initiated by the Bush administration and largely preserved by Obama's has:

1 Been apparently effective in preventing another major terrorist attack by radical Islamists on US soil, except for the small-scale attacks during the Boston Marathon and in Orlando and San Bernardino.
2 Resulted in the widely-publicized killings of Osama bin-Laden, Saddam Hussein, Anwar al-Awlaki, leaders and members of ISIS, the Taliban, and other icons of international terror, and initially drove the Taliban from power in Afghanistan.
3 Installed ostensibly "friendly" and "democratic" governments in Iraq and Afghanistan.

But this counterterrorist strategy has also:

1 Been largely ineffective in reducing the global incidence and lethality of terrifying acts of political violence, which have skyrocketed since 9/11;
2 At the same time, terrorist groups have grown and spread;
3 Lost freedoms in the US have not been restored;
4 US-led wars continue to be waged in many countries.
5 Furthermore, amid huge increases in military spending and big profits for military contractors and armaments manufacturers, many Western economies remain dysfunctional, tottering on the edge of catastrophe.

Based on such circumstances, most Americans do not feel more secure now than on September 10, 2001. Instead, "a majority of Americans believes that over the last decade the US over-invested resources in some of the responses to the 9/11 attacks and that this over-investment has contributed to America's economic problems today," and two in three believe US power and influence have diminished in the world over the last decade.[1]

The victims and costs of the GWOT

Since the beginning of the GWOT, terrorist attacks have dramatically increased outside the US According to the *2015 Global Terrorism Index* and the National Consortium for the Study of Terrorism and Responses to Terrorism (START), there have been stunning recent and post-9/11 increases (up to 900 percent since 2000) in the global number of people who have died from terrorist attacks perpetrated by non-state actors (to about 33,000 in 2014, the highest level recorded); in the incidence of such attacks (up 80 percent from 2013 to 2014, to its highest-ever recorded level); in the global economic costs of "containing" terrorism (c. $53 billion in 2014, also the highest level ever); in the number of hostages taken by non-state terrorist organizations; in the number of perpetrator fatalities, and in the number of mass-fatality (>100 non-combatant deaths) terrorist incidents (up about 400 percent since 9/11).[2]

According to the *2015 Global Terrorism Index*, the most frequent perpetrators of TFB attacks in 2014 were the Islamic State, Al-Shabab (these two groups accounting for more than half the global total of victims of identifiable terrorist groups), Boko Haram, and the Donetsk People's Army; and the countries most victimized were Iraq, Pakistan, Afghanistan, Syria, Nigeria, India, Ukraine, Somalia, Yemen, Libya, and the Philippines. Iraq, for example, in 2014 had the highest level of terrorism ever recorded in a single country for one year—9,929 deaths—which is more than the cumulative total of fatalities from terrorism in the entire world from 1998 to 2000. Globally, the overwhelming majority of victims of contemporary terrorism from below are Muslims; and currently (in contrast to pre-9/11), so are the majority of identifiable perpetrators.

As of the end of 2014, officially about 8,543 coalition troops had been killed in the wars in Afghanistan and Iraq. The US-led Multinational Force (MNA) in Iraq, the NATO International Security Assistance Force (ISAF) in Afghanistan, and the US Operation Enduring Freedom (OEF-A), also in Afghanistan, have carefully kept a running total of fatalities they have suffered: 4,804 MNA soldiers died in Iraq between March 2003 and February 2012, the date when the US body counting stopped. As of the end of 2014, 3,485 ISAF and OEF soldiers had lost their lives in Afghanistan since 2001. Since US and other foreign military boots are only intermittently and secretly on the ground in Pakistan, mainly in the northern tribal areas, there are no body count statistics for coalition force casualties available for that conflict zone.

Officially ignored are casualties—injured or killed—involving "enemy combatants" and civilians. In their joint report called *Body Count: Casualty Figures after 10 Years of the War on Terror*, Physicians for Social Responsibility, Physicians for Global Survival, and the Nobel Prize-winning International Physicians for the Prevention of Nuclear War concluded that this number is staggering, with at least 1.3 million lives lost in Iraq, Afghanistan, and Pakistan alone since the onset of the war following September 11, 2001. However, the report notes, this is a conservative estimate, and the total number killed in the three countries "could also be in excess of two million, whereas a figure below one million is extremely unlikely." Furthermore, the researchers do not look at other countries targeted by US-led war, including Yemen, Somalia, Libya, and beyond. Still, the report states the figure "is approximately 10 times greater than that of which the public, experts and decision makers are aware of and propagated by the media and major NGOs." Importantly, this report does not include deaths among the estimated three million Iraqi refugees, or the millions of Syrian refugees and the estimated 300,000+ Syrian fatalities since Syria's civil war commenced in 2011.

Furthermore, in addition to the approximately one million Iraqi lives lost since the 2003 US invasion, an estimated 220,000 people have been killed in Afghanistan and 80,000 in Pakistan, note the researchers. Similarly, a United Nations report finds that civilian deaths in Afghanistan in 2014 were at their highest levels since the global body began making reports in 2009. These researchers identified direct and indirect deaths based on UN, government, and NGO data, as well as individual studies.[3]

Other researchers report fewer casualties, claiming that at least 150,000 civilians have been killed in Iraq; more than 26,000 in Afghanistan; and at least 21,000 in Pakistan as a result of direct violence as the war in Afghanistan spilled into Pakistan.[4] In Afghanistan, Iraq, Pakistan, Yemen, Somalia, and Syria, millions of persons have been rendered homeless; additional millions continue to suffer from shortages of food, clean water, medicine, electricity, and jobs; and many of them have encamped in Jordan, Lebanon, and Turkey, or are fleeing to Western Europe, engendering in early 2015 the "refugee crisis." Hence, terrorist activity is also a significant driver of refugee activity and internal displacement. The countries that are the greatest sources of refugees and internally displaced people (IDPs) also suffer the most deaths from terrorism, with 10 of the 11 countries that had more than 500 deaths from terrorism in 2014 having the highest levels of refugees and IDPs.

Accordingly, the overwhelming majority of deaths from terrorism *do not occur in the West*. Excluding the September 11 attack, only 0.5 per cent of deaths from TFB have occurred in the West since 2000. Including September 11, the percentage of Western terrorism victims reaches 2.6 percent, mostly (70 percent) victims of lone-wolf perpetrators (except for 9/11), with the other perpetrators being unknown or groups with more than three attackers.

Islamic fundamentalism has *not* been the main cause of terrorism *in the West* during the past decade or so. Eighty percent of deaths by lone-wolf terrorists in the West were driven by right-wing extremism, nationalism, antigovernment sentiment, and by political extremism and other forms of supremacy. The death toll from jihadist terrorism on American soil since the September 11 attacks—45 people (including the 14 victims of the attacks in San Bernardino, CA, in late 2015)—is fewer than the 48 killed in terrorist attacks motivated by white supremacist and other right-wing extremist ideologies, according to New America, a research organization in Washington, D.C.[5]

Additionally, the financial costs of the GWOT have been extremely high. Official US government sources (notably the Office of Management and Budget, or OMB) state that nearly $1.7 trillion has been spent, or is budgeted for, the War on Terror from 2001 through 2016. These are supplemental funds that are in addition to the base budget for the Department of Defense, plus departments that support the War on Terror (Homeland Security, the Veterans Administration, and the State Department).[6] But according to a Harvard University Kennedy School of Government 2013 report, the actual cost of the GWOT from 9/11 until early 2013 was approximately $6 trillion, thus accounting for roughly 20 per cent of the total amount added to the US national debt between 2001 and 2012.[7] And the Nobel Prize-winning economist Joseph Stiglitz estimated the GWOT cost in Iraq alone as exceeding $3 trillion as of mid-2010.[8]

Furthermore, drone, missile, bombing attacks, and other state-sponsored military actions continue to take a toll on civilians. Globally, tens of thousands of innocent persons have been detained by coalition military and security forces, usually without charges and without legal representation, and often without being given minimal standards of humanitarian care. Increased security measures within the United States have by-passed constitutional rights and judicial processes, as is the case with domestic and international wiretapping, surveillance, and spying.

The real killers

In the 15 years of the war on terrorism, the number of deaths on American soil due to terrorist attacks remains at the approximately 3,000 killed on 9/11, averaging out to about 200 deaths per year. From a utilitarian perspective of seeking the greatest good for the greatest number of persons, the high costs of the war on terrorism (most notably, the approximately 8,500 deaths of coalition troops, which averages to about 570 per year, and do not include contractor casualties) are hard to justify based on 200 terrorist-caused deaths per year in the US, when compared to examples of four possibly preventable causes of death that kill at least half a million Americans each year, but which are not afforded a level of national and global attention and resources proportionate to what have been devoted to fighting TFB.

The four categories accounting for at least 531,000 deaths *annually* in the United States are:

1 abuse and neglect causing the deaths of more than 1,740 children;
2 vehicle-related accidents, causing at least 43,000 deaths;
3 medical errors, causing a minimum of 44,000 deaths (possibly more than 100,00); and
4 the use of tobacco, causing 443,000 deaths.[9]

And globally it is estimated that approximately 1.5 million persons will die of tuberculosis this year.[10]

Finally, while the number of civilians victimized by TFB attacks has risen dramatically outside the US since 9/11, approximately 13 times as many people (at least 437,000) are killed globally by homicides than die in terrorist attacks (about 33,000).[11] Furthermore, the costs from officially-designated terrorist attacks are lower than from other forms of violence. The economic losses from violent crime and homicide globally were 32 times greater than losses from terrorism in 2014. And according to the 2016 Global Peace Index, the price tag on global violence added up to $13.6 trillion in 2015, or 13.3 percent of gross world product. On the other hand, investments in peacekeeping and peacebuilding, in contrast, totaled $15 billion.[12]

The GWOT and the politics of fear

Promises that costly national security actions will save unknown numbers of hypothetical persons from potential threats at an unspecified future time sharply differ from the human security priority to protect real persons from actual harms. Citing the interests of national security and self-defense, states make the utilitarian claim that the potential benefits of military violence outweigh the costs.

Accordingly, as tempting as it may be to view the absence of large-scale successful terrorist attacks in the United States after September 11 as evidence that the War on Terror has "succeeded" (at least in part) in its primary mission to protect the United States, there is no demonstrable causal relationship between the war on terrorism and the absence of large-scale successful domestic terrorist attacks since it began—there may have been no successful major additional attacks on the US even if the war had never been waged—and *nonmilitary reasons*, such as good police work and intelligence, may be responsible for this.

But the disproportionate focus Western government-designated terrorist attacks draw in the mass media and their effect on public fear lead to overreactions by governmental, military, and police officials, as well as by vigilantes. That fact that virtually all mainstream Western media and politicians focus on the comparatively small number of Muslim "terrorists from below"—in contrast to the much larger number of victims of state and/or state-sponsored "terrorism from above"—may contribute to the kind of anger and alienation that creates more potential for terrorist recruitment.

Counterterrorism does not counter terrorism: might a law-enforcement strategy be an effective alternative?

The realpolitik strategy of waging a global war cloaked as counterterrorism, put into effect in September 2001—a decade and a half ago—has not defeated radical Islamism, has resulted in, at a minimum, hundreds of thousands of casualties, has led to a global clash between extremist elements within Western and Islamist civilizations, and threatens to escalate to a war of the world in which non-state terrorists and state counterterrorists may both employ weapons of mass destruction. Consequently, it is clear that the GWOT, as a primarily military effort to defeat al-Qaeda and the Islamic State as well as their "affiliates" and "lone-wolf" emulators, and to subdue the Taliban and other insurgents, is not succeeding now and is not likely to succeed in "defeating" "Global Terrorism" in the future.

All wars, including the GWOT, are costly. The disheartening fact that each year brings many thousands of civilian war deaths worldwide points to an urgent need to reconsider the efficacy of lethal military solutions.[13] This applies particularly to what Pope Francis has called the "Third World War," the GWOT.

But in part because terrorists are not manifested in the government of a particular country, against which a declaration of war could be declared, or which could ever be clearly defeated, such a "war" can never be definitively won. The GWOT therefore threatens (or, for its supporters, promises) to go on indefinitely.

Unfortunately, the dominant war narrative, unquestioningly assuming that the "best" and perhaps "only" way to "counter" terrorist violence from below with greater state-initiated counterterrorism violence "from above," is accepted without question in much of the advanced industrial world today and acts as a filter through which the frequency and severity of recent wars and "terrorist" threats tend to be narrowly construed as evidence of this narrative's validity. Without the influence of that narrative, past and ongoing wars might be regarded as evidence of the catastrophic failure of lethal force to save lives and resolve political conflicts. This recognition might free decision-makers to seek, and the public to demand, solutions that have demonstrated long-term efficacy in preventing, reducing, and resolving violent conflicts.

A peace-oriented perspective condemns not only terrorist attacks but also any violent response to them. It is tempting to conclude that under such circumstances, violence is always counterproductive. Nonetheless, an alternative view also deserves respect. Consider a country that refuses to respond forcefully after large numbers of its citizens are attacked. It must be acknowledged that well-meaning, well-informed people honestly disagree as to whether such a policy might actually encourage more attacks, resulting in reduced overall security. Although vengeance is not highly regarded by most civilized persons, justice is.

Accordingly, the best response to such terrible events is often maddeningly unclear, and should not be made precipitously, in the heat of the moment. One course of nonviolent action might be for such international organizations as the United Nations and the International Court of Justice to be empowered to bring to justice the perpetrators of such crimes against humanity as acts of terrorism involving the mass murder of civilians. Implied in such an approach is that "terrorism" should evoke a response involving international police activity, and that "terrorists" should be brought to justice in the same way as other alleged law-breakers.

What might be done to decrease terrifying political violence and to increase human security?

One component of a long-term strategy for decreasing both TFB and TFA would be for the West to recognize that occupation, historically and currently, is probably the principal political reason for terrorist attacks against the occupying powers and their citizens locally and globally. Therefore, the United States, France, Great Britain, Russia, Turkey, and Saudi Arabia, inter alia, might seriously consider dramatically altering their Middle East strategic policy. This would probably necessitate the withdrawal of all Western combat forces from the countries in the region and the redeployment of some of those forces off-shore—until a comprehensive Middle East peace plan could be negotiated by all the affected parties, whereupon those forces would be permanently withdrawn.

Sustainable peace and lasting conflict resolution involve the development and implementation of effective strategies and policies that de-escalate the cycles of violence, promote universal human rights and justice for all, and institutionalize effective nonviolent methods of conflict prevention and transformation. International efforts will be needed to increase "peace literacy" (understanding of these concepts and how they can be applied) in decision-makers and the general public.

Additionally, efforts to encourage best practices in journalism and to promote and protect freedom of the press can provide essential support for nonviolent conflict prevention, conflict resolution, and peace-building policies and practices. A strong, free press dedicated to communicating vital information to the public remains one of the best safeguards against the violence of terrorism and tyranny.

Moreover, Western nations need to make more sustained efforts more fully to integrate Islamic and other immigrants, particularly disaffected young men, and also to wean themselves gradually from dependence on Middle East oil. If successful, the West would then be more insulated from its current perceived need to intervene in Arab and other Muslim states.

Accordingly, there should be much greater human and financial investments in working on the ground with youth, particularly with young Muslim men living in Western cultures who might be tempted to "surf for the sublime," as the anthropologist Scott Atran calls it, in order to address their feelings of alienation and their needs for empowerment, excitement, and group camaraderie.[14]

Atran further claims that:

> Unless we understand these powerful cultural forces, we will fail to address the threat. When, as now, the focus is on military solutions and police interdiction, matters have already gone way too far. If that focus remains, we lose the coming generation. So what might be done? Foremost, continue the important work on problems of development, and on immigration and integration, with the goal of transforming the much-lamented "youth bulge" into a "youth boom" by unleashing youth's inherent energy and idealism...[15]

And as an alternative to the West's vain militaristic efforts to "defeat" militant Islamism, and to prevent further terrorist attacks in Europe and North America by disaffected, "radicalized" Muslim young people, Atran proposes that we:

1   Offer youth something that makes them dream, a life of significance achieved through struggle and sacrifice in comradeship. Sacred values must be fought with other sacred values, or by sundering the social networks in which those values are embedded.
2   Offer youth a positive personal dream, with a concrete chance of realization.
3   Offer youth the chance to create their own local initiatives.[16]

Atran concludes that:

> Social science research[17] shows that local initiatives, begun with small-scale involvement, are better than national and large-scale programs in reducing violence. Imagine a global archipelago of such peace builders: if you can find concrete ways to help and empower them without trying too hard to control them, they could well win the future.

Negotiations between terrorists from below and from above?

Additionally, the Western powers, Turkey, and Russia need to reconsider their official stance of refusing to negotiate with "terrorists." Unfortunately, at the present time direct negotiations between the major adversaries—the US, Great Britain, France, Turkey, Russia and their allies du jour on the one hand, and a shifting congeries of radical Islamist cells ostensibly directed and/or inspired by ISIS, al-Qaeda etc., on the other hand—seem unlikely.

But that was also the case for much of the twentieth century in Northern Ireland and Great Britain. Then came the Good Friday Agreement of 1998, which officially disarmed the "terrorist" IRA organization and brought a fragile peace to Ireland.

Similarly, in 1962, after bloody eight-year war between French government-sponsored TFA and FLN (the Algerian National Liberation Front) TFB, the two sides negotiated France's withdrawal from Algeria.

And few thought that apartheid in South Africa would end peacefully. But after almost a half century of struggle, sometimes armed, in the early 1990s, the African National Congress (ANC)—another one-time "terrorist" organization—and the Afrikaner-led government in Pretoria negotiated a relatively nonviolent transition to black rule and to national reconciliation as well.

The PLO, a longtime "terrorist group" in the eyes of many Israelis and Americans, and the Israeli government has been negotiating for decades, and they appeared to reach a framework for a settlement of their conflict in 1993, in Oslo, Norway. The framework for that aborted agreement might be revived during bilateral Israeli/Palestinian or multilateral talks. It is also probably only a matter of time before Hamas, yet another "terrorist," but democratically elected organization, is also brought into the peace process.

But the mutual demonization of the "evil enemy" by American administrations and by such militant, violent Islamists as ISIS presents formidable challenges not present in the cases just cited. So does the fact that it is difficult to negotiate directly with an adversary far away, decentralized, and without a nation-state to call home.

However, on more than one occasion, al-Qaeda has publicly indicated its willingness to suspend hostilities and to declare a kind of truce with its Western (and Islamic) adversaries. Western governments have officially refused to take up this invitation. But that was also the case for years with the IRA, the ANC, and, more recently, with one spoke of the "axis of evil," North Korea, with whom a temporary nuclear agreement was reached in 2007. And, perhaps ever more unexpectedly, the West and Iran reached an agreement in 2015 to freeze Iran's development of nuclear materials capable of weaponization in return for the termination of crippling sanctions against that Islamic Republic and for the release of Iran's frozen funds.

Good-faith negotiations between the Western powers (possibly including Turkey, Russia, and Saudi Arabia) and militant Islamists—possibly through back-channels conducted by third parties, such as the Arab League, the Organization of the Islamic Conference, and the UN—may or may not result in a reduction of terrorist attacks and counterterrorist operations. But the alternative—an open-ended global conflict with the potential to escalate to the use of nuclear and other weapons of mass destruction—may be so cataclysmic as to warrant that any and all nonviolent efforts should be made to end the "War on Terror."

Certainly, any policy—military, diplomatic, and/or economic—must be chosen with the greatest care and with the utmost respect for human life. And this policy should be based on an understanding and analysis of when, where, how, and why officially designated "terrorist" groups (from below) have ended.

Seeking an alternative to the GWOT: how do terrorist groups end?

There is an alternative to an unending GWOT. To understand what might be a viable, mostly nonviolent alternative to the GWOT, it is essential to know how terrorist groups have ended.

In 2008, at the request of the US House Armed Services Committee, researchers for the RAND Corporation presented the results of a comprehensive study for "Defeating Terrorist Groups," by Seth Jones and Martin Libicki.[18] The RAND researchers examined 648 US-designated terrorist groups between 1968 and 2006. They defined:

> a terrorist group ... as a collection of individuals belonging to a non-state entity that uses terrorism to achieve its objectives. Such an entity has at least some command and control apparatus that, no matter how loose or flexible, provides an overall organizational structure.[19]

Jones and Libicki provide many examples of former terrorist groups which, by cooperating with governments on collective or individual agreements, ceasefires, and peace settlements, have been more successful in achieving their political goals than through the use of force alone. Governments are much more likely to reduce terrorist violence and eliminate insurgencies by reaching political accommodations with their adversaries than by counterterrorist and counterinsurgency military and paramilitary operations.

The RAND researchers found that terrorist groups end for two major reasons: They decide to adopt nonviolent tactics and join the political process, or local law-enforcement agencies arrest or kill key members of the group. "Military force has rarely been the primary reason that terrorist groups end, and few groups have ended by achieving victory."[20] Violence, whether "from below" or "from above," unaccompanied by dialogue, is almost always a losing strategy for all sides.

Another key finding of the RAND report was that the number of terrorist attacks attributed to al-Qaeda went up dramatically between 2002 and 2007, even after excluding from their analysis such attacks in Iraq and Afghanistan. This trend has not been reversed since then, with the Islamic State. Al-Shabab, and Boko Haram replacing al-Qaeda as the principal perpetrators of Middle-Eastern and African TFB, thereby casting into further doubt the efficacy of the primarily military means used in attempting to achieve key goals of the "War on Terror."

Social scientific data accordingly indicate that the incorporation of official terrorist groups in the political process combined with the efforts of police and intelligence services to prevent terrorist attacks result in a success rate (ending terrorist actions) greater than other, more militaristic strategies. So why shouldn't this primarily nonviolent antiterrorist strategy replace the primarily violent, but largely unsuccessful, counterterrorist strategy of the GWOT?

Antiterrorism: a viable alternative to the GWOT?

Antiterrorism is an ethical and possibly effective alternative to the largely unethical and ineffective counterterrorist strategy of the GWOT.

According to Haig Khatchadourian, antiterrorism refers to:

> The administrative, police, psychological resources, tactics, equipment, security, judicial, and political measures employed by governments ... designed to prevent terrorist attacks.... Antiterrorist measures include the use of judicial and penal systems as a whole to bring terrorists to justice. Thus antiterrorism has both a deterrent and a punitive aspect: to deter and so to prevent terrorism, to apprehend and bring to justice suspected terrorists, and to punish convicted terrorists.... *Therefore, antiterrorist measures and strategies are, ideally speaking, nonviolent and in accord ... with extant international law.*[21]

Antiterrorism is a multilateral strategy congruent with human security that advocates ethical, legally sanctioned methods for establishing effective communication and just relations between adversaries, resolving conflicts peacefully, and bringing terrorists to justice. Antiterrorism is a less violent, or even a nonviolent, alternative to counterterrorism (TFA). One possibility is to replace *counter*terrorist violence with *anti*terrorist prevention and interception measures. This may include negotiation with members or representatives of anti-state terrorist groups.

But antiterrorism is only the "negative" component of a long-term process to establish human security. It must be combined with the prevention of terrorism, both from above and from below, which requires the development of a global strategy of peacemaking and peace-building.

The beginning of the end of the GWOT, and of terrorism in general?

Terrorism is simultaneously one of the oldest and one of the most recent incarnations of political violence. Whether employed from above or from below, it has existed for millennia.

Accordingly, it is wishful thinking to believe that terrorism can be ended overnight, or even, perhaps, within our lifetimes.

It is not, however, wishful thinking to believe that we must begin now to struggle forcefully, but nonviolently, against all forms of political violence, no matter the origin, position, or creed of its perpetrators. While we may not see the end of terrorism in the foreseeable future, perhaps by confronting political mass murder with reason, understanding, education, and prevention—rather than with indiscriminate violence that murders the innocent along with the suspect—while we still live we may see the beginning of the end of terrorism.

To end terrorism would mean, among other things, to change the political reality and the mentality that give rise to it. Accordingly, instead of fighting fire with fire, of combating terror with greater terror, why not try the power of dialogue and negotiation to disarm the militants and would-be terrorists instead of the force of arms? What do we have to lose? Nothing. What do we have to win? A more peaceful and equitable world.

Notes

1 Shibley Telhami and Steven Kull, *The American Public on the 9/11 Decade: A Study of American Public Opinion*, The Brookings Institution and Anwar Sadat Chair, University of Maryland Program on International Policy Attitudes (PIPA) (August 9, 2011), 2, 5.
2 Institute for Economics and Peace, *The 2015 Global Terrorism Index*, Sydney, Australia, 2015, available at: http://economicsandpeace.org/wp-content/uploads/2015/11/Global-Terrorism-Index-2015.pdf. National Consortium for the Study of Terrorism and Responses to Terrorism (START), August 2015, available at: www.start.umd.edu.
3 See the Physicians for Social Responsibility Report at: www.psr.org/assets/pdfs/bodycount.pdf; and Sarah Lazare, "Body Count Report Reveals At Least 1.3 Million Lives Lost to US-Led War on Terror," March 26, 2015, Common Dreams Portland, Maine.

Available at: www.commondreams.org/news/2015/03/26/body-count-report-reveals-least-1.3-million-lives-lost-us-led-war-terror.
4. For casualties, see: icasualities.org, 2016, at http://icasualties.org/; Iraq Body Count: "Iraq 2014: Civilian deaths almost doubling year on year," January 1, 2015, at: www.iraqbodycount.org/analysis/numbers/2014/; and Neta C. Crawford, *War-related Death, Injury, and Displacement in Afghanistan Pakistan, 2001–2014*, Costs of War, Watson Institute, Brown University, available at http://watson.brown.edu/costsofwar/files/cow/imce/papers/2015/WarRelatedCasualtiesAfghanistanandPakistan2001-2014FIN.pdf.
5. Peter Baker and Eric Schmitt, "California Attack Has U.S. Rethinking Strategy on Homegrown Terror," *The International New York Times*, December 5, 2015: www.nytimes.com/2015/12/06/us/politics/california-attack-has-us-rethinking-strategy-on-homegrown-terror.html?ref=todayspaper&_r=0.
6. Kimberly Amadeo, "War on Terror Facts, Costs and Timeline," October 26, 2016, at: http://useconomy.about.com/od/usfederalbudget/f/War_on_Terror_Facts.htm.
7. Global Research News, "US Wars in Afghanistan, Iraq to Cost $6 trillion," *Global Research*, February 12, 2014, at: www.globalresearch.ca/us-wars-in-afghanistan-iraq-to-cost-6-trillion/5350789
8. Joseph E. Stiglitz and Linda J. Bilmes, "The True Cost of the Iraq War: $3 Trillion and Beyond," *Washington Post*, September 5, 2010: www.washingtonpost.com/wpdyn/content/article/2010/09/03/AR2010090302200.html.
9. See, inter alia: U.S. Department of Health and Human Services, "Child Abuse and Neglect Fatalities" 2010: www.childwelfare.gov/pubs/factsheets/fatality.cfm#children. U. S. Census 2011, "Table 118. Deaths and Death Rates by Selected Causes: 2006 and 2007": www.census.gov/compendia/statab/2011/tables/11s0118.pdf. U.S. Agency for Healthcare Research and Quality, "Twenty Tips to Prevent Medical Errors" February 2000: www.ahrq.gov/consumer/20tips.htm. American Cancer Society, "Cancer Facts and Figures 2010," April 18, 2011: www.cancer.org/Cancer/CancerCauses/TobaccoCancer/tobacco-related-cancer-fact-sheet.
10. David G. McNeil, Jr. "Vietnam's New Battle with Tuberculosis," *The International New York Times*, March 30, 2016, 9.
11. 2015 *Global Terrorism Index*, op. cit., 4.
12. Institute for Peace and Economics, *Global Peace Index 2016*, Sydney, Australia: 2016, at: http://static.visionofhumanity.org/sites/default/files/GPI%202016%20Report_2.pdf.
13. Milton Leitenberg, "Deaths in Wars and Conflicts in the 20th Century," *Occasional Paper #29*, Cornell University, 2006.
14. Scott Atran in Tom Bartlett, "The Rode to ISIS: An unorthodox anthropologist goes face to face with ISIS. Is the payoff worth the peril?" *The Chronicle of Higher Education*, May 20, 2016.
15. Atran, ibid.
16. YouTube Video, Posted by "Nizar Abboud," April 23, 2015, www.youtube.com/watch?v=qlbirlSA-dc.
17. Atran, ibid., citing Eli Berman, Joseph H. Felter, Jacob N. Shapiro, and Erin Troland, "Modest, Secure, and Informed: Successful Development in Conflict Zones," *American Economic Review*, May 2013. www.aeaweb.org/articles?id=10.1257/aer.103.3.512.
18. Seth Jones and Martin C. Libicki, *How Terrorist Groups End: Lessons for Countering al Qa'ida* (Rand Corporation: Santa Monica, 2008), www.rand.org.
19. Ibid., 3–4.
20. Ibid. 9.
21. Haig Khatchadourian, *The Morality of Terrorism* (New York: Peter Lang, 1998), 113–114.

Index

2001 Authorization for the Use of Military Force (AUMF) 167, 253, 257, 261, 265
9/11 terrorist attacks 1–3, 6, 13–15, 24, 33, 45–6, 49–55, 58, 67–8, 100, 108–9, 128–9, 137, 145, 147–8, 152, 154, 158, 163–6, 169–70, 172, 174–5, 177–9, 204–5, 216, 219, 224, 229, 233, 238, 242–3, 253–5, 257, 259, 261–5, 273–7
Abduh, Muhammad 112
Abu Bakr [al-Siddiq] 123, 125
Abu Bakr Naji 125
Afghānī, Jamāl al-Din al- 112
Afghanistan 2, 3, 9, 11, 14–16, 20, 58, 77, 91, 97, 99, 102, 105, 115–17, 129, 137–42, 146, 152, 156, 159, 160, 164, 167, 168, 173, 176, 177, 197, 199, 207, 208, 228–5, 254–6, 258, 259, 261, 262, 273–5, 282
Alawi 93, 115
Albania 8, 112
Aleppo 64, 66, 68, 75–8, 118
Aleppo Artillery School massacre 115
Al-Jazeera 61–4, 69, 128
Alloush, Zahran 133
Antiterrorism 3, 282–3
Apostasy 111, 114, 116, 123–4, 126
Apostates 91, 110–11, 116, 120, 122–4, 126
Arab–Israeli wars 108, 1948; Arab–Israeli war 113
Arab League definition of 123–4
Arab Spring uprisings 57, 62, 87, 93, 98, 103–4, 115–16, 226
Arabian Peninsula 112, 126–7
Arabize Islam, movement to 113
Army of Islam 68, 77, 109, 115, 118, 131
Asad, Bashar (Assad) 61, 64, 67, 69, 72, 119; regime 93, 98
Asad, Hafez 77
Azīz, Abd al- 112

Badr Brigades 85, 88
Baghdadi, Abū Bakr al- 70, 118–19, 225
Bani Qurayza 126
Bannā, Hasan al- 113, 114; *see also* Muslim Brothers
behavioral experiments 221
Biden, Joe 69, 70, 88, 103
Bin Laden, Osama 14, 15, 70, 86, 97, 100, 117, 129, 137, 139, 152, 174, 176, 208, 209, 225, 231, 232, 254, 261, 263, 265, 273
blowback 163–4
Book of Monotheism 110; *see also* Wahhāb, Muhammad ibn Abd al-
Brussels attack 234–5
Bush, George W. 7, 14, 15, 85, 86, 89, 90, 97, 98, 102, 169, 170, 177, 244, 261; administration 1, 68, 148, 154, 155, 166–8, 196, 200, 209, 243, 259, 265, 273

Caliphate 62, 91, 108, 114, 120, 126, 128, 177, 221, 224, 225
capital punishment 110, 116, 204
Cheney, Dick 14, 15, 85, 90, 98, 170
Christians 91, 94, 102, 108, 216, 231, 233
CIA 9, 11, 14, 66, 139, 168–70, 174, 175, 176, 199, 209, 259, 260
Clinton, Hillary 61, 99, 100, 140, 196
collateral damage 197–9
conflict resolution/conflict transformation 279
consensus (*ijmā'*) 110, 112
converts 117, 219, 224
counter-narratives 223
counterterrorism 1, 2, 97, 99, 137, 145, 147, 153, 173, 178, 199, 202, 203, 215–17, 214, 234–45, 253, 257, 258, 260, 262–7, 277, 278, 283; counter-insurgency 234–45

Index

critical terrorism approach 24, 38, 39
Cuba 8

Dabiq 219
Dickens, Charles 234, 246
Drones (UAVs/UCAVs) 3, 145, 146, 153, 154, 156, 159, 167, 196, 197–210, 216, 232, 254, 259–62, 265, 266

Egypt 10, 62, 65, 90, 93, 98, 103, 112–16, 120, 171, 179
ethics 152–7, 164–5, 181, 282–3; of the War on Terrorism 156–7
exclusionist 21
extraterritorial volunteer fighting force 226

FBI 14, 15, 174, 178, 243
Fertile Crescent 108, 126, 127
Free Islamic Levant 109, 118
Free Syrian Army 64–6, 68, 116, 118–19
Fromm, Erich 7
Führer 113

genocide 13, 102, 109, 175, 203
God's Law (*sharī'atu allah*) 111, 116, 119–20; see also Muslim Law; Hanbali school of Islamic Law
Golāni (*Jolāni*), Abū Mohammad al- 118–20

Hadith 110, 221; definition 110
Hama Massacre 115
Hamad Āl-Thāni 116
Hanbal, Ahmad ibn 110, 118
Hanbali school of Islamic Law 110, 112, 124
Hashemites 112
heresies 110
Hitler, Adolf 98, 113, 151, 225
holy war 87, 88, 90, 110, 116–20, 122, 125, 126; Voluntary 87
Holy Warriors' Consultative Council 117
human security 157–8, 283
Hussein, Saddam 15, 82, 88–90, 116, 117, 119, 132, 141, 151, 237
hybrid peace process 19, 21, 22, 38

Inghimasi 222
innovation and Islam 110
identity fusion 221
Iraq 2–3, 14, 16, 57–8, 61, 68–9, 71–3, 77–8, 82–109, 112, 115–18, 120–2, 126, 127, 129, 141–2, 146–7, 151–2, 156, 159, 163–4, 169, 174, 176–8, 180, 196–9, 207–8, 216, 220–2, 226–7, 235, 239, 240–6, 254–6, 259, 261–2, 273–6, 282
ISIL 58, 108, 218–20; see also ISIS
ISIS (Islamic State of Iraq and Syria) 2–3, 58, 60, 67–78, 82, 87–8, 93–6, 98, 100, 102, 103, 108–35, 141, 147, 165, 175, 177, 180, 208, 215, 218–27, 235, 238–9, 242–3, 273, 280; recruitment patterns 218, 219
Islam and education: logic, psychology, social psychology, philosophy, comparative religion 73–4, 76, 109, 114, 116–17, 125, 130, 139–42, 225
Islam and reasoning (*ijtihād*) 110, 112; see also Islam and science; *Mu'tazila* School, rationalist intellectual movement
Islam and science 112, 142, 222, 227; see also Afghānī, Jamāl al-Din al-
Islam, dawn of 111
Islamic Caliphate 62, 108
Islamic socialism 114
Israel 7, 30, 31, 32, 92, 99, 104, 113, 127, 146

Jazāirī, Tāhir al- 112–13
jihad 11, 14, 16, 58, 62, 64, 66–71, 75, 77–8, 87–8, 109–10, 115–17, 119–20, 125–6, 128–9, 130, 139, 142, 145, 165, 176, 180, 199–200, 218–19, 222–6, 230, 235, 239, 241, 266–7, 275; see also Salafi-Jihadi groups
Jewish settlers 113
Jordan 83, 85–6, 115–17, 171, 275
just war 154–5
Justice and Development Party 116

Kalbani, Adel al- 123
Khalayleh, Ahmad al- 116; see also Zarqāwi, al-
Khalilzad, Zalmay 84, 86, 98
Khatīb, Muhibb al-Dīn al- 113
King, Martin Luther Jr. 181
Kudilah 222
Kurdeity 221
Kuwait 89, 90–1, 112, 141

Land of Islam 120, 126
Land of Truce 120
Land of War 120
Law and the Global War on Terror 164–81; rule of law 165–6
Libya 10, 11, 61, 62, 65, 66, 68, 69, 72, 77, 103, 115, 152, 156, 163, 164, 180, 196, 208, 262, 274, 275

Index 287

Malik, Nouri al- 82, 83, 85–7, 93, 106
Mandela, Nelson 210
Mecca 88, 112, 123
Medina 110, 112
Monotheism and Holy War Group 117
Monroe Doctrine 9
Muhammad, the Prophet 76, 110–11, 117, 123–6, 128–9, 181
Muhammad Ali 112
Mujahedin 224
Muslim Brothers (Brotherhood): recruiting methods 113, 123, 241; underground militias 61, 65, 77–8, 113; *see also* Qutb, Sayyid; Bannā, Hasan al-
Muslim diaspora 126, 218
Muslim dynasties 113
Muslim Law (*al-Sharia*) 108, 110, 112, 114, 117–20, 126, 128; *see also* God's Law
Muslim–Arab nationalism 112
Mu'tazila School, rationalist intellectual movement 110

Nāsir, Egyptian Abd al-, 113
Nationalist trend 113
negotiations/negotiating 227–33, 280–1
Nicaragua 8
nihilist society 224
nonviolence 158–9
Nuqrāshī, Egyptian Prime Minister Mahmoud al- 112–13
Nusra Front al- 70–1, 73, 115, 118–19

Obama, Barack 1, 12, 64, 66, 67, 71, 87, 104, 155, 167, 168, 170, 172, 176, 196, 198, 199, 200, 201, 202, 204, 205, 209, 220, 232, 233, 257, 259, 260, 265, 266, 273
orthodox terrorism approach 18, 19, 23, 25, 26, 29, 34, 35, 37, 38
Orwell, George 7, 225
Ottoman Empire 112, 116

pacifism 155
Pakistan 137–43, 228–33
Palestine 30, 77, 152, 158, 230; 1936 clashes between Jewish settlers and Arabs 113
peace 155; positive 155; negative 155
peace literacy 279
peacebuilding 18–40, 155, 277, 282–3
peacemaking 155
Persia 89, 92, 99, 112, 137, 236
Peshmerga 220

PKK (Kurdistan Workers' Party) 220
PLO 7
political entrepreneurs posing as religious authorities 109
political violence 3, 155, 283
polytheism 110–11, 126
Popular Mobilization 88
post-liberal [peacemaking] 18–24, 29, 30, 32, 33, 35, 37–40
post-terrorism 18–20, 22, 24, 26, 30, 33–5, 37, 39, 40
Post Traumatic Stress Disorder 51–3
prayer 61, 83, 88, 110, 121, 124, 125–6
psychological conditions 223
Pukhtuns 137–42

Qaeda, al- 3, 13–14, 58, 60, 67–71, 77, 82–4, 86–7, 90–3, 97–9, 103, 108, 109, 115–23, 125, 127–9, 139–40, 152, 165, 167, 169, 171, 176–7, 180, 197, 208–9, 215–20, 224–6, 229, 233, 244, 253–67, 278, 280–2; *see also* Wahhābī doctrine
Qaryatayn, al- 130
Qāsimī, Jamāl al-Dīn al- 112
Qatar 61, 64–6, 70, 78, 93, 100, 115–16
Quran 110, 113, 120, 123–4, 128–9, 132, 136, 221
Qutb, Sayyid 113–14, 123; *see also* Muslim Brothers

"radicalization" 3, 279
Rashid, al- 112
Reagan, Ronald 7, 11–14, 88
Riyadh 78, 112
Roosevelt, Franklin Delano (FDR) 181

Salafi 58, 62, 68–9, 90–1, 106, 109, 112–15, 123, 125, 128–31, 218, 225, 238, 265
Salafi-Jihadi groups 58, 68, 109, 115, 125, 128–31, 218, 225; *see also jihad*
Salafiyya, al-, movement 112–15
Sanders, Bernie 181
Saud, House of ibn 111–12
Saud, Muhammad ibn 111–12
Saudi Arabia, Kingdom of 64–5, 70, 73, 78, 90–4, 100, 105, 110, 112, 114–15, 121–3, 126, 139, 176, 179, 208, 279, 281
sex slaves 102, 134
Sharia, al- 110, 228, 240–1; *see also* Muslim Law; God's Law
Shaykh, House of al- 111, 112

Shīa 69, 82–5, 87–98, 103, 105, 108, 110, 112, 117, 127
shrines, destruction of 76, 97, 112, 117
Sibāī, Mustafā al- 113–14
Snowden, Edward 181
Soldiers of the Levant 109, 117
Sufi 110, 123, 143
suicide bombers 179
Sunni 69, 82, 86–98, 103, 106, 108–10, 116–18, 127, 222, 225, 244; Sunni Muslim Law 108
Syria 2–3, 57–8, 60–83, 87, 90, 93, 95, 98–100, 102–4, 108–9, 112–12, 126–7, 141–2, 152, 156, 159–60, 163–4, 167, 170–1, 177, 196, 204, 207–8, 210, 216, 219–20, 226–7, 236, 238, 241–2, 274–5
Syrian anti-government fighting groups 130–1

Taliban 3, 15, 16, 91, 97, 99, 120, 137, 138, 176, 215, 228, 229, 232, 233, 239, 273, 278
Taymiyya, Ahmad ibn 110, 112
Terror from above and from within 196–210
Terrorism 2–9, 11, 13–43, 45, 52–3, 56–60, 67–8, 70–2, 77, 82–8, 93–4, 96–7, 99–100, 102, 105–6, 108–9, 123, 128–30, 137, 139–42, 145, 147–51, 153, 155–61, 163–4, 166–7, 170, 173, 176–81, 199–200, 202–4, 209, 216–17, 220, 222, 226, 228, 233–4, 236–43, 245, 247, 253–4, 256–8, 260–7, 273–9, 281–3; definition 108; ethics of 153–7; from above (TFA, state terrorism) 149–51, 157, 181, 233, 280–1; from below (TFB, non-state terrorism) 149–51, 157, 181, 280–1; long-term solutions 109; religious roots 109, 128; trauma 45–55; Western concept of 108
Trump, Donald 181

U.S. military presence in the Middle East 109, 118, 139, 141–2, 147–8, 151, 156, 167–8, 170, 173–4, 176–80, 244–6
U.S.–Persian Gulf wars, previous 108, 141, 152, 208
Ukaidy, Abd al-Jabbar al- 130
Umayyad dynasty 76, 113

Wahhāb, Muhammad ibn Abd al- 110–12
Wahhābī doctrine 58, 109–12, 114–15, 123–4
Wahhābīyya 112–16
War on Terror (GWOT) 2–3, 5, 7, 9, 13, 14, 17, 57–8, 70, 82–4, 86–7, 93–7, 99–100, 102–6, 108, 126–9, 140–2, 145–6, 148, 153, 155–6, 158–60, 163, 171, 177, 186–7, 196, 203, 207, 215–17, 274, 276–7, 281–2; failure of 108, 175–8; casualties of 129, 177–8
Waziristan 137–40
Western support for Syrian rebels 78, 108

Yemen 199
Yezidi 108, 130

Zarqāwi, Abū Musʻab al- 14, 86, 97, 106, 117–18, 225
Zubaidi, Baqir al- 85